THE GREAT PASSION

THE GREAT PASSION

An Introduction to Karl Barth's Theology

Eberhard Busch

Translated by

Geoffrey W. Bromiley

Edited and Annotated by

Darrell L. Guder and Judith J. Guder

WILLIAM B. EERDMANS PUBLISHING COMPANY
GRAND RAPIDS, MICHIGAN / CAMBRIDGE, U.K.

This English edition
originally published in German under the title
Die grosse Leidenschaft:
Einführung in die Theologie Karl Barths

© 2004 Wm. B. Eerdmans Publishing Co.
All rights reserved

Wm. B. Eerdmans Publishing Co.
255 Jefferson Ave. S.E., Grand Rapids, Michigan 49503 /
P.O. Box 163, Cambridge CB3 9PU U.K.

Printed in the United States of America

09 08 07 06 05 04   7 6 5 4 3 2 1

Library of Congress Cataloging-in-Publication Data

Busch, Eberhard, 1937-
[Grosse Leidenschaft. English]
The great passion: An introduction to Karl Barth's Theology /
Eberhard Busch; translated by Geoffrey W. Bromiley; edited and
annotated by Darrell L. Guder and Judith J. Guder.
p.   cm.
Includes bibliographical references and index.
ISBN 0-8028-4893-1 (cloth: alk. paper)
1. Barth, Karl 1886-1968.   I. Guder, Darrell L., 1939-
II. Guder, Judith J.   III. Title.
BX4827.B3B8513   2004
230'.044'092 — dc22
2004047166

www.eerdmans.com

Contents

II. INSIGHTS — THE THEMES OF HIS THEOLOGY

Bibliography

Indexes

Preface

Some time ago I surveyed a number of recent writings on the work of Karl Barth.[1] What I read *about* him motivated me to look again at Barth *himself,* especially since his work has accompanied me on many stations of my own path. When I was a student at Basel in 1959, I attended Barth's lectures dealing with the early part of volume 4, part 4 of *Church Dogmatics.* At that time I also devoured volume 4, part 3, which had just appeared in print. I had the impression that the whole work was beginning to speak to me again, demanding my full attention as its distinctive mode of thinking and speaking continued to surprise me. Naturally this new hearing would raise for me a host of questions, many of which have been posed since Barth's death, and especially in the secondary literature. Unavoidably Barth's own work could not simply answer these questions, because in his work Barth was asking different questions and addressing other things. Both then and now Barth's theology raises many questions and has much to say.

As it did then, Barth's theology confronts us with many edges and points and corners, perhaps in new ways. Trimming these off is not the way to actualize his theology or "continue to work on it." Similarly, the frictional encounter with it, with the intention of distancing oneself from it and thus assuring oneself of one's own advance "beyond" his theology, will not necessarily constitute a fruitful encounter with it. Nor will the proclaiming of a new paradigm enable us to protect ourselves against the voice of Barth. This voice is part of the chorus of our predecessors who still have the right to be heard within the contemporary church of Jesus Christ.

We certainly should not forget Barth's reminder that he did not aim to

---

1. E. Busch, "Weg and Werk Karl Barths in der neueren Forschung," *Theologische Revue* 60 (1995): 273-99, 430-70.

make us students of Barth but students of Holy Scripture. Barth took the lead on this point. We find it manifested in the "great passion" with which he delivered his Basel lectures (CL 180ff. = 111ff.). This passion has left an imprint on his theology. It is a passion in zeal for God's glory, which zeal posits this glory in God's "friendliness for humanity." The theology of Barth bears witness to this God. What I believe I have learned in listening to it is passed on in what follows, and I suspect that it might be of interest to others.

I will be quoting mainly from his *Church Dogmatics* (CD). I will include the numbers of the volumes and the pages in the text (the CD citations give first the page numbers in the German original, followed by [=] the page numbers in the English edition; "rev." indicates a revision in the ET translation). Quotations from volume 4, part 4 are listed as CL, *The Christian Life*, published posthumously in 1976 (English translation [ET]: Grand Rapids: Eerdmans, 1981).

Thanks are due to Wolfram Ehlenbroker and to my secretary Margret Lessner for their help in the preparation of this manuscript.

EBERHARD BUSCH
Göttingen, January 1998

I

Pointers — Toward an Understanding of This Theologian

I.1

His Profile

Influences

Barth respected the British for their democratic tradition, for their knowl-edge of humanity as displayed by Shakespeare, and for their lifestyle as de-scribed by the detective stories of Dorothy Sayers. He also liked the Germans[1] and spent fifteen years of his life in Germany. In 1933 Emanuel Hirsch attributed his lack of nationalistic enthusiasm to the fact that he was not a real German from head to toe.[2] In reply Barth stated that he knew why he was truly a Swiss, and he quoted Gottfried Keller, who had said: "Hail to us, for free people are still accustomed to free speech."[3] It was an Alemanian who said this, who was critical of overregulation. Jacob Burckhard expressed the same thought in a saying his grandnephew liked to quote, namely, that "power in itself is bad."[4] Barth's own dictum was that the Holy Spirit does not blow through mass assemblages.[5] He strikes a similar note in Berlin in the fall of 1933 when he publicly quoted the Sempach fighters against an alien superpower: "Strike their spears, for they are hollow!"[6] During the Hitler

---

1. As stated by A. Koechlin at the presentation of the Stuttgart Declaration of Guilt, according to Martin Greschat, ed., *Im Zeichen der Schuld: 40 Jahre Stuttgarter Schuldbekenntnis: Eine Dokumentation* (Neukirchen, 1985), p. 100.

2. Emanuel Hirsch, *Das kirchliche Wollen der Deutschen Christen* (Berlin, 1933), p. 7.

3. Karl Barth, *"Der Götze wackelt": Zeitkritische Aufsätze, Reden und Briefe von 1930 bis 1960*, ed. K. Kupisch (Berlin, 1961), p. 69.

4. Karl Barth, *Der Römerbrief*, 1st ed. (Bern, 1919), pp. 501-2; *Dogmatik im Grundriss* (Zollikon-Zurich, 1947), p. 54; ET: *Dogmatics in Outline* (London, 1949), p. 48.

5. Cf. Karl Barth, "Gespräch mit Mennoniten 1967," in *Gespräche 1964-1968* (Zurich, 1997), p. 424.

6. Karl Barth, *Reformation als Entscheidung* (*Theologische Existenz heute!*, 3) (Munich,

occupation his word to France was that "an ocean of reality does not signify a single drop of truth."[7]

Barth was born on May 10, 1886. His birthplace was Basel, which a resident of Herrnhut had described as "the most fruitful place . . . in the kingdom of God."[8] His parents moved in active Christian circles that had a "positive," not a liberal tradition. Basel, however, had a humanist tradition. Preachers in the Minster pulpit could look out on the grave of Erasmus.[9] Nietzsche began attracting attention when at the university in 1886; Karl's father, Fritz Barth, had learned to respect him as his school teacher. A typical citizen of Basel secretly desired the radicalisms and extravagancies of others,[10] and this attitude helped Karl during his student years to abandon the positivism of his family and to adopt an increasingly zealous liberalism. Mocking laughter was typical of Basel, and Barth related the "cutting speech of the Baseler" to the fact that the people here had always thought a great deal about the transitory nature of everything earthly.[11] Barth always viewed himself as a citizen of Basel even though he went to Bern when he was four years old and did most of his schooling there.

Barth thought it singular that throughout the years two portraits, one of Calvin and one of Mozart, should hang "at the same height" next to each other in his study.[12] This tells us something about his character. From his early days and throughout his life two different sides contested with one another and intercrossed. On the one side was a bitter joy in battle, accompanied by laughter. We find this already in his younger days when he took part in children's street fights in which he always wanted to win. Later, when he was accused of always wanting to be right, he responded, "But I always am right"![13] At ten years old he could sublimate this impulse with enthusiasm for the works of Schiller, who inspired him to compose his own freedom-seeking plays. At fifty-four years old he voluntarily joined the Swiss army,

---

1933), p. 24; ET: "Reformation as Decision," in L. W. Spitz, ed., *The Reformation: Basic Interpretations* (Lexington, Mass., 1972), p. 170.

7. Karl Barth, *Eine Schweizer Stimme: 1938-1945* (Zollikon-Zurich, 1945), p. 150.

8. Karl Kupisch, *Karl Barth in Selbstzeugnissen und Dokumenten* (Reinbek bei Hamburg, 1971), p. 16.

9. Karl Barth, "Gespräch in Bièvres," 1963 (unpublished).

10. Karl Barth, *Die protestantische Theologie im 19. Jahrhundert: Ihre Vorgeschichte und ihre Geschichte* (Zurich, 1947), p. 124; ET: *Protestant Theology in the Nineteenth Century: Its Background and History* (Valley Forge, 1973), p. 145.

11. Karl Barth, *Fürchte dich nicht!* (Munich, 1949), pp. 267, 300-301.

12. Karl Barth, "*Der Götze wackelt,*" p. 209.

13. Eberhard Busch, *Karl Barths Lebenslauf,* 5th ed. (Gütersloh, 1994); ET: *Karl Barth: His Life from Letters and Autobiographical Texts* (London and Philadelphia, 1976), p. 395.

ready to stand up for democracy against the Hitler hordes. He loved openness and abhorred deception. He found no place for compromisers. He
pushed for decisions. He strove "beyond the unholy 'and' and 'at the same
time', beyond the whole world of balance, which is untenable and intolerable" (CL 298 = 177). He could state, in the middle of his *Dogmatics,* that "a
garden path may be circular. But a garden path is not a true way. A true way
has a beginning and an end" (IV/1 622 = 558). He was impressed by trees because it was their destiny is "to stand upright" (III/1 173 = 155). As he said of
himself in old age, he never vacillated. He liked to tackle hot issues, and he
felt well in a storm. Opposition did not get under his skin. Nevertheless, he
was against inopportune initiatives. He preferred to keep his powder dry
and then use it at the right moment. He always had a good nose for scenting
dangers so that he could counter them firmly early on. And throughout, he
could be blunt. The question might have been put to him by his contemporaries, as Calvin's contemporaries put it to Calvin: "Could you not be . . .
rather more palatable, rather more like ourselves?"[14]

Yet there is also the other side, the gentle side, that loved peace and harmony and the beautiful. It was not for nothing that the ancestors of his
mother, Anna née Sartorius, were related to the irenic reformer of Zurich,
Heinrich Bullinger. A picture that did not hang straight irritated Barth. He
was fond of the term "tender feelings." He said that a person "without imagination is more of an invalid than one who lacks a leg" (III/1 99 = 91). He himself had tender feelings. He was thus able either to laugh heartily or to cry, to
listen, and to participate. He would place his visitors so that he could study
them carefully, though he did not like to look in the mirror himself. As a five-
year-old his feelings were roused by a profound encounter with the music of
Mozart. In later years he listened daily to this music before getting to work.
"He plays and never stops playing," even through dark periods. "Before com-
posing, he first listened." "The subjective never becomes a theme . . . ," similar to Botticelli, a painter he greatly admired.[15] His style was that of a child-
like immersion in subtle and mysterious things. He did not regard this
immersion as either tragic or important. Just as a person should "work [and]
stand for the right . . . ," he should also "will to enjoy himself" (III/4 427 =
375). Part of a real sincerity is being able to "laugh at himself" (III/4 765 =
665). Barth was also a horseman, and it was his opinion that "a good horse-

---

14. Karl Barth, *Die Theologie Calvins* (Zürich, 1993), pp. 389-390; ET: *The Theology of
John Calvin* (Grand Rapids, 1995), p. 287.

15. Karl Barth, *Wolfgang Amadeus Mozart* (Zollikon, 1956), pp. 37, 39, 49; ET:
Wolfgang Amadeus Mozart (Grand Rapids, 1986), pp. 47, 49, 59.

man is so completely one with his horse" that he "cannot possibly be an ungodly person" (III/4 400 = 352).

This "man with all his contradictions" was quickly absorbed into the world of Christian faith. He was much influenced by the self-evident way in which the hymns sung by his mother referred to the stories of Jesus as ones that "might take place any day in Basel" (IV/2 125 = 112). He achieved such certainty about the presence of Jesus that he spent a Palm Sunday, as a boy, watching for the entry of Jesus into his own city. When he described his family as mildly pietistic,[16] this expressed a certain withdrawal from his background that came to light in his acceptance of historical criticism and of social questions and feminism. It greatly impressed the son that his parents took him out of Sunday school after too vivid a depiction of hell was presented. He was also impressed by the fact that he had to empty his piggy bank to give money to a sick man, which his father required him to do, citing the verse in James: "When we know what it is right to do, and do not do it, for us it is sin" (4:17). The Epistle of James was never for him a strawy epistle, as it was for Luther.

The Pointing Hand

This third aspect, which early on influenced his life, is illustrated by a painting that from his first theological beginnings hung above his desk. The picture was Grünewald's *Crucifixion*. Visible there "in an almost impossible way" was the pointing hand of John the Baptist, who said: "He must increase, but I must decrease." "It is this hand which is in evidence in the Bible."[17] All proper theology in his view must be like this hand, with which a person does not point to oneself nor at some idea or program but towards the God who for his part completely turns to that person. He wanted his theology to be like that hand. This "man with all his contradictions" found himself under claim to do this one decisive thing, unceasingly and above everything else.

If, over the lengthy course of his way as a theologian, he would often start over again, making many twists and turns, then the profound reason was that he believed that he must constantly attempt, in ever new ways, to

---

16. Cf. Karl Barth, "Nachwort," in *Friedrich Schleiermacher* (Munich and Hamburg, 1968), p. 292; ET: appendix to *The Theology of Schleiermacher* (Grand Rapids, 1982), p. 263.

17. Karl Barth, *Das Wort Gottes und die Theologie* (Munich, 1929), pp. 79-80, 85-86; ET: *The Word of God and the Word of Man* (New York, 1957), pp. 65, 75-76, 84.

carry out the ministry of this pointing hand. And if there was an enduring constant in these twists and turns along his way, then it was most profoundly the fact that he never departed from the one to whom John was pointing. If he had one predominant concern in his time, it was always at root to invite, beseech, press, strengthen the church and theology, whether by criticism or encouragement, to imitate the Baptist. Today, if there is any reason beyond merely historical interest to recall his theology, and if in the future "there will be times in which many will rediscover his message with joy,"[18] then it will be the legacy expressed in this picture.

Barth never spoke about his own conversion to the calling of a Christian theologian. "I and my personal Christianity do not belong to the *kerygma* to be declared by me" (IV/3 776 = 677). Why did he study theology? Briefly, he said, out of "curiosity" in face of this "sphinx!"[19] Theologically he was still totally a liberal when he began his pastorate at Safenwil in the Aargau at the age of twenty-five. Yet his distinctive message was already there when he told his people "that I am not speaking to you of God because I am a pastor. I am a pastor because I *must* speak to you of God."[20] The inversion of thought and the stress upon the divine *must* were typical of him. A member of the congregation with whom the young pastor took his meals would relate some decades later that on Sundays, before preaching, he came to breakfast very pale, silent, and highly tensed and focused, as before the explosion of a thunderstorm. He would pick up a cup of tea, stride round the table, and then hasten away without eating a thing. The young Bonhoeffer also said, after first meeting Barth, now a professor, in his seminar, that "Barth was even better than his books." "He has a frankness, a willingness to listen to criticism, and at the same time such an intensity of concentration on the subject, which can be discussed proudly or modestly, dogmatically or tentatively, and is certainly not primarily directed to the service of his own theology."[21] Even at seventy-five years of age Barth could speak of the great passion by which those who know God are "filled, impelled, guided, and ruled" (CL 180, 184 = 113).

The fire of this passion burned within him. It fed upon the fact that the word "God" is no empty concept. This word is filled with a living and mov-

---

18. Willem Adolf Visser 't Hooft, in *Karl Barth 1886-1968: Gedenkfeier im Basler Münster* (Zurich, 1969), p. 54.

19. *Karl Barth–Rudolf Bultmann Briefwechsel, 1922-1966* (Zurich, 1966), p. 303; ET: *Karl Barth–Rudolf Bultmann: Letters, 1922-1966* (Grand Rapids, 1981), p. 152.

20. Eberhard Busch, *Karl Barths Lebenslauf,* p. 73; ET: *Karl Barth,* p. 61.

21. Eberhard Bethge, *Dietrich Bonhoeffer* (Munich, 1967), pp. 216-17; ET: *Dietrich Bonhoeffer* (London, 1970), p. 133.

ing reality, the all-decisive reality. This word is filled with a force that will carry not just the church but the world as well. It is a word of infinite gravity, not because we ascribe it that, but because it is so intrinsically.

Who is God? This was the question in a 1917 sermon. "He is not the fifth wheel on a cart, but the wheel which drives all the other wheels. Not a sanctuary off to the side, but the one who drives with force in the midst of all that is. Not a dark power in the clouds over against which a person can only be a slave, but the clear force of freedom that must be honored above and in all things, and in humanity first of all. Not an idea or an opinion, but the power of life that overcomes the powers of death. Not an ornament of the world, but a lever that penetrates the world. Not a feeling with which one can play, but a fact that must be taken seriously, a fact on which we can stand with both feet in every circumstance, a fact on which we can feed as we do on daily bread, a fact into which we can retreat as into a fortress, and then break out like those who are under siege, to risk sallies in every direction." That is what it means to say "a living God." Let there be no saying, "that we 'have' him, as we often like to put it. What is the attempt to speak of him but helpless sighing and stammering!"[22]

As early as 1914 Barth stated, "The little clause 'God is' signifies a revolution."[23] For this reason sighing and stammering belong to theology as the Amen does to the church. That "little clause" constantly confronts our stubborn ways of thinking as we grapple with divine things and try to make them serve our own views and purposes. It is truly revolutionary. It sets us before the "*new* world" of God, a world that reaches out to us in order to put us in his service. How could such a theology whose talk about God constantly hastens back to that other way of thinking, how should such a theology which is dependent upon God's making himself known, do its work properly without such sighing and stammering? In 1933 the Jewish theologian H. J. Schoeps regarded Barth's theology as extraordinary because it was permeated by a sense of the danger of one's own talking about God. The result is that we always "have to tremble for the correct expression of the truth." And for that reason, "Barth, in the first hundred pages of his dogmatics, reflects *solely* about wanting to say anything at all about God's Word."[24]

Nevertheless, even with such sighing and stammering, God makes himself known to us. "Man knows God in that he stands *before* God" (II/1 8 =

---

22. Karl Barth, *Suchet Gott, so werdet ihr leben!* (Bern, 1917), pp. 102-3.

23. Karl Barth, *Predigten 1914* (Zurich, 1974), p. 168.

24. Hans Blüher and Han Joachim Schoeps, *Streit um Israel: Ein jüdisch-christliches Gespräch* (Hamburg, 1933), pp. 110-11.

9). This is a basic thesis of Barth. It is not this sighing and stammering that makes our theology false. That happens when it does not take its position "before God," perhaps because it already knows what it intends and only uses God after the fact to affirm its good intentions, or perhaps because it believes that it has already comprehended enough and now only considers how the content it already grasps can be applied or passed on. Theology can depart from its position "before God" only if it overlooks or forgets how it came into this position. It was not by a deliberate resolve to place itself there. It was simply by reason of the fact that God for his part stands before us and indeed *introduces* himself to us. Only in this way is a person placed before God, before this God. One cannot put oneself before God on one's own, nor can one leave this position on one's own without losing everything that would make one a Christian theologian. When it becomes clear to us that we are standing "before God," then we know God.

No Bungling

From the time he began his life as a theologian, Barth had been in conflict with the church and theology because he saw them attempting to deal with God without *really* standing before him, and *constantly* standing before him. He was in conflict with them, we might say, because he heard them talking about God without passing through that transformation of thinking. He was struggling against an attitude that enabled the church and theology to put a hold upon God whereby he could be integrated into our own preconceived and preformulated ideas and goals, or whereby he could be regarded as a commodity to be handled by the church and its theologians in any way they wanted to. Barth was opposed to the assurance and "sprightliness" that was miles apart from the sighing and stammering, and with which we assume with regard to "divine things" that "we spoke thus *of* them because we are able to speak *about* them so uninhibitedly" (I/1 168f. = 162-163). In this sense he opposed, from early on, the "false prophet," namely, the "pastor who sets out to do right by his people"[25] instead of desiring to do right by God, the God who truly does right by us. When this perversion takes place, the church, even though it functions ever so well, is simply a "semblance of a church" (IV/2 698 = 617). What is happening here is "the betrayal of the substance of the evangelical church."[26] Barth stresses again and again that no

25. Karl Barth, *Der Pfarrer* (Zofingen, 1916).
26. Karl Barth, *"Der Götze wackelt,"* p. 28.

atheism outside can threaten the church as does such betrayal within its walls. We may solemnly pronounce the word "God," but it is no more than an empty concept. This is far worse than atheism, for in using the name of God, "God" is being emptied. Truly this is to speak of God "by speaking of man in a loud voice."[27] The word "God" basically does nothing more than to elevate and strengthen a perverted and conceptually godless reality.

Barth championed and loved a church and theology whose talk of God is worthy of the name. In 1934 he visited a revue in Paris. He wrote concerning it: "I thought again of the old question: Why doesn't the church at least try to be as good at what it does as the children of the world are with their singing, miming and dancing?"[28] The question is nuanced rather differently when he quotes A. Bebel: "Strictly speaking, the worker who drains sewers to protect humanity from unhealthy miasmas is a very useful member of society, whereas . . . the theologian who seeks to befog the brain with supernatural, transcendental doctrines, is an extremely harmful individual." Barth added: "We must be careful not to be guilty of what is here stated to be the activity of theologians" (III/4 612 = 534). In his final lecture in 1961 he asked: "Is there not an astonishing disparity between what is important, discussed and more or less victoriously put in action in theology, and the errors and confusions, the sea of suffering and misery prevailing in the world that surrounds theology? . . . Could not theology be a luxury occupation, and could not we all be in the process of fleeing before the living God?"[29]

Theology was useless in his eyes when instead of following in the steps of the "living *God*" it at some point set him aside or left him behind and devoted itself to "other tasks." But it is just as senseless and loses sight of the "*living* God" when it abstractly and generally reflects, as a luxury occupation, on the "ultimate relations of God, man, and the world," rather than on faithfulness toward the living God to serve him so that the church might be "the church of a specific time with its needs and hopes" (I/2 941 = 841). Most of the criticisms of Barth since the 1920s were at their root, with many variations, the objection that the very thing to which he refers is lacking in his theology. In that he took God with such radical seriousness, he neglected or suppressed those whom God addressed: the human race, history, modernity, the world, and the reality in which we all live. He never dealt with the question of method: How is "God" to be communicated to those whom he addresses?

27. Karl Barth, *Wort Gottes*, p. 164; ET: *Word of God*, p. 196.
28. Eberhard Busch, *Karl Barths Lebenslauf*, p. 256; ET: *Karl Barth*, p. 244.
29. Karl Barth, *Einführung in die evangelische Theologie* (Zurich, 1962), pp. 154-55; ET: *Evangelical Theology, an Introduction* (New York, 1963), pp. 140-141.

Is this a justifiable criticism? Perhaps theological outsiders were capable of seeing things more clearly. The Jewish philosopher H. Jonas, for example, thought it worth noting that in Barth's theology "a nonworldly standpoint . . . appears to enable an unwavering and also realistic judgment about the things of this world that could shame many of the devotees of pure innerworldliness."[30] The Peruvian theologian G. Gutiérrez, when comparing Barth's theology and Bultmann's, commented, "The one who starts with heaven is sensitive to those who live in the hell of this earth; whereas the one who begins with earth is blind to the situation of exploitation upon which the earth is built."[31] These comments have observed something that is very relevant.

In fact Barth was convinced that the church and theology do not basically have many tasks among which they then mediate. Rather, they have been given only the *one* task, the task of John the Baptist portrayed in that painting. In the early days of the Hitler regime Barth stated categorically, "There are some things about which there is unanimity within the Church. One is, that there is no more urgent demand in the whole world than that which the Word of God makes, viz. that the Word be preached and heard. At all costs, this demand has to be discharged by the world and the Church itself, cost what it may."[32] Additional tasks that might be set must all be included in this one task, and met in its fulfillment. For Barth, the point was this. If the church regards this universally urgent task as secondary and neglects it, then compared with the dancing children of the world it creates "a piece of theological bungling" (III/4 606f. = 529). Yes, it justifies the complaint of Bebel that it is harmful for society, doing nothing for the society to which it is indebted. Its work is then a mere luxurious preoccupation, in which while fleeing from the living God, it also fails humanity with its "sufferings and hopes."

This point becomes illuminating only when it is clear that the task of theology does not consist of those "supernatural and transcendent doctrines," not even if it tries to communicate them to someone or other. It is not a theology that alleges to be close to life, while in the process perhaps moving further away from its one task; its "object" excludes all this. As we learn from John, its object is God, the God who turns to us in our deepest depths. God is not just *above;* he is also *below.* As such he is the living God.

30. Karl Barth, *Eine Schweizer Stimme,* p. 293.

31. Gustavo Gutiérrez, *Historische Macht der Armen* (Munich, 1984), p. 202; ET: *The Power of the Poor in History* (New York, 1983), p. 203.

32. Karl Barth, *Theologische Existenz heute!,* 1 (Munich, 1934), p. 4; ET: *Theological Existence Today* (London, 1933), pp. 11-12, 13.

He is present to humanity so much that it cannot be our task to make him present but only to believe, to recognize, and to testify that he is present. Barth's answer to his critics was this. The task of theology and the church is not that of doing what they thought Barth had failed to do, namely, mediating God to humanity. Its task is to understand and enter into God's self-mediation to humanity, as it has happened and continues to happen anew.

To say it again: God is not "a concept, an opinion," nor "a dark force in the clouds." He is a "lever that invades the world." Barth stated in 1956 that "it is precisely God's *deity* which, rightly understood, includes his *humanity*."[33] If it is the urgent and sole task of theology and the church simply to point to God, to this God, then it has no other course: then it must be present with the people to whom God has turned. It then sees humans in those deepest depths where God has sought and found them. Then, if God is a living God, theology and the church must stand with human beings "at specific times with their needs and hopes." Then, "more humanistic than the humanists,"[34] it cannot take humanity seriously enough, but in fact will take humans more seriously than they take themselves. More seriously because humanity is not perceived other than through the fact that God has entered into and taken on its cause.

We can thus see more clearly the contours of the way in which Barth understands the service of witness to which the church and Christian theology are called. They must follow the Biblical witnesses. They must adopt the pointing hand of the Baptist as Grünewald depicted him. Barth found here his own calling as a member of the church of Jesus Christ. Theology according to his thinking performed a work not alien to the church, because all its members are summoned into the knowledge of faith. All, then, are theologians. Because Barth perceived that the church was in danger of not doing its "service," he became a theologian in a specific sense. He did so in that he called upon the church to perform its task by pursuing this task himself on the field of theological reflection, the task of such a witness. In 1923, in a notable dispute with Harnack, the Nestor of liberal theology, he declared that "the task of theology is the same as the task of preaching." Out of this arose his great contribution to theology, and at its center his comprehensive *Church Dogmatics*.

---

33. Karl Barth, *Die Menschlichkeit Gottes* (*Theologische Studien* 48) (Zollikon-Zurich, 1956), p. 10; ET: *The Humanity of God* (Richmond, Va., 1960), p. 46.
34. Karl Barth, *Wort Gottes,* p. 53; ET: *Word of God,* p. 303.

Theology in the Service of God

To what may we liken his distinctive theology? It has a character of its own. To come upon it is like entering a light and roomy and beautiful church with wide-open windows and open doors that invite an entrance and welcome the everyday world. Divine service takes place in this church after the manner that Barth described when speaking of a Roman Catholic house of worship during World War I, when the Magnificat was sung without a pause even though a shell exploded through the church roof.[35] His respect for this, and his suspicion that it would not have happened in a Protestant worship service, had nothing to do with deficient sensitivity to the threats of grenades and other symbols of this age. He was convinced that the church does not serve people aright, or protect them properly against dangers, if in doing so it is diverted from its own worship *of God* and interrupts it.

His theology is focused on such worship as the community's service of God. It is itself an act of worship and service, related to the reformers in the conviction that it is worship in the field of thought. Not by coming up short intellectually! When asked concerning the significance of reason in his theology, he said: "I use it."[36] Regarding laziness of thought, he said that "stupidity is also sin" (IV/2 462 = 412). Yet theology draws its life from the Holy Spirit, who is "an express friend of a healthy human understanding."[37] But: the service of God on the field of thought! Theology carries out this worshipful service in that it understands clearly that "theology can be performed . . . only in the act of prayer."[38] It is no pious flourish if his *Church Dogmatics* opens by quoting the prayer with which Thomas Aquinas begins his *Summa Theologica*: "Grant me, most gracious God, that I will desire and wisely seek and truly know and in all things fulfill that which is pleasing to thee, to the praise of thy name" (I/1 23).

Worship services have good reason to be beautiful. Similarly a theology that combines work and prayer, even though it involves sighing and stammering, will have to be "a particularly beautiful science. Indeed, we can confidently say that it is the most beautiful of all the sciences. . . . It is an extreme form of Philistinism to find, or to be able to find, theology distasteful. The theologian who has no joy in his work is not a theologian at all. Sulky

---

35. Karl Barth, *Wort Gottes,* p. 109; ET: *Word of God,* pp. 112-113.

36. Karl Barth, *Briefe, 1961-1968* (Zurich, 1975), p. 474; ET: *Letters, 1961-1968* (Grand Rapids, 1981), p. 294.

37. Karl Barth, *Christus und wir Christen* (*Theologische Existenz heute!,* n.s. 11) (Munich, 1948), p. 10.

38. Karl Barth, *Einführung,* p. 177; ET: *Evangelical Theology,* p. 160.

faces, morose thoughts and boring ways of speaking are intolerable in this science" (II/1 740 = 656).

Barth's theology does not only query theology regarding its spiritual substance. For all the questioning, theology has its own distinctive quality. Even where it is modern, it repudiates what is coquettishly novel. Even where it stands in the tradition of the church, it plows a new furrow. When speaking about what concerns it deeply, it refrains from subjective emotionality. And yet when it thinks "strictly objectively," it does so with perceptible warmth. It speaks often in an elementary way yet avoids catchwords. It goes into detail at times but steers clear of what is unimportant. It focuses on the singular center of faith yet sees it from different concrete angles. It does not address a detail without keeping the total picture always in view. It gets down to the root of things yet keeps in mind the possible and necessary ramifications. It steadfastly puts to scripture the question whether this is how it is, and it does not separate from dogmatics the ethical question: "What shall we do?" It professes a definite knowledge but does not ride certain principles to death, because it is always engaged in a long march forwards, without ever roving around short of breath and purpose. Even in difficult movements of thought it never loses the childlikeness of faith. Starting with faith, it relentlessly seeks insight, enlightenment. It never flees from problems, and it recalls forgotten issues. In the flow of thought it anticipates possible objections yet also has the courage to ignore purportedly relevant challenges because — and here Barth praised his unorthodox teacher, C. Blumhardt — "other things were more important to him."[39] In addressing its temporal context, his theology was more like the needle of a compass than a weather vane. Reflecting on the eternal truth of God, it spoke not from the rocking chair but from the trenches of the church militant. It looked at the church's present status but also looked beyond the horizon at the presence of worldwide church history, the history of our Christian forebears — "What a lot of remarkable things, long assigned to the lumber room, I have come past all along the way and really, I have found almost everywhere that in each of them there was something that was worth saying again."[40] His theology was looking ahead, strengthening the church to continue its existence as an "unassuming . . . mobile brotherhood" even when it had lost its "acknowledged position" (IV/4 184 = 168). Theology was for Barth a "free science."[41] He

---

39. Karl Barth, *Suchet*, p. 176.

40. *Karl Barth–Eduard Thurneysen Briefwechsel,* 2 vols. (Zurich, 1973, 1974), II, 302; ET: Eduard Thurneysen, ed., *Revolutionary Theology in the Making: Barth-Thurneysen Correspondence, 1914-1925* (Richmond, 1964), p. 202.

41. Karl Barth, *Einführung,* p. 15; ET: *Evangelical Theology,* pp. 8-9.

knew that it was tied to the object of its knowledge, and yet it moved in the air of freedom in which it could appropriate the insights even of non-Christians. It distrusted the force of its own logic and asked always whether its efforts of thought might not involve a "flight from the living God." Nevertheless, it was always sure of its subject matter. It questioned much yet never doubted the divine "presupposition." Adopting a phrase of Nietzsche, we might call Barth's theology a "joyous science." We can look calmly at its weaknesses, and as Barth said of Calvin's theology without overlooking *its* faults, we can affirm that it has a powerful "flow."[42]

42. Karl Barth, *Calvin als Theologe,* p. 3.

Path

Constant Beginning

Whoever engages Barth's theology does not enter a building of ideas but embarks upon a path. In his view, this has to do with the "object" of theology, which is not a principle that, once we have happily grasped it, must then only be developed. The object is the living God, whom theology must attentively follow in ever new ways. In 1947 Barth said: "If I had gone on saying the same thing that I had always done, I would have remained true to my theme, my system. But the point was to remain true, not to my theme, but to the Word of God, which is a living Word."[1] Again in 1957 he observed: "As far as I can recall there was no stage in my theological career when I had more than the very next step forward in mind. . . . I saw myself" set before "some subject. . . . It was always something new that got hold of me, rather than the other way round. I then tried to cope with this thing as well as I could. . . . I hardly had anything like a program to follow at all costs. My thinking, writing and speaking developed from reacting to people, events and circumstances with which I was involved with their questions and riddles. I prayed for my daily bread, got it and ate it, and let the next day look after itself."[2] Then in 1962 he wrote that one doing theological work "cannot proceed by building with complete confidence on the foundation of questions that are already settled, results that are already achieved, or conclusions that are already arrived at . . . [he cannot] live today in any way on the interest from a capital amassed yes-

---

1. Karl Barth, *"Der Götze wackelt": Zeitkritische Aufsätze, Reden und Briefe von 1930 bis 1960,* ed. K. Kupisch (Berlin, 1961), p. 116.

2. Eberhard Busch, *Karl Barths Lebenslauf,* 5th ed. (Gütersloh, 1994), p. 436; ET: *Karl Barth: His Life from Letters and Autobiographical Texts* (London and Philadelphia, 1976), p. 421.

terday. His only possible procedure every day, in fact every hour, is to begin anew at the *beginning*. In theological science, continuation always means 'beginning once again at the beginning.'"[3]

Barth's own theological existence was in keeping with that, in that both outwardly and inwardly he trod a broad and dramatic path, and both outwardly and inwardly he always stood in a context. This path of his took surprising turns and involved many breaks, reversals, and new beginnings. It was a path on which there were certainly continuities, a path on which he could maintain what he began with, or later bring to light things he was initially only groping after. What surfaced early on would sometimes be later withdrawn, only to be taken up again in another guise at a later stage. These findings make it very difficult to grasp Barth's theology, and in particular to quote from his own works in a meaningful way. The result is that very different and even contradictory interpretations are given. The prolific secondary literature will testify to this.[4] Barth's own works are superabundant.[5] The *Church Dogmatics* itself amounts to almost ten thousand pages. We certainly cannot understand his work unless we study his path both inwardly and outwardly.

His path began when, as a young adult, he studied theology between 1904 and 1909 with Harnack in Berlin and Herrmann in Marburg and was a decided champion of liberalism as a co-worker with Rade in editing the journal *Christliche Welt*. He acquired from Herrmann a distinctive combination of Kant's philosophy and Schleiermacher's religion. As he then saw it, the unassailable modern sense of autonomy leaves room only for the "knowledge of critical rationalism." We thus have to reject all "authoritative" dogmas, including the biblical canon.[6] Faith, then, is simply an "individual vitality," an "inward experience," the "impress made on our self-consciousness by the eternal content," "the actualization of possibilities in our consciousness resulting from an *a priori* function."[7] God exists for us not as an "outward norm but as the individual inward certainty."[8] That God is alive "is the

3. Karl Barth, *Einführung in die evangelische Theologie* (Zurich, 1962), p. 182; ET: *Evangelical Theology, an Introduction* (New York, 1963), p. 165.

4. Cf. Hans Markus Wildi, *Bibliographie Karl Barth,* vol. 2: *Veröffentlichungen über Karl Barth* (Zurich, 1992).

5. Cf. Hans Anton Drewes and Hans Markus Wildi, *Bibliographie Karl Barth,* vol. 1: *Veröffentlichungen von Karl Barth* (Zurich, 1984).

6. Karl Barth, "Der christliche Glaube und die Geschichte," *Schweizerische Theologische Zeitschrift* 29 (Zurich, 1912), p. 17.

7. Barth, "Der christliche Glaube," pp. 59, 63, 72, 51.

8. Karl Barth, "Antwort an D. Achelis und D. Drews," *Zeitschrift für Theologie und Kirche* 19 (1909), p. 485.

experience of the one who is himself alive."[9] With Angelus Silesius he could say that "It is not out there,/there the fool seeks it,/it is within thee,/thou dost eternally bring it forth."[10] Or he could say more cautiously that it "is mediated to us by people who have come to life,"[11] who show us in some way that "Christ wills to live in you."[12] Someone who values liberal theology as Barth did will neither have misunderstood it in his later critique nor merely rejected it, even though one may not discount either the harm that he perceived in it or the seriousness of the change for which he wanted to be the champion. What caused Barth to move away from his earlier views was the recognition that this kind of religious person, for all the stress upon his or her sensitivity, is a lonely I-person, threatened as well as threatening. Barth made it his task to find for this kind of person a real counterpart. The key would be found in the insight that we must needs rediscover *God* as this counterpart.

To be sure, Barth still preached the liberal line when he was assistant minister at Geneva in Calvin's church, and after 1911 as pastor in Safenwil. Yet at Safenwil he experienced some changes when he saw the economic problems of his workers and farmers and confessed that "I was touched for the first time by the real problems of real life."[13] He took the side of the workers, instructed them politically, acted as spokesman in strikes, joined the socialist party as "Comrade Pastor," founded labor unions, and came into conflict with the local manufacturers. He made this defense: "Because I believe in God and his kingdom, I place myself where I see this kingdom breaking through," and today this is not the church, notwithstanding its "religion," but socialism, for all its lack of religion, for socialism carries the hope of a new and just society and shows solidarity with the deprived.[14]

At this point we note a portentous shift from his liberal position. What he had previously called "religion," namely, that individual inward life, is now viewed negatively. It shuts off access to "*real* life" and sanctions a poor kind of reality. It is thus a betrayal of God whom, as early as 1911, Barth had called "the social God of solidarity" proclaimed by Jesus.[15] This God is manifest and "breaks through" only in the breaking through of the terrible reality of those who live for themselves, in the hope for a social kingdom, and in the

9. Karl Barth, *Predigt* [Sermon], no. 47, August 7, 1910, unpublished.

10. Karl Barth, *Predigt* [Sermon], no. 21, November 21, 1909, unpublished.

11. Barth, "Der christliche Glaube," p. 66.

12. Karl Barth, *Predigt* [Sermon], no. 43, July 3, 1910, unpublished.

13. *Karl Barth–Rudolf Bultmann Briefwechsel, 1922-1966* (Zurich, 1966), p. 306; ET: *Karl Barth–Rudolf Bultmann: Letters, 1922-1966*, ed. B. Jaspert (Grand Rapids, 1981), p. 154.

14. Karl Barth, "Religion und Sozialismus" (1915), unpublished lecture.

15. Karl Barth, *Vorträge und kleinere Arbeiten 1909-1914* (Zurich, 1993), p. 405.

formation of human solidarity empowered by this hope. The non-religious people outside the church are closer to God than the religious within it. For this reason Barth joined the Swiss movement of religious socialism promoted by Ragaz and Kutter. Yet he was still true to his earlier principle that the vitality of God shows itself in our own vitality, understood now as social and not just individual life. It was then a further step that caused him to vacillate about this principle.

The new insight came through the shock when he saw both his liberal teachers and the German Socialists approve of the German entry into World War I.[16] At the time this shock did not really produce a new insight but a long and exciting *search*. What was new — a typical thing for Barth — was the new kind of questioning with which he began to deal with the shock. He did not, like Ragaz, contrast a "right" ethical decision with the "wrong" one. He inquired rather into the material presupposition that made it possible that the invocation of God, or of the social kingdom, should have added nothing to this awful reality other than its endorsement. As an answer to his questioning there came with increasing clarity a recognition that such an ethic could endorse the existing reality only because it stood upon a premise laid down by "religious" or socialist people *themselves*. The core problem of modern humanity, and one that neither religion nor socialism could penetrate, was seen more and more clearly to be that of human subjectivity, which has nothing with which to challenge the given situation because it is itself a part or a product of the given situation. No new reality *can* be generated out of the present reality. Even what we call "revolutionary" is a product of the old world.[17]

This critical insight was for Barth the reverse side of a positive recognition that he derived from the eschatology of C. Blumhardt, whom he visited at Bad Boll in April 1915. "God" is in fact the designation of the true "revolution,"[18] the reality that is a *"new"* world in contrast with the present one. The new reality which the old world cannot itself posit can be posited only *from outside* of it, and it is posited by God. Only God can posit it, for, according to an unconditionally new and essential understanding, God is not simply a humanly *constructed* presupposition. God *posits himself* prior to all human reality. He does so by both setting himself against this reality ("judgment") and by setting himself in relation to it ("grace"). Along these lines Barth would later describe God as the "object" of theology. As the reality or "new world"

---

16. *Briefwechsel*, pp. 306-7; ET: *Barth–Bultmann: Letters*, p. 154.

17. Karl Barth, *Der Römerbrief*, 1st ed. (Bern, 1919), pp. 42-43.

18. Karl Barth, *Predigten 1914* (Zurich, 1974), p. 168.

of God is posited from without in relation to the reality of the world, it constitutes both a critical questioning and a promise of renewal for existing world reality.

Of basic significance was Barth's statement in January 1916 that "it will then be, above all, a matter of our recognizing God once more as God. . . . It is a task beside which all cultural, moral, and patriotic duties . . . are child's play."[19] Also important is the way in which Barth tackled this task. Looking back, he said that "I gradually turned back to the Bible."[20] He remained true to this procedure when later as a dogmatician he also gave exegetical lectures and finally included exegesis in his dogmatics, something no other dogmatician has done. In the summer of 1916, sitting under an apple tree, he began to read Paul's Epistle to the Romans. He read the text in a new way. He discovered that the Bible, so long as we do not read out what we read in, introduces "into our old and customary world" a "completely new world — the world of God" — "not the right human thoughts about God . . . but the right divine thoughts about men, . . . not how we find the way to him, but how he has sought and found the way to us."[21] Here was the new way of reading the Bible. It was not because of their criticism that Barth reproached the historico-critical exegetes. "The critical historian needs to be *more critical!*"[22] They must be critical of their procedures that analyze the text without being confronted by it, without seeing the "Word . . . in the words."[23] This Word is neither a timeless kernel within its temporal husk nor some historical past that we can make use of at will. It is the Word of God that, because it *spoke* as it did then and there, *speaks* thus both here and now. The first task of Bible exposition is to understand this, and it is understood only when we hear it *speaking* to us rather than *our* trying to actualize a relative human word of the past. We must not seek to "experience all kinds of things about Paul" but rather to hear and "think" "with Paul."[24]

The hearing of Paul produced *Der Römerbrief* [*Epistle to the Romans*] in 1919, but Barth quickly found his work to be so unsatisfactory that in 1920

---

19. Karl Barth, *Das Wort Gottes und die Theologie* (Munich, 1929), p. 15; ET: *The Word of God and the Word of Man* (New York, 1957), p. 24.

20. Karl Barth, *Letzte Zeugnisse* (Zurich, 1969), p. 19; ET: *Final Testimonies* (Grand Rapids, 1977), p. 23.

21. Karl Barth, *Wort Gottes,* pp. 21, 24, 28; ET: *Word of God,* pp. 43ff.

22. Karl Barth, *Der Römerbrief,* 2nd ed. (Munich, 1922; 12th ed., 1978), p. xii; ET: *The Epistle to the Romans* (Oxford, 1933), p. 8.

23. Karl Barth, *Der Römerbrief,* 2nd ed., p. xiii; ET: *The Epistle to the Romans,* p. 8.

24. Karl Barth, *Der Römerbrief,* 1st ed., p. 644.

and 1921, "like a drunk man,"[25] he completely revised it in eleven months. He found in Paul "something very ancient, early oriental, indefinably sunny, wild, original."[26] Barth's style of speaking was also "somewhat wild." The tale went around in Safenwil that a lightning flash had come down from the clear sky and through the open window had struck Barth's writing desk. In its soon famous second edition the book had the effect of the unsettling word of a wilderness prophet. It called Christendom to a thoroughgoing conversion because it had lost its way in every direction. It complained that the church was saying "God" when it simply meant "non-god," a mirror image of self-assertive humans. It enjoined the church to distinguish God from everything supposedly divine. It called the "religion" of the believers an illusion because it imagines that it forms an exception to the solidarity of all sinners and to the fact that we are all of us just *human* in the presence of God. It also hammered home the fact that the *relation* between the divine God and us humans, that divine redemption and our divine sonship, is an impossibility within our human possibilities, only possible as we are invaded by the dawning "new world" of God. Basically Barth made this threefold argument already in the first edition. But there, he did it in such a way that the divine, instead of making demands upon us and thus promoting an individualism that asserts itself in mutual self-assertion, worked *organically* as an imparted power "in Christ." The result was the development of a human "organism" that overcame such God-denying individualism. The second edition contested this view.[27]

The divine does not initiate any human possession; it destroys it as illusory. It is not a widening and lengthening addition to an old and perverted world; it abolishes that world. It is something absolutely new that does not grow "organically" into the old world but always *remains* something absolutely new, "altogether thoroughgoing eschatology."[28] His use of the concept of "the invisible"[29] is directed against Schleiermacher's "highest formulation of religion": "intuition" [*Anschauung*],[30] which knows the divine only as "al-

25. *Karl Barth–Eduard Thurneysen Briefwechsel,* 2 vols. (Zurich, 1973, 1974), I, 508; ET: Eduard Thurneysen, ed., *Revolutionary Theology in the Making* (Richmond, 1964), 59.

26. *Barth-Thurneysen Briefwechsel,* I, 236; ET: *Revolutionary Theology,* p. 43.

27. Cf. Karl Barth, *Der Römerbrief,* 2nd ed., p. 223; ET: *The Epistle to the Romans,* p. 241.

28. Karl Barth, *Der Römerbrief,* 2nd ed., p. 298; ET: *The Epistle to the Romans,* p. 314.

29. Karl Barth, *Der Römerbrief,* 2nd ed., p. 67; ET: *The Epistle to the Romans,* p. 92.

30. Friedrich Schleiermacher, *Über die Religion: Reden an die Gebildeten unter ihren Verlächtern* (Berlin, 1799), ch. 2; ET: *On Religion: Speeches to Its Cultured Despisers* (Cambridge, 1988), ch. 2; cf., e.g., p. 104.

ready posited from the outset" in the religious self-consciousness.[31] It is also directed against the concept of the "organic" insofar as this involved a *subsequent* positing of the divine in the consciousness. His criticism was now directed no longer against individualism but against "religion." We cannot escape religion,[32] but we ought to see that, in its assertion that there is such a positing or possessing of God in us, it drives sin to its most extreme point. God mocks such assertions, in that He is *alien* to us, the "*Wholly* Other."[33] God is not one of the concepts which we apply to him; "God is *God*,"[34] not merely "beyond," but that which is beyond "both 'here' and 'there.'"[35] He is not just distant but alien *in that* He approaches us, hidden *in that* He reveals himself, establishing a relationship with us that is "absolute paradox," "the impossible possibility,"[36] the "standing place in the air,"[37] the "void,"[38] finding us "vertical[ly] from above."[39] This he does without finding any predisposition toward him present in us, justifying us in that he unmasks us as sinners. He does not develop the potential already present in our "life," but is rather the *death* of humanity as it knows itself, and the resurrection of the new humanity that is always totally alien to us.

What we find here is a rediscovering of Luther that the influence of Kierkegaard and Overbeck has helped to shape. Mozart's "strange guest of stone" in "Don Giovanni" also played a part.[40] Barth pressed far beyond the anthropocentric thinking that had become almost fateful for modern theology. But could the new path that he was taking ever succeed? By means of an unceasing chain of negations of everything humanly possible? The trace of the gospel surfacing in the first version disappeared here behind this dis-

---

31. Friedrich Schleiermacher, *Der christliche Glaube nach den Grundsätzen der evangelischen Kirche im Zusammenhange dargestellt,* 3rd ed., 2 vols. (Berlin, 1835/36), p. 57.

32. Karl Barth, *Der Römerbrief,* 2nd ed., pp. 237, 105, 163; ET: *The Epistle to the Romans,* pp. 254, 129, 184.

33. Karl Barth, *Der Römerbrief,* 2nd ed., p. 90; ET: *The Epistle to the Romans,* p. 115; *Wort Gottes,* p. 85; ET: *Word of God,* p. 74. The familiar "Wholly Other" is rendered as "Wholly Distinct" in the ET.

34. Karl Barth, *Der Römerbrief,* 2nd ed., pp. 324, 326; ET: *The Epistle to the Romans,* pp. 339, 342.

35. Karl Barth, *Der Römerbrief,* 2nd ed., p. 118; ET: *The Epistle to the Romans,* p. 141.

36. Karl Barth, *Der Römerbrief,* 2nd ed., pp. 69, 80, 175, 186, 197, 316; ET: *The Epistle to the Romans,* pp. 94, 105, 195, 205, 216, 332.

37. Karl Barth, *Der Römerbrief,* 2nd ed., p. 68; ET: *The Epistle to the Romans,* p. 94.

38. Karl Barth, *Der Römerbrief,* 2nd ed., p. 32; ET: *The Epistle to the Romans,* p. 57.

39. Karl Barth, *Der Römerbrief,* 2nd ed., pp. 25, 77; ET: *The Epistle to the Romans,* pp. 50, 102.

40. Karl Barth, *Wort Gottes,* p. 133; ET: *Word of God,* p. 149.

mal judgment. A judgment abstracted from the gospel, however, can hardly
be the judgment of *God*. No position results from pure negations — which
was his intention. Its "cry of 'Not I! Rather God!' actually directs all eyes on
itself instead of on God."[41] Did Barth take seriously enough something he
already knew,[42] that this "not I" is still the I, the "isolated lonely" I, the modern I that hopes to overcome, that fails to see itself as God's counterpart —
not one of the "members of the church"?[43] As Barth quickly detected, he
needed to say the same thing in another way. Thus he entered upon a new
search.

This search developed as Barth pursued the theological orientation
suggested by his commentary on Romans as Professor of Reformed Theology in 1921, in company with his friends Thurneysen, Bultmann, Gogarten,
Brunner, and Merz, and at a distance Tillich. The journal *Zwischen den
Zeiten* gave them a wider hearing. The circle was agreed in criticizing so-
called "neo-Protestantism" that its talk about God "dealt not with God but
with man."[44] They were called the Dialectical Theologians because of the
awkward problem to which they gave consideration. If we cannot presuppose God because he always presupposes himself over against us, we can
speak about him only paradoxically, only dialectically. As Barth put it, "We
ought to speak of God. . . . We are human, however, and so cannot speak of
God. . . . We ought, therefore, to recognize both that we should speak of God
and yet cannot, and by that very recognition give God the glory."[45]

The Word That Leads to Thinking

This dialectic began to open up for Barth with the insight that we "cannot"
talk about God because only God talks about God. Because he does, however, we can then do it in our own way, although not as something we

41. Hans Urs von Balthasar, *Karl Barth: Darstellung und Deutung seiner Theologie* (Cologne, 1951), p. 92; ET: *The Theology of Karl Barth* (San Francisco, 1992), p. 84.

42. Karl Barth, *Der Römerbrief,* 2nd ed., p. 84; ET: *The Epistle to the Romans,* pp. 109-
110.

43. Cf. Adolf Schlatter, "Karl Barth's Römerbrief," in *Anfänge der dialektischen
Theologie,* part 1, ed. J. Moltmann (Munich, 1962), p. 218, ET; *The Beginnings of Dialectical
Theology* (Richmond, 1968), vol. 1, p. 121.

44. Rudolf Bultmann, *Glaube und Verstehen: Gesammelte Aufsätze,* vol. 1 (Tübingen,
1933), p. 2; ET: *Faith and Understanding,* 6th ed. (New York & Evanston, 1966), p. 29; cf. Karl
Barth, *Der Römerbrief,* 2nd ed., p. 20; ET: *Epistle to the Romans,* pp. 44-45. In the Bultmann
citation, the term used is "liberal theology," not "Neo-Protestantism."

45. Karl Barth, *Wort Gottes,* p. 158; ET: *Word of God,* pp. 186, 198, 212.

"should" do. Hence the "Word of God addressed to man"[46] became the center of the theology of both Barth and his circle. A unique feature of Barth's first work in dogmatics was his understanding that *the sermon* was "the starting point and goal of dogmatics."[47] Dogmatics was now neither the monologue of the devout self-consciousness (as in neo-Protestantism) nor an individual effort of thought (as in his *Epistle to the Romans*). It had its place in the *church,* a dimension whose scope first began to clarify for Barth when he encountered the theology of Roman Catholicism at Münster, where he became Professor of Systematics in 1925. Barth found the prevailing approach of Protestantism to that theology a wholly impossible one, for "on the one hand it gives away too much of what we have to join the Roman Catholics in affirming, and on the other, it tacitly takes over from them too much about which we should be arguing."[48] As one of the things that should not be surrendered he discovered the church itself as the setting of theology. This link to the church was the abiding concept of his theology — theology presupposes churchly praxis to which it relates critically, aiming at new praxis for which it prepares the way constructively. The praxis of the church is at its core proclamation of the Word of God. The purpose of this proclamation is that the *Deus dixit* [= God speaks] find expression.

The central formula of *Deus dixit*[49] implies three things that capture in a new way the threefold basic insight of *The Epistle to the Romans.* (1) Where *Romans* had opposed a reduction of theology to the pious subject by postulating the over-againstness of God, what was intended then now becomes fully visible. *Deus dixit:* God is a free subject, not the object of human speculation. He is his own I, an active and speaking I, an eternal I. Far from being our own creature, he is himself the one who created us, who addresses us, who communicates with us, who makes us those who are addressed, who are hearers of his Word and who thus know and acknowledge him. (2) The *Deus dixit* has a *present tense* significance, as proclamation makes plain. Yet it is based, preceding all churchly activity, on a *perfect tense,* for God *has* spoken, first of all in the *concrete and particular* history of Israel and Jesus Christ to which the Old and New Testaments bear witness. Acceptance of this truth involves a turning away from "modern" theology, for this sought to integrate biblical truth into a *general* framework of ideas in order to show that it was

---

46. Karl Barth, *Ethik,* vol. 1 (Zurich, 1973), pp. 19-20; ET: *Ethics,* ed. D. Braun (New York, 1981), p. 13.

47. Karl Barth, *Unterricht in der christlichen Religion,* vol. 1 (Zurich, 1985), p. 28; ET: *Göttingen Dogmatics* (Grand Rapids, 1990), p. 23.

48. Eberhard Busch, *Karl Barths Lebenslauf,* p. 185; ET: *Karl Barth,* p. 179.

49. Karl Barth, *Unterricht,* vol. 1, pp. 53ff.; ET: *Göttingen Dogmatics,* pp. 45ff.

"possible." This understanding focused either upon what could be integrated as "possible" or upon the concrete history, as no more than an "example" or "symbol" of what can be recognized as universal truth. The loss of the Old Testament was typical of this procedure. (3) The God of *Deus dixit* is not one who can be thought of in the abstractness of a being in itself. He is the God who *sets himself in relationship* with us. Hence the theme of Christian theology is the fulfilling of this relationship based upon the divine initiative, namely, the "covenant" that is proclaimed in both the Old Testament and the New;[50] the theme is thus neither God per se nor humanity per se, in order then to relate them to each other as a *later* step. We can speak of God only as we also speak of ourselves as those whom God addresses and claims. To speak of claims reminds us that dogmatics must also be an ethics. In this regard Barth parted from the tendency in neo-Protestantism to detach ethics from dogmatics or to leave ethics to the secular world.

These insights, attained in the twenties, remained basic for Barth even later. He regarded his first works as inadequate and preliminary. He never published his first course in dogmatics, and he broke off the publication of the second (*Die Christliche Dogmatik* [*Christian Dogmatics*], 1927) after the first volume. He also held back the publication of the 1928-29 *Ethik* [*Ethics*]. The reason for all of this was that the articulation of these three points was permeated by a lack of clarity.[51] He was motivated to tackle this lack of clarity by the fact that the "leaders of the Dialectical Theology were as disunited as the revolutionary Chinese generals."[52] An urgent question for his contemporaries was how the Word of God addressed to humanity relates to the presuppositions which humanity brings. The task as they saw it was to investigate these presuppositions as such, in order then to be able to relate the Word of God to them, thus making it "understandable." Perhaps it was as the Reformed theologian schooled by Calvin[53] that Barth became concerned lest nontheological insights should become prescriptions for the Word of God. Nevertheless, he was open on this question, as he had to be in view of the category of paradox. For if the coming of the Word of God addressed to humanity is paradoxical, that is, contrary to human expectations, then, if we are to avoid a sheer absurdity, these expectations must be described in such a way that the Word of God can be related to them meaningfully.

In fact Barth could speak in a way that reminds us of Tillich. "God's

---

50. Karl Barth, *Unterricht in der christlichen Religion*, vol. 2 (Zurich, 1990), p. 381.

51. Cf. his self-criticism in CD I/1 128ff. = 125ff., 177ff. = 171ff.

52. Karl Barth, *"Der Götze wackelt,"* p. 64.

53. Karl Barth, *Die Theologie Calvins* (Zurich, 1922), e.g., pp. 170-71; ET: *The Theology of Calvin* (Grand Rapids, 1995), pp. 126-27.

revelation . . . is the answer to our question how we can overcome the contradiction in our existence . . . which we know that we cannot overcome."[54] Along these lines Barth in his 1928-29 *Ethik* worked with the idea of the orders of creation, but he then rejected it as useless.[55] As he saw it, "an anthropology . . . was thus being advanced as the supposed basis on which we know decisive statements about God's Word. . . . I was paying homage to false gods" (I/1 130 = 127). If theology presupposes an anthropology of its own concoction *apart* from its knowledge of God, and if its knowledge of God is suspended even temporarily in favor of its knowledge of humanity, then theology sets itself under conditions that will dominate its knowledge of God and have indeed the quality of a prior human knowledge of the divine. It must then be granted that the human can indeed provide information about God, but about a god who is necessarily other than the God who addresses his Word to us. Even if this information is described as "the question of God," the Word of God is allowed only to correct it. God's address to us in his Word will then be seen as a more precise but incidental definition of God. It will then be subjected to the suspicion that it is only one of our human pictures of God, that is, one of the "false gods."

In order to find a place for those three positive insights, Barth had to alter the form of his own knowledge. He therefore changed that form, moving from "dialectics to analogy," which in effect ended the circle of "Dialectical Theology."[56] The shift took place while he was teaching dogmatics at Bonn, in his book *Fides quaerens intellectum* (1931). The "ontological proof of God" of Anselm of Canterbury, which he took up, had been heavily freighted by Descartes's version of it: The fact that *I* can *think* a supreme being leads to the conclusion that it *exists;* otherwise it would not be supreme being. Barth thought that Kant's criticism of this version was convincing. The proof does not support the existence of God; it simply demonstrates that the thinker can conceptualize God. Descartes was for Barth the father of the modern crisis regarding the knowledge of God. For here God is rendered dependent upon the self-conscious human I that conceives of him, thus making God a part of that I. "This God is hopelessly within" (III/1 412 = 360), namely, within us. He is a human construct and not God.

Seeking to *vanquish* this line of thinking, Barth took a fresh look at Anselm's proof and turned it upside down. The issue was to demonstrate that

---

54. Karl Barth, *Unterricht*, vol. 1, p. 82; ET: *Göttingen Dogmatics*, p. 69.

55. Karl Barth, *Ethik*, vol. 1, pp. 365ff.; ET: *Ethics*, pp. 215-216.

56. Hans Urs von Balthasar, *Karl Barth*, p. 71; ET, *Karl Barth*, pp. 63-64; but cf. Michael Beintker, *Die Dialektik in der "dialektischen Theologie" Karl Barths: Studien zur Entwicklung der Barthschen Theologie und zur Vorgeschichte der Kirchlichen Dogmatik* (Munich, 1987).

God cannot be proved on the basis of his being thought, for it is impossible to think of him as merely being thought. The key lies in the title, *Fides quaerens intellectum* [= faith seeking understanding]. Knowledge does not begin with the I who knows. The *intellectus* must follow after the *fides*. "Intelligere [= understanding] comes about by *reflection* on the Credo that has already been spoken and affirmed,"[57] in the "analogy of faith" (I/1 11, 25f. = 12, 23), in correspondence to what is believed to be true, as discipleship on the level of thought. This does not mean that "I, the Christian, am the innermost material for the discipline that I, the theologian, pursue."[58] We are not to take it that what *I* believe, or even what the *"church"* believes, its unquestioningly accepted doctrines, is true. No, that *in which* the church believes, the presupposition of its faith that posits it as such, is the Word of God whereby God *gives* himself to be known. The fact that understanding follows faith corresponds to the fact that faith comes from hearing this Word of God.

Knowledge corresponds to faith, for what grounds faith, what faith acknowledges, is indeed *truth*, God as truth disclosing itself to us. "Deum veritatem esse credimus" [= We believe that God is *truth*].[59] The human as such does not already have the truth, so that one can use that truth to determine the truth of God. Yet in the encounter with God one *receives* the engagement with the truth, so that then one seeks to relate to it appropriately in the search for *knowledge*. We have to deal with the truth in correspondence with our search for understanding. We cannot know God except through the *faith* that God's disclosure of the truth calls forth, that faith that perceives the truth as true, acknowledges it, and responds to him. Our knowledge of God lives on the acknowledgment that we can think of him only because he has given himself to our thinking as the truth. He is not God simply because we have thought him. That faith precedes knowledge means that knowledge, then, has to do with *the* one true and authentic *object* that it cannot ever ground or prove or posit. That *object* is itself the presupposition of knowledge, proves itself to knowledge, and grounds knowledge. Knowledge, then, can only follow the disclosure of truth that faith acknowledges, "verifying" it,[60] seeking to correspond to it with the

---

57. Karl Barth, *Fides quaerens intellectum* (Munich, 1931), p. 26; ET: *Anselm: Fides quaerens intellectum* (London, 1960), p. 27.

58. Cf. J. C. K. von Hofmann in Karl Barth, *Die protestantische Theologie im 19. Jahrhundert: Ihre Vorgeschichte und ihre Geschichte* (Zurich, 1947), p. 555; ET: *Protestant Theology in the Nineteenth Century: Its Background and History* (Valley Forge, 1973), p. 609.

59. Karl Barth, *Fides quaerens intellectum*, p. 17; ET: *Fides quaerens intellectum*, p. 18.

60. Wolfgang Ullmann, "Barths zweite Wende: Ein neuer Interpretations-vorschlag zu Fides quaerens intellectum," in *Theologie als Christologie: Zum Werk und Leben Karl Barths*, ed. H. Höckert and W. Krötke (Berlin, 1988), p. 79.

question not whether but *"to what extent* is reality *as* the Christian believes it to be."[61] It is only in this way that we can speak of the *existence* of God. We cannot derive the truth of God from our own thinking anymore than we can derive his existence from our own existence. On the contrary: Because God is the truth, "then following from that [he] exists."[62] He discloses himself to us as he who is the *truth,* and *is* in truth. He thus grounds both our knowledge *and* our existence. Therefore we not only *know,* but correspondingly we *are* those who are ac-knowledged in faith. And thus we not only know who *God* is, but also who *we as humans* are.

In his book on Anselm, Barth worked out the cognitive basis for his *opus magnum,* which like "the medieval cathedrals," remained an *opus imperfectum* (IV/4 vii = vii): the *Church Dogmatics.* The first volume came out in 1932, and the twelfth of the bulky volumes appeared in 1967, one year before Barth's death. Much of his life's energy went into the countless "lucubrations" (nocturnal labors) that produced this work.[63] He viewed this formally as his primary "occupation." He could say that "more important than everything else I tackled was the movement I had to carry through here."[64] He was called a "Jerome in the hermitage" (IV/1 i = ix), referring to Dürer's painting which depicts the scholar with a lion at his feet, a skeleton in front of him, and an hourglass to the rear. "Moby Dick" was Kornelis Miskotte's name for *Die kirchliche Dogmatik,*[65] not merely for its gigantic scope but in remembrance of Melville's legendary whale, which, bold and undeterred, sailed most disconcertingly across the seas and in the depths and was never caught. Barth himself once called his work "the lady in the hoop skirt"[66] because it advanced so slowly, while charmingly twisting and turning.

His work remained "unfinished." As he saw it, the task of dogmatics consists not of "an offering of all sorts of material . . . but of the *movement* of this material" (I/1 298f. = 282-83). Dogmatics does not have many *"objects"* but basically only one, namely, the revelation of God to which the Bible has borne witness and to which the church now must witness. Dogmatics must deal with each point in such a way that, from each different angle of perspective, it always keeps in view the totality of the Christian confession of faith.

61. Karl Barth, *Fides quaerens intellectum,* p. 26; ET: *Fides quaerens intellectum,* p. 27.

62. Karl Barth, *Fides quaerens intellectum,* p. 94; ET: *Fides quaerens intellectum,* p. 92.

63. Oral communication.

64. Karl Barth, *"Der Götze wackelt,"* pp. 198-99.

65. Kornelis Heiko Miskotte, *Über Barths Kirchliche Dogmatik (Theologische Existenz heute!* n.s. 89) (Munich, 1961).

66. Karl Kupisch, *Karl Barth in Selbstzeugnissen und Bilddokumenten* (Reinbek bei Hamburg, 1971), p. 106.

This dogmatics, therefore, though with rare references to previous state-ments, constantly makes retractions of earlier content in order again and again to formulate it in a new way. For its *object* is not static, but continually speaks afresh and is alive and dynamic. For this reason, and not just because "the times change and we within them," the *object* has to be seen again and again from new angles. Because its *object* is moving, the dogmatics that deal with it must also be moving. There can be no end to it. It will never arrive at a result. It can never be a system. It will always be open (I/2 860 = 769). It will neither always say the same thing nor always say something different. Rather, again and again it will say *the same thing,* and again and again it will say the same thing *differently.*

Thus, when Barth began his major work, he had not, based on his work till then, arrived at a happy end to his search, so that he could now simply ex-pound his findings. "No, in a remarkable way life was really only just begin-ning."[67] As he often remarked, this was to be an arduous venture, feeling his way into unknown territory. As he was preparing to start his last volume he sighed, "It is curious still to be so much a beginner at the age of seventy-three."[68] The searching was not, of course, a blind poking about. Some basic decisions had become clear to him. He was amazed "how it was possible that I had not learned and said that much sooner. Why are we so slow when it is a matter of the utmost importance?"[69] He had ruled out some theological pos-sibilities as digressions and distractions. Even if he had no precise "plan" in mind, he had discovered the direction in which he was to proceed, one step at a time, always prepared to be surprised and to correct himself.

He abandoned his earlier title, *Die Christliche Dogmatik* (1927) [*The Christian Dogmatics*], and now entitled his work the *Die kirchliche Dogmatik* [*The Church Dogmatics*]. The title signifies that theological work is not done by a single Christian individual who thinks through what he has been able to acknowledge as the truth. The title signals that the thinking of Christian the-ology can be responsibly done only by a member of the church of Jesus Christ. This included, for Barth, the affirmation of the "confessional" form of the church in which this thinking takes place. What he also saw at the time, namely, that "what consciously belongs only to the sect or to the pro-vincial Church cannot as such belong to the Church" (I/2 925 = 827), became increasingly evident to him. The ecclesial character of a dogmatics carries with it responsibility in the "ecumenical church" (IV/2 7-8). What Barth had

---

67. Karl Barth, *"Der Götze wackelt,"* p. 182.
68. Eberhard Busch, *Karl Barths Lebenslauf,* p. 457; ET: *Karl Barth,* p. 441.
69. Karl Barth, *"Der Götze wackelt,"* p. 185.

in view was not a dogmatics of the clergy, nor a summary of the dominant state of consciousness of the church, nor what is embedded in church tradition. He thought that he had been led here "to an intensified *critical* debate with the church's tradition and even with the Reformers."[70] The use of the word "church" denotes his taking seriously that theology cannot give to itself its own *object;* that *object* is only given to it in that it precedes theology in accordance with the church's faith in God who has revealed himself in his Word, the witness to which is the meaning and task of the church. Theology is "ecclesial" as "a function of the Church" (I/1 1 = 3), in which it examines the agreement of the church's witness with the *object* of the faith to which it bears witness. In this way it prepares for a new orientation of that witness.

It was now much clearer in the *Church Dogmatics* that the *object* of theology, that is, what Barth calls the "Word" or "revelation," is truly identical with the person of *Jesus Christ.* Alongside him are those who belong to him, in Israel and in the church, but this person is in the center. He is not divorced, of course, from the action of the Triune God. Yet precisely in the revelation of the Trinity we have the incarnation of this person as God's Word. God does not merely "reveal" something in him. He reveals that he himself *is* what he *does* — he is none other than the God who takes us to himself. And God does not simply "direct" his Word "to" humanity in him. Rather God determines that he will be precisely that which he then experiences, the human accepted by God and no other. "The saying in John 1:14 is the center and theme of all theology. . . . I have no christological principle and no christological method. Rather, in each individual theological question I seek to orient myself afresh to some extent from the very beginning — not on a christological dogma but on Jesus Christ himself *(vivit! regnat! triumphat!)* [= He lives! He reigns! He triumphs!]. On each occasion I then have to go about answering any particular question in a quite special way, or rather, to allow myself to be led in a special way in the direction towards which I am looking. The methods must keep being renewed, changed, modified. I am very attracted to a remark by Hilary of Poitiers: *Non sermoni res, sed rei sermo subjectus est* [= the word serves the content, not the content the word]. There is a whole theological revolution in this saying, and if people had noticed it, many errors, much barrenness and much boredom in theology would have been impossible. The question of christological theology is first of all a question of *life* — the question of the confrontation of theology with the *res* [= content], i.e. the one who is the *imago Dei invisibilis, primogenitus omnis creaturae, caput corporis ecclesiae*" [= image of the invisible God, firstborn of all creatures, head of the

---

70. Karl Barth, *"Der Götze wackelt,"* p. 186.

body of the church, Col. 1:15-20].[71] He is not a principle from which statements can be deduced. He is the one who is alive, one whom our knowledge can only *follow*, openly and nimbly. This is not one of our own self-fabricated presuppositions that then hedge us in; it is God's prior decision in our favor, the beginning he has made with us with which we can only *begin* again and again. "Within theological thinking generally unconditional priority must be given to thinking which is attentive to the existence of the living person of Jesus Christ" (IV/3 200 = 175). Only thus can we perceive and reflect upon everything else. Therefore, "Saying 'yes' became more important to me than 'no.'"[72] "My experience has been that in this concentration I could say everything much more clearly, much less ambiguously, much more simply, much more worthily of the confessions, and also much more openly, much more freely, and much more comprehensively than before, when I was hampered in part at least by the eggshells of philosophical systems."[73]

The Church Conflict

At the time when Barth was working on his *Church Dogmatics* he was outwardly pressured by many external responsibilities on which he adopted pointed, fearless, and often offensive positions. Undoubtedly the two lines of activity, the internal and the external, were related. What took place outwardly was a kind of commentary on that to which he was devoting himself at the inner level. He had refrained from taking up such positions in the twenties because he did not sense at the time that he was challenged to do so. But that does not mean that his critique of Neo-Protestantantism made him a supporter of the anti-liberal authoritarianism of the day, thus undermining the Weimar Republic.[74] It is not only the fact that his political ethic as early as the *Epistle to the Romans* was aimed at an "honest humanitarianism" and a "calm reflection about justice and injustice" within political relativity.[75] His critique of the neo-Protestant idea of an absolutely self-positing human sub-

---

71. Eberhard Busch, *Karl Barths Lebenslauf,* p. 394; ET: *Karl Barth,* p. 380; cf. CD III/3 v = xi; IV/3 199f. = 165ff.

72. Karl Barth, *"Der Götze wackelt,"* p. 191.

73. Karl Barth, *"Der Götze wackelt,"* p. 186.

74. Cf. Friedrich Wilhelm Graf, "'Der Götze wackelt'? Erste Überlegungen zu Karl Barths Liberalismuskritik," *Evangelische Theologie* 46 (1986): 443ff. Klaus Scholder, "Neuere deutsche Geschichte und protestantische Theologie: Aspekte und Fragen," *Evangelische Theologie* 23 (1963): 510ff.

75. Karl Barth, *Der Römerbrief,* vol. 2, p. 472; ET: *The Epistle to the Romans,* p. 489.

ject did not then lead to an appeal for some kind of human authority to restrict this subject, as was the case with Emanuel Hirsch and Friedrich Gogarten. Barth's critique appealed to the *spiritual* authority of the Word *of God*. As he saw it, God's Word, which is outside any human grasp, challenges all human attempts to posit oneself as absolute. It should be clear that, coming out of that process, he was equipped for the challenges which the year 1933 presented. For it was his thesis that the new authoritarian regime was not a ("justified") reaction to liberalism, but a violent and aggressive fruit of the idea of a humanity that posits itself as absolute, which he had already criticized. He thus thought that this new disorder could be resisted only if at the same time an older historical error was also disputed.[76]

Since the Nazi state, before attacking the Jews, first proceeded against its critical political opponents, Barth, who unlike Tillich[77] kept up his membership in the Social Democratic Party, expected that he would quickly be dismissed as a professor at Bonn. He used the time that remained to seek clarification in the church. He was even more shocked by the church's full agreement with the new regime than he was by the regime itself. On the basis of the first commandment that we should serve God and not other authorities, he appealed in March 1933 for an understanding that the authorities should be interpreted "according to the standard of revelation and not that revelation should be interpreted according to the authorities." He called this approach "natural theology."[78] In June his statement that the urgent task now was to do theology "as if nothing had happened"[79] was properly understood as a rigorous focus on the fact that the new political slogans could not in any way be obligatory for Christian thought.[80] Barth was primarily opposing the German Christian movement. Opposing the German Christians' conformity to the Nazi-State, Barth made *one* question into the "key to all the church controversies": the issue is not "whether theology is capable of making political judgments but rather . . . whether these political judgments had been made in a theologically correct way."[81] This he denied, because the theologically binding norm in this context had been rendered inoperative by another norm alien to it.

76. Cf. esp. Karl Barth, *Der deutsche Kirchenkampf* (Basel, 1937).

77. Cf. the correspondence of April 1933 and Karl Kupisch, *Karl Barth*, pp. 75-76.

78. Karl Barth, *Theologische Fragen und Antworten* (Zollikon, 1957), pp. 136, 139, 143.

79. Karl Barth, *Theologische Existenz heute!* (Munich, 1933), p. 3; ET: *Theological Existence Today! A Plea for Theological Freedom* (London, 1933), p. 9.

80. Thomas Mann, *Tagebücher 1933-1934*, ed. P. de Mendelssohn (Frankfurt, 1977), p. 167; ET: *Thomas Mann — Diaries 1918-1939* (London, 1983), p. 168.

81. Klaus Scholder, *Die Kirchen und das Dritte Reich*, vol. 1: *Vorgeschichte und Zeit der Illusionen* (Frankfurt, Berlin, and Vienna, 1977), p. 547.

We really begin to understand his position when we see that his comparatively isolated struggle was directed "no less sharply"[82] against the centrist faction of the church, which had drawn a line between itself and the German Christians in 1933. It decisively resisted any state intervention into the church's interior life, but in the political area it just as decisively affirmed the state of the *Führer* and the *Volk*. It could condemn the ousting of Jewish Christian pastors and yet at the same time welcome the State's anti-Jewish laws. In 1933, looking at the emerging injustice toward both Jews and Socialists, Barth called this "one of the worst illusions in an age that was rich in illusions" — as though one could politically be "united with the 'German Christians'" with a "Yes to Hitlerism" and then "in opposition to them could have a pure church."[83] Only if the church let the Word of God be its *sole* norm, and did not suspend it in its position towards Nazism, would it be freed from the stance of defending its self-preservation in a State otherwise greeted with "joyous assent,"[84] and thus freed to witness to God's Word *over against* this state. The text that guided him in all this was Matthew 6:24: "You cannot serve God *and* mammon."

This is the sense[85] of the Theological Declaration largely composed by him in May 1934, with its confession of Jesus Christ as the "*one* Word of God" that the church must hear and trust and obey.[86] The Confessing Church was founded with the unanimous recognition of the Declaration at the first national synod of the German Evangelical Church, which met at Barmen. This was a surprising move, for the Declaration excluded the thinking of the centrist party as well as the German Christians. Barth then began to draw out the demanded consequences of such a confession in relation to the state. He demonstrated what this stance meant by declaring that, even though he was a *state* official, "as an evangelical *Christian* he could not take the required unconditional oath of obedience to Hitler."[87] This led to ten-

---

82. Karl Barth, *Theologische Existenz heute!*, 1 (Munich, 1934), p. 30; ET: *Theological Existence Today!*, p. 62; "no less sharply" renders the German original literally.

83. Werner Koch, "Karl Barths erste Auseinandersetzungen mit dem Dritten Reich," in *Richte unsere Füsse auf den Weg des Friedens*, ed. A. Baudis (Munich, 1979), pp. 500-501.

84. Karl Barth, *Theologische Existenz heute!*, p. 31; ET: *Theological Existence Today!*, p. 65.

85. Cf. Karl Barth, *Texte zur Barmer Theologischen Erklärung* (Zurich, 1984).

86. Alfred Burgsmüller and Rudolf Weth, eds., *Die Barmer Theologische Erklärung: Einführung und Dokumentation* (Neukirchen, 1983).

87. Cf. Heinrich Assel, "'Barth ist entlassen . . .'. Neue Fragen im Fall Karl Barth," in *Zeitworte: Der Auftrag der Kirche im Gespräch mit der Schrift* (Nürnberg, 1994), pp. 77-99, who says that this is how E. Hirsch understood Barth's refusal to take the oath and thus why he actively supported Barth's removal from his professorate.

sions between Barth and the Confessing Church, which was retreating to the line of the centrist group at Barmen. In November he was forced out of his leadership position in the Confessing Church and the state deposed him as a professor. A court in Cologne condemned him for "treacherous conduct" against the state, proven in part by his criticism of the discrimination against the Jews.[88] When the Confessing Church withdrew an invitation to him to a synod in June 1935, he found no place for himself in Germany and accepted a call to the University of Basel. After a parting address to the Confessing Church at Wuppertal in the fall of 1935, he was arrested and deported. In this address, in opposition to the prevailing idea in the church that the "authorities" are an expression of God's law, he declared that "gospel and law" are indissolubly united and must both be confessed against the reality of the state.

Going back to Switzerland did not narrow his field of action. His friendship with W. A. Visser 't Hooft opened him to the ecumenical horizons and gave his theology an ecumenical hearing. He traveled extensively through Europe and encouraged the churches to stand with the Barmen Declaration. He still remained in contact with the Confessing Church and helped to set up an aid organization in Switzerland to aid refugees who were victims of racist persecution. In 1938 he came to a politically sharper "application"[89] of his views. His lectures in Scotland coined the phrase "political service of God."[90] He developed this concept in his work *Rechtfertigung und Recht* [*Justification and Law*], arguing that a legal democratic state is compatible with the gospel, and that threats to such a state may be justifiably resisted.[91]

After the Crystal Night's events he declared that Hitler was Antichrist because he was anti-Semitic,[92] and soon thereafter we find in his doctrine of election an express recognition that Israel and the church are together the one elect community of God (II/2 218 = 198). Thus an attack upon the Jews is also an attack upon the church "at its roots." He thought, therefore, that Christians ought to see more clearly than others that the power of Hitler *had to be* resisted by military force.[93] Barth thus supported the war against the German military with all his powers. He was persuaded that this was a "po-

---

88. Hans Prolingheuer, *Der Fall Karl Barth, 1934-1935: Chronographie einer Vertreibung*, 2nd ed. (Neukirchen, 1984), pp. 286ff.

89. Karl Barth, *"Der Götze wackelt,"* pp. 186-87.

90. Karl Barth, *Gotteserkenntnis und Gottesdienst* (Zollikon, 1938), pp. 203ff.; ET: *The Knowledge of God and the Service of God* (London, 1938), pp. 222ff.

91. Karl Barth, *Rechtfertigung und Recht* (Zollikon, 1938), pp. 42-43.

92. Karl Barth, *Eine Schweizer Stimme: 1938-1945* (Zollikon-Zurich, 1945), pp. 69ff.

93. Karl Barth, *Eine Schweizer Stimme*, pp. 102-3.

lice action" that was being waged on behalf of the Germans, too, "defending a just state" and "restoring an order that had been injured and destroyed by the common guilt."[94] In this regard Barth came into conflict with the Swiss government, which largely gave in to the wishes of the German Goliath and prohibited Barth from issuing political statements.

Renewal and Reconciliation

When Germany was defeated, Barth again swam against the stream, resisting the widespread hatred of the Germans. He now pleaded in the other countries that one should treat the Germans as "friends in spite of everything"[95] — not, of course, to minimize the German guilt nor to move quickly on to other things, now that the war was over. His concern was how they could become people who would *take responsibility* for their guilt. After helping to frame the Stuttgart Declaration of Guilt in October 1945,[96] he gave even stronger support to the Darmstadt Declaration (1947),[97] which says that only on the presupposition of an already valid divine reconciliation, which is not merited by enforced penitence, will people become capable of recognizing their guilt and, as a result, of being converted for renewal. An abstract demand for repentance will result only in the suppression of guilt and regression into earlier patterns of behavior and countercharges.[98] Barth was also fighting for a needed and patient learning of democracy "from below" in Germany.[99] In doing so, his real concern was the practical realization of a sense of responsibility that would then be capable of confessing guilt. This was then an illustration of Barth's thesis that democracy is what in the secular world corresponds to reconciliation.

Reconciliation must precede repentance. This was Barth's point when, in the keynote lecture assigned to him at the first meeting of the World Council of Churches in Amsterdam in 1948, he read the conference theme, "The Disorder of the World and God's Plan of Salvation," in reverse order. Only then would we see the real damage of the "disorder of the world." And

---

94. Karl Barth, *Eine Schweizer Stimme,* pp. 279-80.

95. Karl Barth, *Eine Schweizer Stimme,* p. 305; cf. p. 297.

96. Martin Greschat, ed., *Im Zeichen der Schuld: 40 Jahre Stuttgarter Schuldbekenntnis. Eine Dokumentation* (Neukirchen, 1985), pp. 10-11.

97. Martin Greschat, *Im Zeichen der Schuld,* pp. 82-83.

98. Karl Barth, *Eine Schweizer Stimme,* pp. 357, 361; Karl Barth, *Die christliche Lehre nach dem Heidelberger Katechismus* (Zollikon-Zurich, 1948), pp. 38ff.

99. Karl Barth, *Eine Schweizer Stimme,* pp. 372ff.

then we would see the saving fact that God has the world in his hands, and we are not those "who transform this evil world into a good one. God has not abdicated his dominion to us. That we should be his witnesses in the midst of the political and social disorder of the world is all that is demanded of us."[100] Nothing less is expected of us, as Barth showed in his contribution to the second meeting of the World Council of Churches at Evanston. Participating in the hope of Israel, the church bears witness to the great hope with which it greets "the coming King in its hungry, thirsty, alien, naked, and imprisoned brothers" and sisters.[101]

Shaped by the context of the special thematic that in his view was posed by the postwar period are the very definite positions that Barth adopted about West German rearmament and about participation in the cold war between the West and the East. These caused such offense that for a long time especially in Switzerland Barth was stigmatized as a Communist. He was in fact an opponent of Communism: "None of us wants Communism."[102] Yet in the hysteria of those years no one apparently noted his opposition or his warning to the churches of the East not to adjust to the ideology of their states.[103] But why was he also warning the churches of the West against "anti-Communism" as the greater and more imminent danger? Why did he no longer equate the brown shirts with the red shirts as he had done to irritate the Nazis?[104] Why did he now summon the church to a "freedom" that smacked of neutralism, to a freedom that did not take sides as it had done in the past, but that would avoid doing so as it evaluated the new situation?

The decisive reason, conceptualized on the basis of the divine reconciliation, was that "war is . . . something other than the 'ultima ratio' [final resort] of the political order. In itself war is murder, homicide, and so is everything that makes for war instead of counteracting it."[105] Behind this stands the thesis that war is rooted in the inhumanity of the prewar period and that it brings this inhumanity to light (III/4 525 = 458ff.; IV/2 474 = 421). This thesis is critical of the argument that *military* weakness provokes aggression and that peace can be secured only by increasing armaments. The logic here, that "if

---

100. *Amsterdamer Dokumente* (Bielefeld, 1948), p. 146.

101. *Evanston Dokumente,* ed. F. Lupsen (Witten, 1954), p. 55.

102. Karl Barth, *"Der Götze wackelt,"* p. 154.

103. Karl Barth, *Offene Briefe 1945-1968* (Zurich, 1984), pp. 274-89.

104. Cf. Karl Barth, "Kerl und die Bekenntniskirche," *Basler Nachrichten,* Basel 1, Beilage zu Nr. 333 (1935); Karl Barth, *Die Kirche zwischen Ost und West* (Zollikon-Zurich, 1949), pp. 19-20.

105. Karl Barth, *"Der Götze wackelt,"* p. 153.

one wants peace one must prepare for war" [*Si vis pacem, para bellum*], is deceptive (III/4 517 = 452). This logic provokes war, and doubly so in that the inhumane damage on one's own side is thus suppressed while it is excused by cheap accusations against the opponent. This logic, whose inhumanity is really true godlessness,[106] is exemplified for Barth in atomic armaments in that proponents are prepared to accept the destruction of everything which they promise to "protect."[107] With the cold war as a concrete example in view, Barth inverted the logic: "If you don't want war, prepare for peace" [*Si non vis bellum, para pacem*] (III/4 517 = 452). If the cause of war is a deficit in humane relationships, then in the postwar period neither armament nor disarmament can be "the first concern, but the restoration of an order of life which is meaningful and just" — in correspondence with God's reconciliation "the fashioning of the state for democracy, and of democracy for social democracy" (III/4 525f. = 460-61). This means "that in relation to Communism . . . there can only be the positive defense of the creation of just and tolerable social relations for all classes of the population."[108] This was the "freedom" to which Barth wished to summon at least the Christian churches.

It is intriguing that in these years, when Barth was making such statements, he came to the midpoint of his *Dogmatics*, to "the *heart* of the message received by and laid upon the Christian community": the doctrine of reconciliation. The ethical arguments that formed the basis of Barth's public decisions were intended as implications of this message of reconciliation. The message proclaimed "the free act of the faithfulness of God in which He takes the lost cause of man . . . makes it His own in Jesus Christ, carrying it through to its goal and in that way maintaining and manifesting His own glory in the world" (IV/1 1 = 3). This reconciliation involves our own *vocation* to be its messengers and an ethics in which, *calling* upon God, we achieve maturity, and in which, being "zealous for God's glory" and "fighting for human justice," we look ahead to the kingdom of God that will come in Jesus Christ and renew all things. The *Dogmatics* broke off here. At almost seventy-six years, Barth concluded his professorial work, during which he had taught and studied with innumerable students from all parts of the world, with a lecture course entitled *Evangelical Theology, an Introduction*. The last lecture was on love.

Retiring as emeritus, Barth embarked on a lecture tour through the United States. His chief aim was to develop a "theology of freedom" which

---

106. Karl Barth, *Offene Briefe*, p. 444: the denial of all three articles of faith — as in Nazism (*Eine Schweizer Stimme*, p. 246).

107. Karl Barth, *Offene Briefe*, pp. 206-7.

108. Karl Barth, *"Der Götze wackelt,"* p. 153.

would demythologize the concept of arbitrary freedom ("liberty") and prepare a path for the freedom in coexistence made possible by God's initiative.[109] It was related to his recently announced intention to work on a theology of the Holy Spirit.[110] What Barth had in view was not a shift in paradigms but the expectation that what he had worked on for years now needed to be said in a different way and with new tongues. Forty years before, Barth had remarked, "Veni, creator Spiritus [= Come, Creator Spirit] . . . you have been introduced to my theology if you have heard this sigh."[111] Then again, in one of his last sermons, when he was preaching only in the Basel prison, he stated that the four little biblical "words: 'My grace is enough,' say much more and say it better than the whole pile of paper with which I have surrounded myself. They are enough — something that I am very far from being able to say about my books."[112]

A second and final journey in the fall of 1966 took him to "the tombs of the apostles" *(Ad limina apostolorum).*[113] He went for talks with the Vatican about the consequences of Vatican II. The trip crowned his irenically critical[114] dealings with the Roman Catholic Church and its theology. He regarded the council as a sign of hope during the sixties, because he sensed that they had discerned a renewal in the "form of 'conversion' — not to a different church, but to Jesus Christ, the Lord of the one catholic and apostolic church," in readiness to let themselves "be called in his church to faith in the one Lord and into his service."[115] Only a general renewal of this kind on all sides would be the promising way to the unity of the divided.[116] Barth had a difficult time finding something similar in the Protestant churches. His final words, uttered on the evening of December 9, 1968, spoke to this concern. He said to his oldest friend, Thurneysen, "We shall not be downhearted! Never! For 'he reigns.'"[117]

---

109. Karl Barth, *Gespräche 1959-1962* (Zurich, 1995), pp. 279, 489.

110. Karl Barth, "Nachwort," in *Friedrich Schleiermacher* (Munich and Hamburg, 1968), pp. 310-11; ET: appendix to *The Theology of Schleiermacher* (Grand Rapids, 1982), p. 278.

111. Karl Barth, *Wort Gottes,* p. 123; ET: *Word of God,* pp. 134-35.

112. Karl Barth, *Rufe mich an!* (Zurich, 1965), p. 79; ET: *Call for God* (New York, 1967), p. 78.

113. Karl Barth, *Ad limina apostolorum* (Zurich, 1967); ET: *Ad limina apostolorum* (Richmond, 1968).

114. Karl Barth, *Ad limina apostolorum,* p. 41; ET: *Ad limina apostolorum,* pp. 43-45.

115. Karl Barth, *Ad limina apostolorum,* p. 18; ET: *Ad limina apostolorum,* p. 18.

116. Karl Barth, "Kirche in Erneuerung," *Freiburger Zeitschrift für Philosophie und Theologie* 15 (1968): 161-70.

117. Karl Kupisch, *Karl Barth,* p. 135, quoting the last words of J. C. Blumhardt.

Primary Work

The Church Dogmatics

This dogmatics is a gigantic work that can frighten off even the well-disposed and discourage them from reading it. Its very appearance often gives the impression of something unapproachably monolithic, a heavenly metaphysics remote from time.[1] Even when it does find readers, they are often fleeting readers who find a few phrases and terms here and there, and are done with the matter before they arrive at any real understanding. They can easily block their own access to the *Dogmatics*. It must also be said that an age when everything goes by so quickly, when what is desired is a fast-food theology, is not a time when access to a work of this kind is easy. Those who say that they have no time, those who are content with slogans, do best to ignore these volumes. Nevertheless, for those who will take the time, some hints might be appropriate as to how to handle this work.

1. As stated already, this dogmatics is always seeking to say the same thing differently. At every point, from various angles, it focuses on the one totality of the Christian confession of faith. The liveliness of this one thing propels the discussion to constantly new approaches from different vistas. This lies behind the distinctive style of thinking and speaking that colors the lengthy sentences which seem at times to form a microcosm. Barth moves ahead by constantly circling around his subject, in order to follow it in the dynamics which inheres in it. Thus, it is relatively unimportant where one chooses to start reading. It is much better to read a small portion and under-

---

1. Cf. Heinz Zahrnt, *Die Sache mit Gott: Die protestantische Theologie im 20. Jahrhundert* (Munich, 1966), pp. 141-54; ET: *The Question of God: Protestant Theology in the Twentieth Century* (New York, 1969), pp. 112-122.

stand it well than to read a large part superficially. One will certainly need to go slowly, even when reading a small section, if one is to follow the train of thought and move and think along with Barth on his circular course. Whoever is quarrying for quotations, either to confirm one's own views or as a dark background for one's own views, will learn nothing from this work. For people doing that, Barth's twelve volumes will simply be "his coffin," and they will not comprehend that "what he once *said* he still speaks, saying what he once *wanted* to say."[2] We really first understand Barth's work only when we do not merely understand his work but what it is that motivates it.

2. "You eternal cornucopia"[3] was Hans Urs von Balthasar's comment to the aging Barth when he pressed ahead with his dogmatics. Yet we need to understand more than the psychological motivation that kept him going. We will not gain an objective view of all that Barth did unless it is clear to us — clearer than in much of the literature concerning it — that a work of this magnitude would soon have been halted, or "shifted into neutral gear," if the author had been involved here in an endless monologue, rather than in an ongoing and many-sided dialogue. If we take note of the fact that there is discussion with many named or silent partners, the impression of the monolithic will disappear. In this dialogue the author is first of all the one who understands, listens, and receives, who thereupon speaks, answers, considers, and questions again. Since this is a theology in which prayer and study belong together, the dialogue is first of all with God, and then with the Holy Scriptures of the Old and New Testaments, with an abundance that is remarkable in a dogmatician. There is also dialogue with Christian and secular contemporaries, with what we read in the newspapers, and, just as importantly, with his students. With increasing intensity there is also dialogue with figures in theological and intellectual history. For Barth our predecessors are "not dead, but living. They still speak," so we should give them a "hearing" in our theology, "not only . . . favourite voices" but also "quite unwelcome voices" and "even avowed pagans."[4]

3. We should stress once again that this dogmatics is not "only" a dogmatics. It contains detailed explicitly exegetical passages. Much of the doc-

---

2. Cf. Karl Barth, *Die Theologie Calvins* (1922) (Zurich, 1993), p. 9; ET: *The Theology of Calvin* (Grand Rapids, 1995), p. 7.

3. Eberhard Busch, *Karl Barths Lebenslauf*, 5th ed. (Gütersloh, 1994), p. 457; English translation: *Karl Barth: His Life from Letters and Autobiographical Texts* (London and Philadelphia, 1976), p. 441.

4. Karl Barth, *Die protestantische Theologie im 19. Jahrhundert: Ihre Vorgeschichte und ihre Geschichte* (Zurich, 1947), p. 3; ET: *Protestant Theology in the Nineteenth Century: Its Background & History* (Valley Forge, 1973), p. 17.

trine of creation is an exposition of Genesis 1 and 2, and Barth's so-called "doctrine of Israel" in CD II/2 consists largely of an exposition of Romans 9–11. There are also many broadly nuanced discussions of theological and philosophical history. It contains also an extensive ethics. That the work has a homiletical aim is indicated by the fact that sermonic meditations on the lectionary of pericopes were included in the Index volume. The fullness of this dogmatics also demonstrates how all the theological disciplines are inter-related and inter-dependent. This does not deny the distinctive character of their various tasks, but it makes us aware of the fact that theology becomes "unhealthy and more dangerous than useful" when there is a "disintegration" of its disciplines "into a relationship of indifference or concealed or open hostility." Theology "is sound and healthy when in all its [disciplines] . . . it keeps its eye fixed on its problem and theme" (IV/3 1009 = 880). Since this dogmatics integrates the disciplines, it can be used from many different points of view, such as its widespread use for sermon preparation.

4. As has already been said, Barth's dogmatics offers "no system," "no comprehensive views, no final conclusions and results" (I/2 971 = 868). It seeks to open up a dialogue and not to have the last word. Yet at the same time, we should now emphasize, it is not a wild concoction of stray thoughts. It should not be compared with a cabinet that has many drawers, for its intention is to proceed along its way with logical steps as a train of thought that one can follow. If we detach individual sayings from this train of thought, we will easily make nonsense of it. We have to see that its statements follow one another in an inner sequence and are structured with a characteristic rhythm. In large measure this contributes to the beauty of the presentation: the shaping of the expounded content by a well-arranged order. If we are to understand appropriately, we must pay more attention than is usually given to the order as well as the content, to the location at which "something" is said or not said in a certain context, and to the larger and finer structures that give form to the contents. At first glance the work can appear to be old-fashioned — and many never get beyond that first impression. Its structure is deliberately unspectacular: Prolegomena (I/1 and 2), then the doctrine of God (II/1 and 2), then creation (III/1-4), then reconciliation (IV/1-4), and finally, though Barth never got this far, redemption (V). Only upon closer and more exact examination of the work will its original character be revealed. It is disclosed in the perspectival approaches within which a particular "content" is moved back and forth and considered, and in the style and typical sequence of the steps with which the consideration of the subject matter proceeds. C. Frey remarked in a comparison of Barth with Tillich, that Tillich "builds the old half-timbered building with new beams, . . . whereas Barth

takes the old beams and builds a new structure with them."[5] To shift meta-phors, we shall now attempt to draw a map of the landscape through which this dogmatics moves, and of the roads upon which it makes its way.

What Must Be Said First

The dogmatics of the 19th century understood the "prolegomena" with which it began as a preamble addressing the general human and human-religious presuppositions which would make a "doctrine of faith" *possible.* Barth, however, begins his work with a crash of the drum by understanding prolegomena in precisely the opposite sense: It has to do with "the *first part* of dogmatics rather than that which is *prior* to it" (I/1 41 = 42). Theology gets bogged down in preambles if it does not begin with the "major content." It will never get to the real theme if it does not deal with it from the very first. Moreover, it can never speak about God at all except for the fact that God *be-gan* to speak to humanity. It can speak about God only when it sees that it "must continually begin again at the beginning" (I/2 971 = 868), at *this begin-ning.* What we "say first" comprises both our respect for and seriousness about the fact that *God* speaks, and must speak, first. Barth's prolegomena, then, comprises his total dogmatics in brief, or more precisely, a comprehen-sive doctrine of the *Word of God.*

For Barth the "Word" or revelation of God is the event in which "God speaks" so that he is heard (I/1 136ff. = 132ff.). The Word of God does not merely mean that God says "something"; it means the "speaking God" (I/1 141 = 136). This Word is not something different, then, from God himself, but is God himself, God defined in it, so that we are dealing with God him-self in it. God is no one other than he who discloses himself in it. Further, the Word of God does not mean that hearers already exist or that there are those who are ready to hear and able to do so. Nor does it mean that it is an open question whether there will be hearers or not. Rather, the Word involves the creation of a human counterpart to whom it is addressed. "Revelation means the incarnation of the Word of God" (I/1 175 = 168). This revelation is not the transformation of the Word into a man but the Word's *assumption* of human-ity in one man so that it may be perceived by him. The Word of God is finally an event, an action. This does not mean that God acts without words, nor that his naked word is complemented by his action. The meaning is that "God's Word is itself God's act" (I/1 153 = 147). On the side of the hearers,

5. Christopher Frey, *Die Theologie Karl Barths* (Frankfurt am Main, 1988), pp. 239-40.

then, hearing and acting and being must not be separated! Barth then makes three further points.

1. The Word of God is the *reality* of the fact that God has made and does make himself known to us in the *concrete* history of Jesus Christ, which summarizes the history of Israel, and which is imparted to us by the Holy Spirit, *attested* to in Holy Scripture, and then *proclaimed* to us in the church in accordance with Scripture. Here we have Barth's doctrine of the threefold form of the Word (I/1 114 = 111). The Word or revelation of God is not simply an idea that we can regard as realized in what is attested and proclaimed, although always and only partially; it is identical with the reality that God himself *speaks* in what is attested and proclaimed. We *can* know God only as we *do* know him. Yet we *do* not know him merely because we *can* do so, but rather because God *gives* himself to be known in his speaking.

2. The Word of God contests the idea that humanity as such possesses the possibility of knowing God. It is not self-evident to the human person that the true God is concealed from him. This has to be said to her by the Word of God. We may thus say that "God conceals Himself in revealing Himself" (I/1 341 = 323; cf. 175 = 168-69). His concealment and revelation are not two phases that can be detached from one another. God is concealed even *in* his revelation. Otherwise, Barth stresses, his revelation would not be the revelation *of God*. God's hiddenness does not rest on an inadequacy of human knowledge that revelation would only correct, and then only partially. It rests on the fact that it is and remains a possibility *of God* alone when the human actually has to do with God in the encounter with him. Without the divine concealment understood in this way, humanity cannot in fact have dealings with God in his revelation.

3. The fact that, in God's real speaking, humanity begins to deal with God, and that God deals with the human person, is made possible by God alone — there is no possibility for this present in the human. The point is that God can be known only *through* God, but through God *can* truly be known (I/1 312 = 296; cf. II/1 200f. = 179-80). This defines for Barth the meaning of the doctrine of the Trinity. For this reason it is one of the things that "must be said first" in dogmatics. Barth finds in the doctrine of the Trinity "a *necessary* and *relevant* analysis of revelation" (I/1 326f. = 310). He can then translate the Trinitarian terms "Father, Son, and Holy Spirit" with the triad Revealer, Revelation, and Revealedness (I/1 311 = 295). God is to be understood then as "triune" in the sense that he is the Subject, the Act, and the Goal of revelation. As the Triune God he can do what humanity cannot do, but which he in his revelation does: he turns to the human person, causing a turning in response, in order to *show* himself as knowable by humans and to

give himself to be known by them. Three times there is this same free, kind, and effective grace, that God *gives* himself to be known, so that he *is* known by the human person.

When theology begins at the beginning it puts what God says first and before everything else, in order constantly to reflect upon it, to pursue it, to follow it, and to let one's thinking be formed and shaped by what precedes it. Balthasar's criticism that for Barth "the Trinity . . . do[es] not play a central role" for dogmatics[6] is to a certain extent correct. For Barth refused to derive the structure and development of dogmatics from the *doctrine* of the Trinity. Its object would then be a "controllable principle . . . for the construction of a 'system,'" whereas its real object is the "being of God in His work and activity . . . the actuality of the Word of God, freely preceding and underlying all views and dogmas" (I/2 983 = 879). This implies of course the event of the Word of the *triune* God.

In the dogmatics Barth views each of the themes he addresses as an aspect from which to reflect on the being of God in his Word and work. He structures his train of thought, with a certain freedom and yet with a recognizable constancy, with a three-step sequence, in both small and large contexts. This threefold step is obviously an implication of the way he understands the doctrine of the Trinity. As a rule he speaks first of the subject of the divine Word and work, then of the act, and finally of the goal. Again and again his train of thought seeks to correspond to God's movement to humanity, to his turning to humanity and of humanity, in order to disclose himself to the human and the human to him. In so doing he not unwittingly begins up "above" with God. *We* cannot do this on our own, he stresses. Yet we must because of the reality that God has already trodden this path and addressed us in his Word. For this reason, before taking that threefold step, he usually first has a "hermeneutical" discussion in which he explains how far, on the basis of the preceding reality of revelation, the knowledge to be explored in the subsequent three steps has been given and shaped.

The train of thought with its threefold structure reflects upon the way of God toward humanity. It thus reflects upon the work of the Triune God. God is, however, always the *One* in Three, so that in all that he is and speaks and does, the Triune God must always be thought of as the One God. Barth's form of knowledge seeks to do justice to this in that the steps in his thinking are set up in a threefold pattern not only in *sequence,* one following the other, but also *parallel,* one next to the other. We see here the authentic structure of

---

6. Hans Urs von Balthasar, *Karl Barth: Darstellung und Deutung seiner Theologie* (Cologne, 1951), p. 272; ET, *The Theology of Karl Barth* (San Francisco, 1992), p. 160.

his thinking, in which a threefold line intertwines and corresponds both vertically and horizontally.

A good example might be found in the doctrine of God (II/1-2), outlined in Table 1 (on p. 46). To see how the characteristic vertical and horizontal three-step sequence shapes the content of Barth's thought in detail, we provide in Table 2 a further example, the subdivision of the middle item in Table 1. Once we see clearly the structure of Barth's doctrine of God we can understand the material task that he had set for himself. If in volumes III-IV he planned to speak of the threefold work of the Trinity in creation, reconciliation, and redemption, it is a characteristic of his dogmatics that he *precedes* all of them with the doctrine of God first in volume II. This arrangement of his material emphasizes the fact that we can do justice to the work of God *toward* us and *for* us and *with* us only if we *first* know God as the *Subject* of his work, and indeed if we do not know that, then we will not recognize this threefold work of the Triune God as in truth the work of *God*. By putting the doctrine of God before that of his work, is Barth metaphysically thinking of an abstract God "in Himself" who lies behind his work? So, as one common objection puts it, if we do not want to be subject to groundless speculations, can we make any statements about God at all, because we *humans* can never know God (or anything else) except in relationship to *ourselves?*

Fundamentally, however, Barth still aims to discuss God in relation to ourselves. Yet he contests the idea that this relation rests on a weakness or limitation of human knowledge. His emphasis is that the relation about which Christian theology has to speak lies beyond the problem of the limitation of human knowledge and rests on the fact that *God* graciously sets himself in relation to us (cf. II/1 204, 217 = 182, 193). If we think along that other line we will make the center of theological thought the *human person* who relates everything to it*self.* We will then do precisely what Barth is criticized for doing: to the extent that the human cannot relate God to itself, God would have to be thought of as such an abstract being "in and of itself." Barth conceives of this relationship differently. It is grounded in and by God, not in the self. It is graciously created by God. This is made clear by putting the doctrine of God before that of his work.

The meaning is not that we should talk of an abstract being of God *behind* his work but that in free grace God is the *doer* and *initiator* of his work. He is the Subject of his action. He "is" not outside it, for it would not be his action if he were not its subject. If we do not attend first of all to this subject, then it would be doubtful whether the relationship with God is with a real *counterpart,* with the one who first establishes us, and it would be debatable whether this relationship came about solely through God's sheer *grace.*

Table 1. The Doctrine of God

	II/1: God's Reality	*II/2: God's Gracious Election*	*II/3: God's Command*
God's Reality	God's Being in Action	God's Self-Determination for the Covenant of God and Man	God's Claim Enclosed in God's Assurance to Us
God's Turning	Perfections of God's Love	Temporal Fulfillment of Election	The Goodness of God's Decision
God's Claim	Perfections of God's Freedom	Recipients of Election	God's Judgment Whereby He Accepts Sinners

Table 2. Doctrine of Gracious Election

	God's Election	*Revelation of and Testimony to Gracious Election*	*Recipients of Election*
God's Election	God's Eternal Covenant Decree	The Witness to God's Free Grace: The One Community Israel/Church	Solidarity of the Elect with the Reprobate
Revelation of and Testimony to Election	Temporal Fulfillment of the Covenant	Witness to Election: Heard and Believed	The Elect as Witness to the Gracious Election
Recipients	The Human as Covenant Partner	The Goal of Witness: The Human Who No Longer Contradicts God	The Reprobate as Recipient of the Testimony to Elections

This helps us to understand why, as the tables show, Barth structures his doctrine of God along Trinitarian lines. The structure demonstrates that God as the Subject of his work is not a mere being "in and of itself," so that he needs the human and is dependent upon the human in order to enter into relationship. How would this relationship be sheer grace? No, God is himself rich in relationships. He is a relational being. In the freedom of his grace he can thus set himself in relation to us. He can initiate this relation. We can thus understand why the Trinitarian permeation of the material contents of the doctrine of God is so meaningful.

The contents deal with (1) the reality of God. The first point (1.1) is that God "is," and he is in such a way that his being is not a special case within a general concept of being. The point is not that God *is,* but that *God* is. Nor is his being static, so that his activity would be something external and over against him, which he could do without. Rather, because and in that God is grounded in himself and moved by himself (II/1 303, 339 = 270-71, 301), he is "being in act," yes, he is the one who "alone in His act . . . is who He is" (II/1 305 = 272). As the *subject* of his *act,* God "is" not outside it. If he were, the act would not be *his* act. The second point (1.2) is that God's "attributes" are to be viewed as the fullness of his perfections, which are not attached to him externally but in which "the eternally rich God" is his own essence. They are first the perfections of his love *insofar* as he exists in his act and works, in which he founds and perfects relationship and fellowship. The third point (1.3) is that they are the perfections of his *freedom,* which is not contrary to his love. It is not an arbitrary freedom, not a freedom in which he sets aside his love, but in which he is totally himself in his love. In this freedom, his love is always *totally* his own love, in which he is free to determine what his love is and what use he should make of it. His being is that of "the one who loves in freedom" (II/1 288 = 257).

2. The next chapter deals with the election of grace ("predestination"). This is a high point in Barth's dogmatics. Barth sees election not as the "terror of Christian thinking in every age" (Heinrich Barth) but as a pervasively gracious election, the "sum of the gospel" (II/2 9 = 12). First (2.1) it is the self-determination of God, at the beginning of all his movement beyond himself, that brings about fellowship with the human race, which as such carries with it the determination of that race for fellowship with God. Second (2.2), it reaches its fulfillment in time with the consummation of the covenant with Israel in Jesus Christ. It is the divine election of fellowship with sinners in which he consigns the judgment of sin to himself and life to the sinner. It is witnessed to the rejected for their salvation by the "one community," which has the double form of Israel and the church of Jews and Gentiles. Third (2.3), the

recipients of election are the rejected sinners whom God has chosen as his covenant partners in Christ, as the "one elect community" bears witness.

3. That dogmatics should include ethics is for Barth based on the fact that the God of grace is also the God who commands. If the election of grace corresponds to the love of God, the *command* of God corresponds to his freedom, which is identical to his lordship (II/1 338 = 301). The command of God is his (3.1) *claim* upon humanity, which is a just claim because the gospel implies the law, and the total grace implies the total right of God to humanity. Yet the command is also (3.2) God's *gracious decision* for the human, which is then not a disposition over him to be blindly accepted, because God's command is his announcement and explanation of what is *good* for us. It is then (3.3) God's *judgment* upon those who are addressed by God's command. Barth has a new formulation of the concept of judgment. It is a gracious judgment, for in it God separates sinners from their sins but does not separate himself from sinners, instead defining and claiming them as his.

Faith in the Creator

Volume III (in four books) deals with the doctrine of creation. It is not as finely structured as the other volumes (III/3, V). Nevertheless, the form principles are recognizable which correspond to those that Barth discerned in his understanding of God's revelation of grace. The material approach to the doctrine makes this evident. We cannot know the world as *creation* if we do not know the *Creator*, know *God* as its Creator, and know the creation in *faith* in him. If God has revealed himself, then knowledge comes with this relation. It is twofold. First, we must take seriously that no other god holds sway here, only the God who has disclosed himself in his revelation, in his Word. The Creator is not an Anti-God over against the Reconciling God and the Redeeming God, nor is he a partial God, say, the "God of the patriarchs," who finally distinguishes himself in his revelation in Christ as a supplement to the first revelation in creation. No, the Triune God is the Subject at the creation of heaven and earth (III/1 52ff. = 48ff.).

Second, we need to make it clear in what way and to what extent this God, who is the same in all his works, does different things in creation from what he does in reconciliation and redemption. Barth's explanation is this: we must see creation *in terms of* revelation, and therefore in relation to the covenant between God and humanity viewed in the context of the biblically attested history of Israel and Jesus Christ. "It is precisely in view of creation that we cannot possibly ignore Jesus Christ" (III/1 49 = 46). That is the meaning of the Biblical discourse about creation "through the Word" which the New Testament equates with Jesus Christ. We must *understand* creation in terms of the covenant, because materially the covenant *precedes* creation. God's "yes" to his creature precedes its existence. The fallen creature's "no" cannot negate this "yes." God's "yes" to his fallen creature in the covenant of reconciliation reveals that God affirms its existence.

On this view the divine creation is to be understood as a work that corresponds to God's covenant will and covenant decision, which the fall contested but did not negate. All this comes to expression in Barth's structuring of the substance of the doctrine both as a whole and in detail. We again have a three-step sequence both horizontally and vertically (III/1 25ff. = 22ff.). (1) God is the Creator by giving existence to, by favoring, and guaranteeing a reality different from himself, a true counterpart, other and distinctive. (2) The existence of the created world, and particularly humanity, since it is from *this* God, is a conferred existence, proving the benevolence of God. (3) The two-sided but one reality is the truth that is made known to us by the history in which God announces himself to us in his Word according to the witness of Holy Scripture. This three-step sequence determines the arrangement of the doctrine of creation as a whole.

Volume III/1 speaks of the subject of creation, of the *Creator,* but in terms of his deed, his creative action. This happens in a further three-step sequence. (1) Faith in the Creator is the pre-condition of the possibility whereby we can speak of the "world" as his creative work. (2) The work of the Creator, the act of his creating, is presented in a differentiated treatment of the relation between creation and covenant, by means of a detailed exposition of Genesis 1 and 2. And further, (3) it is said that God's work is not a silent one; it is joined to his Word, by which he discloses the good meaning of his work — his "yes" to his creatures.

Volume III/2 deals with the product of God's action, the creature. For Barth, this focuses particularly upon humanity, not because of a preference of the human over all other creatures, but because the human is recognizable in the Word of God as its first responsible (i.e. capable of responding) recipient. For this reason the structures of human existence cannot be recognized in themselves, but only in the Word of God itself, concretely in the one who is not only "true God" but also "true man," which means for Barth "real man." In this second step the benevolence of the divine work of creation is also to be considered, for the human person does not exist alone but essentially in relationships, first to God, then to our fellow-creatures, then to ourselves as made up of body and soul, and finally to the limitations of time in which the creature as such always exists.

Volume III/3 deals with the history of Creator and creature in which the reality and goodness of the creation are authenticated and guaranteed. Once more we have a threefold process. (1) God in his love as Father, and in his freedom as Lord, preserves, accompanies, and reigns over his creature, in that he draws it into the covenant with all his elect. This is the meaning of the so-called "doctrine of providence." (2) Surprisingly, at the point where we would expect Barth, following the pattern of the three-step sequence, to speak about the benefits of God's action, he deals instead with the question of evil. This does in fact fit in here, for Barth defines evil as "nothingness." It is that which God negated at the very outset. It did not come from God nor is it a creature of God, and thus it has no legitimate place in God's creation. (3) Again surprisingly, where we would expect Barth to discuss the historical disclosure of this twofold reality, he treats instead of the kingdom of heaven and the angels as God's messengers. Yet this also fits well here, since it has to do with the statement (III/3 426 = 369) that God claims the upper world for himself. That upper world was created, but in principle it is beyond the reach of earthly creatures and is a limitation for them. From there, God sends messengers as authentic witnesses to his will and revelation on earth.

Volume III/4 deals with *creation ethics.* The thematic term freedom here replaces the customary language of "orders of creation." The reference is to the free affirmation of the human person as the good creature of God in that he functions humanely in basic and defined relationships. That this affirmation is a benefit is stressed by the fact that ethical priority is given not to duties and norms but to the Sabbath commandment. Its meaning is the release from the necessity of earning one's right to life, so that, based on the right to life already given to us, the activity we are commanded to do is to be understood as a free and liberating activity. As creatures, we are commanded to live in correspondence to the basic relationships in which the human is a creature, and thus to practice our freedom as freedom in *fellowship:* with God, and in relation to others, to ourselves, and to our delimited time.

Faith in the Reconciler

The books in Volume IV are devoted to the doctrine of reconciliation, which is the inner core of the work. Barth first saw the very artfully structured plan in a dream. On awakening in the night, he committed it to paper at once.[7] In the arrangement three vertical lines correspond twice to three horizontal

---

7. Busch, *Karl Barths Lebenslauf,* p. 391; ET: *Karl Barth,* p. 377; cf. CD IV/1 83ff. = 79ff.

lines. Before we present this content schematically, however, some preliminary remarks that will contribute to our understanding will be helpful.

1. Originally Barth had thought of calling this volume series the doctrine of the *covenant.* The covenant is indeed the inner theme, summarized in the "Immanuel, God with us" (IV/1 2ff. = 4ff.). He understands the classic designation of Jesus Christ as "true God and true man" as the designation of the covenant made in him. This is not a "new" covenant as compared to the "old" covenant with Israel, but is rather the *fulfillment* of that covenant made by God with Israel and now in its fulfillment completed for all people.

2. The covenant fulfillment in Jesus Christ is not to be understood as a reaction to sin but the execution of the original good will of God with his creatures. If his covenant had been *only* a reaction to sin, then it would have been defined by the condition of sin and would have become invalid when sin was vanquished. If it did not *also* react to sin, it would never be "fulfilled" because of the failure of the human covenant partner. If, as Barth says, it is *also* a reaction to sin, then this reaction is to be characterized as a factual "incident" (IV/1 72 = 68) that does not arrest God's original covenant will but can only signify that he fulfills it *all the more decisively* in spite of sin. The fulfillment of the covenant is thus an *action* of God that, because of sin, has the form of a *reaction:* the form of the *reconciliation* of sinners with God.

3. In this event we are not to separate the person and work of Jesus Christ. Barth has reservations about the so-called "doctrine of Christ's two *natures*" (true God and true man). It is his *nature* to be in *action.* We cannot know his person apart from the execution of his work. At the same time we would not know his work properly if we were to see his person as totally absorbed in that work, if we were to fail to discern his person as the irreversible and irreplaceable subject of that work. Hence we have to distinguish between the person and the work so as to make it clear that in that work we have an authentic, divine human counterpart who acts in and for us, and that that work rests on his pure and gracious initiative.

4. In his understanding of the *person* of Jesus Christ Barth interweaves three doctrines that were formulated alongside one another in classical teaching. (a) The first is that of the two natures of Christ as both true God and true man in *one* person. (b) The second is that of his two states of humiliation and exaltation. (c) The third is that of his three offices as priest, king, and prophet. He does it in this way: (a) Christ is true *God* in that he *humbles* himself and is *priestly* in his action toward us. (b) He is true *man* in that he is exalted to fellowship with God and thus is the *kingly* man. (c) He is *one* person in that, in the *Holy Spirit,* he imparts himself to us as the *pledge* and *witness* to what he is and does, and thus acts *prophetically.*

5. Since Barth understands God's work in Christ not as defined and conditioned by sin, but only as the later reaction to it, the consequence is his distinctive *doctrine of sin.* Sin is not *in its essence* wrong conduct over against divine or human laws but rather is *opposition* to the God who in grace and love encounters sinners to reconcile them. It is, then, not only that which is forbidden, but that which has no grounding at all, and is in its presumptuous reality so incredibly empty that the divine reconciliation alone is a match for it. It can be truly known only where God in his kindness sets himself in opposition to it. It must therefore be discussed after Christology, not before.

6. Because what God does in Jesus Christ, when carried out, has the form of a reaction to sin, it is also a means to heal the damage done by sin. *Soteriology,* as the older dogmatics called it, deals with this: the doctrine of salvation. In classical style one speaks here of the divine justification and sanctification of sinners by God. Barth adds to these two themes a lengthy discussion of a third perspective, the vocation of humanity to be witnesses to God's reconciliation.

7. In classical dogmatics, the section on the doctrine of the provision of salvation would be followed by the doctrine of the personal *appropriation* of salvation, which is by faith. Barth has several corrections at this point. (a) He sees this entire theme decisively as the work of the *Holy Spirit.* (b) He stresses that salvation through the Spirit is made known first to the Christian *community,* so that individuals can be Christians only within that community. (c) This means that the "church" does not mediate salvation between Christ and individuals. Thus, the church cannot be divided into two essentially different groups, the clergy and the laity. All those in it carry the full responsibility of members. (d) There is only a *provisional* difference between Christians and all other people, which consists of the fact that Christians know salvation in Christ, but not that it is valid for them alone and not for the others; their task is to witness to it to the others. (e) Therefore, faith alone is not the proper and responsible "appropriation of salvation" but rather with faith also love and hope.

Table 3 (on p. 53) should help us to understand the formal structure of Barth's doctrine of reconciliation. In it we see once more how Barth's thinking is shaped by the Triune God and how God makes his way to humanity. This dogmatics, we repeat, is not a system, nor is it directed towards producing "results." The important thing is the forward-moving handling of the dogmatic "material," from theme to theme. In point of fact, its writing never did reach its conclusion, but was interrupted as he was moving into the doctrine of ethics (IV/4) which was to follow the doctrine of reconciliation. Entitled *The Christian Life* and in correspondence with the theme of the "cove-

Table 3. The Person of Jesus Christ

	IV/1 God's Turning to Humanity	*IV/2 Human Turning to God*	*IV/3 Revelation and Witness*
Two Natures (Subject)	Jesus Christ as True God	Jesus Christ as True Man	Jesus Christ in the Unity of His Person
Two States (Act)	Humbling Himself as Man	Exalted by God	Pledge of Reconciliation
Three Offices (Goal)	As Priest Reconciling Man	As King in Fellowship with God	And as Prophetic Witness Enlisting Man in His Work
Work of Jesus Christ	(God's Humiliation as Man)	(Man's Exaltation by God)	Revelation of Reconciliation
God's Judgment on Our Opposition	Sin of Pride	Sin of Sloth	Sin of Falsehood
God's Changing of Our Opposition	Justification	Sanctification	Vocation
The Work of This Change by the Holy Spirit	(a) The Gathering of the Community	(a) The Building Up of the Community	(a) The Sending of the Community
	(b) Faith	(b) Love	(b) Hope

53

nant" fulfilled in the reconciliation, it was to address the interaction between God and us, between ourselves and God, and the action that is graciously commanded of us therein and thereto. Three chapters were planned.

1. The first deals with *baptism* as the *founding* of the Christian life. As the contradiction of sin, baptism involves a person's *renunciation* of the old life, made possible by God's descent and turning to that person. As the appropriate response to God's action in a person's life, it is that person's *mature* "yes, " one's answer to the new life which God has promised him. It thus entails as well one's incorporation into the gathered community.

2. The second and main chapter on ethics was intended to address the living of the Christian life as action in the *invocation* of God. For Barth this is the essence of all action of the reconciled person, because in the human response to God's gracious covenant fulfillment in Jesus Christ, the interaction with God from the human side is concretely fulfilled. This ethic was to involve the closest possible interweaving of the ancient admonition to "pray and work," the presentation of which was to follow the Lord's Prayer, that prayer of Jesus that enables and inaugurates human response. Obviously for Barth prayer does not replace action, but through prayer this action is pervasively characterized as activity that both responds to reconciliation and is dependent upon it. The dogmatics breaks off after two sections which expound the first two intercessions of the Lord's Prayer in discussions of "Zeal for the Honor of God," and "The Struggle for Human Righteousness."

3. The closing chapter would have dealt with the Lord's Supper seen in analogy to the departure for the promised land in the Passover, as the departure of the community which is nourished for its journey at this meal. Its journey is moving both towards the coming kingdom of God and simultaneously into the world around it.

Barth did not leave any indications on how he would have handled volume V and its theme of eschatological redemption. He would certainly have developed this doctrine in Trinitarian fashion and added an ethics.[8] It is also well known that he would have understood the eschaton brought about by the Holy Spirit in particular as an "apocalypse," a definitive, total, and universal "revelation"[9] of the eternally decreed and beneficent counsel of God fulfilled temporally in Jesus Christ, that is, of his covenant with created humanity as its eternal validation. With this validation God sets aside forever all human opposition against himself, and his work is thus consummated as all creation gives him thankful praise.

8. Karl Barth, *Ethik*, vol. 2 (Zurich, 1973), pp. 359ff.; *Ethics* (New York, 1981), pp. 461ff.
9. Cf. CD IV/3, 1053ff. = 917ff.

II

Insights — The Themes of His Theology

The Wonderful Beginning — The Doctrine of Revelation and of the Knowledge of God

Perplexities

At the early stage of his path Barth quoted Overbeck's saying, "Theology cannot be re-established except with audacity."[1] Where was the problem for Barth? "Many things can be meant by the word 'God.' For this reason there are many kinds of theologies. There is no man who does not have his own god or gods as the object of his highest desire and trust, or as the basis of his deepest loyalty and commitment. There is no one who is not to this extent also a theologian."[2] Did perhaps theological pluralism disturb Barth, and did he seek then to make his Christian theology the dominant one? He saw it as characteristic of *all* these theologies that each "considers and represents itself as the best . . . because even should it not be the only right one, it claims to be still more right than the others." In his view, it was the task of Christian theology neither to "participat[e] in this competition,"[3] nor to encourage all of them to moderation and tolerance. For him the problem was at a different point. He once remarked, "What is meant by the word ['God'], what does it say to me, what am I supposed to do about it? Didn't a great philosopher . . . say that God was dead? Well . . . even if God were in fact a dead God for many people and sometimes for all of us, that is very far from saying that he is dead. But there is something in it; while the word 'God' is certainly not

---

1. Karl Barth, *Die Theologie und die Kirche* (Munich, 1928), p. 23; ET: *Theology and Church: Shorter Writings, 1920-1928* (New York, 1962), p. 72.

2. Karl Barth, *Einführung in die evangelische Theologie* (Zurich, 1962), p. 9; ET: *Evangelical Theology, an Introduction* (Grand Rapids, 1963), p. 3.

3. Karl Barth, *Einführung*, p. 10; ET: *Evangelical Theology*, p. 4.

dead, it is ailing, ailing badly, because it has been wrongly used and abused so often."[4]

How seriously sick is it? It was seriously sick for Barth because so many theologies today have fallen under the shadow of the suspicion that even *if* they speak so very ardently of God, they are not really speaking about God but only about *the human*. They do not delineate an authentic divine counterpart confronting humanity, but rather only the human's own concepts and desires and needs, no matter whether they think of God as transcendent or immanent within humanity. Feuerbach, who died one decade before Barth was born, had declared that "Theology had long since become anthropology."[5] He acknowledged that theology reads into the term "God" our noblest experiences and concerns. Far from rejecting all that, Feuerbach wanted to preserve and nourish it all on the condition that theology concede that its term "God" was speaking about nothing other than the human person. "I, on the contrary, let religion itself speak. I constitute myself only its listener and interpreter. . . . It is not I, but religion, that worships man, although . . . theology denies this. . . . I have only found the key to the cipher of the Christian religion," which is, "that atheism . . . is the secret of religion itself; that religion itself, not indeed on the surface . . . in its essence, believes in nothing else than the truth and diversity of human nature."[6]

What could Christian theology in good conscience reply to its interpreter? It might declare bankruptcy, as D. F. Strauss did when he responded to the double question, "Are we still Christians?" and "Are we still religious?" by flatly negating the first and affirming the latter![7] What if Mauthner's thesis were correct, that the modern godlessness in this interpretation of theology "was simply an irruption of the same thinking which had lived on strongly enough in a hidden stratum of the European spirit through all the preceding and ostensibly Christian centuries" (IV/1 681 = 610)? Should we assert in response to Feuerbach's provocation that the statements of Chris-

---

4. Karl Barth, *Rufe mich an!* (Zurich, 1965), p. 7; ET: *Call for God* (New York & Evanston, 1967), pp. 10-11.

5. Ludwig Feuerbach, *Das Wesen des Christentums* (Leipzig, 1957), p. 35; ET: *The Essence of Christianity* (Boston, 1881), p. xi (reference to citation from 1st ed.); cf. Karl Barth, *Die Theologie und die Kirche*, p. 225; ET: *Theology and Church*, p. 226.

6. Ludwig Feuerbach, *Das Wesen des Christentums*, p. X; ET: *The Essence of Christianity*, p. x.

7. David Friedrich Strauss, *Der alte und der neue Glaube* (Leipzig, 1872), pp. 94, 146-47; cf. Karl Barth, *Die protestantische Theologie im 19. Jahrhundert: Ihre Vorgeschichte und ihre Geschichte* (Zurich, 1947), p. 497; ET: *Protestant Theology in the 19th Century: Its Background and History* (Valley Forge, 1973), p. 48.

tian theology are not a human illusion because they rest on *revelation?* This was not good enough for Barth because the concept of revelation was part of the very theological legacy that ignited Feuerbach's thesis. Even in his liberal youth Barth had made generous use of the concept to the point of "ennui with revelation" (II/1 78 = 73), describing all kinds of people such as Goethe and Beethoven as God's revelation.[8]

Barth began to question this usage in 1914 when he heard his liberal teachers contend "seriously that war was a *revelation* of God."[9] As early as 1914, and again in 1933 in response to the interpretation of "the German hour" as "a new revelation of God in the German Christians,"[10] he began to investigate not how far the political position was right but how far such religious statements were *theologically* correct. What did such a description of the war or of the German hour really add to the view of these events that these people already had, except that it sanctioned their opinion? Were not human thoughts and interests already formed without revelation reflected in what was now called "revelation"? Furthermore, if leading theologians could talk along these lines, was not this the result of a long exercised if wrong habit of thought rather than a minor collapse? Barth *warned* against a theology that "with [its] magic key of the 'concept' (revelation) put into the hand of man the instrument with which . . . man becomes wholly master even of the self-revealing God."[11] If Barth has been described so often as a theologian of revelation, then that must mean that he subjected this concept of modern theology to a critical revision and only then regarded it as theologically usable.

Barth's fear was that modern theology — and not just "merely modern theology," for Feuerbach "could so often choose to cite Luther"[12] — could not truly in any of its forms stand up to Feuerbach's objection — he was the "thorn in the flesh of the newer theology. . . ."[13] In typical fashion Barth's own thinking found that this objection worked decisively against modern theology, which demonstrated that Christian theology cannot participate in a competition for the most correct theology. Most disturbing to him was the

8. Karl Barth, "Der christliche Glaube und die Geschichte," *Schweizerische Theologische Zeitschrift* 29 (Zurich, 1912), pp. 69-70.

9. Karl Barth, *Predigten 1914* (Zurich, 1974), p. 523.

10. Cf. Karl Barth, "Lutherfeier," *Theologische Existenz heute!* 4 (Munich, 1933), p. 20.

11. Karl Barth, *Die Theologie und die Kirche*, pp. 227-28; ET: *Theology and Church*, p. 228.

12. Karl Barth, *Die Theologie und die Kirche*, p. 229; ET: *Theology and Church*, pp. 229-30.

13. Karl Barth, *Die Theologie und die Kirche*, p. 231; ET: *Theology and Church*, p. 231.

disproportion between the lack of concern about the question, Are we "*really* talking about [God] when we are *allegedly* doing so" (I/1 169 = 163), and the weight of the suspicion that theology only ostensibly talks about God when in reality it is dealing with the human, with his desires and their satisfaction, with her goals and her innate or acquired ability to reach them. Barth believed that the newer Christian theology represented by Schleiermacher provided more than enough reason to be suspected of having made it unclear that to speak of God means *something other* than "speaking of man in a loud voice."[14] "Whether the 'matter'" for which one "unceasingly" engages oneself with the claim that it is about God is "really *God's* matter, whether *God* himself wills all this, is something that no one every seriously wanted to question, for this was always a dangerous question. It was always the case that everything was already complete without God. God should always well suffice to execute and crown what humans had already initiated on their own. Objectively the fear of the Lord was *not* the beginning of our wisdom. Rather God's assent here had to be picked up in passing." But if that fear is not there as "the beginning," "then what follows from it can not be divinely new and helpful. Instead, it will be at best a reform, merely a new garb for the old world relationship, which from God's point of view will do more harm than good."[15]

If Barth's assessment was cautious because the theology he had in view might not have been meant as he himself thought he was hearing it, then his criticism of a "God" understood in this way was ruthlessly radical. "It is high time for us to declare ourselves thorough-going doubters, skeptics, scoffers and atheists in regard to him. It is high time for us to confess freely and gladly: this god, to whom we have built the tower of Babel, is not God. He is an idol. He is dead." In the place of the living God now stands "the unquestionable fragment of our own thoughts. . . . It will then be, above all, a matter of our recognizing God once more as God. . . . It is a task beside which all cultural, moral, and patriotic duties, all efforts in 'applied religion' are child's play." The issue now is to "begin with him anew."[16] Indeed, theology cannot be re-established except with audacity. This is possible only in a situation that involves "an inconceivably impressive sharpening of the commandment, Thou shalt not take the name of the Lord thy God in vain."[17]

Barth compared this task to that of the "rider on Lake Constance," a

14. Karl Barth, *Das Wort Gottes und die Theologie* (Munich, 1929), p. 164; ET: *The Word of God and the Word of Man* (New York, 1957), p. 196.

15. Karl Barth, *Der Römerbrief*, 1st ed. (Bern, 1919), p. 299.

16. Karl Barth, *Wort Gottes*, p. 14; ET: *Word of God*, pp. 22-24.

17. Karl Barth, *Die Theologie und die Kirche*, p. 3; ET: *Theology and Church*, p. 57.

"mortally dangerous undertaking . . . in which we have reason not only at the beginning but also in the middle and at the end to take the last resort of invoking the name of the Most High." "We are a generation that has to learn again, sometimes even by name, what are the presuppositions that a Thomas, an Augustine before him, and a Calvin after him could quietly take for granted." "But the task is posed for us as for previous generations. None of the laughter or head-shaking of our contemporaries and none of our faint-heartedness ought to keep us from at least recognizing the task. And when we do so, we shall have to address it in some way."[18]

God's Beginning with Us

How do we arrive at the knowing of God? The answer is to be found, in Barth's view, by a reversal of the question. We don't arrive at such knowledge, and as long as we try to do so, we will always make images of God that are in truth only reflections of ourselves. That we don't arrive there is, however, not the despairing conclusion of our self-knowledge, leading to the postulate that there must be some other way to arrive at such knowledge. For we will always contest the claim that we cannot, if we wish to, arrive there. Even if this is not our contention, we remain, with that postulate, still within the limits of those images we create. The statement that we do not arrive at the knowledge of God is for Barth a negative consequence that can be grasped only in the light of the preceding positive statement, namely, that we can know God only as God comes to us. "The beginning of our knowledge of God . . . is not a beginning which we make with him. It can be only the beginning which He has made with us" (II/1 213 = 190). Gaod is the presupposition of our knowledge of him, that we cannot posit with our own knowledge and presuppose ourselves in it. God is *his own* presupposition, and he thus presupposes that we can and do truly know him. In this way alone our knowledge of faith has to do with God himself and not with some reflection of humanity.

The enabling and actualizing of the authentic knowledge of God is an act of pure *grace*. The *fact* of this knowledge and not just its *content* is already grace. The fact "*that* God speaks with us," and not just what he says, "is al-

---

18. Karl Barth, *Unterricht in der christlichen Religion,* vol. 1 (Zurich, 1985), pp. 3ff.; ET: *Göttingen Dogmatics* (Grand Rapids, 1990), pp. 3-5. The reference to the "Rider on Lake Constance" alludes to Gustav Schwab's ballad, "Der Reiter und der Bodensee" (1826), on p. 6 in the ET; the phrase emphasizes the risk of the venture.

ways in all circumstances already grace."[19] Barth believed that at this point theology should not go beyond what the reformers said about the knowledge of grace, but in view of the modern problem of the knowledge of God, it should "expound it more sharply than they did." They did not see clearly enough "the decisive connection between the problem of justification on the one hand and the problem of the knowledge of God, between reconciliation and revelation." "They saw and attacked the possibility of an intellectual work-righteousness in the basis of theological thought. But they did not do so as widely, as clearly and as fundamentally as they did with respect to the possibility of a moral work-righteousness in the basis of Christian life."[20] Delimiting the former possibility, however, means that our ability to know can no more set us in a relationship with God than our works can. In the last analysis we owe this to the free grace of God. In his criticism of the reformation outlook Barth looked at the question, How shall I find a gracious God? and perceived here the danger of a "narcissism" that obscures our social interconnectedness (IV/1 588 = 527). Yet he regarded that statement that "16th-century man was occupied with the *grace* of God" while "modern man is much more radically concerned about God *Himself*" to be "one of the most superficial catchwords" (IV/1 591 = 530). For if God were not gracious, we would not be dealing with God at all and would not know him.

This means *negatively* that we bring no presupposition to our knowledge of God, upon which it could be built as though on some kind of foundation, or to which it would submit itself as a condition imposed somehow upon it. To ideas of this kind Barth said a radical "no."[21] This "no," however, is not the judgment of a skeptical human reason that, while it can be generally affirmed and thus relativized, is skeptical about its own possibilities. Nor is it a general Platonic wisdom relating to the final human inability to comprehend the infinite. It is the "content of a statement of faith" and hence already of a true knowledge of God, for it recognizes "that the capacity to know God is taken away from us by revelation" (II/1 206f. = 184). This is the barrier against Pelagianism in the human knowledge of God. Barth also rejects semi-Pelagianism, namely, the notion that even though the human has no innate capacity to know God one may still arrive at the knowledge of God by means of a capacity to know that is graciously infused in the human person. We know

---

19. Karl Barth, *Evangelium und Gesetz* (*Theologische Existenz heute!* 32) (Munich, 1935), p. 4.

20. Karl Barth, *Nein! Antwort an Emil Brunner* (*Theologische Existenz heute!* 14) (Munich, 1934), p. 38; ET: E. Brunner, *Natural Theology* (London, 1946 [with Brunner's article]), p. 102.

21. Cf. Karl Barth, *Nein;* ET: *Natural Theology.*

God "in consequence of His giving Himself to be known by us," but God "remains the One whom we know only because he gives himself to be known" (II/1 43f. = 40-41). And so we *remain* dependent on God's prior gift of our knowledge. It cannot be transformed into a given that we hold in our hands, nor into an ability of ours in virtue of which, once God has presupposed himself, we can then presuppose God ourselves and *make* this the positing of our own knowledge, which we can manipulate at will. Precisely in regard to this decisive presupposition theology finds itself with empty hands, for there is no basis for this presupposition. Theology cannot prove it, let alone produce it. God posits it. He does so in such a way that it is always his positing. God alone produces it, and God guarantees that it is not a "dream . . . if [man] supposes that a second entity standing over against him" is the foundation and justification of his talk about God.[22] What we say about God would have nothing to do with God if it were not defenseless when challenged with the question we cannot answer, the question whether "we are really talking about Him when we are allegedly doing so" (I/1 169 = 163). Theology must *always* simply "begin at the beginning,"[23] which means that all true knowledge of God lives by the beginning that God makes with us, not that we make with God.

These negative statements thus result from a positive statement that cannot be understood unless the negative consequence is perceived. The positive statement is that all true knowledge of God rests on the prior gift of God's *giving* himself to be known, so that it is a "divine gift" (II/1 220 = 196). Yet what does that mean? Only when this is clarified will we understand what we mean by revelation. Revelation is not merely the event in which God is known by us. That is, of course, what is at stake: that the human person engages with "God himself," that he begins to know that he is engaging God and no other. But the decisive point is that "in the knowledge of God we have to do . . . with God Himself *by God himself*" (II/1 202 = 181), for "God is known by God" (II/1 202 = 180). The idea that we engage God through some capacity of our own is thus excluded. Barth calls this exclusion the concealment of God in his revelation. "It is because the fellowship between God and us is established and continues by God's grace that God is hidden from us. All our efforts to apprehend Him by ourselves shipwreck on this" (II/1 211 = 188). That revelation is *grace* means precisely that in his hiddenness God makes himself known through himself, that for us he enters into the means of communication in such a way that he becomes known to us. Again, the fact that in revelation we engage God "by God himself" means that "al-

---

22. Karl Barth, *Die Theologie und die Kirche,* p. 221; ET: *Theology and Church,* p. 223.
23. Cf. Karl Barth, *Einführung,* p. 182; ET: *Evangelical Theology,* p. 165.

though we are men and not God, we receive a *share* in the truth of His knowledge of Himself" (II/1 55 = 51). Regardless of how well we might understand this, we may cling to the fact that God's revelation is reliable, that in it God gives *himself* and not something else to be known, and that he is not someone other than whom he gives himself to know.

Revelation for Barth is not something to be postulated in order then to investigate whether it might "exist" somewhere. That the beginning of all knowledge is this beginning that God makes with us is a conclusion that simply does justice to the *reality* that God has already made this beginning with us. It is not an example of an idea deduced from elsewhere, the idea, that is, of a general possibility of similar processes. It is grounded in an event that expounds and interprets itself in this way. That event is for Barth the *Easter event.* "If there is any Christian and theological axiom, it is that Jesus Christ is risen, that He is truly risen." This "central statement of the biblical witness," announced to us and repeated by us "in the enlightening power of the Holy Spirit" (IV/3 47 = 44), is "for the New Testament witnesses of this event . . . the revelation of God in Him," Jesus Christ: ". . . the true, original, typical form of the *revelation* of God in Him and therefore of revelation generally, the revelation which lights up for the first time all God's revealing and being revealed (in Him and generally) . . . the infallible mediation as unequivocally disclosed in a new act of God, of the perception that God was in Christ (2 Cor. 5:19), that is, that in the man Jesus, God Himself was at work . . . going to His death, and that He acted as, and proved Himself, the one high and true God, not in spite of this end . . . but in His most profound humiliation, at the place where an utter end was made of this man" (IV/1 332 = 301). For those witnesses this was the revelation, the mediation of an otherwise hidden knowledge that we too cannot have apart from this revelation, even if it is concealed in the form of the learned interpretation of "historically" secured fragments that are all that remains for us if we do not perceive the texts of these witnesses as the testimony to revelation. Since the issue is this *particular* event, we have to do with a "'prehistorical' happening" that "cannot be grasped historically" (IV/1 371 = 336); it becomes immediately unrecognizable when the attempt is made to understand it "historically."

This knowledge was communicated to the witnesses when Jesus "came amongst them again in such a way that His presence as the man He had been (had been!) was and could be *exclusively* and therefore *unequivocally* the act *of God* without any component of human will and action; that it was and could be understood by them only and exclusively as such, exclusively and therefore unequivocally as the self-attestation of God in this man without any cooperation of a human attestation serving it. . . . God in Christ became *conceivable* to them in the *inconceivable* form of the unmediated presence and action of its origin and subject-matter without any other mediation at all" (IV/1 333 = 302). "To say death is to deny any future to the one who existed. Death is the frontier . . . beyond which there is no one and nothing save God the Creator, beyond which the creature . . . can be, if at all, only from God and for God" (IV/3 358 = 310). These witnesses hear at this point a word that "is spoken out of the great, conclusive and absolute silence in which all the words of all other men reach their end and limit, namely, the silence of the death of this man. God alone as the only Lord of life and death can break this silence. . . . But the crucified, dead and buried man Jesus Christ does speak. Those who hear him, hear God" (IV/3 474 = 410-11).

That God speaks and can be heard is pure grace. For one thing, the humanity which might be able, of itself, to hear him does not exist. In the death of the one man God has brought its life to an end. Yet when God speaks at Easter, he graciously awakens the human who can hear him. Moreover, the word that God speaks is not a neutral word. It is the "word of the cross." In that God's Word is *this* word it says that what happened on the cross is *God's work*. Because God has transferred this rejection of humanity separated from him to himself, God's Word as the Word of this work is his unconditional *Yes* to humanity. It is the word that speaks of "the conclusion of peace on both sides in which God fulfils the covenant between Himself and man on both sides, delivering man, and in him all creation, from his exposure to the assault of nothingness, and rescuing him for participation in His eternal life." A further point: It is *exclusively* God who speaks here, and his gracious "yes" is not just *one* word; it is the *only* word. "In this action God has expressed Himself, His innermost being, His heart, His divine person, His divine essence, Himself as the One He is. As the One who has done this, He has distinguished Himself from the God or gods of all the general notions and concepts of divinity invented and projected by man. As the Doer of this act, He is the one true God. He is this, therefore, in the death of the man Jesus Christ." And so "He reveals not only the work done, but in and with this Himself, His divine essence. . . . God Himself is needed to reveal this work, and especially to reveal Himself, His divine person and essence" (IV/3 475 = 412).

In the unity of this work the crucified and risen Lord "is the one Word of God that we must hear, that we must trust and obey, both in life and in death" (IV/1 382 = 346). His community takes this Word alone seriously. There is no

> other word that God might have spoken before or after or side by side with or outside this word, and that he willed to have proclaimed by it. . . .

In it it hears the Word of all God's comfort, commandment and power. . . .
It interprets creation and the course of the world and the nature of man,
his greatness and his plight and the promise of the kingdom wholly in the
light of this Word and not *vice versa*. It does not need to accept as normative any other voice than this voice, for the authority of any other voice depends upon the extent to which it is or is not an echo of this voice. As it
seeks to know this voice, it is certainly allowed and commanded to hear
other voices freely and without anxiety; as an echo of this voice they may
certainly share its authority. But it will always come back to the point of
wanting to hear first and chiefly this true and original voice, and wanting
to give itself to the service of this voice. (IV/1 383 = 346)

Holy scripture bears witness to this voice. It witnesses to "God's past
revelation" in that it is moved by it "just as the water was moved in the Pool of
Bethesda" (I/1 114 = 111). It does this in a twofold way, as the witness of expectation and the witness of recollection, in relation to this revelation (I/2 77 = 70). It
is not because the authors speak that God reveals himself (the view of
biblicistic orthodoxy). It is because God reveals himself that they are witnesses. To bear witness means "pointing in a specific direction beyond the self
and on to another." "What makes a man a witness is solely and exclusively that
other, the thing attested" (I/1 114f. = 111-112). We cannot, therefore, understand
what they wrote unless we "take part" in the thing attested, unless we know
God as "one's own God," unless "the Spirit Himself who has spoken to the
biblical writers" also speaks "to their hearers and readers" (III/1 101 = 92). If we
detach the biblical texts from their intention, they are plunged into a confusion
of the differing religious conceptions of past ages, and then Lessing's "gaping
and wide chasm" opens up between the "accidental truths of history" and what
is binding for us today (IV/1 316ff. = 289ff.). In that case the relevant meaning
of the texts will be arrived at only through a subjective selection or, more to the
point, through value judgments we assign to them. Then the essential connectedness of the New to the Old Testament will become unclear.

Barth thought that the question of Lessing was wrongly put. For the
"past revelation" testified to in Scripture is not just a past event, but an event
that took place "once and *for all*." It contains within it the promise, as an event
that happened once, now to take place again and again in the power of the living Jesus Christ. This promise underlies the fact that the revelation that
Scripture attests to the church is then *proclaimed* in it (I/1 114 = 111). We have
here, briefly, Barth's doctrine of the threefold form of God's Word. The point
is this: revelation is not present because the church proclaims it; because Jesus
Christ lives, and because he makes himself present, the past revelation is pro-

claimed in her as the presently happening revelation, in accordance with the Scriptures. Lessing's question is thus turned upside down. The urgent problem is no longer what we can do with the historical past. It is whether we with our "unclean lips" can stand in the presence of the present Revealer (IV/1 319 = 290). If there were not the beginning that he makes with us, if he did not cleanse us and put the Word of proclamation on our lips, how could we speak of him without stumbling and stammering! And even if we are now allowed to do it, how can we speak without astonishment, "never ceasing to be astonished"? "We are startled at the nature of the reality to which we refer and on which we rest. We are surprised by the unexpected thing which enlightens and motivates us. We are thankful for the grace which frees us to go further." This astonishment brings to light the distinction between "serious, fruitful and edifying thought and utterance in the Church and its theology" and that "which may seem to be learned and edifying but is basically and in its effects banal, trivial and tiresome" (IV/3 330f. = 287).

Rejection of Natural Theology

The statement about Jesus Christ as the "one Word of God that we must hear" is a citation of the first thesis of the Barmen Theological Declaration of May 1934. It repudiated the German Christians who saw, alongside the revelation attested in Scripture, the "German Hour of 1933" as a kind of divine revelation. Barth saw in this delimitation a rejection of "natural theology," "a purifying of the Church not only from the concretely new point at issue, but from all natural theology" (II/1 197 = 175). This rejection does not dispute the fact that theology must speak not only of the reconciling work of Christ (the second article of the Creed) but also of the work of the Creator (the first article) and that of the Holy Spirit (the third article). The rejection, however, raises the question: How are *all* three articles to be truly understood? Again, the rejection is not maintaining that God reveals himself *exclusively* in the Easter event and not in all his works. His "one Word" is not once and for all in the sense that the rest of the time he is silent. "God may speak to us through Russian Communism, a flute concerto, a blossoming shrub, or a dead dog" (I/1 55 = 55). Immediately after the Confessing Church had accepted the Barmen Declaration, Barth commented, "We are not denying the statement that God holds the whole world in his hands, including all the individuals, events, and powers, and that he reveals himself in them."[24]

24. Karl Barth, *Texte zur Barmer Theologischen Erklärung* (Zurich, 1984), p. 19.

Against what, then, was this repudiation directed? Note the continuation of the above remarks. "We do not recognize God in these individuals, events, and powers in such a way that we can point to them and say, Here is God, so that this knowing could become knowledge next to the knowledge of God in Jesus Christ — as an example, the knowledge of the German hour! We have no certain knowledge of that. God has unambiguously spoken in *one* place. When we ask, Where is God's Word?, we must cling to *this* fact. Any word that goes beyond this is a betrayal of the church. Even to stretch out a little finger to such a word is to surrender completely. Confessions will not help us if we put alongside them a second element, a second source of revelation."[25]

The point is this. Only after we have recognized God where he has unambiguously revealed himself, can we then, afterwards, recognize the extent to which he may have revealed himself elsewhere, or that we might be mistaking him for a demon. "Afterwards" means that we do not relate these "figures" to the divine and thus regard them as its revelation, but that the God who reveals himself in the biblical witness relates himself to them and them to him. Then we can recognize him there, perhaps with a new aspect for us, but still as the *same One* and not as another, the one who revealed himself unambiguously at that one place.

The distinction between natural theology and a theology of revelation is not that for the latter God is knowable in only *one* event and for the former God is knowable *everywhere*. The distinction is that God is knowable here and there in a diametrically opposed way. The distinction is demonstrated in their contradictory basic principles of knowledge. In a theology of revelation (1) *reality* has absolute precedence *over possibility*.[26] We know God because he *has given* and *still gives* himself to be known, and only in following that sequence can we attempt to understand the extent to which it is "possible." Natural theology reverses this relation by constructing a general possibility of the knowledge of God or of "revelation," thereby giving humanity a standard by which to measure what may or may not be counted as true. "Revelation" must subject itself to this standard and is accountable to the humans who wield it. It can be regarded as only *one* among many possible approximations of the constructed concept of the possible knowledge of God. Its reality depends upon the validity conferred by those who are equipped with the standard. In that the human determines in advance who God "can" be for

25. Barth, *Texte zur Barmer Erklärung,* p. X.

26. Kornelis Heiko Miskotte, *Über Barths Kirchliche Dogmatik* (*Theologische Existenz heute!* n.s. 89) (Munich, 1961): 39.

him, he may well thereafter worship a God. But is he bowing down to anything other than his own product?

A theology of revelation also gives (2) unconditional priority to the *specific over the general.* Barth often quotes the saying *Deus non est in genere* [= God does not belong to a particular human category] (II/1 349 = 310) and *Latet periculum in generalibus* [= Danger lurks in generalities] (II/2 51 = 48). If our knowledge of God rests upon his self-declaration, it is tied to the concrete "there and then" witnessed to in Scripture, in order that only then may we ask how far this once is also a once and for all. This concreteness is not a mere shell that we can peel away in order to reach the timeless idea, which *we* then would have to make "concrete"! The knowledge of God is inseparably attached to the "there and then." For Barth this means that the revelation of Christ can never be detached from the history of Israel. For him, the separation of Israel from the church is characteristic of natural theology. It thus misunderstands the New Testament by putting the general above the specific and thus classifying it within the context of general values already posited by humans — which can be confirmed with examples provided by the Bible, now reduced by "material criticism."

A theology of revelation also acknowledges a principle that goes with the two former ones, that (3) of *Esse sequitur operari* [= Being follows work] (II/1 91 = 83). It knows God solely in the concrete reality of his *action.* In this action he turns to humanity in order to make it known that God *is* "who He is in the act of His revelation" (II/1 293 = 262). "For where do we ever find in the Bible any other being of God than that of the Subject of His work and action toward man, of the God of Israel, who is also the Father of Jesus Christ, who is also the Word made flesh, who is also the Holy Spirit and who is not, in and for Himself, another God?" (II/1 91 = 83). When natural theology inverts this principle, then that means that that God is other than who he is in and for himself, one whose action is not essential to him. He could be very different from the one who is at work here. He is accessible to humans even without the act of turning to them. He is then identical with the image they make of "God."

The two theologies do not follow the different paths of knowledge yet still conceive of the same God by different routes. Their differing approaches point to a *different* God. For natural theology the beginning of our knowledge of God is one "that we make with God." For the theology of revelation the beginning has to be the one that "God has made and still makes with us." In natural theology the knowledge of God is always possible for the human, always accessible. The human is open to it or can open herself to it, regardless of whether she only has a hunch about God or has a very concrete grasp of him, regardless of whether this ability is innate or learned. Either way the human knows God without coming to know him "by God," because God can be known on the basis "of a union of man with God existing outside God's revelation in Jesus Christ" (II/1 189 = 168). In distinction from the theology of revelation, which refers its knowledge wholly to the grace of God, natural theology relies upon "the affirmation that even *apart from* God's grace" man can know God (II/1 150 = 135). This theology *is* the work of *that person* who would live without the grace of God, is closed to it, hates it as the enemy. "On that soil and in that atmosphere the growth of natural theology is *inevitable*" (II/1 151 = 136). "Natural theology is no more and no less than the unavoidable theological expression of the fact that in the reality and possibility of man as such an openness for the grace of God and therefore a readiness for the knowability of God in His revelation is *not* at all evident" (II/1 150 = 135).

Barth goes one step further. If we *really* have to do with *God* only where he graciously initiates our knowledge of him in his revelation, then this discloses that we only appear to be dealing with God when we initiate our knowledge of God, as in natural theology. "For . . . man as he thinks he can understand and rule himself without God, it is the meaning and content of life to master himself and the world and regard the goal and origin of this endeavor as a first and last thing and therefore as his god" (II/1 93f. = 86). Yet as the quintessence of the highest that humans themselves can choose and make, this god is in truth only "an element in our own existence" (II/1 157 = 141), a non-god, "a false god . . . known to him" that "will not lead him in any sense to a knowledge of the real God. . . . On the contrary, it will keep him from it. Its knowledge . . . will make him an enemy of the real God" (II/1 94 = 86), "blind to the real God" (II/1 99 = 91). There can be no "connection" between the revelation of God and the knowledge communicated by natural theology, as though "idolatry [were] . . . but a somewhat imperfect preparatory stage of the service of the true God."[27] It can only break off its efforts and replace them with a new and different beginning. "The real God, where He is known, kills the natural man with all his possibilities, in order to make him alive again" (II/1 99 = 90). He joins himself, so to speak, to "a corpse" (IV/1 535 = 481).

When the revelation of God encounters us in making this beginning with us, natural theology then, but only then, removes itself. "From the standpoint of a theology of the Word of God which has a true understanding of itself we do not contest natural theology as such." Conversely, it will al-

---

27. Karl Barth, *Nein!*, p. 19; ET: Brunner, *Natural Theology*, p. 82; cf. CD II/1 96 = 88-89.

ways be true that the human person will seek to "defend himself" in this theology; he will struggle to assert that "in this position outside the grace of God he is not in any sense godless." How should one argue against this without persuading him that he is what he really is not: "free to renounce this undertaking which is so necessary to him. . . . in a sort of self-disillusionment to free himself from natural theology. The grace for which we think we ourselves can decide is not the grace of God in Jesus Christ. The illusion that we can rid ourselves of our illusions ourselves is the greatest of all illusions. And a theology which thinks it can persuade man against natural theology . . . is still itself definitely natural theology." The only thing "that can help him is that the grace of Jesus Christ Himself in its revelation comes triumphantly to him, freeing him from the illusion and therefore from natural theology" (II/1 189f. = 169 rev.).

The theology of revelation will enter the lists only when natural theology, "disguis[ing] . . . its position of monopoly" over against a theology based upon the grace and revelation of God, portrays itself as "*Christian* natural theology," and seeks to combine the two under a *single* cover as it "places itself at the side" of the knowability of God out of the grace of his revelation, as a kind of preamble that seeks only "to prepare an understanding of it" (II/1 152f. = 137-38). We must contest this view, for it obscures the alternative opened up by revelation; indeed, as a rule it does not lead to revelation at all, but unwittingly leads away from it. "If grace is alongside nature, however high above it it may be put, it is obviously no longer the grace of God, but the grace which man ascribes to himself. If God's revelation is alongside a knowledge of God proper to man as such, even though it may never be advanced except as a prolegomenon, it is obviously no longer the revelation of God, but a new expression (borrowed or even stolen) for the revelation which encounters man in his own reflection" (II/1 154f. = 139).

As Barth sees it, natural theology can take many forms. Among them is the Roman doctrine of the *"analogia entis"* [= analogy of being] that he describes as "the invention of the Antichrist" (I/1 viii = xiii, though cf. II/1 90 = 82-83). He is not contesting that there is a similarity between the self-knowledge of God and our human knowledge of God. His debate is with the thesis that the basis of this similarity is an existing *essential* relationship between God and us, so that we can begin with ourselves and then move on to God. If an analogy is present, it is because God first gives it, bringing our knowledge into line with his through his Word (II/1 254ff. = 226-227).

Another form is the program of *contextual* theology. He does not contest a relationship of theology to the nontheological contexts. He allows that such a theology sees "revelation in relationship to reason, existence, creation, or whatever the instance might be called — and both in thought and speech does this relating, as it must!" He contended, however, "that this theology should interpret these other instances in terms of revelation, and not revelation in terms of these other instances."[28]

Then there is the form of a *correlative* theology (Tillich), which tries to see revelation as answer to the questionable character of human existence, as evidenced by the questions humans formulate. "What the Word of God talks us out of is only the positive possibility of receiving revelation. And at the same time we talk ourselves into the possession of a great negative possibility; in fact, we must." But this is not what happens. The Word itself speaks to us about the latter, and makes us truly poor. "This poverty . . . is the gift of the Holy Spirit, the work of Jesus Christ" (I/2 287f. = 264-65).

Yet another form is a theology that sees its theme in the human person's new self-understanding against the background of a previously ascertained "pre-understanding" (Bultmann). We do, of course, all work with "some kind of preconditions. . . . We all have our prior notions of possibility, truth and importance. We all know what we think is our capacity to understand," and thus we seek to "confine" the "strangeness" of the Gospel texts "within the strait jacket of our prior understandings." But this approach cannot be elevated "into a methodological principle," because the text challenges us to "accept the New Testament's understanding of ourselves before we take our own self-understanding too seriously and try to force it on the text. If we adopted this procedure, we should find our understanding of the text enhanced."[29]

In brief, the Word of God rejects natural theology in *all* its forms.

Objectivity[30]

Barth calls God the "object" of theology. In his view, the "objective" knowledge of God is the only true knowledge of God. "Biblical faith lives upon the objectivity of God" (II/1 13 = 13). When theology turns aside from this, as

28. Karl Barth, *Theologische Fragen und Antworten* (Zollikon, 1957), pp. 139-40.

29. Karl Barth, *Rudolf Bultmann* (*Theologische Studien* 34) (Zollikon-Zurich, 1952), pp. 49-50; ET: *Kerygma and Myth* (London, 1962), pp. 124-25.

30. Barth's use of the German term *Gegenstand* builds on its root meaning, "that which stands against," and it is thus precisely the opposite of an "object" that one can have in one's hand and manipulate. This "Objectivity" is not at humans' disposal, opposes them, and moves towards the human for the purpose of encounter. There appears to be no appropriate English translation for Barth's distinctive usage of *Gegen-Ständlichkeit*. See CD I/1, viii.

happens when its god is only a reflection of the self-absolutizing self, it is literally groundless ["object-less"](II/1 76f. = 70-72). If the theological knowledge of God is not objective, then for Barth there are two consequences: it does not know *God*, nor does it *know* him. The fact that God is the object of theology does not, of course, mean that he is a mere something in the hands of the human subject who controls and manipulates him. The reverse is the case — God is the Opposite, who does not merely evade the human grasp in passing, but who permanently obstructs and counters that grasp in his revelation. Theology loses its objectivity the moment "we turn our backs on God's Word" (I/1 249 = 236), thinking we ourselves can grasp it in order now to ask about its application or communication to others. "For of what use would be the purest theology based on grace and revelation to me if I dealt with the subjects of grace and revelation in the way in which natural theology usually deals with its soi-disant data derived from reason, nature and history, i.e. as if one had them pocketed . . . ?"[31]

If we understand God as the "object" of theology, this does not mean, on the other hand, that we ascribe to God's reality the objectivistic "character of transcendental exclusiveness."[32] The real question is whether the confrontational character of this object is such that it "could never conceivably be interrupted except by God; or whether man is conceived as possessing by nature or by acquisition the power himself to end this encounter."[33] The object envisaged is to be seen in *relationship,* but in one that he himself constitutes. In it, God is certainly "outgoing and communicative" to others (IV/3 9 = 10), but the relationship is based solely on grace. "His *objectivity* is always *grace* even in His revelation" (II/1 232 = 206). Thanks to this grace God becomes knowable to humanity. The term objectivity carries the thought not only of confrontation but also of *encounter.* If theology views God as object in this twofold sense, then its effort stands under the promise that in it *God* is known and God is *known.* Yet what precisely does this mean?

In his younger days Barth would not apply the term "object" to God. He used the argument of Kant that only our experiential knowledge knows "objects," and then only as finite phenomena given for us in the knowledge forms of perception and concept. For Kant God could not possibly be an object of our experiential knowledge. For Barth this meant that "there is no object apart from our thinking of it; nor has an object any clear characteristics

31. Karl Barth, *Nein!,* p. 14; ET: Brunner, *Natural Theology,* p. 77.

32. Jürgen Moltmann, *Theologie der Hoffnung* (Munich, 1964-66), p. 48; ET: *Theology of Hope: On the Ground and the Implications of a Christian Eschatology* (London, 1967), pp. 42ff.

33. Karl Barth, *Die Theologie und die Kirche,* p. 192; ET: *Theology and Church,* p. 207.

save when we are able to recognize them by some quick-moving previous knowledge. Therefore if God be an object in the world, we can make no statement about Him . . . which does not proceed from some previous superior knowledge. If therefore God were . . . an object among other objects . . . He would then obviously not be God."[34]

The later Barth appeared to take a different view, and thus became subject to his own earlier criticism, when he now described revelation in this way: "God comes into the picture, the sphere, the field of man's consideration and conception in exactly the same way that objects do" (II/1 13 = 13). In fact, however, Barth was simply giving a more precise shape to his earlier thinking. What must still be maintained is that ". . . knowledge of this object can in no case . . . mean that we have this object at our disposal. Certainly we have God as an object, but not in the same way as we have other objects. . . . We have all other objects as they are determined by the pre-arranged disposition and the pre-arranged mode of our own existence" (II/1 21 = 21). "We *resemble* what we can apprehend . . . we are *masters* of what we can apprehend . . . we are originally and properly *one* with what we can apprehend" (II/1 211f. = 188-89).

In spite of these critical distinctions, Barth keeps the term "object." One reason is that in the revelation of God the human engages an object sui generis, or rather an object that is true and genuine in every way, an object that certainly disposes himself toward us, but in such a way that we can never dispose over him. It discloses itself to us in a way that we can learn to respect it in its mystery. A distinctive feature of the self-revelation of God is that the "giving of a name (Exodus 3:13-14) is in fact and content the refusal to give a name" (I/1 335 = 317). The revelation of God also involves his concealment (cf. II/1 209ff. = 186ff.). This does not mean that he is not present in his revelation (H. Gollwitzer), nor that his revelation is conditioned by our human weakness (W. Pannenberg). The reason for this is that, in his revelation, *God* in free grace, quite apart from any claim or capacity of ours, posits himself as an object of our human knowledge. He does this in such a way that, *because* he is God, he opposes any human attempt to gain control of God. If he were not an object in this sense, we would not be engaging God.

Another reason for the fact that the term "object" is indispensable is that God in his revelation would not be known as he intends if he did not enter the field of our human perception and comprehension and thereby encounter us, if he did not become in that sense "one object among others." If the word "object" connotes perception and comprehension, then this im-

34. Karl Barth, *Der Römerbrief*, 2nd ed. (Munich, 1922; 12th ed., 1978), pp. 56-57; ET: *The Epistle to the Romans* (Oxford, 1933), p. 82.

plies that God becomes perceptible and comprehensible to us only indirectly, not directly as he is perceptible and comprehensible to himself, that is, as he is an "object" to himself (II/1 62 = 57). "Indirectly" means that we cannot perceive and comprehend God unless he allows us to participate in that knowledge by which he sees and grasps himself. "Indirectly" also means that God lets us participate in such a way that he permits certain earthly "objects" to represent him, in which he desires to become perceptible and comprehensible to us. This movement of God toward us means in a new sense God's concealment in his revelation, yes, even his humiliation on our behalf (II/1 59 = 55). The indirectness means that he may be perceived and comprehended by us only as he is concealed in earthly objects. The human person stands "directly before *another* object, one of the series of all other objects.... This other object ... is the medium by which God gives Himself to be known and in which man knows God." Indirectly means also that this object is not automatically a medium of this kind. It represents God insofar as it is "determined, made and used by God as His clothing, temple, or sign; insofar as it is peculiarly a work of God, which above and beyond its own existence (which is also God's work, of course) may and must serve to attest the objectivity of God and therefore to make the knowledge of God possible and necessary." The one who knows God in this way "does not arbitrarily choose objects to set up as signs, in that way inventing a knowledge of God at [one's] own good-pleasure." That would be idolatry! We know God "by means of the objects chosen by God Himself" (II/1 16f. = 16-18).

What is true of earthly "objects" is also true of the "human views, concepts and words which as such can be applied only to the creaturely" (II/1 257 = 227). How can these signify divine things? Or, if one is willing to accept that they do, is not the truth of the matter that they can never really signify God but can only be our *images,* our *ideas?* Are we not replacing God with idols made of our concepts, with something that can only be "inauthentic" with regard to God and only "authentic" with regard to us? "God is *God.*"[35] When he made this statement the younger Barth was protesting against the common fault of describing God by a value concept that we had desired and sought and come to know. We pretend that this is God. We substitute for God words like love or spirit or power or father or mother. In applying such terms to God, are we not projecting into God things that (without God!) we regard as valuable and worth seeking or defending? And by doing this are we not confirming what is known to us already without God? Does not this

---

35. Karl Barth, *Der Römerbrief,* 2nd ed., pp. 324, 326; ET: *Epistle to the Romans,* pp. 339, 342.

procedure make God superfluous, in that we mean, when we use these concepts for God in this way, not truly God but ourselves?

Barth's solution to this problem involves turning everything upside down. Our concepts can "indirectly" describe God just as God is "indirectly" objective to us. Nevertheless, not so indirectly that they could not "really" describe him properly but only us and our creaturely reality! We have to relate our concepts to the fact that in his revelation God "comes into his own." He himself "has every — the best-founded and most valid — claim *on us* and on all our views, concepts and words, that He should be their first and last and proper subject . . . not because they are appropriate for it or because they originally mean Him apart from this one truth. As our own they simply do not do this. When He claims them, He does not confirm us but Himself. . . . Our words are not our property, but His. . . . The use to which they are put is not, then, an improper and merely pictorial one, but their proper use. We use our words improperly and pictorially . . . when we apply them within the confines of what is appropriate to us as creatures. When we apply them to God they are not alienated from their original object . . . but . . . restored to it" (II/1 258f. = 229).

This process of restoration places us, in our knowledge of God, before the permanent task of not using our concepts and views in their general sense and then transferring them to God, but of letting them be *corrected* time and again in the light of revelation. The possible consequence will be that a "God" will not correspond to what those concepts might otherwise denote, but rather, they will be brought into correspondence with the Word of God! A saying of Hilary that was greatly esteemed by Barth pointed to this task: *Non sermoni res, sed rei sermo subjectus est* (= The word serves the content, not the content the word). Barth's comment was that "he who does not adopt this statement as his own methodological axiom is no theologian and never will be" (I/1 354).[36]

Thinking After

The aim of God's revelation is the grounding of the human knowledge of God in the confidence that we, when we speak of God, are speaking in all

---

36. Cf. Eberhard Busch, *Karl Barths Lebenslauf,* 5th ed. (Gütersloh, 1994), p. 394; ET *Karl Barth: His Life from Letters and Autobiographical Texts* (London and Philadelphia, 1976), p. 380. Hilary's dictum is translated in Busch: "The word serves the content, not the content the word."

our indirectness really of God and not merely about ourselves. The point is that we should acquire a share in the knowledge that God has of himself. Since God is always revealed to himself, his revelation to humanity is no gain to him. It is humanity's gain. The human is not just to acquire further insights. She is to enter into fellowship with God. Revelation is *grace,* the revelation of divine reconciliation. The human is to enter into fellowship with the God who through his work reveals himself as the one who wills this his work and can do it. Fellowship with God thus means the knowledge of God. Grace is also *revelation.*

Knowledge is not merely

> the acquisition of neutral information, which can be expressed in statements, principles and systems, concerning a being which confronts man, nor does it mean the entry into passive contemplation of a being which exists beyond the phenomenal world. What it really means is the process or *history* in which man, certainly observing and thinking, using his senses, intelligence and imagination, but also his will, action and "heart," and therefore as whole man, becomes aware of *another history* which in the first instance encounters him as an alien history from without, and becomes aware of it in such a compelling way that he cannot be neutral towards it, but finds himself summoned to disclose and give himself to it in return, to direct himself according to the law which he encounters in it, to be taken up into its movement, in short, to demonstrate the acquaintance which he has been given with this other *history* in a corresponding alteration of his *own* being, action and conduct. (IV/3 210 = 183-84)

For Barth *knowledge* means *conversion* (IV/3 226ff. = 198ff.). It means the human's conversion to God through the God who begins something with him. It means converting away from beginning with self to beginning with God's beginning with him. Knowledge is not here the appropriation of an object by the knowing subject, but rather "takes place as it is set in motion by its living object which seizes and retains the initiative in relation to man. . . . The whole man with all his possibilities and experiences and attitudes is grasped by the object . . . and turned right about face to this object, to be wholly orientated upon it" (IV/3 251 = 220).

In relation to the knowledge of God Barth does not focus upon the knowing subject as a form that might be filled with different contents, for example, God as a possible object of knowledge that might be chosen at our own good pleasure. The reverse is the case. We may well have other objects "because we first of all . . . have ourselves," but we have them as "defining conditions of our own already established existence" (II/1 21f. = 21) — modern subjectivity comes into view! But if we certainly cannot have God in this way, then we receive him only as an object in that we do *not* "first of all have ourselves," that is, that we first receive ourselves through him. "The precedence which alone comes into consideration here . . . is the precedence of this object. Only because God posits Himself as the object is man posited as the knower of God." "The position of the knowing man in relation to this object is the position of a fundamentally and irrevocably determined subsequence . . . which can in no way be changed or reinterpreted into a precedence of man. It is the position of *grace*" (II/1 21f. = 21-22). Revelation is grace; thus the issue here is the application of the doctrine of grace to the question of the knowledge of God. There is, here as well, the grace of God which comes before ("prevents") the human, and therefore there is here no *homo gratiam praeveniens* [= man coming before grace] but only *homo gratiam sequens* [= man following grace]. Let us consider the scope of these statements as they relate to the problem of the knowledge of God.

    1. For us, coming to the knowledge of God means that God in the sending forth of his Word creates us as its recipients — a kind of resurrection of the dead (II/1 99 = 90). The possibility of knowing the Word of God is "proper to the Word of God and to it alone. . . . God's Word is no longer grace . . . if we ascribe to man a predisposition towards this Word, a possibility of knowledge regarding it that is intrinsically and independently native to him" (I/1 201f. = 193-94). "But as faith has its . . . unconditional beginning in God's Word independently of the inborn or acquired characteristics and possibilities of man, and as it, as faith, never in any respect lives . . . by anything other than the Word, so it is in every respect with the knowability of the Word of God. . . . We can establish it only as we stand fast in faith and its knowledge, i.e., as we turn away from ourselves and turn our ears to the Word of God" (I/1 249 = 236). "This knowledge first of all creates the subject of its knowledge by coming into the picture" (II/1 22 = 21). Revelation, then, is the opening up of human subjectivity by and for the divine counterpart, and in this opening the new grounding of human subjectivity. This subjectivity is grounded not in itself but in its relationship with God, and so it is rescued from its perverted being and established in its true being. Revelation offers humanity together with the possibility of knowing God the possibility of knowing oneself, and of doing so in a new way that the human has not known before, but which is in fact the way he truly is in God.

    2. This possibility consists of a conferred freedom to be able to do what humans earlier thought they could do but in fact could not — which they now realize in the light of the gift of freedom. That previous inability in fact

was due to sin and not merely to creaturely limitations from which one would have to flee or for which one would have to receive a new organ in order to know God. Barth did not see the person who is drawn to the knowledge of God as an unwritten slate, but as one shaped by many biological, historical, sociological, psychological, economic, and political factors (III/4 710ff. = 618ff.). These influences mean that the human person is a mixture of one's possibilities and impossibilities. It is clear, however, that the creaturely possibilities do not amount to a capability to know God. Unless God gives the human freedom, the creature cannot know God. On the other hand, the creaturely impossibilities, one's limitation because of such factors, form no obstacle. The freedom need not be and is not a freedom from limitation but a "freedom in limitation" (III/4 648 = 565) through such factors. In this freedom the human "must not wish to jump out of his own skin" (III/4 717 = 624). "Man is not to run away, to flee from his situation with its limitations, problems, tensions and tasks. Accepting this situation and orientated by it, he is to move on from it. For he is not caged in it or chained to it. His situation is not his grave; it is rather his cradle" (III/4 714f. = 622).

3. Freedom for the knowledge of God is a freedom *given* us with the Word of God, a freedom we can neither have of ourselves nor obtain by ourselves. The knowledge of God is based upon the beginning that God makes with us. It does not contradict this freedom — it is no caprice — that it consists fundamentally of a definite *acknowledgment* or, Barth would say, of a definite *obedience,* an acknowledgment of the beginning that God has made with us and obedience to that beginning. Just as faith is essentially faith *in,* for it is rooted in a counterpart that we did not posit but that posits itself in relation to us and therefore posits us as believers, so similarly the knowledge of faith is an *ac*knowledgment, a "respect for the fact that takes place in God's Word" (I/1 215 = 205). "Knowledge of God is in *obedience* to God" (II/1 38 = 36).

This acknowledging obedience is not what we often otherwise associate with obedience, that is, the replacement of one authoritarian lord through another even more authoritarian one. As the knowledge of God is owed to the beginning that God has made with us, it is also owed totally to the grace of God. We know God as we let this gracious beginning be the beginning of our knowledge of God, that is, we acknowledge him. The grace of God's beginning with us aims not to destroy but to give a "new grounding to human subjectivity," which generates our true subjectivity in that it is grounded in God's relationship to the human person.

This subjectivity becomes active in our acknowledgment, although it is not limited to that. Our acknowledging is no blind submission, for in acknowledging knowing is already present. Our obedience is "free obedience," not a perverse acceptance of slavery but an activation of our freedom, and "for this very reason it is a real obedience" (II/1 39 = 36). Its contention is that any other unfree and enforced obedience conflicts not only with freedom but with authentic obedience itself. Obedience to God means listening to the one to whom we belong and through whom we truly belong to ourselves. If all true human knowledge of God has its basis in the grace of God's beginning with us, then the question of the possibility of knowing God cannot be answered until we know God. This is effectively a circle, that we always and only *can* know God in that we already do in fact *know* God. We can know God only when we do know God. We can arrive at the knowledge of God only when we begin there, and we can begin there only as we seek to know God.

4. In this free obedience, theological knowledge responds to this prior gift made to us in God's beginning, to this prior movement of God which precedes and prepares our knowledge of him, by following *after* it, pursuing *after* it, thinking *about* it, repeating *back* what God's Word has already said — in a continuing journey. In this process of knowing the human confirms that *after-ness* in which the knowing subject is established by the object that gives himself to be known. For Barth theological thinking is "thinking *after*.[37] It is logic responding in human fashion to the "Logos," the Word of God. Its relation to that Logos is that of a "human ana-logy . . . not a creative act but only a praise of the Creator and of his act of creation."[38]

Barth does not reject the term analogy. He is opposed to the *analogia entis* [= analogy of being], which brackets God and humanity together under the one word "being" and empowers the human to think his way to God. Instead, analogy is to be understood as the *"analogia fidei sive revelationis"* [= analogy of faith or revelation] (III/3 59 = 51; cf. I/1 257 = 243-44), as a "mode" of revelation, "as the work of his grace." *He* gives to creatures "the thing which by nature they cannot have — in their creatureliness the character of an analogy to Himself as the Creator." What is at issue is a "similarity . . . which is promised and bestowed by God's revelation, and is not arbitrarily discovered and affirmed," an analogy or a correspondence. There is no third thing between God and humanity through which this similarity exists. The self-revealing God evokes through his speaking creaturely correspondences to this speech, which are to be recognized in theology's knowledge of faith. Theological knowledge can appropriately know God and such

---

37. Cf. *Zürcher Woche*, 6.14.1963.
38. Karl Barth, *Einführung*, p. 25; ET: *Evangelical Theology*, p. 17.

creaturely correspondences only when its *own* terms correspond to the revelation of God (II/1 261-263 = 232-33).

5. How can theology's knowledge of faith be communicated to those who do not believe or who believe differently? This is for Barth not a question of what but a question of how, and he does not contest that "obvious point" that theology "constantly" faces this double question.[39] Barth does not accept, however, the common answers, for example, that after clarification of the "what question" the "how question" becomes an independent problem, or the assertion that the use of the right method for how one is to say something will automatically clarify what one has to say. If I know God only in that I "think after" his beginning with me, then, unless I want to stop talking about God altogether, I will never be able to exit from this process of "thinking after." I can never act as though I had a given result in my hand and could now turn to the special question of its dissemination. For Barth the problem is solved differently, "under the assumption that there is a solidarity between the theologian and the worldling."[40] In analogy to the reformation slogan that we are sinners and righteous at the same time, this is a twofold solidarity. On the one hand, the theologian, confessing that the beginning of the knowledge of God is not a beginning that we make with God, never has to make that move towards the others because he is already one of them, in that he "will find unbelief first and foremost in himself" (II/1 104f. = 95). On the other hand, the theologian, confessing that the beginning of the knowledge of God is a beginning God makes with us, does not have to establish the "connection" with the other because that is God's affair, and therefore he can deal with the other in the hope that this other person, by virtue of the Word of God addressing him, will be someone "inside" rather than an outsider. If we suppress this twofold solidarity, the twofold danger arises of either "patronization" or "neglect" of those we are addressing (IV/3 949f. = 829-30).

---

39. Karl Barth, *Nein!* p. 57; ET: *Natural Theology*, pp. 122-23.

40. Karl Barth, *Fides quaerens intellectum* (Munich, 1931), p. 67; ET: *Anselm: Fides quaerens intellectum* (Cleveland & New York, 1962), p. 68.

The Fulfilled Covenant —
Israel and Christology

The Question of God

In 1962 Barth stated that "the word 'theology' fails to exhaust the meaning of 'evangelical theology.' . . . 'Theanthropology' would probably better express who and what is at stake here."[1] He coined a word that signifies talk about God and humanity, talk about the God-man. The point is that theology cannot talk about God at the cost of humanity, but only in such a way that humanity is honored. The point is also that theology cannot talk about humanity at the cost of God. It most emphatically talks about humanity when it talks first about God. Citing Titus 3:4, Barth summarized what he meant with the term "the humanity of God,"[2] which for him had the same meaning as the biblical concept of the *covenant* (IV/1 36 = 35-36), and the same meaning as the Old Testament term, cited in Matthew 1:23, "*Emmanuel* (which means, God with us)" (IV/1 2-4 = 4-6).

This "Emmanuel," according to Barth, is "the [epitome] of the recognition in which the God of Israel reveals Himself in all His acts and dispositions. He is the God who does not work and act without His people, but who is with His people as their God and therefore as their hope" (IV/1 4 = 6). When the name "Emmanuel" is given to Jesus, this emphasizes that that recognition is the epitome not of an idea, but is epitomized in a *Name* in which "God with us" is embodied for Israel and all peoples. Certainly Christian

1. Karl Barth, *Einführung in die evangelische Theologie* (Zurich, 1962), p. 18; ET: *Evangelical Theology: An Introduction* (Grand Rapids, 1963), p. 12.

2. Karl Barth, *Die Menschlichkeit Gottes* (Theologische Studien 48) (Zollikon-Zurich, 1956); ET: *The Humanity of God* (Richmond, Va., 1960).

theology "can and must at once declare" his name. "In and with His name it can and must at once declare His cause, but . . . only as His cause. This cause of His has no . . . validity of its own apart from Him. Everything that is said about it is measured by whether it faithfully reflects Him. . . . It is not, therefore, the case that properly . . . the Christian message is concerned about its own affair and introduces His name only as the One who is responsible for it" (IV/I 21 = 20-21).

Barth was well aware that both "God" and "humanity" can be given very different meanings. But it was even clearer to him that Christian theology is not free to play fast and loose with these terms. It has to take seriously the fact that we have in the name "Immanuel" not a possible but the only knowledge of both God and humanity directed to us. It tells us that only "God with us" is truly God, and that *only* the human person included in that "us" is truly human. Just as in the Old Testament the "uniqueness of Yahweh . . . is not merely laid down but argumentatively *expounded*" (IV/3 117 = 105), the name of Jesus Christ proclaimed in the New Testament as "the one Word of God" is not merely to be asserted. What is to be shown is the extent to which "in light of its particular *content* [this Word] is quite distinctive in relation to all other words." Theology certainly does not have to be ashamed of this. "We may quietly listen to others. We may hear what is said by the whole history of religion, poetry, mythology and philosophy" (IV/3 120f. = 107-8). In doing so, one will surely not encounter only darkness. Yet it will become quite evident that this name sets itself apart from all others, by virtue of the content it bears. The crucial issue is that theology must "argumentatively expound" this content.

It was the view of Eberhard Jüngel[3] that Barth's theology was wrestling here with the atheism of modern secularism (both with *it* and with "religion" in that he regarded religion to be useless in the debate with it since religion basically strengthened that secularism!). Many have debated this position. But what is of interest is *how* his theology does it. His theology sees it as meaningless to counter atheism with a theism that asserts, "there is a God." "As though there were such a thing as God Himself and as such, or any point in seeking Him!" (IV/I 591 = 530). Atheism might have some justification, and in a certain sense it does. The younger Barth could demand that, over against a God "who exists," "it [is high time] to declare ourselves . . . atheists."[4] Joining with the labor movement of that day he could quote approv-

3. Eberhard Jüngel, *Barth-Studien* (Zurich, Cologne, Gütersloh, 1982), pp. 332ff.

4. Karl Barth, *Das Wort Gottes und die Theologie* (Munich, 1929), p. 14; ET: *The Word of God and the Word of Man* (New York, 1957), p. 22.

ingly Heinrich Heine's scoffing of the "*eiapopeia* of heaven with which we still the whining of the people, the great oaf."[5] His intention was not, as a self-deprecating theologian, to curry favor with the atheists in order to join them in declaring the death of "religion" for the higher purpose of saving the God of the Christians.

What had atheism correctly sensed? People speak about God, he said, and "far too often what is meant by it is . . . the unsubstantial, unprofitable and fundamentally very tedious magnitude known as *transcendence,* not as a genuine counterpart, nor a true other, nor a real outside and beyond, but as an illusory reflection of human freedom, as its projection into the vacuum of utter abstraction" (III/4 549 = 479). The God against whom atheism objects is merely a reflection of ourselves and is not God. Barth further clarifies the thesis: Atheism shares with the theistic acceptance of the general givenness of God the conviction that, in the words of E. Bloch, the word "God" bespeaks "Something up there where humans are not present."[6] Bloch's expression relates to a traditional way of thinking that is deeply rooted in the church. According to it, our thinking about God is purer the more we think of him as beyond thought and therefore on the far side of humanity. God is the supreme being, the absolute, the one who is disconnected from us, the non-human being. Humanity conceives of God here by acknowledging that one is totally excluded from God, "rather like the subject, once upon a time, who acknowledged the absolute monarch over him from whose highest power he was expressly excluded in the very act of acknowledgement."[7]

This thinking has left deep imprints upon theology. It may begin with the being of God that excludes humanity in order then afterwards somehow to relate it to humanity, or it may limit itself to a knowledge of God the way he appears to us, presupposing that God in and of himself is an Other, the absolute being. Whether the one or the other, God himself is always the one who is "something up there where humans are not present." This is the theistic view of God. A-theism derives from it the conclusion that if God *in and of himself* is such a non-human, even inhuman "something above," then humanity cannot reach full maturity unless it breaks free from this God. By becoming godless, humanity emancipates itself. Against the "something above" which excludes humanity, atheism sponsors a "below" that excludes God. Thus, for Barth, it was senseless to counter this atheism simply with God as

---

5. Heinrich Heine, *Werke* (Berlin and Weimar, 1967), pp. 2, 95; cf. Karl Barth, *Vorträge und kleinere Arbeiten 1909-1914* (Zurich, 1993), p. 394.

6. According to Jüngel, *Barth-Studien,* p. 334.

7. Ibid.

long as God continued to be thought of as such a highest, non-human being. At this point he took a turn that is characteristic of his thinking. He approached the problem of modernity *theologically.* He grappled with atheism by directing his critique not *directly* at it but instead self-critically at *Christian theology.* He attacked atheism at its roots by challenging the presupposition on which it made its deductions. He assaulted the notion that God is to be understood as the absolute, as an abstract concept that is the contrary concept to the human. This God was for Barth a greater evil than no God at all.

Then he merges into his criticism of this theistic concept of God his other criticism of an ostensible "God" who in truth is simply a reflection of *humanity.* The God who is "something up there where humans are not present" is a self-projection of humanity onto the heavens. This is the nature of the false gods whom we invent, namely, to be up above and in and for themselves. "In their otherworldliness and supernaturalness and otherness" they are not God. They are "a reflection of the human pride . . . which will not stoop to that which is beneath it" (IV/1 173 = 159). According to Genesis 3 pride is the sin of wanting to be like God. For Barth the evil here is not just humanity's overvaluation of itself. The evil here is that humanity is involved in a far-reaching error in thinking about *God.* We think of God as a being that wills only itself, as an independent and absolute being that is there for itself alone — and we would like to be like that. We depict God according to our own desires, but in so doing we miss the real God. The true God does not want to be without humans. He is not that independent being that we want to be like, and that we are much too similar to, to our great misfortune. The concept of God that T. Rendtorff attributed to Barth, the God who wants to be victor over humanity, who wants to be absolute,[8] has nothing to do with God, according to Barth. It "makes God into the devil" (IV/1 469 = 422).[9] "For if . . . there 'is' a devil, he is identical with a supreme being which posits and wills itself, which exists in a solitary glory and is therefore 'absolute.' The devil is that being which we can define only as an independent nonbeing" (IV/1 469 = 422).

The weighty consequences of this error concerning God are demonstrated by the fact that the human person herself bears the damage it causes. For in trying to be an independent and absolute being herself, she is wrong both about herself as well as about God. In making God into "the devil" and

---

8. Trutz Rendtorff, "Radikale Autonomie Gottes," in *Theorie des Christentums: Historische-theologische Studien zu seiner neuzeitlichen Verfassung,* ed. T. Rendtorff (Gütersloh, 1972), pp. 164ff.

9. Cf. Karl Barth, *Dogmatik im Grundriss* (Zollikon-Zurich, 1947), p. 54; ET: *Dogmatics in Outline* (London, 1949), p. 48.

wanting to be like God, she makes herself into the "devil."[10] Barth acknowledges that atheism's critique is right insofar as it unmasks the picture of an independent divine being as a projection of the human's own being made by humanity. He makes this acknowledgement, however, by offering a theological criticism of atheism. For what the human finds mirrored in heaven is not only not the true essence of God, but it is also not the true essence of the *human.*

Ludwig Feuerbach, it is true, thought that we only need to decipher the process as a projection in order for humanity to come to its senses. But this removal of illusion rests on a new illusion that humans have of themselves. It does not cure humanity of its self-alienation, but instead actually causes an alienation from the *self.* The illusory notion of a self-existent being does not get one whit better when it is applied to the human rather than to God. That is only to fall from the frying-pan into the fire. In theological terms this notion that merely mirrors the human heart is the product of the human fall into sin. It is a terrible delusion, because those who cling to it, or chase after it, are *both* alienated from God and from themselves. By ascribing an independent being to themselves rather than to God, they step into the chains of captivity. They "free" themselves from that image of God, but now that they ascribe this image to themselves, they cannot free themselves from the devilry of that ill-fated absolute nonbeing. In a new and naked way humanity remains alienated from itself. Theism and atheism suffer from the same evil and must be cured together.

The Human God

For good reason, Barth does not proceed by showing, on the basis of his analysis of modernity, that the positions of theism and atheism constitute a dilemma that he then resolves by postulating a position beyond both. To do so would have meant the construction of a new mental image of God. We have already learned the basic principle that reality precedes possibility. A fact, not a postulate, is the starting point of Barth's theology: The event of God's encounter with humanity. This encounter heals alienated humanity. Thinking does not.

This healing opens the door to knowledge, including the knowledge that the problem of modernity is derived from the conviction that salvation will be found in an independent and absolute being, whether humanity defines that as God or self. It helps us to see that a false presupposition lies be-

10. Ibid.

hind our assuming either an unattainable "above" where we are not present or a "below" where God is not present. We are also helped to see the fatal consequences of these false presuppositions: either God is made into the devil or the human is sent to the devil. Barth observed "that in no historical sphere has common lying flourished so grandly as in the Christian era" (IV/3 521 = 452). His meaning is this: Only when the message of God's union with humanity was proclaimed so clearly as here could its obstinate contradiction surface with the insistence on some absolute being, divine or human.

With what does the reality of the God who encounters us oppose this? How does it contradict this so that we are healed of our alienation from God and from ourselves? Barth states that "while there is a godlessness in the human, in view of the Word of reconciliation there is no humanlessness in God" (IV/1 133 = 119 rev.). We still have to investigate whether that "human godlessness" which "exists" is all that enduring. At any rate, the statement means that over against the historical thesis that atheism developed out of theism we must set the material thesis that human godlessness can be broken open only when the assumption of an absolute and divine "above in which the human is not present" is contested. That assumption can and must be contested. Otherwise Christianity would forget the God whom it is to confess. Barth does indeed think that that kind of theism, with its assertions that "God exists," is a theology without God and is thus powerless against atheism. The God whom Christianity confesses is Emmanuel, God *with us*. This God is to be thought in no other relationship than in relationship to the human person. Christianity does not have "any interest" whatever in the statement that "God exists" (IV/1 591 = 530). All its interest focuses upon the statement "There is no humanlessness in God."

This statement has implications, first of all, for the understanding of God. Not in the slightest can theology find room for the idea that God is a being that wills itself alone and defines itself by differentiation from us. God's being is a being in encounter and connectedness. It would be a mistake to see the reason for this in the *weakness of our human knowledge*. On its account we can know everything we know only as it relates to *us*, so that we know God only in those aspects of him that are comprehensible to us. It is a mistake because God's encounter with us is not just an instance within the range of what is otherwise conceivable to us, that which is only and always subjectively conceivable. It is a mistake because we are then conceding the possible existence of *another* God, as he does not appear to us, the existence of a concealed God in himself, who has nothing to do with us — the existence of a God who is cut off from humanity (II/1 206ff. = 182ff.). Barth's meaning is that it is not just God as he appears to *us* but God even before we ever think of him, God *in and from himself,* who is Emmanuel. This helps us to understand in a new light his rejection of natural theology. He does not contend against divine revelation in nature and history, even outside the witness of the church.[11] His contention is that a knowledge of God abstracted from the revelation of "Emmanuel" ends up being the knowledge of *another* God, a God for whom it is not essential to be "God with us" in every relationship, but who is still supposed to be "God" or a preliminary stage of the Emmanuel, an undefined and general being that only becomes God for us *through us.*

Yet how can we say that *in his essence* God is "God with us"? What counts here is a right understanding, gained when we proceed from the priority of reality over possibility, that God has *revealed* himself, and revealed himself *in the way* that he did it. We know God in no other way than on the basis of this revelation — otherwise God would be a human projection. God reveals *himself,* not just a "part" of himself, causing us to search for other parts in order to amplify and integrate and relativize and in truth correct what we already know, so that in that one part we would not be reliably dealing with God and, further, so that we would still have to count on some other God than the "Emmanuel." Never mind that here and everywhere God *always* and only reveals himself partially, that God "in and of himself" is always another than the one who communicates himself to humanity. God reveals himself, which means that God reliably *says,* in a binding way for both himself and us, *defines* who he is, who he is for us, and who we are for him, validly for all times and places. In revealing *himself,* God does not tell us "something." He really does impart *himself.* In this way God encounters us, and he thus tells us that he is the God who turns to us, the God who encounters us.

It is decisive that, in so doing, God is "binding . . . Himself in relation to man" (IV/1 172 = 158). This decisive emphasis cannot even be articulated wherever God's relationship to us is understood as being based on the weakness of our knowledge. In this case, God does not bind himself, but we ourselves bind God to our own possibilities of knowledge. Then, to the extent that he does not completely reveal himself, which is conceded, he is the God who has nothing to do with us, the God who does not bind himself to the human person. Since in his encounter with us, God is revealed as the one who "binds himself to his human opposite," that human does not exist alone here "below" where humanity is present. God is then present here, not God alone but God *with* the human person. "God shows Himself to be the . . . true God . . . capable and willing and ready for . . . this far journey" (IV/1 173 = 159).

---

11. Karl Barth, *Texte zur Barmer Theologischen Erklärung* (Zurich, 1984), p. 19.

It is a journey into the *far country* because the human person, existing for itself, is alienated from itself and from God because of its image of God tailored after the likeness of man. And it is a *journey* into the far country because it is God's goal to find humanity in that far place and to bring it home. He can do this, not because he can do anything but because as "God *with us*" he meets us and sets aside this twofold alienation. He does not, however, *become* "God with us" through this encounter. He clearly encounters us because he is "capable and willing and ready for this," because he is already "God with us." If he goes into the far country, he does not find it strange to be with humans (IV/1 196 = 180). Nor does he alienate himself from himself, as though he could "cease to be God" (IV/1 173 = 158). He simply shows himself to be the one who has always turned to humanity. This means that the reason God is present below where humanity lives is that humanity is already present in God's "above." If God binds *himself* to humanity, then God *is* himself with humanity.

Barth is cautious here. He does not say, as Hegel does, that we are eternally in God. This would mean a divinization of humanity and a dedivinization of God. It would take issue with the view that we owe God's binding of himself to us to his *free and gracious resolve.* God binds himself to humanity but does not become our captive. What he does rests on his own *free* decree. He executes this in time, but it is a decree of the *eternal* God who precedes all time. It is not a decree of fate nor a ruthlessly arbitrary choice. "It cannot be a *decretum absolutum*" (II/2 172 = 158). It is a resolve in keeping with God's eternal *love.* It is a *decretum concretum,* a decree that already takes account of an another who is external to God. It is a decree in which he is not alone but ready to bind himself to this other. Even before we existed this resolve meant that God was the God "from eternity" who had determined to be with us (III/2 173f. = 152). "In no depth of the Godhead shall we encounter any other but Him. There is no such thing as Godhead in itself" (II/2 123 = 115). "There was no time when God was not the covenant partner of man" (III/2 260 = 218).

The statement that God is the God of humanity is in the first instance a statement about God, namely, that he is "capable and willing and ready" to link himself with us and that he is thus resolved to "limiting . . . Himself" in this way (IV/1 172 = 158). We thus have to rethink certain things in our concepts of God. We must not imagine that God is an unlimited and "absolute" power. Barth was not ready to abandon the term "absoluteness" in relation to God, but he used it only in the sense that the God who makes that decree is the one who entirely determines himself. If, however, absoluteness meant merely a desire for complete independence, then God would negate what is external to himself, or rather, he would be dependent upon that other in order to be able to delimit himself from it. We would then have only described what "we would gladly ascribe to ourselves" or, as we transfer this to God, it would be no more than "man's own reflection" (II/1 347 = 308-9). The true God stands opposed to this reflection. His being does not consist of demarcation from others. He "uses" his own being to bring himself into relationship with them.

Naturally we do not contest the mightiness of God, nor is evil power contested by declaring God to be weak, which alongside that mirror image is just another form in which the human declares his independence from God. God does indeed have power, but this power so limits itself as to *make possible* the authentic *being* and *action* of God. Limited in that way, it is no real limitation, for God "has all the real power" (II/1 597 = 531). God's power means "that . . . He can not do everything, that the possibility of the impossible . . . [is] excluded from his essence and activity" (II/1 599 = 533). *God's* power is his ". . . capacity . . . which is . . . utterly *concrete*" (II/1 598 = 532). It is not the fact that he has *power* that makes him God. "Power in itself is evil" (II/1 589 = 524). If we do not have to reckon with "an essentially different omnipotence from that which God has manifested in His actual choice and action," we will then have to contest Luther's concept of the *Deus absconditus* [= hidden God], who is supposed to have a power *independent* of this "actual choice and action" (II/1 609f. = 541-42). Against the medieval concept of a *potentia absoluta* [= absolute power] posited in God, namely, an unlimited power, we have to assert that this does not make "Him the divine Ruler that [is] ruling with infinite power in an infinite sphere; that is the very thing which He does not do." That is ". . . rather the characteristic of the government of ungodly and anti-godly courts. God Himself rules in a definite sphere and with a definite power. What makes Him the divine Ruler is the very fact that His rule is determined and limited: self-determined and self-limited, but determined and limited nonetheless" — by a "primal decision" to make himself the God of humanity (II/2 52-54 = 50). In God's use of his power, in his actual choice and action, the truth is demonstrated that God's power is true as it is activated in a real display of will and action. "There is no humanlessness in God."

The God-related Human

There is "a godlessness in the human," says Barth. And yet it cannot really "exist" as little as there exists "a humanlessness in God," *because* there is no humanlessness in God. If the presupposition of atheism is disputed, the "above where the human is not present," then there is no "above" in that sense at all. Then there is also no "below" shut off from God. Atheism is then attacked on its own ground, there in "that below where God is not present" — not because of some conclusion in logic but because of the fact of the humanity of God. In that God is not humanless, it is questionable whether humanity is godless. "In the absurd way which is all that is possible in this connection, man is able to be . . . relatively, although not absolutely and ontologically, godless. It is bad enough that he can do it and, in fact, does." But "his godlessness . . . cannot make God a 'manless' God" (IV/1 534 = 480 rev.). Barth teaches an essential God-relatedness on the part of every human, based in the grace of God and not in human "nature," nor in an immanent goodness of the human reflecting an optimistic over-valuation of a human core untouched by sin. Instead, the basis for this conviction is that the godless human cannot render God humanless.

The relativity of the "relative godlessness" rests entirely on the *relation* of God to humanity, which the godless person cannot set aside. This does not make human godlessness relatively harmless. It is "bad enough," because humans who are not abandoned by God do not have the *capacity* to be godless, and their *actual* godlessness is a flagrant contradiction not only of God but of their own humanity. The truly godless person is not merely a human who is still lacking "something." Her humanity itself is put into question. "Even in its noblest forms humanity without the knowledge of God has in it always the seed of discord and inhumanity, and sooner or later this will emerge" (IV/2 474 = 421). The ungodly person is for Barth the one who as such *posits herself absolutely.* Nothing is changed if she claims that her thinking is valid only for herself and not generally true, and in this sense "relativizes" it — all of which only increases the number of human illusions. In no way does this erase her godlessness. In severing herself from God the human absolutizes herself.

The self-absolutizing of the godless is for Barth more than evil arrogance. Naturally it is "bad enough" that such persons should be driven to excesses. They will almost unavoidably arrogate to themselves what is God's, they will function as creator, reconciler and redeemer, will re-interpret the holy Trinity as a law of world history that they supposedly control. They will elevate themselves to be judges of humanity and managers of providence. Yet when applied to themselves all these assumed titles become destructive and self-destructive. This is not accidental. For self-absolutizing means not only existence in excess but also, and above all, the negation of the "other," that is, *lonely existence, solitude.* The solitary person stands behind such excesses.

"The solitary man is the potential, and in a more refined or blatant way the actual, enemy of all others" (IV/2 474 = 421). For solitariness means restriction, *anxiety* that the human does not merely have, but which has him (IV/3 770 = 671-72), has him in such a way that he is always trying to break out of it but fails to do so. "In what he takes to be his successful hunt, he is himself the one who is hunted with terrible success by anxiety" (IV/2 523 = 463). Alienated from God, the human dissolves her humanity in this loneliness and anxiety initiated by her, and is at odds with her neighbor as with herself. The solitary person is "inhuman" (IV/2 487 = 433-434), and in the disintegration of her physical and mental drives hateful (IV/2 514 = 456).

"In this state of anxiety, he may become [*pious*]." "It would be an independent task to [document] this in the light of the history and phenomenology of religion (including the Christian), but also of the concealed religions." *"Timor fecit deos"* [= It was fear that first created gods] (IV/3 924 = 807 rev.). Barth formulates an apparent paradox: piety is also a possibility of the absolute human who is separated from God. The only thing is that the gods that he may well have are the products of his solitariness and anxiety, which is evidenced by the fact that they maintain him in his anxiety and solitariness; they leave him ab-solute. The reason that Barth so decidedly opposed neo-Protestantism was that he always had the suspicion that its ultimate outcome could be that it would seek to overcome the self-absolutizing person, the person in relative godlessness, by making the claim that part of *one's* psychological equipment is a disposition for religion. If he was right in suspecting this, then the attempt *could* never achieve its objective. The consequence perhaps would be that the "Cartesianism" of the absolute individual would be enhanced by "the Cartesianism of the believing Christian" (I/1 223 = 213). It would also disguise the fact that the attempt remains entangled in the system of absolutizing.

What heals such a person is not she herself, not even when she interprets herself as a bearer of the divine; it is the human God who heals her. What sets aside his loneliness is the fact that God no longer leaves him on his own. What sets her godlessness aside is that fact that God does not let go of her. Since there is no "humanlessness" of God, the human person can, to be sure, posit himself as absolute, but cannot posit his godlessness. A relative or subjective godlessness does indeed "exist," and it is so great that we cannot "subjectively" overcome it, for example, by upholding the existence of a religious area in the soul of the "absolutized" person. Therefore, there is no absolute or "objective" godlessness of the human. This statement is fully grounded in God's assertion that he is the God of the human person and that the human is therefore God's, which is the "objective" God-relatedness of the human. We as humans are *involved* here, for when we absolutize our-selves we are shown that this contradicts our very essence. God does not as-sert a claim to "absolute" power in doing this, but he does assert that the hu-manity of the human is saved by this.

To put it another way, in that the human projects onto God the image of an absolute and self-existing being, in order to be like him, he is in "error . . . concerning himself" (IV/1 467 = 421). The human who wants to deify her-self in that way is not only in opposition to God; she is inhuman, the enemy of humanity and despiser of humanity. God, however, shows himself to be true God by being the God of humanity, and he thereby also demonstrates that the true human is God's human. Thus, the human *cannot* let God "be God in His sphere in order in his own sphere to try to be man 'in abstracto' and on his own account." In that God Himself "becomes man for men," the decision is made that "men have a character, we can call it a *character indelibilis*" [= indelible character]. When God reveals "that from the very be-ginning he willed to be . . . the God of man . . . He reveals that man is *His* man, mans belongs to Him, is bound and pledged to Him. The man for whose sake God Himself became man cannot be basically neutral. He can only face God as a partner in His activity" (IV/1 43-44 = 42 rev.). The true person, the per-son with God, is more original than the absolute person, alienated from God and oneself. If we cannot conceive of God in any other way than as the one who never lets us *go,* then we cannot think of ourselves in any other way than as those who never *leave* God.

But this true God is *really* God. Thus the true human person given by him is also *real* and not an ideal to be attained. The fact that God is our God who will neither let us go nor let us leave, is the real potential for questioning and ultimately removing the absolutizing human, the relative godlessness that alienates us from God and our own self-alienated loneliness. These will be removed in a way that does not deal arbitrarily and manipulatively with hu-manity — otherwise, the event would be inhumane and an admission that the absolutized person is humane. The human's relative godlessness is overcome only where she herself *affirms* that she is God's human. God convinces her of that in that he encounters her as her God and clarifies thereby that the person who is subject to *him* is the *true* human. But "he does not force or suppress or disable us," when convincing us of this and seeking our own free agreement. "He is not the rampaging numinous which strikes man unconditionally so that he can only be petrified and silent before it, yielding without really want-ing to do so. He does not humiliate or insult man. He does not make him a mere spectator or puppet" (IV/3 607 = 528). The human person "is declared accountable and treated as such" (IV/4 25 = 22-23 rev.).

That the human with God is the true human is proved, for Barth, in that fact that she is *human.* This takes place in the *relationship* which the humane God enables. In this relationship the human person is removed from her self-alienation. Through this God she not only moves from her godlessness into a connection with God; but in God's coming to her, she also and emphatically comes *to herself.* She is neither a subject in herself nor does God treat her as an object. Through God's *relationship* to her, she *becomes* a subject. She is who she really is not alone. Corresponding to God's being, she *is* being in relationship, both with God and with fellow humans. "Thus the incarnation of God corresponds soteriologically to the humanization of the human (*homo homini homo* [= the human becomes human to the human])."[12] "Since God himself became man, man is the measure of all things."[13] Knowing the humanity of God we are "from the very start . . . humanists" (CL 463 = 267). If the humanity of God is not merely *one* of God's many faces, if God *Himself* is the one turning to humanity, then the understanding of the human as the one turned toward God is neither a reshaping of his being nor an incidental definition added to him, without which he could still exist. Then *this* human person is the human *himself.*

Those "humanists" are convincing for the following reason: "The *a priori* of what they think and speak and will . . . is the *man* who is loved by God, his right and worth — solely and simply man" (CL 464 = 268). Thus they resist the subjection of people to overbearing systems. Bureaucracy, in which "men are grouped . . . according to specified plans, principles and regulations" so that they "are invisible to one another," is a typical example of "inhumanity" (III/2 302 = 252). "No idea, no principle, no traditional or newly established institution or organization, no old or new form of economy, state, culture . . . no prevailing habit, custom, or . . . moral system, no ideal of education and upbringing, no form of the church, nor . . . any negation or contesting of certain other ideas and the social constructs corresponding to them" shall be allowed to dominate over the human person. Otherwise from all of these there can emerge absolutes that are distinct from humanity. "Where do we meet one another more like wolves swallowing one another up than when we come in the name of absolutes, no matter what we call them?" (CL 464f. = 267-268).

These "humanists" refuse to tie man down to the "garbs and masks" —

---

12. Eberhard Jüngel, *Barth-Studien,* p. 345.

13. Karl Barth, *Christengemeinde und Bürgergemeinde* (*Theologische Studien* 20) (Stuttgart, 1946), p. 33; ET: "The Christian Community and the Civil Community," *Community, State, and Church: Three Essays* (Gloucester, Mass., 1968), p. 172.

be they vain, or poor, or aggressive, or groundless — with which he likes to surround himself. "It will be no accident that he bears them and that he bears this or that particular one of the many that are available. To see him it may be helpful to see him also in these disguises." Christians, however, "cannot stop here." The masks "are not man himself. . . . In, with, and under all the apparatus by which he is surrounded and with which he . . . usually hides himself, he himself is the being who, whether he knows that God is on his side or not, [would like] to achieve his right, live in dignity, and enjoy freedom, peace, and joy." To do so, he chooses "inept" and "wicked" ways and secretly suffers because he "does *not* achieve his purpose. . . . He acts — this is the point of his disguises — as if he does not suffer. The one who suffers is man himself whom God loves." The task of the "humanists" is to look with mercy on those behind the masks (CL 466-468 = 269).

Finally these "humanists" take note of the context. Where the individual in his attempts particularly "to equate God with himself and himself with God does not know *God*," there he "does not know his *fellow man* either. . . . He regards him as an object to whom he as subject may or may not be in relation according to his own free choice and disposal, whom he may pass by as he does so many other objects, or with whom, if this is out of the question, he may have dealings as it suits himself." If he does know God, he knows his fellow human "as a fellow subject whom God has set unavoidably beside him, to whom he is unavoidably linked in his relation to God, so that apart from him he cannot himself be a subject, a person" (CL 216 = 131).

God's Covenant with Israel

The truth of the humane God is not that of a simple *idea,* as though the mere thinking of it would be capable of doing away with the theological presupposition of atheism and with it atheism itself as its consequence. All thinking here can only be a "thinking after," in view of the fact that this truth is the truth of a specific *reality.* This reality has the capacity to overthrow both the presupposition of atheism and atheism itself. In this reality, the *fact* of the God who is not separated from humanity and the human who is not separated from God encounters us. This is no postulate. The issue here is to "read" that truth in the reality of this fact, as Barth likes to put it. It forces us to think that truth and to take cognizance of the rebuttal of both the presupposition of atheism and its consequence. The reality of this fact is for Barth the covenant that God concluded with Israel on the basis of which it lived, and still lives, as a special people among the peoples. This covenant is not an illustration of the *general* concept of a humane God and of a humanity sub-ject to him. On the contrary, the very *special* fact of God's covenant with Is-rael is what *leads* us to this concept in the first place.

Barth stresses that this fact encounters us even outside Scripture, as an unmistakable phenomenon in the midst of world history. "Here a part of world history gives the most direct witness to the biblical witness of revela-tion, and therefore to the God who is attested in the Bible" (I/2 567 = 510-11). We come upon it in the special existence of this special people. Unlike other peoples, often powerful peoples, who rose and fell, this people obviously cannot be destroyed. The Third Reich *had* to come to its own downfall be-cause it tried to extinguish Israel.[14] "In spite of the destruction and persecu-tion, and above all the assimilation . . . the Jews are still there, and perma-nently there" (III/3 239f. = 212). *Modernity's* response to the encounter with this phenomenon was to be offended by it, in order then to dispute its dis-tinct testimony to God. The "liberal solution" tries to do this by "evading" it (I/2 567 = 511), i.e., by absorbing the peculiarity of God's people, elect solely by God's grace, into the generality of every possible kind of religious concep-tion. The "plague" of anti-Semitism (III/3 289 = 220) tries to do it by furi-ously punishing and banishing the Jews for their distinctiveness, while fail-ing to realize that "in rejecting the Jew he rejects God" (I/2 567 = 511). Whether the one way or the other, what Israel testifies to in its distinctive-ness is "hardly seen by Anti-Semites and liberals" (I/2 567 = 510). In Barth's view the two "solutions" are connected, and the plague cannot be healed by way of that "liberal solution." The judgment on both is that "anti-Semitism in all its forms means rejection of the *grace* of God,"[15] *covenant grace!* In a Christian theology that detaches itself from the Jews there lurks the core of both a cult that asserts a nonhuman God, a God who is "almighty" without grace, and the inhumanity of the self-centered individual who asserts himself against his fellow man. The existence of Israel is the factual reality that testi-fies to the truth of the God who is bound to humanity and of the humanity that is bound to God. Hence any attempt to do away with Israel would be the root of what is both ungodly and inhuman and thus the destruction of the message of the church.

We cannot understand the mystery of the existence of this people with-out the Word of God according to the Scriptures (III/3 256 = 226). It can give us sufficient and competent information about them, because it is "necessar-ily" (I/2 566 = 510) written by Jews. We can indeed understand the mystery

---

14. Karl Barth, *Eine Schweizer Stimme: 1938-1945* (Zollikon-Zurich, 1945), pp. 321-22.
15. Karl Barth, *Eine Schweizer Stimme,* p. 90.

when, taught by Scripture, we see what the issue is: "From the existence of this people we have to learn that the elect of God is [Another], not a German nor a Swiss nor a Frenchman, but this Jew. We have to learn in order to be elect ourselves, for good or evil we must either be Jews or belong to this Jew" (III/3 255 = 225). This becomes clear when we see that the innermost mystery of the existence of this people is its election from among all people by God to be joined with him in the enacted *covenant*. What does "covenant" mean? The meaning of the concept must be "read" from the history of *the* covenant to which "the whole Bible bears witness"; we must not "import" a prior concept of the covenant (IV/1 59 = 55-56). A covenant of grace might make no sense when set in the light of a general concept. The point is to be found in *this* covenant, so much so that we must insist that the term "covenant" in its *precise* and *original* meaning is at stake here.

So what does covenant mean *here?* "It is with this freely electing love that according to the witness of the Old Testament Yahweh concluded His covenant with Israel." Election means "not that Israel has chosen Him but He Israel" (IV/2 871 = 768). Israel's own electing can consist only of acknowledging after the fact the covenant that has been made — or not doing so. The covenant is two-sided to the extent that — regardless if Israel were worthy of it, or how Israel relates to it — its connectedness with God is enclosed in God's connectedness with it. The covenant is "the historical reality with which the Old Testament is concerned whether it actually uses the word or not." It rests on the divine pronouncement: "'I will be your God, and ye shall be my people' (Jer. 7:23; 11:4; 30:22; 31:33; 32:38; Ezek. 36:28)" (IV/1 22 = 22). In this pronouncement God defines exactly our modern problem as Barth perceives it, namely, that "just as there is no God but the God of the covenant, there is no man but the man of the covenant" (IV/1 40, 45 = 37-38, 43). In this pronouncement God has pledged himself to this people and thus first placed a commitment *on himself* — he has *bound* himself. And in this promise God has then also bound *this people* to himself, making it what it is: the partner in his covenant, the people *of God*. This covenant "does not discover Israel already existing as such. . . . It creates Israel" (I/2 88 = 80-81).

The covenant "cannot be something *given* apart from the act of God and man." It takes form as the *history* of the covenant, in such a way that "the conclusion of the covenant in the Old Testament represents a series of many such events." The covenant "remains — and it is in this way and only in this way that it does remain — the *event* of . . . divine and human choice, just as God Himself *exists* to the very depths of His being, and is therefore a (personally) living, active, acting and speaking God, and just as His human partner, His Israel, is actual only in its *history*, in the doing of its good and evil deeds, in the acting and suffering of the men who compose it" (IV/1 23f. = 23-24). Hence the covenant is a *lasting* covenant. The word about the "covenant of peace which will not be removed (Is. 54:10) stand[s] over everything that takes place in the relations between Yahweh and Israel." This statement is grounded solely in the faithfulness of God who is committed to his promise. No unfaithfulness on the part of the partner can "dissolve" the covenant (IV/1 23 = 23). "God does not cease to be the . . . covenant-partner" of humanity. Thus, the human has never ceased "to be the covenant-partner of God. . . . As he has not instituted the covenant, he cannot destroy it or even contract out of it" (IV/2 547 = 484). For Barth the promise of a new covenant in Jeremiah 31:31-34 cannot mean the replacement of the old covenant with Israel by a different one. It has to mean the "confirmation of what He had always willed and indeed done in the covenant with Israel" (IV/1 34 = 34). The promise, however, aims at a "radical change in structure" of that covenant, of which it is "capable," because it is the history of the *covenant,* and "which it will actually undergo in the last days" (IV/1 32 = 33). It will then be so "filled" with grace that "the covenant with Israel is made and avails for the whole race" (IV/1 35 = 35).

From the very first it is a covenant of *grace.* For this reason, and not because of an abstract distinction between a superior God and a subordinate human, the covenant is between two highly *unequal* partners. They are unequal "because God is the merciful Lord, and because man is the covenant partner who shares but also needs this divine mercy" (III/1 177 = 158). Therefore the covenant is not based on human fitness for it, nor can human unfitness set it aside. The two-sidedness of the covenant rests totally upon the fact that it comes about and endures only through God's grace. This means for God something very difficult — He has as his partner not a peer but a human in dire need of mercy. "God will lose so that man might win" (II/2 177 = 162 rev.). The human gains as God makes himself into the "fellow and friend" of humanity, thus making the human into his "fellow and friend" (IV/1 53 = 50-51). Grace is present in both the fact that he makes the human person worthy of fellowship with him *and* in the fact that the covenant is grounded solely on God's goodness and not on human worthiness. The inequality of the partners can, thus, not threaten the covenant. That is the reason that the signs of divine judgment in the covenant displayed in the history of biblical Israel are signs that Israel belongs to the covenant and is not ejected from it (II/1 438 = 392-93). "It is quite incontestable that God *receives* him in this judgment" (II/2 820 = 734).

What might threaten the covenant of grace is apparent when one observes that "the gods of the ancient world surrounding Israel also had their own *peoples,*" in such a way that both stood "in a reciprocal relationship of solidarity and control" (IV/2 871 = 768). Wherever the relationship with God is thus thought of and shaped, the covenant of *grace* is disputed. "Natural theology" takes over (IV/2 112 = 101), which must deny the initial election of *only* Israel to the covenant of grace, just as that election itself denies such a theology. When the covenant of "two partners who are from the very first and unchangeably unequal" is replaced by the "notion of a continuous coexistence of the two" — with an appeal to the Holy Spirit as the "impelling force" for this! — there the human resists the covenant of grace (IV/3 512f. = 444-445). Suppose Israel sees the relationship with God along these lines?! Then "it is unfaithful to its own election as His (God's) peculiar people and to its own electing of God. It has already fallen away to the worship of false gods and the transgression of all His commandments" (IV/1 26 = 25). What Barth sees here is the *breach of the covenant* in the midst of the covenant people, which that people constantly does according to the Old Testament, and then confirms in its No to Christ, placing itself on a level with those other peoples. The fault is not a moral one, evaluated in terms of a lex naturae [= law of nature] (IV/1 154f. = 140). It is the No to the grace on which the covenant with the people rests. According to Barth *this* is a sin that can be committed only on the basis of the covenant, and it would threaten it if God were not himself faithful to his unfaithful partner *in spite of it* (IV/2 547 = 484), faithful not in the sense of impotently tolerating that unfaithfulness but faithful in a new act that genuinely involves a fulfillment of the covenant with grace.

Jesus Christ

This end-time fulfillment of the covenant by grace takes place in Jesus Christ. This is Barth's basic thesis. *This* is the issue for him, and not that the covenant with Israel is *replaced* by a different one. Nor is it that the covenant portrayed "in the Old Testament as a sequence of *many* covenant decisions" (IV/1 24 = 24 rev.) now receives further continuations, since it now becomes *definitive* because it is "fulfilled." The Christ event is thus the "confirmation" of the covenant with Israel (IV/1 71 = 67) in the intensive sense that apart from it the covenant would fall "in the void" (IV/1 72 = 68). It is not left in the void, because its fulfillment is *decisively* grace in that it "shows itself and acts . . . as grace for lost sinners" (IV/1 73 = 69). God remains thus emphatically faithful to his unfaithful partner. Hence the negation by non-Christian Israel of the fulfillment in Christ of its own covenant with God cannot set that covenant aside but instead only confirm it. Because Israel's covenant is fulfilled *in this* way — and in that Israel confirms its distinctive fulfillment by saying No — the covenant now opens itself up for *other* sinners *outside* Israel and thus becomes the covenant "between God and *man*" (IV/1 22 = 22). In Christ we do not have a different covenant that is made with the nations; "there can be no question of anything but their inclusion in the one covenant" (I/2 115 = 105). The church of *Jesus Christ,* which on the basis of that inclusion gathers together both Jews and Gentiles, can be certain of the validity of that "grace for lost sinners" for it only by confessing the *eternal* election of Israel (II/2 225 = 200f.). For Barth the Christ event as the basis of the abiding election with Israel also constitutes the basis of the inclusion of the *world* in the divine covenant of grace. Just as the existence of that special people among all the peoples bears testimony to God's *covenant of grace,* the existence of the church of Christ among the peoples bears decisive witness to the *fulfillment* of the covenant through grace.

To what extent can we say this of Jesus Christ? Barth refers to both the Old Testament and the New: "What . . . was God's covenant with man, is here, in the fulfillment, God's becoming man" (I/2 114 = 103). This is not a contradiction, but a covenant event intimately connected to what has gone before. Under the name of Jesus Christ "God Himself realized . . . the self-giving of Himself as the Covenant partner of [His] people" (II/2 57 = 53 rev.). The incarnation of God is the fulfillment of the covenant as a radical form of the relationship between God and Israel, Israel and God. God has not, of course, *transformed* Himself into a man, nor a man into God (IV/2 68 = 63). What has happened is that God has *assumed* human form, not just *a* man, but in the *one* man Jesus *the* man (IV/2 51f. = 47-48), and that in this one man humanity as a whole is *assumed* and *accepted* by God, and yes, accepts God Himself. Insofar as this event is inseparably linked to Jesus Christ, he rightly bears the name "Emmanuel," fulfilling what this name means. And again, this name can be uttered only when the *story* is told that is inseparably linked with his name. He, the Son of God, "in His divine essence takes part in *human* essence — so radical and total a part that He causes His existence to become and be also the existence of the man Jesus of Nazareth. Again, He gives to the human essence of Jesus of Nazareth a part in His own *divine* essence as the eternal Son who is coequal with the Father and the Holy Spirit" (IV/2 67 = 62). In the unity of the fact that God assumes humanity and humanity is assumed by God, God assumes humanity *itself* to himself. He does this in order to put right the wrong that humanity has done. More precisely, he does it in order to heal the broken covenant and to set aside the "dissolution" which threatens, precisely in that place where the covenantal breach occurs and at which the covenant is threatened by "dissolution" (IV/1 22 = 22).

The Christ event takes place with "divine necessity" (IV/1 184 = 168) in the context of the covenant with Israel. "The Word did not simply become any 'flesh,' any man humbled and suffering. It became Jewish flesh. The Church's whole doctrine of the incarnation and the atonement becomes abstract and valueless and meaningless to the extent that these come to be regarded as something accidental. . . . The New Testament witness to Jesus the Christ, the Son of God, stands on the soil of the Old Testament and cannot be separated from it" (IV/1 181f. = 166). Only *because* this witness stands on this soil and testifies to the *fulfillment* of the covenant taking place on this soil, must we say that it is speaking of the event that is valid not *only* for the Jews, for in Jewish flesh God has assumed *all* "flesh," and this witness is the end of a covenant history "to the exclusion of all others" (III/3 239 = 211). Jesus Christ as "the Messiah of Israel becomes the Saviour of the world" (IV/2 288 = 260). For as the Word, who is God himself, becomes Jewish flesh and assumes it into unity with himself, God *conclusively* displays grace in this "flesh," to which testifies the fact that God accepts those who have just as *conclusively* not merited such grace, the Gentiles. The existence of these Gentiles points backward and "brings to mind" the incarnation of God, where what was still "unfulfilled" on the soil of the Old Testament but was "expected" *in* the covenant made there, now took place (I/2 77, 112 = 72, 101; IV/3 54 = 50).

The nonfulfillment of the covenant in the Old Testament does not mean that it might be a dissolvable covenant. Nor does the fulfillment of the covenant mean that it was replaced by another. Its fulfillment confirms it in the very fact that the threat to it caused by the human partner was removed. The incarnation of God is no other and no less than the covenant of God with Israel that has now become truly a "perfect covenant" (IV/1 34 = 33), perfect in that it is now God's covenant not only with Israel but with humanity in general. In the incarnation we are encountered by the One who is no other than the "covenant God" who bound himself to Israel, but now his definition as the covenant God has become *definitive,* in that it is made precise in a *deepened* sense. In Jesus Christ God has shown that he is *"truly God"* [= *vere Deus*], so that what took place in the action and passion of Jesus Christ is, in Luther's words, "a mirror of the fatherly heart of God" (CL 106 = 67). The true God is he who, unwilling to be without us, *humbled* himself in relation to us. "Who the one true God is and what He is, i.e., what is His being as God and therefore His deity, all this we have to discover from the fact that as such He is very man and a partaker of human nature, from His becoming man . . . and from what He has done and suffered in the flesh" (IV/1 193 = 177). "He, the electing eternal God, willed Himself to be rejected and therefore perishing man" (IV/1 191 = 175). He is so much in solidarity with humanity that he took its place and accepted and overcame that which separates us from him in a truly gracious *contradicting* of that which would detach us from God, tackling the root of the breaking of the covenant, the graceless notion that the covenant rests in part upon our human worthiness and readiness for it. The incarnation does not lessen but truly demonstrates the deity of God even in such humiliation.

In the very same event that demonstrates God's deity, God also shows who is *vere homo* [= true man]. ". . . As God condescends . . . to man and becomes man, man himself is exalted, not as God or like God, but to God, being placed at His side, not in identity, but in true fellowship with Him" (IV/2 4 = 6). The human, "in and for himself," and as we know ourselves, is the alienated person, not the authentic human — just as a "God in and of himself" who is not the God of humanity is a figment of our alienated human imagination and not true God. The "human in and of herself" can only vary her self-alienation but cannot remove it — just as a "God in and of himself," whom this human may "have" as a figment of her heart, can only preserve the alienation but not rescue from it. Thus, true humanity is no distant ideal that we can only strive after and only approximately attain. True man is the *real* man who is real in the incarnation of God in Jesus Christ. Jesus is *vere homo* [= true man] not because he is like us but because he is "different" from us (IV/2 29 = 27-28), so that we might become truly human in him and like him. The man truly *accepted* by God in his incarnation is true man. As Jesus takes our place and acts on our behalf, the new and true man who, exalted in God's acceptance in a *grace that cannot be gainsaid,* is now *truly there.* The *"vere homo"* [= true man] is thus inseparable from Jesus Christ, for he is inseparably "enclosed" (IV/2 4 = 6) in the fulfillment of the covenant in the incarnation of God.

"Man has not fallen lower than the depth to which God humbled Himself for him in Jesus Christ" (IV/1 534 = 480-81). For this reason he cannot, ultimately, truly fall. In the positive sense he is rather lifted up. We have here a demonstration of the fact that the humanity of the human person consists essentially and not just subsequently or incidentally (as though one could be human without it) in one's being accepted by God. In that God in Jesus Christ revealed that from the very beginning he willed to be the God of humanity, he also revealed that the human person is his human and belongs to him (cf. IV/1 46f. = 45).

Barth finds the "incarnation of God" decisively consummated in the "it is finished" of the *event of the cross* (John 19:30). "His death on the cross was and is the [*perfected* consummation] of the incarnation of the Word and therefore [of] the humiliation of the Son of God and [of the] exaltation of the Son of man" (IV/2 157 = 140-141 rev.). *Two* things happened at the crucifixion. First, in the self-offering of the Son of God into the depths (John 3:16; IV/1 76 = 71), in his suffering "for us" and for our sins (2 Cor. 5:21; IV/1 80 = 75f.), God has shown his deity in his acceptance of the sinner and her misery. Second, the human, liberated from her Godforsakenness (Mark 15:34; IV/2 187, 693 = 164-165, 612-613), accepted by God and transferred into indissoluble unity with God, is the "exalted" human (IV/2 325 = 292).

But what does the *Easter story* mean then? It is not just the "noetic converse" (IV/1 335 = 304) of the crucifixion event, through which the reality hidden there can be believed and acknowledged by humans. It is also this, but only subsequently. If it were only this, then our belief and acknowledgment would be no more than an *interpretation* of the event added by *us* to Good Friday. The true basis of our belief and acknowledgment is the fact that Easter is a "new act of God" (IV/1 335 = 304). "His resurrection. . . *confirmed* His death. It was God's *answer* to it. . . . It was God's *acknowledgment* of Jesus Christ, of His life and death . . . His judicial sentence that the action and passion of Jesus Christ were not apart from or against Him, but according to His good and holy will, and especially that His dying in our place was not futile but *effective,* that it was not to our destruction but to our *salvation*" (IV/1 336f. = 305). His resurrection is the "directive" with which Jesus Christ "reaches out to us," causing us to be "told" by him that in him we are the new and true humanity (IV/2 338 = 303-304 rev.), thus believing and acknowledging what has taken place in him.

For Barth this means that the truly human person is the one who is accepted by God and who thereupon *accepts* him in return. The human does not *make* herself into the true human by accepting God, thus rendering the covenant a two-sided one. The human can only correspond to the two-sidedness of the covenant initiated by God, and thus be a "witness" of the covenant (III/4 80 = 73-74). When we accept God we are simply acknowledging that in Christ we have first been accepted by him and are truly human as such. In accepting God we correspond to the man Jesus, who as the man accepted by God was the man who accepted God. "The circle of the covenant which in its earlier form is open on man's side will in its new form be closed" (IV/1 33 = 32), in that Jesus as God's human partner is faithful to God precisely at the place where the covenant was and is broken. For by a "free choice" he became obedient to God "unto death, even death on a cross" (Phil. 2:8; IV/1 211 = 193). In this free "obedience" that open circle is closed, for in him the true man is present whose faithfulness corresponds to God's faithfulness, responds to it, and thus relates with him.

In Barth's eyes, however, the decisive act by which the covenant is closed, and the true man acts accountably as God's partner, is the *prayer* of Jesus (II/2 134 = 124-125). The covenant aims finally at an accountable human partner whose *answer* is sought. This answer has to be *prayed* for. The covenant concludes in prayer, for by prayer we ourselves lay upon God the burden of being God, who "is God in the fact that he lets man apply to Him in this way, and wills that this should be the case. Here, then, we stand before the innermost center of the *covenant* between God and man" (III/4 102 = 93). Following the prayer of Jesus we ourselves can come forward as God's covenant partners and act accountably as the true humans that we are in him. For Barth such prayer becomes the event of "the primal and basic form of the whole Christian ethos" (CL 144 = 89). For prayer is the first "work of obedience" (III/4 103 = 94) that defines all the other acts of "covenant people." It is our human correspondence to the work of God.

That God has *in fact* accepted us in Jesus Christ is attested in the world by the visible "community" of those *accepted* by God who are gathered together by him and through him. These exist in order to *bear witness* to the world that they belong to him. "To say 'Christ' is to say 'Christ and His own' — Christ in and with his fullness, which is His community. As His community (His body), this cannot be merely a passive object" of all that God does to it within his covenant and its fulfillment (IV/2 717 = 634). It sounds surprising, but is logical in Barth's train of thought, that he lays much stress on the fact that "the *people of Israel* in its whole history *ante et post Christum* [= before and after Christ] and the *Christian Church* as it came into being on the day of Pentecost are two forms . . . of the *one* inseparable community in which Jesus Christ has his earthly-historical form of existence, by which he is attested to the whole world, by which the whole world is summoned to faith in Him. For what the Christian Church is, Israel was and is before it — *His* possession (Jn. 1:11), *His* body. . . . It is the bow of the *one* covenant which stretches over the whole. . . . To try to deny *this* unity would be to deny Jesus Christ Himself" (IV/1 747-749 = 669-71).

The church that confesses Jesus Christ would deny him and make its witness "pointless" if it did not confess its unity with all Israel and instead saw itself in detachment from Israel (II/2 213ff., 318 = 213ff., 267). "For what does the Church have which the Synagogue does not also have, and long before it (Rom. 9:4-5) — especially Jesus Christ Himself, who is of the Jews, who is the Jewish Messiah, and only as such the Lord of the Church?" (IV/1 749 = 671). "The Gentile Christian community of every age and land is a guest in the house of Israel" (IV/3 1005 = 877). Furthermore, the two are not just passive objects in the Christ event. They both *bear witness,* even Israel

that was elected for the covenant but denies both its fulfillment and implementation in the church. Indeed, in their different positions in the one covenant of grace — this is Barth's thesis (II/2 215-336 = 195-305) — the one community bears witness to itself and to the world, and both forms of the
community bear witness to each other of the twofold shape of the one covenant of grace. The existence of Israel shows that the covenant rests only upon
God's gracious self-determination for fellowship, upon his readiness to turn
aside and take upon himself his No to the unworthiness and anti-grace hostility of the covenant-breaking partner. The existence of the church shows
that all the sin and remoteness from the covenant cannot prevent God from
receiving humanity and honoring it with his fellowship with it, so that humanity has no other option than on its part to accept God. The two witnesses need one another. When they both speak, the one community bears
testimony to the one covenant of grace. That they, puzzling as it is, do not
speak together is for Barth "a wound, a gaping hole in the body of Christ."
"Jewish missions" is not our real need. What is needed is a credible confession by the church of its unity with the synagogue, "a unity which does not
have to be established but is already there ontologically" (IV/1 749 = 671).

The Divine Freedom —
Trinity and Predestination

Threatening and Threatened Freedom

Barth created an offense with a turn of thought that frequently emerges throughout his thinking. He claimed that God does not need humanity in order to be God. We hear, for example, the following statements, in which he even uses the concept of an absoluteness of God: "God confronts all that is in supreme and utter independence, i.e., He would be no less and no different even if they all did not exist or existed differently. . . . If they belong to Him and He to them, this dual relationship does not spring from any need of His eternal being. This would remain the same even if there were no such relationships. . . . He would be who he is even without this connection" (II/1 350 = 311-312).

What are we to say to this? Is Barth not contradicting all that he seemed to have clarified in the previous section? Is there, after all, a "humanlessness" of God? Is Barth not making a distinction here between a hidden God who has nothing to do with us and a revealed God who concerns us? Is God's revelation unreliable after all, because we have to deal with another God than the Emmanuel? Notwithstanding all the reassurances elsewhere, is not God now presented as an absolute and independent being, as the one "above where no human is present"? If we are to measure this by what Barth says in other places, is he not himself making God into the devil? Are not the critics correct who argue that Barth regards God as an autonomous God who in a battle against autonomous humanity puts an end to that autonomy?[1] Is not the further criticism justified that Barth presents

1. Trutz Rendtorff, ed., *Die Realisierung der Freiheit: Beiträge zur Kritik der Theologie Karl Barths* (Gütersloh, 1975), p. 170.

God as a monarchical and authoritarian God who will simply rule over us and can never set up any mutual relationship?[2]

An answer can be given to all these questions that will set aside these reservations just articulated, and it will be an answer that will offer greater precision to the insights already discussed. To achieve this answer we need to dig deeper and explore in particular Barth's understanding of the term "freedom." We need to note, in doing this, that the context within which his theology stands is marked not only by the controversy with the problem of modern atheism but also with the problem of the Enlightenment. Their decisive watchword according to both T. Rendtorff and Barth is that of autonomy, the human person's free self-determination. We should also note, however, that Barth is contending with the destructive threats to twentieth-century humanity that might easily give the impression that we are going "to the devil." He traced these threats back to a specifically modern understanding of human freedom. In his debate with it he does not denounce freedom as such but criticizes a perverted view of freedom, persuaded that its perversion can be corrected only through a properly understood concept of *freedom.* In his *Epistle to the Romans,* alleged by some to be responsible for the authoritarian thinking of German theology in the Weimar years,[3] he says that the kingdom of God is a "kingdom of the free and the freed" in which the human "has found himself with his free will."[4] Yet Barth is not agreeing in principle with that perverted view of freedom and just making one or two differentiations. There is a fundamental dispute here: What is freedom?

He defines the perverted human freedom that underlies modern thinking as the "freedom of choice" of Hercules at the crossroads (cf. IV/1 834, 499f. = 746, 449-450). In this view freedom is a purely formal possibility that is so indefinite and without content that it can "freely" choose the good as well as the bad. It is left to the human to will either the one thing or the other. In this freedom the human understands himself as an independent and isolated being, as an individual.

> "I am" — this is the forceful assertion which we are all engaged in making and of which we are convinced that none can surpass it in urgency and importance; the assertion of the self. . . . "I am" means that I stand

2. Jürgen Moltmann, "Schöpfung, Bund und Herrlichkeit," *Zeitschrift für dialektische Theologie* 3 (1987): 191-214.

3. Klaus Scholder, "Neuere deutsche Geschichte und protestantische Theologie: Aspekte und Fragen," *Evangelische Theologie* 23 (1963): 510-36.

4. Karl Barth, *Der Römerbrief,* 2nd ed. (Munich, 1922; 12th ed., 1978), pp. 156-57; ET: *The Epistle to the Romans* (Oxford, 1933), pp. 178-180.

under the irresistible urge to maintain myself, but also to make something of myself, to develop myself. . . . "I am" means further, however, that in every development and activity outwards I must and will at all costs maintain and assert myself. . . . 'I am' means that I may and must live out my life in the material and spiritual cosmos, enjoying, working, playing, fashioning, possessing, achieving and exercising power . . . within my limits — and who is to say where these are to be drawn? — have my share in the goods of the earth, in the fullness of human knowledge and capacity. . . . Originally and properly within I am still alone by myself: in my freedom in relation to the whole cosmos . . . with the question of my needs, . . . as my own doctor, as the sovereign architect, director, general, and dictator of the whole, of my own earth and heaven, my cosmos, God, and fellow-men . . . in first and final solitude. Within this total conception there is naturally an infinite range of colours and contours. . . . It is a unity only in general. (III/2 274-275 = 229-31)

This "I" stands as an ultimate reality over against the "things" over which it exercises the power of control. With this power it can treat them as "objects" over which it can freely dispose. Freedom means "that this man, the man who I feel myself to be, is given authority to be the secret judge, the secret authority over all things." This freedom, which is not capable of limiting itself, equips man with the possibility and the right of "making inward of what is external, objective to man, by which it is robbed of its objectivity." "One could conversely speak of externalization . . . man projecting what is within him externally in such a way . . . that he obtrudes himself upon the object." Either way it is appropriated and made a private possession.[5] Barth derives the word "private" from the Latin *privare* = "to rob" (cf. IV/2 498 = 442). To rob is to seize what is not at our disposal and by an individual freedom of choice to change it into something that is at our disposal, whether it be to appropriate it for myself or, after it is plundered or appears to be useless to me, to throw it away.

Barth finds this idea at work in the modern scientific and technological attempt to master the world, which proceeds without ever asking whether what *can* be done *should* be done, or — and "which is far worse" — assumes that what *can* be done apparently *should* be done (II/2 733 = 658). The way it works is first to regard the world as a great machine, in order

---

5. Karl Barth, *Die protestantische Theologie im 19. Jahrhundert: Ihre Vorgeschichte und ihre Geschichte* (Zurich, 1947), pp. 92-93; ET: *The Protestant Theology in the Nineteenth Century: Its Background and History* (Valley Forge, 1973), p. 113.

then to transform it "theoretically and practically" into a "machine world" (III/1 466 = 405).

In modern technology humanity beholds, as though it were a miracle,

> the human capacity and ability to harness and control the materials and forces of nature. . . . And like a storm there has come in a corresponding and comprehensive will for this power, followed by achievement in every sphere and the opening up of the most fantastic prospects of further achievement in the future. But one thing has failed to keep pace with this whole development, namely, the conscientious answering of the simple question whether all this capacity and will are vitally necessary. . . . The abundance of technical possibilities . . . has brought with it a corresponding abundance of requirements. . . . But how many of our modern requirements are really necessary, justified, sensible or even genuinely felt? (III/4 450 = 395).

How can we find a place for this question, however, when our primary concern is "becoming [our] own lord[s]" (III/4 314 = 314)!

For Barth this concept of freedom as a power of individual control is to be found at work everywhere in modern society. Freedom here means individual independence together with the desire to secure one's assets. By nature it is *competitive,* and its problem is how to limit the claims of the individual in relation to the claims of other participants in the general battle of competition, so that "a quite fortuitous contract or arrangement . . . [for] the solid organization of the struggle for existence . . . should proclaim itself to be the peace which all men yearn after and which all should respect."[6] Competition means, however, that "the one aims to be better off than the other simply for the sake of being better off than the other. By doing better he hopes to secure easier and ampler access to that for which the other also strives. He does it for his own advantage, and therefore inevitably to the disadvantage of the other and at the cost of the partial or even perhaps the total exclusion of the other from that which both desire. . . . There is no fun in this contest. . . . It is not merely a matter of competition but of serious conflict" (III/4 619 = 540).

Freedom understood as the striving for individual independence means that individuals will be in competitive battle with one another, but as long as the smooth organization of this battle is successful, the fact is concealed that this battle is a war, which then not accidentally can explode into

---

6. Karl Barth, *Der Römerbrief,* 2nd ed., p. 463; ET: *The Epistle to the Romans,* p. 479.

hot wars. The competitive struggle carries with it the potential that "the dreadful pagan saying [will become] true that war is the father of all things" (IV/1 501 = 451). Indeed, so necessarily will this freedom subject society to the domination of competition that it will necessarily spawn the forces that threaten *freedom*, the forces that make the individual "a marionette pulled by wires in a group of men who all share the same illusion of independence" (IV/1 517 = 465). In Barth's view, no "purely formal democracy" can offer real protection. He puts this question to democracy: "Where else but in your great banks are the wires being pulled to which you dance in your supposed freedom and upon which your employment, your unemployment, and your very livelihood depend?"[7]

Some critics ascribe to Barth a view of the human as one who, in supposed freedom, is in fact a "puppet" in the hands of a ventriloquist,[8] or a replaceable "pawn in God's chess game."[9] But Barth regarded this view of the human as the great danger. How could he have sanctioned such views, since he carried out his own critical analysis of the modern concept of freedom based upon another approach, his theological understanding of the character of freedom?

For Barth, it is important to see precisely that freedom as the individual power to control does not become distorted accidentally and subsequently, at that point when it obviously chooses the wrong thing. In that case one could conceivably rely upon the competitive battlefield to produce those cleansing powers that could restrict such wrong choices. This might succeed in part and for a time, but it essentially cannot rule out the destructive potential latent in the conflict. We have to see that this kind of freedom as such is corrupt, evil, tyrannical, destructive. The very fact that I, in the sense of this controlling freedom, think that I can choose for myself what appears to be good and right for me, the very fact that in such freedom I am the authority to decide about good and evil, right and wrong, means that "I am already choosing wrong," and objective evil results — even as I contend that I meant it only for good. In doing so, "I divide myself and I break the fellowship between myself and others." "When our eyes are opened to the possibility of

7. Karl Barth, *Die Kirche zwischen Ost und West* (Zollikon-Zurich, 1949), pp. 13-14.

8. Wilfried Härle, *Sein und Gnade: Die Ontologie in Karl Barths Kirchlicher Dogmatik* (Berlin and New York, 1975), p. 121.

9. Dorothee Sölle, *Stellvertretung* (Stuttgart and Berlin, 1965), p. 116; ET: *Christ the Representative* (Philadelphia, 1967), p. 90; but cf. Wolf Krötke, "Gott und Mensch als 'Partner': Zur Bedeutung einer zentralen Kategorie in Karl Barths Kirchlicher Dogmatik," in *Theologie als Christologie: Zum Werk und Leben Karl Barths,* ed. H. Köckert and W. Krötke (Berlin, 1988), pp. 106-30.

our own exaltation in judgment, we become truly blind to what is right and wrong.... And there begins ... the whole misery of the moral battle of everyone against everyone else," in which we are "sowing and reaping discord as the children of discord" (IV/1 500f. = 451). "Is there a worse threat to freedom itself than the establishment of man as his own lord and lawgiver? Who can exercise a worse tyranny over us than the god in our own breast? And what further tyrannies does not this first and decisive one drag in its train?" (I/2 749 = 668).

Nevertheless, the real point for Barth is that Christian theology opposes this questionable concept of freedom by *emphatically* asserting freedom, but a freedom correctly understood. Barth's question was not that of restricting freedom but that of finding a right basis for it. He was serious when, in 1935, he announced that "we should learn to be *more* liberal than the liberals!"[10] He did not join the anti-liberal front of theologians like Friedrich Gogarten and Emanuel Hirsch who argued that it was providential that the thrust toward individual independence should have been checked by the authoritarianism of the Hitler regime. Barth's view was that "the Church in its behaviour and discourse before the world must interest itself in that idea of freedom which is now opposed and persecuted in the worldly sphere ... nor does it neglect to become the asylum of the truth which today is on the losing side — and that is the truth of the idea of freedom. The power and authenticity of its struggle against a philosophy of pseudo-freedom depend wholly upon its refusal to take part in the secular attack on secular liberalism, upon its not being affected by the relatively justifiable criticisms with which liberalism opposes authoritarianism" (I/2 745 = 665).

Conflict could not be avoided. Barth could not see in Nazi authoritarianism, however, a means to restrict an individual's arbitrary freedom because he judged that system to be itself the fruit of a "false concept of freedom." In 1937 he had pointed out that where freedom means living "in free competition of persons, systems, and ideas, under the motto, 'Make way for the competent,'" there the secret or open "battle of all against everyone, ... which will never be without harshness and suffering," is in full sway. They have already started down "the slippery slope ... at the end of which is authoritarianism."[11] Later Barth merged this criticism with his criticism of Communism. He wrote that "the individualism of the West obviously cannot evade responsibility for the formulation of this concept" — of the *Führer*

---

10. Karl Barth, *Das Bekenntnis der Reformation und unser Bekennen* (*Theologische Existenz heute!* 29) (Munich, 1935), p. 67.

11. Karl Barth, *Der deutsche Kirchenkampf* (Basel, 1937), pp. 7-8.

or of any collective domination. "All the brutality, all the murderous insolence of the usurper have been involved in it from the very outset" (II/2 342 = 311). The "usurper" is the one who preempts for himself alone all the conditions of arbitrary freedom and thus robs all others of their freedom with the result that they become a mass society or a *"Volk."* In such situations, the individuals go under and become the willing helpers of the usurper as he seeks to fulfill his desires, willing because they recognize in the figure of the usurper what they all secretly want.

God's Self-Determination for Coexistence

Barth takes issue with this perverted concept of freedom, and he does so on *theological* grounds. Theology cannot evade doing so because it bears responsibility for the formation of this concept of freedom. If the thesis advanced from various sides is correct,[12] one can understand the formation of this concept of human freedom as described above as a reaction to the concept of God in late medieval Nominalism. There, God was understood as the essence of absolute freedom as *"potentia absoluta"* [= absolute power], i.e., the almighty divine arbitrariness and independence, bound to no law. God was seen here as the perfect stronghold of what Barth called freedom of choice. According to Barth's thesis, Enlightenment thinkers revolted against such a God and freed themselves from him, but they did so in such a way that, using the idea of the human's divine likeness, they ascribed to themselves what had previously been ascribed to God. The freedom and autonomy that the human person now claimed were thereby deeply permeated with the hallmarks of a *potentia absoluta*. If this view is correct, then Barth's interpretation of the modern concept of freedom is in agreement with it.

In point of fact, he thought that as long as theology carries in its legacy a concept of God as *potentia absoluta*, it cannot countervene modern humanity as it equips itself with the corresponding power to control. Barth's first step was to submit this understanding of God defined in terms of absolute powerfulness to criticism, thinking that he would thereby tackle the wrong theological root of the wrong concept, and thus lay the foundation for a new definition of what human freedom really is.

His criticism was directed against the Reformers, especially Calvin, for he believed that "notwithstanding all the theoretical protestation against

12. Cf. Günter Howe, "Gott und die Technik," in *Die Verantwortung der Christenheit für die wissenschaftlich-technische Welt,* ed. H. Timm (Hamburg and Zurich, 1971).

potentia absoluta," they had brought this legacy into Protestant theology (II/2 52 = 49). What he was criticizing was a view of God that equipped him with this kind of absolute power, a God who was thought of as "an unconditioned God, a God who is free *in abstracto,"* whose being is an "*abstract* absoluteness or *naked* sovereignty" (II/2 52 = 49) — "in the sense that His caprice as such constitutes His divine being and therefore the principle of His world-government!" It is a fundamental mistake "that to conceive of God Himself we need only conceive of a being which rules absolutely" (II/2 52-53 = 49-50). The statement, There is no humanlessness of God, corresponds precisely with the statement, There is no divine *decretum absolutum* [= absolute decree] (II/2 172 = 158), no sheer wielding of power on the part of God. These statements come from Barth's doctrine of election in which he subjects the ideas of a freedom of divine preference and of an omnipotent control to searching criticism.

Nevertheless, he carefully frames his criticism of *potentia absoluta,* be it applied to God or conceived as the grounds of human freedom, as part of the process of his development of a positive theological thesis. He does not proceed by first engaging in a pretheological analysis of modernity in order then to hunt around for theological concepts with which to meet the resultant problems. He would have been doing precisely the kind of theology that he believed it was his task to repudiate. He would have made theology's necessary discourse about God dependent upon the (contestable) correctness of a non-theological interpretation of the world. This would then expose Barth's positive theological thesis to the suspicion that he was countering the problems of the age with a mere postulate about how everything could or should be different. For Barth, theology could not hang its craft on a nail for a while, in order to pick it up again at an appropriate opportunity. Our discussion demonstrates that his theology is not located in a vacuum and that it enables a profound analytic look at the contemporary situation. It never engages, however, in supposedly neutral observations that can then be later related to theological themes. Conversely, in his view, theology must be done in such a way that it relates its knowledge to its context. Furthermore, his positive thesis is what first provided him the clarity with which he saw the fatal developments, and the clarity to discover how the switches were wrongly set at the beginning of an incorrect theological thought process. The power of his thesis was its capacity to see the fatal developments that contradicted how God reveals himself in Christ. Further, its power rested in the recognition that God's revelation corresponds to our life so that our life can be brought into correspondence with it. Barth's conviction was that a theology of this kind does its part in bringing about the necessary conversion in modern thinking.

Barth indeed believed strongly that the *free God* himself, not a new concept of freedom, even when projected upon God, would bring true deliverance and hope in the midst of the powers of destruction that afflict our modern world. This free God must not be thought of in terms of *potentia absoluta!* "If we inquire how, according to His revelation in Jesus Christ, God's lordship differs in its divinity from other types of rule, then we must answer that it is lordship in freedom. . . . There *are* other sovereignties, but freedom is the prerogative of *divine* sovereignty" (II/1 339 = 301). The freedom of God does not simply mean that he is subjected to nothing else, to no pressures or necessity. For Barth the freedom of God means that he is no prisoner of himself or of his own freedom. He is "free also *with regard to* His freedom" (II/1 341 = 303). Hence he is not defined by his freedom, rather he defines his freedom. "God is not *free; God* is free"; "the accent does not fall on 'free' but on 'God'" (II/1 360 = 320). His freedom is simply demonstrated by the binding use he makes of it, and on this basis it may be known to be binding on us. This freedom functions as God is "free not to surrender Himself to it," "yes, in that He confirms it," "but to *use* it to give Himself to this communion (with the partner who is different from Him) and to practise this *faithfulness* in it, in this way being really free, free in Himself. . . . In the absoluteness in which He sets up this fellowship, He can and will also be conditioned. . . . This ability, proved . . . in His action, constitutes *His* freedom" (II/1 341 = 303).

What use does God make of his freedom? Barth's basic thesis is that he reveals himself to us in Israel and in Christ in such a way that he makes a definite *choice,* not an accidental one that he might later disavow, but a binding one, so that we can say that God has made this choice from the very beginning of all his ways, a choice that is God's intention for the reality that is different from himself. God did not originally exist in a state of (indecisive) rest, in order then to make this choice later! God's being is in this act, and in this act God "is" (II/1 291 = 260). The choice that he makes precedes and anticipates everything else. We must never think God except in the revelation in which he chooses, or in this choice in which he reveals himself. To choose, or as the classic term for *praedestinare* renders it, "to elect," is for Barth synonymous with such modern terms as freedom, self-determination, and autonomy. To choose is the primal act of freedom or self-determination. Whoever does not choose is controlled from outside oneself and is not free. The one who is free chooses. But how and what does God choose? Barth's answer is that the choice of God is the *election* of grace. It consists of the fact that "God has elected fellowship with man for Himself" and simultaneously "fellowship with Himself for man" (II/2 177 = 162). This is in brief Barth's basic thesis about the freedom of God, or how we are to think of God as free.

According to the first part of the formula, God defines in his election, in the act of his freedom, "primarily about himself" — "Primarily God elected or predestinated Himself" (II/2 176 = 162). What is meant is that God's freedom is not in this first moment a willfulness in which he disposes over others as he wishes, not at the outside a determination about others which would unavoidably treat these others as objects of his arbitrariness. God's freedom is, to begin with, his exclusion of all arbitrariness from his freedom (cf. II/1 358 = 318). In his freedom God makes a self-determination, but he determines himself for *something specific.* It is not as though his choice of something specific contradicted his freedom! His practice of his freedom consists of his determining himself for something specific, and that he obligates himself to it. Barth goes so far as to say that "God decides for Himself . . . His determinedness" (II/2 108 = 101 rev.). God's freedom is thus God's repudiation of a *potentia absoluta,* yet this repudiation does not mean that God would then not be free. He is truly free by excluding a *potentia absoluta,* an unlimited power of control. His freedom is self-determination but not of a random kind. It is essentially self-determination for *fellowship.* Freedom is thus something radically different from independence that permits interaction with others only in terms of competition. It is not a power of control that treats others as objects of its control. It is not a capricious freedom of choice that as an intrinsically neutral act comprises an openness both for good and for evil.

As freedom for fellowship, God's freedom is essentially *communicative,* committed to solidarity, social freedom, freedom not in competition but rather in coexistence, freedom not at the cost of others but for their benefit, for them and with them, not autonomous self-assertion seeking to have its away versus others. When one considers that God wants to coexist with sinners, then his freedom includes his willingness "for the sake of man" to "hazard Himself wholly and utterly" (II/2 179 = 164). This was by no means a masochistic or altruistic self-offering. God's *freedom,* his self-determination is actualized here as his self-determination for *love.* God, for Barth, is the one who has his being as "the one who loves in freedom" (II/1 288 = 257). To say it another way, Barth's concern is to explain the action of God in his revelation. If revelation means that God defines himself in it, then we are to expect no other freedom of God than the one in which he is free for coexistence.

But coexistence, or existence in love, does not replace or abrogate freedom. Nor is it the case that God is free until he makes his choice, and thereafter he is bound. God is free not only *for* coexistence but also *in* coexistence. The issue is not, in the latter instance, a freedom in which what he has chosen, the fellowship, could constantly be challenged again. This is a freedom in which God is always free as he defines himself, free to say who he is, who he is for his partner, and what form the fellowship with this partner will take.

> God is free to be provoked and to be merciful, to bless and to punish, to kill and to make alive, to exalt us to heaven and to cast us down into hell. God is free to be wholly inward to the creature and at the same time as Himself wholly outward . . . and both . . . as forms . . . of the *relationship* and *communion* chosen, willed and created by Himself between Himself and His creation. . . . His revelation in Jesus Christ embraces *all* these apparently so diverse and contradictory possibilities. They are all *His* possibilities. If we deny Him any one of them, we are denying Jesus Christ and God Himself. Instead of recognizing and adoring God, we are setting up an idol. For we are imposing upon Him — in defiance of the freedom which He has actually proved to us — a bondage which can be only that of our own self-will that would like to deny God and put itself in the place of God. (II/1 354 = 315)

The Destining of the Human for Freedom

According to Barth this divine "freedom for and in fellowship" is not to be understood as an ideal that humanity should take as a goal worth striving for, in order to get a grip on the problems of modernity. This "concept" of freedom is a divinely created *reality*. If it were just an ideal then the human person would encounter it with that freedom of choice with which she could opt to appropriate it or not. If it is a reality, then for Barth that means that as a unique and distinctive moment it contains a destining of the human person, whether she knows or wants to perceive it or not — on the human side, this is still for Barth an open question. Before the human can choose, God has made a choice for humanity as well as for himself. In electing himself for fellowship with man, "God has elected fellowship with Himself for man" (II/2 177 = 162).

Yet is not this a Christologically based authoritarian form of control over humanity? According to Barth (cf. IV/3 98ff. = 88ff.) only when considered totally from the outside, which means concretely, as though located in that area of the freedom of choice and disregarding its content. The content might be summed up as follows, "God's Choice: Our Freedom."[13] This

---

13. Cf. Peter Eicher, "Gottes Wahl: Unsere Freiheit: Karl Barths Beitrag zur Theologie der Befreiung," in *Aufbrechen-Umkehren-Bekennen*, ed. Evangelische Akademie (Baden and Karlsruhe, 1986), p. 31.

means, of course, that we owe "our freedom" to God and his choice, not to a choice of our own. That means that true freedom is not that which humans claim to have innately, or that one must simply take in order to have it. Genuine freedom is the freedom that is granted to us, that is a *gift* to us.[14] "If the Son makes you free, you will be free indeed" (John 8:36; cf. IV/1 832 = 744-745). For if freedom is that which God exercises, and exercises in relation to us (his freedom for and in coexistence), then we do not have this freedom on our own. It will be given to us in such a way that he is free to initiate and cultivate a relationship of fellowship with us. There is freedom for us only on the basis of *liberation*. And there is liberation for us on the basis of the fact that God maintains fellowship with us. Indeed, for Barth a detached and "absolute" and capricious type of freedom makes us into "slaves" (IV/1 483, 499f. = 436, 450). That applies not only to those who are controlled under such freedom, but also to those who think that they are able to maintain that control themselves. This freedom of choice is the *servum arbitrium* [= captive will]. The human person, the I-centered person who is effectively isolated and alone in this freedom, is like a captive in a cavern, "imprisoned in his own arbitrariness" (IV/1 108 = 100), out of which he cannot find his way "alone." We can only get out in that God brings us out, which means that he enacts his freedom for co-existence upon us.

What God rescues us *for* is no less freedom than that which we had in the situation *out of which* he brought us. In contrast to that freedom of choice, it is now truly and authentically *freedom*. If God's freedom is freedom for coexistence with others, then he himself *wills* and *causes* these others to be capable of coexistence, and therefore free and independent. The determining of the human which emerges from God's self-determining for fellowship with man is thus no abstract act of control over the human but rather the determining of the human for freedom: "freedom of thought and will and movement and action" (IV/3 1080 = 940). "The electing God creates for Himself as such man over against Himself. And this means that for his part man can . . . elect God. . . . There is, then, a . . . comprehensive autonomy of the creature which is constituted originally by the act of eternal divine election and which has in this act its ultimate reality," certainly on the basis of the divine initiative, but in such a way that "the motive for this establishment of the kingdom is not in any sense an autocratic self-seeking, but a love which directs itself outwards, a self-giving to the creature. . . . But He wills (and) fulfills . . . Himself . . . in willing and recognizing the distinct reality of

14. Karl Barth, *Das Geschenk der Freiheit* (*Theologische Studien* 39) (Zollikon-Zurich, 1953).

the creature, granting and conceding to it an individual and autonomous place side by side with Himself. Naturally the individuality and autonomy are only of such a kind as His own goodness can concede and grant. . . . An independent individuality or autonomy could be only devilish in character." But that does not contradict the fact that God did give to the creature, with which he wills to coexist, its own autonomy, "not that these gifts should be possessed outside Him, let alone against Him, but for Him and within His kingdom, not in rivalry with His sovereignty but for its confirming and glorifying." What is to be glorified is "His love, which did not will to exercise mechanical force" or "rule over puppets or slaves," but wills to triumph, "not in their overthrow, but . . . in their own free decision for Him" (II/2 194f. = 177-78). Thus, "God is not exalted in the suppression of the creature" (III/3 147 = 130). "The concern of God active and visible in the encounter with Jesus Christ is His concern for the man who is himself to be freed, not for a puppet or a chessman" (IV/3 551 = 477).

Freedom of this type is a divine gift, and thus God does give it. There is need, then, to rethink the concept of divine grace. Barth accepts the Reformation teaching on grace — we cannot cooperate with the gifts of God — but then he adds the further thought: not that God gives and the human is the passive recipient of his grace, but that God speaks and gives and the human responds and receives. For Barth, God's fellowship with the human person grounded, to be sure, solely on God's grace would not be true fellowship as long as the human part in it were as a passive object and not as an accountable subject. At baptism we "are not engulfed and covered as by a divine landslide or swept away as by a divine flood," not "even partially . . . left out" as "if their free decision is crowded out, replaced, or made irrelevant by the overpowering word and work of God." The grace of God treats us as "active subjects" (IV/4 179 = 163). The revelation of God involves "true *intercourse* between God and man. If it undoubtedly has its origin in God's initiative, no less indisputably man is . . . taken seriously as an independent creature of God" and liberated (IV/4 25 = 22). The fact that prayer is permitted is a proof for Barth that we may and should take seriously that the essential characteristic of God does not consist of his "being the only one at work." We are not "marionettes who move only at his will," but in his love, God is ready to "let his action be codetermined by his children" (CL 167f., 170 = 102, 104).

The *essence* of this freedom — not its limit for it would be misunderstood as freedom from the very outset if its essence were understood as its limit and external control — is that, in correspondence to the freedom of God, it is itself freedom toward and in fellowship with God. It is freedom only when it *corresponds* to God's freedom, or, as Barth says with the biblical term, it "obeys." True human freedom is obedience, not obedience to some kind of government but obedience to the God who determines himself for coexistence with us. Therefore, this obedience toward God is also freedom (IV/1 257). "He is a free man — free in his thinking and deciding and acting — when he regards that which God has chosen for him as self-evident and indeed the only thing which is possible, when he accepts and is perfectly satisfied with this divine choice without . . . (having) to ratify it by his own choice. He is a free man when . . . his decision is simply and exclusively a repetition of the divine decision" (IV/1 499 = 449). "Freedom means being in a spontaneous and therefore willing agreement with the sovereign freedom of God" (IV/1 108 = 101). "The human self is no cave dweller who might one day decide to leave his cave and go hunting and fishing. It is the self which is already summoned, which has already been called out of its cave and is thus active in responsibility toward God." The issue is his "freedom which is exercised in the fulfillment of responsibility before God. . . . It is certainly freedom of choice. But as freedom given by God, as freedom in action, it is the freedom of a *right* choice. The choice is right when it corresponds to the free choice of God." It is choice "not between two possibilities, but between his one and only possibility and his own impossibility, and thus between his being and his nonbeing, between the reality and the unreality of his freedom" (III/2 233-235 = 196-97). This does not mean any diminution of human freedom; it rules out a pseudo-freedom that from the very first is in truth nonfreedom. That capricious freedom of choice is excluded as an empty capability of choosing good or evil. Freedom is certainly a choice for Barth, but only in the sense that I can choose only what God has already chosen. Everything else that I might choose is already unfree. "Every one who commits sin (is not using his freedom but) is a slave to sin" (John 8:34).

This helps us to understand why Barth is so critical of a concept of individual freedom that is emancipated from one's commitment to God. With such a freedom, the human person must necessarily become an isolated, lonely individual. That loneliness is most ambivalent. "Even in society with others he secretly cherishes his own fears and desires." Since "it is just the same with them too," distrust and disillusionment disturb and destroy our mutual coordination. "Behind disappointment and distrust there lurks, ready to spring, hostility" (IV/2 539 = 477). "The solitary man is the potential, and in a more refined or blatant form the actual, enemy of all others" (IV/2 474 = 421). He can be the aggressor but also the victim of others, and all this will be the very opposite of what he was seeking. In his individual freedom "he is simply a chessman," "not a living man, but one whose life is passing. The individual who wants to help himself forfeits his individuality" (IV/1 518 = 466).

As it corresponds to the divine freedom, our human freedom has two aspects. On the one side it is freedom *for* fellowship both with God and with our fellows. It is not independence, which at the individual level is an act that is intrinsically not humane and at the communal level reduces society to competition in which people work against each other, seek to outdo each other, live in anxiety and mistrust of one another. In the freedom that God has given we are brought out of that "cavern of . . . isolation," of a "nakedly private existence," into the "open country of fellowship" (IV/3 761 = 664 rev.). "It is as though a cave dweller were brought out into the open, blinking a little because the sun shines so brightly, and concerned a little because there is also wind and rain, but at any rate emerging." His life becomes "an 'eccentric' life, i.e., one which has its centre outside itself" (IV/2 893 = 787-788). Instead of attacking others we can *love* them, giving of ourselves, open to the needs of neighbors, not to use them for our advantage, and also without any fear that they might seek to take advantage of us, but always with *joy,* which is for Barth much more than bravery as opposed to fear. "The man who genuinely loves is also a cheerful man, and the genuinely cheerful man is also one who loves," and this is true of him "even when his love beats against a stone wall, receiving no answer, or only a more or less hostile answer. . . . He does not love him for the sake of his answer, but because he is made free to do so by God" (IV/2 895 = 788-789). "We cannot insist too sharply that we do not love for any external reason. . . . The one who loves does not want anything except to love . . . to give himself, to enter into relationship with the loved one. If he has any other plan or project — however noble — it means that his love is betrayed and ended" (IV/2 894 = 788). In such love "free people [are] . . . signs of hope, comfort and encouragement for many who are still unfree."[15] "What would be the good to the Christian of all his knowledge of forgiveness . . . if he lacked this element of humanity, and he were not present gladly and . . . concretely in the freedom of the one man for the other" (III/2 339f. = 282).

On the other side human freedom, like the divine, is a freedom *in* fellowship, so that the fellowship in which freedom perished would become a mass of people in which the individual person "as a free citizen" becomes a "driving wheel in a machine," so that "his will to live, his conscience and understanding . . . and ultimately even his body, have all to die" (II/2 343 = 312). If Christians are to be free in society, they must be really *free.* "They have to go

---

15. Karl Barth, *Freiheit,* pp. 3-4.

their own way in great and little things alike, and therefore in their thought and speech and attitude they are always at bottom . . . aliens and strangers who will give plenty of cause for offence in different directions. To some they will appear to be far too ascetic. To others they will appear to affirm life far too unconcernedly. . . . On the one hand they will be accused as authoritarian, on the other as free-thinkers . . . on the one hand as bourgeois, on the other as anarchists. They will seldom find themselves in a majority. . . . Things generally accepted as self-evident will never claim their absolute allegiance. . . . Nor will they command their complete negation, so they can hardly count on the applause of the revolutionaries of their day. Nor will their freedom . . . be exercised by them in secret, but revealed openly in free acts and attitudes which will never be right in the world" (IV/2 690 = 610). Since they will never be excessively rigid and unbending, they can also be free in relation to themselves and therefore "laugh at themselves from time to time."[16] Therefore they "cannot proceed by building with complete confidence on the foundation of questions that are already settled, results that are already achieved, or conclusions that are already arrived at," but they must be prepared "every hour . . . to begin anew at the beginning."[17]

God's Unique Freedom

If God's freedom is then his freedom toward and in coexistence with humans, then the question is certainly germane as to what the meaning of Barth's statements is in which he says that God would be "the same" even without his "relation and connection" with us, yes, even if there were no creatures at all. Barth is not contradicting what we have just presented, but he is making a necessary elucidation without which it would all ultimately become erroneous. We must pay attention here, for it is basically at this point that the accusation of authoritarianism in his theology is brought against Barth. It can certainly be said that if Barth's thesis appears to stand near to more recent anti-authoritarian concepts, then he is raising a critical objection to them.

Barth also thinks it worth discussing whether concepts like free coexistence describe conceptual *principles* that the partners in question would have

---

16. Karl Barth, *"Der Götze wackelt": Zeitkritische Aufsätze, Reden und Briefe von 1930 bis 1960,* ed. K. Kupisch (Berlin, 1961), pp. 160-61.

17. Karl Barth, *Einführung in die evangelische Theologie* (Zurich, 1962), p. 182; ET: *Evangelical Theology: An Introduction* (Grand Rapids, 1963), p. 165.

to accept, or the *act* in which God alone and of himself forms with humanity a fellowship of the free. In other words, may the concept of free coexistence be a "higher comprehensive term" (II/1 349 = 310) under which we subordinate both God and humanity, or must it be rather, as Barth thinks, formed by the reality of God's turning to humanity, as he has described it? If "free coexistence" derives from a preexisting concept, then God would be only one possible address among many for such human coexistence. Coexistence would thus be conceivable and practicable even without God. Yet if its meaning is shaped by the event of the divine turning to us, then over all that we have said there reigns the principle: "The eternal correlation between God and us, as shown in God's revelation, is grounded in God alone, and not partly in God and partly in us" (II/1 315 = 281).

This principle implies that we have to speak of a unique freedom in God that is proper to him alone. This freedom Barth equates with the biblical designation of God as the "Lord" (II/1 338f. = 301). We must count on this particular freedom of God because in the correlation between God and the human as free partners, "as it is visible in God's revelation," there is a fundamental and irremovable distinction. God is the Creator and not a creation made by humans, and the human person is God's creation and not a creator. As Barth puts it, God is "grounded in one's own being, to be determined and moved by oneself" (II/1 339 = 301) and not by an other external to him. If an other external to him does also exist, then only because this other is grounded by God and not in and of itself. This distinction between God and humanity does not have the fact of human sin as its cause, so that it would become moot if sin were removed. The fact of human sin does give emphatic emphasis to that distinction, for as a result the partners in this correlation are the human who has fallen into sin and is held captive by it, and the God who alone can free him and in mercy does free him. A further accentuation of the distinction is that God does not abandon the creature founded by him and the sinner liberated by him but claims that creature for his good purposes for him, so that the partners in this correlation are to be seen as the God who graciously commands and his children who are called to responsibility by him. We must speak of these ineffaceable distinctions when we talk of God's unique freedom. The fact that such a correlation arises in and in spite of these differences is based on this special freedom of God and its initiatory ability.

If in speaking of that correlation we ignore the distinctions, then in Barth's view we fail to see the biblically attested events through which the distinctions are introduced and sustained. Then the meaning of correlation will necessarily be something very different from the testimony to it recorded there. Then the human does not need God's special turning to her, nor his grace, in order to *become* his free partner. Then she already *is* his partner and is located on the same footing as he is. The distinctions between God and creature, Reconciler and sinner, the one who commands and his children, become blurred. For Barth this is basically the approach of panentheism, which originated in the Ionic beginnings of Greek philosophy and which tells us that everything is permeated in God or by God as an all-pervasive world soul. Barth points to the true problem of this position when he states: "God does not form a whole with any other being" (II/1 351f. = 312). Barth does not contest that God is together with an other. What he contests is the interpretation that claims that God only *becomes* God when he is together with a created other. He contests that God needs the human person in order to be *God*. In such a case he would be bound to humanity, not because he willingly loves us but because he has to actualize himself, because he has to submit to a higher constraint, namely, the supreme law of "totality." That would mean not just that we are dependent upon God and his grace but that God would also be dependent upon us and our grace with him. With that, the human deifies himself. This was what the mysticism of Angelus Silesius maintained: "I know that without me God cannot an instant be. He needs must perish at once were death to come to me" (II/1 316 = 281). But to the extent that the human deifies herself, she "robs God of His deity" (II/1 316 = 281).

That debatable statement that God would remain the same even if we never existed should now be understandable. Naturally what is at issue is not a reasserted abstract independence of God or a rejection of his self-determination for fellowship with us. The principle is stated in the context of the assertion, the lack of which would result in one's being drawn into the wake of panentheism and mysticism, namely, that "the correlation between God and us" is constantly and not merely initially "grounded in God *alone*." In God alone! God does not *need* the human for this. That is not to say that he does not want that human: he wants him, he wants him as his partner and wants to be his dependable partner. Yet all this can take place only because God wills it, and not under the dictate of a higher necessity. For this reason God neither needs us nor needs to negate us in order to be God. He does not need to create us, nor does he need us in order to relate himself to us nor to be gracious to us. To contest this statement would be to contest God's *deity* itself by conceiving of it as constituted by the human's good conduct. The grace of God would also be contested, as well as its power to deal with our captivity to sin and to give us a new freedom. Instead of beginning with ourselves, we can only begin at the beginning that God is making and has made with us. Yet in all that God is and does, God does not presuppose anything outside himself, whether it be a question of his existence, or his creating a reality outside himself, or his setting himself in relation to it, or his contesting sin and commanding humans. God can only and always "begin with Himself" (II/1 342 = 304). *That* is the unique freedom of God, and that is the point of the principle that God would remain the same even if he did not enter into fellowship with us and even if we had never existed at all.

But who would God then be? "The very same One"! — This is Barth's decisive answer. Even then, God would not be a being living for itself alone, not the mirror of the lonely and isolated "I am" that is for Barth the root of the perverted modern idea of a capricious freedom. Even then he would not be a despairing or defiant self-sufficient God, an arbitrary God who stands in no relation to anyone. He would still be "the *loving* God." God does not need the human in order to be *God* as we need him in order to be human. For God is God by himself alone. That being said, God is not merely different from humanity — he *loves* the human person. Yet God does not need the human in order to be able to *love,* for the very reason that God is love in himself. That is why he can also love outwardly, loving us dependably in fellowship with us. God would be an essentially lonely and isolated and loveless being if he needed us first in order to be a loving being capable of fellowship. "The god of all synergistic systems is always the absolute, the general, the digit 1, the concept" (III/3 157 = 139). *That* God cannot love unless we help him to do what he cannot do of himself. *That* God cannot truly have mercy on his creatures in the freedom of grace. *That* God cannot set up a free coexistence with what differs from himself. *That* God certainly cannot liberate isolated humanity from the "I am" of its perverted and capricious freedom. Yet if God *is* love in himself, he *can* do all these things. Then, in order to do them, he can "begin with himself." This "can" is for Barth the freedom of God (cf. I/1 337 = 319-320), which is not that neutral and arbitrary "can" that allows of other options. That God is free for coexistence with a reality created by him that is different from him, that he "can" love these creatures, means that God *must* do this of himself. Only by and through himself can he be moved to do these things. The recognition of the free grace of God must also have its impact upon our doctrine of God himself. If he had to do these things, he would no longer do them of himself, but in subjection to a law alien to him. Yet when he does them, then he does so as he *himself* and in free and overflowing grace. In doing what he does he does not follow an arbitrary caprice because as God he can only act in correspondence with his being, so that he practices that love outwardly which he is, in and of himself.

According to Barth, this is what the *doctrine of the Trinity* is all about. It says, in Barth's view, that God is so free that truly of himself in grace he becomes *our* God and thus, in spite of our sin, makes *us* his children. Whoever contests this is also contesting the doctrine. As Barth sees it, this doctrine is the legitimate interpretation by the church of the biblically attested revelation of God in Jesus Christ (I/1 325 = 308). "The doctrine of the Trinity states that our God, namely, He who makes Himself ours in His revelation, is really God" (I/1 401 = 380). Who is God, if he who is eternal and endures can take on temporal form, the form of one who was humiliated and gave himself up to death, and all this for our salvation? Obviously the one who "can become unlike himself" without ceasing to be God in that unlike form, is wholly God, God himself (I/1 337 = 319-320). The otherness of form as such clearly is not really alien to God; he does not have to suppress it or rid himself of it. God did not need a world in order to be other. Before the world was, he was eternally differentiated in himself (I/1 320). These statements, again, are not claiming an abstract independence for God nor maintaining his indifference to his creatures. They are upholding the ability of God to do what he does do for his creatures, in creating them, in entering into fellowship with them, and in revealing himself to them — God's "ability" in this twofold sense. It is first of all his freedom as his self-determination, solely in and through himself, in everything that he is and does, wills and does not will, says and does not say. Without diminishing any of that, we must emphasize that his self-determination includes all that he alone can accomplish and confirm and preserve; it includes the fact that through it all he is and remains God in all he does; upon the basis of it we are engaged even in his humiliated form unmistakably with the one God and with no other one than him, and by virtue of it we ourselves effectively engage him. Along these lines the doctrine of the Trinity tells us that "God reveals Himself as the Lord," as the one who is free (I/1 323 = 306).

The ability also consists of the fact that God, whose lordship must not be misunderstood as arbitrary rule, does what appropriately corresponds to that ability in relation to all that is outside himself, to that reality posited by himself and different from him; he does that which "repeats" his ability (III/2 261 = 218). He "can" posit an outside relationship, enter into this relationship, and love within it, for "antecedently in Himself" (I/1 404 = 384) he possesses that otherness, and because therefore relationship and love in such a relationship are most authentically he himself and not alien to him. According to Barth we must abandon any notion of God as the "Absolute," the Number One, the *Mon*arch. The doctrine of the Trinity tells us that "God already negates in Himself, from eternity, . . . all loneliness, self-containment, or self-isolation. Also and precisely in Himself, from eternity, in His absolute simplicity, God is orientated to the Other, does not will to be without the Other, will have Himself only as He has Himself with the Other and indeed in the

Other. He is the Father of the Son in such a way that with the Son He brings forth the Spirit, love, and is in Himself the Spirit, love. . . . The love which meets us in reconciliation, and then retrospectively in creation, is real love, supreme law and ultimate reality, because God is antecedently love in Himself" (I/1 507 = 483-84).

Abandoning the idea that God is the Absolute means that there is a need more precisely to define "monotheism." That "God is one" is certainly true in the battle against all human deifications. "It was on the truth of the sentence that God is One that the 'Third Reich' of Adolf Hitler made shipwreck" (II/1 500 = 444), wrote Barth in 1940 when Hitler was at the height of his power. Yet this truth does not imply an "absolutizing of uniqueness," which necessarily provokes a Prometheus-like rebellion against it. "Necessarily" because "it is the reflection of . . . the claim to mastery on the part of the human individual" or "the various cosmic forces" (II/1 504 = 448). God is one, however, as the living God in the history of his address to the fallen creature and in the exalting of this creature to himself. He is the one God in that he as the Triune has the freedom in himself to do that. "God is *God*" in the interrelations and actions of his three "modes of being" and not in a "neutral godhead" that bypasses them. This pure and empty neutral godhead, with its claim to be truly divine, is the well-known delusion of an abstract "monotheism" that most effectively dupes people when pagan religions, mythologies, and philosophies are at the peak of their development. The true and living God is he whose Godhead consists of this *history*, who is in it "the One God, the Eternal, the Almighty, the Holy, the Merciful, the One who loves in His freedom and is free in His love" (IV/1 222 = 203).

Barth closely links the doctrine of *predestination* to the doctrine of the Trinity. In his view, that doctrine says that what God *does* in his turning to us is based upon what God *wills* from the very beginning, what he eternally can do. What is at stake in what God wills is his relation to the temporal creaturely reality that is different from himself. He who is eternally loving and not alone "wills" to disclose himself outwardly and for this purpose he posits this other reality which is based upon the decision of his will, upon God's election. Apart from that election we might conceive of this other reality either as eternal and divine or as fundamentally detached from God. We know what God wills and can do solely from the event in which God both *shows* what he can do and *accomplishes* what he wills to do, namely, from his approach to us, and our approach to him, to which the Bible bears witness (II/2 154ff. = 145ff.). Yet because it is *God* who does this, room must be left for the conclusion that what is done is no accident. It was planned and chosen from the very first, before he carried it out within time, even before the earthly counterpart was there on whose behalf it was done. "There is no 'outward' except that which is willed and posited by God in the presupposing of all his ways and works. There is no 'outward' except that which has its basis and meaning as such in the divine election of grace." (II/2 102 = 95 rev.). Preceding and anticipating everything that exists on earth and in time, all human self-determination, "at the beginning of God's dealings with the reality which is distinct from himself," God, "in an act of free unconditional self-determination," decided and willingly purposed to coexist with this reality, to love it, and therefore to will its existence, to create it, to affirm his own 'determinedness' through this good will, and hence to oppose and reject anything that contradicted his will" (II/2 108f. = 100-102 rev.).

Barth uses the term *"election of grace"* for this decision, for "predestination." Two elements are to be noted. First, it is a real *choice,* "his free decision." "God would not be God, He would not be free, if this had to be so" (II/2 108 = 101), if he were under a compulsion imposed upon him and made his decision on the basis of a human claim. The distinctiveness of the freedom of his choice may be seen in the fact that God first made a determination about himself and only then allowed the partner in this choice to make a corresponding self-determination. "In a free act of determination God has ordained concerning Himself; He determined Himself; without any obligation, God has put Himself under an obligation to man" (II/2 108 = 101). In precisely this way, his grace in no way contradicts his free choice. For he makes his election under no compulsion nor does he exercise the "the caprice of a tyrant." ". . . In the mystery of His freedom God always does that which is worthy of Himself" (II/2 22 = 22), that which is in keeping with his own Trinitarian love, that which in his temporal revelation he faithfully executes toward the partner in his work. His free election, unlike our "supreme form of electing posited as absolute," is "the active demonstration of his love. . . . As electing love it can never be hatred or indifference, but always love: 'God so loved the world that he gave his only begotten Son, that whosoever believeth in him should not perish, but have everlasting life' (John 3:16)" (II/2 25f. = 25-26).

The doctrine of predestination, wrapped in much obscurity, likens God's electing decision to the arbitrary ruling of some blind fate. For Barth, however, the doctrine contains "good news." It is "the sum of the Gospel" (II/2 11, 13 = 10, 12). It speaks of this unique "freedom in which He is the One who eternally loves" (II/2 9 = 10), and of the power with which God, and God alone, can set and keep in motion the covenant between himself and the creation, between himself as the one who freely coexists and the creature as the one who is freed for coexistence.

The Disconcerting Truth —
The Problem of Religion

Difficulties with the Truth

Barth was stimulated to considerable reflection by the title picture of the book that C. Wolff wrote "for lovers of truth" in 1720, namely, *Rational Reflections on God, the World, and the Human Soul* [*Vernünfftige Gedancken von Gott, der Welt und der Seele des Menschen . . .*]. This picture portrays "a sun whose powerful rays pierce a mass of black clouds, and spread light upon mountains, forests, towns and villages. The aureole of this sun is obviously not considered to be insupportable to the human gaze, for it takes the form of an exceedingly friendly and pleasantly smiling human face, whose owner seems to be extremely pleased to see the clouds in the heavens and the shadows on the earth dissipate everywhere."[1] Barth found here a picture of the spirit of the *Enlightenment* in which that lover of truth set out to shed light on the darkness of prejudice, hypocrisy, superstition, fanaticism, and ignorance. Immanuel Kant defined "enlightenment" as "man's emergence from a self-inflicted state of minority."[2] Thus it put the issue of truth first on the agenda of modern thinking. It made the free research into truth the motto of science, but also, and not accidentally in Barth's view, it produced journalism, the age of the media (CL 388 = 227).

What should be the approach of theology to this? Barth makes the following point: "Ignorantly or stubbornly to ignore the anxieties and hopes of

1. Karl Barth, *Die protestantische Theologie im 19. Jahrhundert: Ihre Vorgeschichte und ihre Geschichte* (Zurich, 1947), p. 16; ET: *Protestant Theology in the Nineteenth Century: Its Background and History* (Valley Forge, 1973), p. 33.

2. Karl Barth, *Protestantische Theologie,* p. 238; ET: *Protestant Theology,* p. 268.

the immediate present is something which we do not expect of theology for the sake of the church. It is [one thing] openly to champion the predominant interest or even the demonism of an age, [and quite another] openly to identify oneself with that interest and to become the prisoner of that demonism. This is the very thing which theology must not do" (I/2 319 = 293 rev.). Discussing the way in which the modern age deals with the question of truth, Barth adopted a dialectical position.

The one side of his position was *positive!* This was not because historical forces might have made the question unavoidable — there were no such inevitabilities in Christian theology in Barth's eyes — but because the question, though never treated this way previously, was a justifiable one.[3] At the age of twenty-six Barth had stated that the church must be the place "where the truth is both spoken and heard, . . . the unadorned truth. One need not be afraid, one conceals nothing, glosses over nothing, misrepresents nothing. One does not generate clichés and offer unreasoned statements as one constantly must hear in life otherwise. One simply says it as it is." For, "humanity needs the truth more than its daily bread."[4]

Thus, Barth said later, the sermon has to answer the question, "Is it true?"[5] We must learn to see "man himself" as he really is and not in the "garbs or masks" in which she hides herself (CL 466f. = 269). "Against the basic proposition that truth must be freely investigated even in the field of theology, there is nothing to be said. . . . The man who rejects that proposition will inevitably and rightly cut a poor figure" (I/2 317 = 291). Referring in 1948 to Kant's definition, Barth expressed the hope that "after the first half of the twentieth century had brought us so much sinister madness, it would be good if the second half became a time of such 'enlightenment.'"[6] Already in 1941, speaking of a Swiss censorship whose peculiarity was that "it claimed not to be such," he said "that for the sake of the freedom of the press and the right of public speaking it would even be worth it to run the risk of war."[7] In brief, the church "at the risk of providing opportunities for empty, useless, and dangerous words, . . . will therefore do all it can to see that there is at any rate no lack of opportunity for the *right* word to be heard."[8]

3. CD IV/3 32ff. = 31ff.

4. Karl Barth, *Predigten 1913* (Zurich, 1976), pp. 594-95.

5. Karl Barth, *Das Wort Gottes und die Theologie* (Munich, 1929), p. 106; ET: *The Word of God and the Word of Man* (New York, 1957), p. 108.

6. Karl Barth, *Christliche Gemeinde im Wechsel der Staatsordnungen* (Zollikon-Zurich, 1948), pp. 12-13.

7. Karl Barth, *Eine Schweizer Stimme: 1938-1945* (Zollikon-Zurich, 1945), pp. 222-23.

8. Karl Barth, *Christengemeinde und Bürgergemeinde* (*Theologische Studien* 20) (Stutt-

On the other hand, however, where does such "sinister madness" come from, in spite of the Enlightenment? Why was the age of the Enlightenment also the age of absolutism?[9] "Is it not one of the remarkable characteristics . . . that the darkness . . . to which on the one hand it so eagerly opposed the light of reason . . . was something which on the other hand it . . . desired . . . ?"[10] Did not the issue of truth, which it had made into its watchword, experience more darkness than illumination? So much so that whoever refers to this state of affairs usually has to "swim against the current"![11] Is not this "man himself," in that the new sciences have illuminated him to his very marrow, not all the more totally concealed in all kinds of "garbs and masks"? And what did the free research into truth do for theology, in view of results that *certainly are not* "the results of free, theological inquiry into truth?!" (I/2 218 = 292). And what about the media and their freedom of speech? They "join in the sham and are often its front line"[12] with their "interpretations, insinuations, commendations and calumniations in the service of a one-sided interest, at once the slave and the master of public opinion," with a press which is "meant to be 'impressed' upon our minds and hearts and consciences" day in and day out (IV/3 521, 881f. = 452, 770-71). Thus Barth saw the distinctive insidiousness of the Third Reich in the "systematic lie with which its press poisoned German life as a whole."[13]

Yet this was only the symptom of a more far-reaching problem. What we need to understand is why the modern age, in its search for truth, has helped "propaganda" to blossom, "the particular art and masterwork of ideologies. What they have to push systematically is their own excellence and usefulness, and by way of background they must show how utterly valueless and harmful their rivals and opponents are" (CL 388 = 227). Truth was announced but lying triumphed, "all the wickedness and folly of man . . . and all the affliction which he brings upon himself" reaching here "their climax" (IV/3 500 = 434).

It was no accident, according to Barth, that the Enlightenment, in that it wanted to shed light on things — and made many good discoveries — nevertheless threatened to obscure the truth in new darkness. This was due to the manner in which it attempted to achieve its legitimate purpose. The hu-

---

gart, 1946), p. 39; ET: "The Christian Community and the Civil Community," in *Community, State, and Church: Three Essays* (Gloucester, Mass., 1968), p. 177.

9. Karl Barth, *Protestantische Theologie*, p. 19; ET: *Protestant Theology*, p. 36.

10. Karl Barth, *Protestantische Theologie*, p. 18; ET: *Protestant Theology*, p. 35.

11. Karl Barth, *Predigten 1913*, p. 595.

12. Karl Barth, *Predigten 1913*, p. 594.

13. Cf. Karl Barth, *Der deutsche Kirchenkampf* (Basel, 1937), p. 64.

man sought to clarify what was to be regarded as true, and did so by removing it from God's hands into his own, so that in the process that truth was revealed to be something which the human can form in accordance with his views and intentions. The result was that the human was not certain, or only supposedly certain of that truth. Thus truth began to disintegrate into relativized conceptualizations or technically useful functionalisms. In Barth's view, it was only the attempt to make a virtue out of *this* necessity when, both outside and then inside theology, one established "the rather barren law of toleration, i.e., of refraining from all absolutizing, and therefore in fact of avoiding all positive statements concerning binding content and direction" (III/4 549 = 480; cf. IV/3 97ff. = 92ff.). This law evades the question of material truth and decrees of "all positive statements" that all of them, whatever they say, are relative truth, possible opinions, alongside which other opinions can just as well be asserted — for Barth this was "the worst kind of intolerance."[14] This law puts the immanent truthfulness of a human in place of the truth that claims us,[15] what a person *regards* as true at the cost of the question of what *is* true. So this law is only a symptom of the modern crisis with regard to the truth, but no help in it. With it, humanity settles down in the crisis without asking either about its causes or its solution.

Barth has only one question to raise here: How does one *distinguish* between truth and falsehood? For him, this is *the* fundamental problem which the modern thematic treatment of the question of truth surfaces. It has to do with the fact that for us there persists a fundamental inability to differentiate between the truth and the false truth that purports to be and is presented as "truth," which looks deceptively like truth, and may appear to be more attractive than truth. For Barth such sham truth is the most dangerous form of falsehood. The reduction from absolute to relative "claims to absoluteness" is of no help at all in dealing with that falsehood. By settling on the determination of what one genuinely regards to be true, at the cost of the question of what is true, one is at the mercy of that falsehood, with no defences.

How did this basic problem of the question of truth, this apparent indistinguishability of falsehood from truth, arise in the first place? It happens when we initially do not take seriously and then ignore the fundamental principle that enabled Barth at the very first to see the problem truly as a problem: "God is the truth. . . . *The* truth — not *a* truth" (II/1 73 = 68). As soon as God is viewed as "a truth," the disaster has happened. For then one

---

14. Karl Barth, *Der Römerbrief,* 1st ed. (Bern, 1919), pp. 546-47; cf. CD I/2 326 = 299.

15. Cf. Karl Barth, *Briefe, 1961-1968* (Zurich, 1975), pp. 508-9; ET: *Letters, 1961-1968* (Grand Rapids, 1981), pp. 317ff.

assumes a truth independent of God which, not only hypothetically but in principle, can be detached from God. In concordance with that principle, one can then understand the existence of God as a truth, perhaps even a supreme truth, but a truth that one has first arrived at in abstraction from God, whose validity and criteria are established first for us without reference to God. This is a truth that the human thinks she can find on her own, which she can grasp, lay hands on, so that it becomes a commodity that she can manage and manipulate, that is being manipulated already in the process. It need occasion no surprise, then, if it becomes a sham truth that is both deceived and deceiving, that it becomes falsehood, for in order to succeed it must deck itself out with the appearance of truth. Falsehood "doesn't differentiate itself." "In his prime the liar confesses the truth with the greatest emphasis and solemnity. . . . The only thing is that it has become untruth, . . . which is taken in hand and inspired and directed by him" (IV/3 505, 503 = 438, 437). When truth is taken into service by the liar in this way, when *he* makes it into *his* truth which suits him and which he makes suitable, then for Barth it has become *the* untruth. It is such a source of anxiety because it can have the appearance of "truth" and thus find acceptance by us. Does not this explain why the Enlightenment's search for truth has promoted "so much sinister nonsense" rather than preventing it? And why the resultant problem is obscured rather than solved by the reducing of truth to personal truth and by the distinction made between absolute and relative claims to truth? As though, in spite of the greatest effort at sincerity, we could not be deceived by sham truths! As though a "relativized claim to truth" were not always a humanly made claim that all the more radically deceives us because it obscures the fact that we are dealing here with a sham truth, the distorted result of our human attempt to grasp the truth!

What Is Truth?

Modernity's question of truth and our crisis in relation to it call for a deeper investigation, which must be a *theological* examination. What we need is "Enlightenment . . . by the light of the gospel."[16] If we accept the principle that "God is the truth," then it is *His* truth and not ours (II/1 233 = 208). We cannot take hold of truth any more than we can take hold of God — to think that we can is self-deception. Truth for its part seeks to take hold of us. "If a

---

16. Eberhard Jüngel, *Karl Barth zu Ehren* (*Theologische Studien* 100) (1969): 48; ET: Eberhard Jüngel, *Karl Barth: A Theological Legacy* (Philadelphia, 1986), p. 20.

man tries to grasp at truth of himself, he tries to grasp at it *a priori*" (I/2 330 = 302). Truth always lays claim to us, and we cannot make either an absolute or relative claim to it. Even a relative truth is "absolute" to the extent that it is divorced from the fact that God is the truth and that we cannot even take partial hold of it, but rather that it always "reaches" out for us.

Yet do we not have to "possess" the truth so that we can get rid of that indistinguishability between the truth and the lie, which is so important to the lie that it presents itself as a sham truth? Do not Christians "possess" the truth in such a way that they can oppose and unmask sham truth as a deception? Certainly only where the truth makes itself known can it be distinguished from sham truth, and can the latter be unmasked. It is only on this presupposition that we can truthfully say that "we are liars." Moreover, the announcement of the truth includes within itself the unmasking of the fact that as those who live in the lie we only apparently live in the truth, that we are in truth liars. When God "reveals" himself as the truth to us, when his revelation is "the truth of the truth" (II/1 73 = 68), then this truth documents itself by making clear that "God is true and all people are liars" (Rom. 3:4; cf. II/1 234 = 208).

For Barth this makes it impossible for Christians to encounter others as the possessors of the truth. The truth of the revelation that has happened to them makes itself known in the unmasking of *their* life as lived in sham truth. Indeed, says Barth, because in this revelation truth engages us, lying is "the specifically Christian form of sin" (IV/3 432 = 374), "much more evil and dangerous than lying in the moralistic sense" (IV/3 500 = 434). Compared to Christian falsehood, secular lying is no more than an "epiphenomenon," so that "Christianity has again good cause to beat its own breast before it can describe as falsehood the falsehood of the world, . . . and before it can make honest use of the truths of the world" (IV/3 522 = 452). Christians can be witnesses to the truth to others only if "they are perfectly clear and are prepared to confess that . . . in them as Christians the unbelief, superstition and error, and therefore the falsehood of man, have their true and original form." Hence "they will be kept from all pride, never throwing stones at others, but [they will be] with them and for them, and thus authorized to tell them the truth, looking to the justification and sanctification which they also need, which they need first, and which they can as little as others ascribe to themselves" (IV/3 520 = 451).

In reply to the question, What is truth?, Barth states that Christians, instead of describing either a relative or positive truth held in their hands or their own sincerity, must point out how the truth of God in revelation is in controversy with *Christian* "liars" concealed behind sham truths, and now unmasked. This controversy, he thinks, is of exemplary significance if we are to understand what is true and what is untrue in the world.

What is truth? If "God is truth," then the answer must be that we cannot know the truth in abstraction from God. Or rather, we can know it when God does not abstract himself from us and thus gives himself to be known by us. "Truth means unhiddenness" (II/1 73 = 68). That God, who is the truth, reveals himself to us, means that he makes himself unhidden to us, but does so indirectly because this challenges us in our desire to "have" the truth without God, abstracted from him, and thus not living in the truth. What is truth? Truth is that in which God discloses himself as the truth contesting the "counter-revelation" (IV/3 432 = 374) of liars who conceal themselves in sham truth. It continues to be the case that we "cannot in [ourselves] express His truth" (II/1 219 = 195). "The accomplished work of truth will always be God's own work and not ours" (II/1 234 = 208 rev.). Only by God's self-disclosure and his imparting of truth to our own knowledge can we recognize the truth in its conflict with our falsehood and in spite of it. What unmasks our falsehood and contests it, differentiates itself from it, is the truth. Barth offers a more precise exposition from three angles.

1. The truth encounters us in its identity with a specific *person* who is its witness (IV/3 507 = 440). "It is certainly not an idea, principle or system (whether constructed by the integration of views and outlooks or the combination of concepts . . .). Nor is it a structure of correct insights, nor a doctrine . . ." (IV/3 434 = 375). If such were the case, then we could grasp it, and it would become something we could manipulate. "Indeed, falsehood loves to take the garb of doctrine, idea, principle and system" (IV/3 434 = 376). It "transforms [identity] into nonidentity" (IV/3 508 = 441). Yet this is all ruled out if that specific person is the truth. The truth is someone who encounters us, and who can encounter us only in and of himself, so that we cannot "have" the truth in that encounter. Thus, the truth in that self-disclosure is a mystery which opens itself up from within, which is not forced to open itself, and which we can not open. "*Jesus* said: I am the truth" (John 14:6). This statement has for Barth, beyond the negative aspect just discussed, positive significance in two ways.

First, because the truth is identical with this one person, it is not a silent truth that achieves articulation only as we make various interpretations of it, with the result that in our encounter with it we would really be dealing only with our own interpretations. It is a speaking truth, which "speaks for itself" (IV/3 472 = 409; IV/1 158 = 143-44). It is not dependent upon our apologetics, but is truth that helps itself, that expresses itself in words. It is a truth that speaks, that "speaks where all others think they do, but in reality only lisp and stutter" (IV/3 472 = 409), which "transcend[s] the frontier of death which puts an end to all the speech of all other men," breaking "the silence of His death . . . from the place from which God alone has the power to speak" (IV/3 474 = 411). "To be of the truth means to hear first *His* voice in encounter and confrontation with Him" (IV/1 277 = 252 rev.).

Second, since the truth is identified with a person, it is indissolubly linked to a specific content, to *what* this person says: "He speaks of the work of God . . . of the *reconciliation* of the world to God effected in His death and passion" (IV/3 475 = 411). Not everything is true that is "correct." "It is behind the great truths that man usually conceals the truth, or rather conceals himself from the truth" (IV/1 446 = 403). Truth is not a mere form that can be filled with any contents of our own choosing or that can express any thought we might have. It is true as it is filled with this one, this good content, which is that the truth is grace and "this grace is truth, the first and final truth behind which there is concealed no other or different truth," so that the human can "be and live absolutely by this truth" (IV/1 54 = 51).

2. Precisely in this way truth encounters the human not "as a phenomenon which is immediately and directly illuminating, pleasing, acceptable and welcome" (IV/3 376), but as "*strange*, shocking and quite opposed to what we might for once call the natural feelings and desires and thoughts and beliefs and dreams of man" (IV/3 478 = 415): as the "Word of the *cross*" (IV/3 436 = 377-78). "In the first instance it does not address him; it contradicts him and demands his contradiction" (IV/3 435 = 377). It is an "offense" to us (IV/3 509 = 442), an "offense" that we "fear" (IV/3 439). The human lie, seeking to escape the painful thorn of the truth, will be "to render it innocuous, to work it over, to translate and reinterpret and transform it . . . into a less troublesome" word (IV/3 510 = 442).

Why does it have such thorns? Because the event in which God speaks the truth to us is truth's conflict with falsehood, and because this conflict reveals that we have covered ourselves with our sham truths; the truth is that we live in the lie. The event is, to be sure, a gracious one, but not in the sense that it leaves the lie unchallenged, but rather in the sense that the one who is the truth profoundly contends with those who for their part contend against the truth. The grace of the event is evidenced in that the lie is laid open to the light as it is contested, in order to remove it. In this event God so contends with falsehood that "we shall not find God where we think we should look for Him, namely, in a supposed height," but instead "in direct confrontation with and at the very heart of our own reality," there at "the one painful point where each of us is stripped and naked" (IV/3 480 = 416). In that God has engaged the wrongness of the human who lives in the lie, he does indeed accept her, but only in such a way that the truth about us is said, and we liars must look at "the reflection of our human reality divested of all illusion." "This is how man deals with God and therefore with man. . . . How can we rejoice to see him?" — to see one for whom really the story should be over now. "Hence the Crucified speaks the truth," and he does so only as the Crucified (IV/3 479f. = 416).

3. The truth encounters us as the crucified person who speaks a word "which *claims* us as those who are pledged to hear and obey" (IV/3 511 = 444). Once again it contradicts our falsehood and is contradicted by this lie that, beyond whatever it can receive as truth, cannot accept this: truth's claim on us. The lie makes every effort to evade this claim by reinterpreting the truth, by domesticating and "nostrifying" it [= adapting it to ourselves] (IV/3 510, 513 = 442, 446). It makes every effort to ensure that the human person takes control of the truth, has it at her own command, to fashion and manipulate it in accordance with her own interests, so that it becomes her intellectual property and her product. She advances its own claims on the truth (be they demanding or, where conflict with others threatens, more moderate), founded on a standard derived from herself and applied to others. The human thus lives in the lie from her very first step and not only then when she makes questionable use of his own capacity.

Life in the truth begins at the point where it makes its uncompromising claim on us, not with the fist but with the defenselessness of the one who is "the King crowned with *thorns*" (IV/3 450 = 390), the Lamb upon the throne (IV/3 459 = 397) yet nevertheless the King upon the throne. Since he does not leave us to ourselves and our "foolish freedom" (IV/3 517 = 449), and since he binds us to himself so that we are left with an "obedience which advances no claims" and does not want to see the truth as our "own stock of knowledge to be advanced or defended" (IV/3 473 = 410), the truth encounters us effectively and we are liberated to affirm it wholeheartedly in "self-determination" and not as "a puppet or chess-man" (IV/3 515 = 447). "The truth will make you free" (John 8:32). The truth is never the product of our own arbitrarily selected and enacted freedom.

The Power of Illusion

The truth alone can unmask the lie. The lie "will take good care not to characterize itself as falsehood." And whoever would like "in his own power . . . to differentiate it from the truth" should be sure that he is not representing "as the truth what is perhaps only another form of falsehood. . . . The truth itself, Jesus Christ as the true Witness infallibly differentiates falsehood from the truth" (IV/3 505 = 438-439). He unmasks the lie as the contradictory opponent to the truth. In its contradiction of the truth, it presents a picture of itself that is similar to the truth. The serious lie is not simply untrue, which makes it all the more dangerous. "It has taken and swallowed and so far as possible digested and assimilated the truth. . . . The true and succulent lie always has something of the scent of the truth." It has "a radiant aspect of righteousness and holiness, of wisdom, excellence and prudence, of zeal, austerity and energy, yet also of patience and love for God and man. . . . The short legs of lies, that are doubtless very strong legs, carry them very far" (IV/3 504f. = 438 rev.). The nearer that the truth approaches us, the greater and more devastating is the danger that we will pervert it into a lie. For this reason, and contrary to our modern belief in humanity's progress, we must assume that "the sphere of our time and history is not then the theatre of a decrease of darkness as we might suppose . . . but rather of its intensification and increase" (IV/3 453 = 392). Since Christians, by reason of the revelation made to them, have to do with the truth, the Christian lie is the "primary phenomenon" of falsehood (IV/3 521 = 451), in comparison to which all other lies are only "epiphenomena" (IV/3 521 = 453). Thus, those who know the truth are recognizable by the fact that they do not really struggle critically enough with the transposition of truth and untruth, to which they are very susceptible.

It is of the nature of falsehood to take on the appearance of truth. Barth emphasizes that this is *just* an appearance! But this makes its power, as terrible as it is, into a powerless power from the outset — not in and of itself, but in the relationship of truth to it (IV/3 505 = 439). That proves that the lie is obviously too "unoriginal" to set up an autonomous alternative over against the truth. And "one little word — a little word on the part of the One whom he, i.e., the lord of this supposed counter-power, would replace — can fell him" (IV/3 504 = 437). Nevertheless, the lie can do many things against us. It takes on the appearance of truth because it presupposes the truth (that truth which unmasks it!), and because it only knows how to hold its ground in that it does not directly deny the truth, but by "apparently" acknowledging it, it conceals itself in the truth. In this way it attains the quality of a sinister and overwhelming power. It thereby receives the character of an illuminating "counter-revelation" (IV/3 432 = 374), i.e. of the opposite to the revelation of the truth of God as the disclosure of his unhiddenness. This counter-revelation is essentially the humanly irreversible *concealment* of the lie, the process of making it invisible as a lie. In taking on the appearance of truth it renders invisible the fact that it is a mere sham truth, an untruth. It obscures with a clever maneuver what its work of lies consists of and to what purpose it uses the truth under the illusion of truth. "[Man] manages . . . to use the truth to silence the truth, or the true Witness, by . . . all the time patronizing, interpreting, domesticating, acclimatizing, accommodating, and gently but very definitely and significantly correcting Him while drawing Him into his center" (IV/3 504 = 437 rev.). It perverts the truth into falsehood by the most thoroughgoing removal of its thorn possible. In contradicting the truth, the lie handles it (1) as a neutral idea that we can fill at our pleasure with anything we might think of. (2) It makes a picture of the truth that awakens in us the impression of something we would wish for, something useful to us, something that meets a need we have. (3) The lie reinterprets the truth's claim upon us into a claim that we can make, using the truth as something we control and manage.

When truth is handled in this way it is transformed for us. Rather than something over against us that confronts us, it is something in our hands. It becomes what we *hold* to be true on the basis of its agreement with our own concept of it. It becomes for us the result and product of our own determinations. What is true is what we define as true. What seems to be true to us, that is, what appears to be probable, is what counts as true. When we look at things "tolerantly," this means that the truth exists for us only in the different versions of what we hold to be true, or alternatively, that we should stick to that version which is able to muster the greatest success among the largest majority of people. When we look at things in an authoritarian manner, then truth exists only in what the external institution tells us that we *must* regard as true, and that may happen in our saying this command to ourselves in its internalized form.

Barth thought that these two approaches were not as far apart from each other as they each claimed to be against the other. Further, Barth was of the opinion that modern authoritarianism has its source in modern liberalism.[17] "Who can exercise a worse tyranny over us than the god in our own breast?" (I/2 749 = 668). He may present himself outwardly as ever so tolerant, but he still represents "the worst form of intolerance" (I/2 326 = 299), because he is, in and of himself, the human subject that posits himself as *absolute* and separated from God. The "freedom" of this subject does not lead to truth, but at best, in view of the endlessness of its freedoms, to attempts to limit itself and even to the willingness to submit to imposed and dictatorial limitations. Although tyrannies do not necessarily have to emerge from the source of the subject which posits itself as absolute, they can always do

17. Karl Barth, *Der deutsche Kirchenkampf* (1937).

so, as long as the source itself is not clogged. The truth stands under the patronage of what the human person in her heart of hearts would like to regard as true.

Although one's satisfaction with what we have just described might seem to be similar to that "obedience to the truth that makes no claims," both are as different from each other as night from day. In the former case the human is dealing not just relatively with the truth, but with what one holds to be true, whether it is posited to be absolute or relative — that is, with the *appearance* that the human produces in designing his sham truths, the picture that one makes and then presents as true. "Man is *forced* to *live* with this distorted image which he has set up by his *falsehood* and which corresponds to it. As he *sees* things, so they *are,* not in themselves, but *for him.* So, then, he must have and experience them, and so they must have their effect on him" (IV/3 540 = 469). This helps us to understand how violent the sham truth is. It is violent in that the human person is both its agent and its victim. On the one hand, the more our projections have the scent of truth, and the more we hide the fact that they are just our own fabrications, the more powerful they are and the more they dominate things. As we now see these things, so they *have* to be. The human now tries to conform everything to the way he sees things. On the other hand, that image thus gains power over the human person. Although her hands have formed it, it now *takes control* of her and she becomes its product. "The distorted image has, as such, reality and power in relation to the one who stirs it up by his falsehood. It controls, determines, limits and characterizes his existence. He is forced to have and experience the world and himself in the defaced, distorted and corrupted form in which they represent themselves to him in this image. He exists in a subjective reality alien to and contradicting his objective reality" (IV/3 540 = 469 rev.).

In this ambivalence, the mendacious sham truth participates in the sinister dialectic in which Barth sees all the products of the human person who is estranged from himself because he is estranged from God (CL 363-366 = 213ff.); the "lordless powers" is the way he describes them very early on.[18] The human is lordless when she is alienated from God; when she abstracts herself from God, she ceases to be the "free lord" who she might be in God's realm and in orientation toward him. Thus the human unleashes a "catastrophic" chain reaction of a dreadfully powerful illusion. In trying to exist in "absolute" fashion, he does not become a lord of the world as he intended. That is "the *myth,* but only the . . . *illusion* of the person who thinks and claims that he . . . is now sovereign. . . . In thinking this — and the more

18. Karl Barth, *Der Römerbrief,* 1st ed., pp. 20, 27, 34, 219, 348, 466.

self-consciously . . . he does so, the more . . . he is overtaken by the *opposite*. . . . Parallel to the history of his emancipation from God there runs that of the emancipation of his own possibilities of life from himself: the history of the overpowering of his desires, aspirations, and will by the power, the superpower, of his ability. His capacities when he uses them . . . become . . . lordless indwelling forces. To be sure, he thinks he can take them in hand. . . . In reality, however, they escape from him. . . . they act at their own pleasure, as absolutes, with him, behind him, over him, and against him . . ." (CL 365 = 215).

The untruth that is camouflaged as sham truth is an example of this dialectic. The reshaping of the truth into a manipulable ware begins immediately to manipulate the human person (CL 388 = 227). It is more than an example of this; in this dialectical process it is itself effective: they are called "lordless powers" because they only *appear* to be lords. They do not really have humanity in their own power. God has the human in his hand, and they are powerless against him. If, indeed, they do have power over the human person, then only as lordships imagined and fabricated by him, placed in the saddle by him. But as "lordless *powers*" they exercise real lordship. "They are not just the supports but the motors of society . . . the real *factors* and *agents* of human progress, regress, and stagnation in politics, economics, scholarship, technology, and art" (CL 368f. = 216). Like wild and rampaging "lordless" beasts, they fraudulently exercise an illegitimate lordship that, in contradiction to the kindly lordship of God, is "hostile to humanity." These powers are destructive of both individuals and human society. In that "they *break away* from man even as he breaks away from *God*" (absolutized!), they become so powerful over him that he can not redeem himself from them (CL 397 = 232-33). Only God can redeem him from them, and he does so as he allows the kingdom of his reconciliation, his peace and thus of his truth to come to us and thus scatters the lordless powers "to the winds like the mists of the hypostatized fictions that they are, restoring to man the freedom over his abilities of which they had robbed him" (CL 405 = 237). "Anything other than or less than the truth is no match for them, whether it take the form of mental purification, zealous good will, knowledge or techniques. . . . Only the truth is strong enough to meet them. This is so immediately, basically and conclusively. Yet it must be the whole truth, the real truth, the truth of God and His kingdom and angels, the truth which they have attempted to imitate and in the imitation of which they are so powerful. Other truths . . . are of no value. . . . The truth of God dispels them. . . . It does so simply by speaking for itself as the truth, and thus separating itself from the lie as such and showing it to be a lie" (III/3 620 = 528-29).

The Deceptiveness of Religion

Barth finds that the "exchange of the truth about God for a lie" (Rom. 1:25; cf. I/2 335 = 307) takes place in its most sinister way in *religion*. His criticism of religion is the crown of the very same criticism that he brings against the political "Leviathan" and the moneyed establishment as its "close relative" (CL 379 = 222). His criticism of religion comes within the structure of his critical analysis of falsehood pretending to be the truth. What he has to say about this kind of lie applies with even greater force to religion. What religion comprises is, in contrast to what it purports to be, "never the truth. It is a complete fiction, which has not only little but no relation to God. It is an anti-God who has first to be known as such and discarded when the truth comes to a human. But it can be known as such, as a fiction, only *as* the truth does come to one" (I/2 331 = 303 rev.). "The divine reality offered and manifested to us in revelation is replaced by a concept of God arbitrarily and willfully evolved by man" (I/2 329 = 302), to which then he subjects himself because it establishes dominion over humanity. "In religion man bolts and bars himself against revelation by providing a substitute for it" (I/2 330f. = 303). Religion "is the *one* great concern of *godless* man" (I/2 327 = 300). These statements by Barth, whose severity he never retracted (CL 212ff. = 129-132), have always caused such offense that there has seldom been any attempt to understand them. Let us attempt to understand them!

First, we should note that in these statements Barth is not presenting "Christianity's" criticism of the religions. Christians do not conduct a critique of religion; they themselves are subject to it. Indeed, the criticism especially "affects ourselves . . . as adherents of the Christian religion." It must first concern "us" because it is "the judgment of divine *revelation* upon all religion." For all its severity this is certainly also a merciful judgment, not a blind and barbaric "contesting of the true and the good and the beautiful which a closer inspection will reveal in almost all religions, and which we naturally expect to find in abundant measure in our own religion" (I/2 327 = 300). Whoever thinks about this judgment will discuss the problem with *"patience."*

> This patience must not be confused with the moderation of those who actually have their own religion or religiosity, and are secretly zealous for it, but who can exercise self-control, because they have told themselves or have been told that theirs is not the only faith, that fanaticism is a bad thing, that love must always have the first and last word. It must not be confused with the clever aloofness of the rationalistic Know-All . . . , who

thinks that he can deal comfortably and in the end successfully with all religions in the light of a concept of a perfect religion which is gradually evolving in history. But it also must not be confused with the relativism and impartiality of an historical skepticism, which does not ask about truth and untruth in the field of religious phenomena, because it thinks that truth can be known only in the form of doubt about all truth. (I/2 326 = 299 rev.)

This is a patience that derives "from the knowledge that by grace God has reconciled to Himself godless man and his religion. It will see man carried, like an obstinate child in the arms of its mother, by what God has determined and done for his salvation in spite of his own opposition. In detail, it will neither praise nor reproach him. It will understand his situation . . . not because it can see any meaning in the situation as such, but because it acquires a meaning from outside, from Jesus Christ" (I/2 326 = 299).

To be sure, that judgment of God is to be understood as strict as well as loving, for at this point Barth presupposes a concept of religion that, not accidentally parallel to the shift in the understanding of truth, was formulated by the Enlightenment, and in the words of P. de Lagarde was in "the most decided opposition" to the concept of revelation (I/2 309 = 284). "Opposition" here does not necessarily mean elimination; it means that religion is now understood as the presupposition, the criterion, and the necessary framework of revelation, and revelation is understood as a predicate or one possibility among many others within the range of the given, as something that we can have and know "apart from revelation" (I/2 315 = 289). That is precisely what religion is according to the modern definition: "the relationship with God which we can and actually do have apart from revelation" (I/2 315 = 289). "Religion" means thus to observe the *human person* with the confidence and purpose of discovering in her a "province" (Schleiermacher) in which she finds the divine present in herself, or at least a capacity that is open to the divine, that can set her in relationship to it, that can grasp after it. It is not that after which she grasps but the *grasping itself,* and then what is grasped, that is the aim of religion. If there is reference to revelation in this context, it is not something new but simply an expression for something already given in this framework. For Barth this understanding of religion defines what is meant by speaking of *the* "religion" within the religions.

It also expresses what the human whom God relates to himself in his revelation is. Is he or she the godless human, separated from God? Indeed they are, but they themselves deny this in that they are so religiously engaged and thus give the appearance of having long since been involved with God.

They conceal this from themselves in such a way that for them "the revelation of God is . . . the *hiddenness* of God in the world of human *religion*" (I/2 307 = 282). Revelation does not confront us "in a neutral condition," but as *religious* people who deny that they are ungodly and contest their dependence upon God's revelation. That is, revelation "reaches us in the attempt to know God from our standpoint," and not "in the activity which corresponds to it" but in our "*opposition* to it" (I/2 329 = 301). It, however, emerges from its concealment in the world of human religion as unhiddenness, as truth, in that as *revelation* it uncovers what the human has hidden from himself in *religion*. It does not reveal what the human already knows, or even partially suspects and desires, but rather, in its confrontation revelation uncovers what the human denies in her religion, contradicts in it, and seeks to evade with the assertion that such a religious person does not need it at all. "In a worse form . . . than . . . in theoretical atheism" (CL 129), the human denies in his religion that he needs and yet is unworthy of forgiveness, and that precisely *in* his religious being. The Church "must be continually reminded of the most serious of all symptoms. It was the Church, not the world, which crucified Christ."[19] Revelation can encounter us only in that it contradicts us. It does this by showing that it is a fiction that humans would already somehow have what it must first give them, that religion is "a kind of outstretched hand which is filled by God in His revelation" (I/2 330 = 303), with the result that the human can willfully manipulate what she has in her hand. Revelation tears off the mask with which the human conceals his godlessness under the appearance of religion.

There are two aspects, for Barth, to the way revelation makes this disclosure. First, revelation tells us that when we speak about God, we are only deceiving ourselves that we are speaking about God. "The external satisfaction of the religious need . . . will never be anything more or other than a reflection of what man is and has" (I/2 345 = 316). "When we set God upon the throne of the world, we mean by God ourselves. In 'believing' on Him, we justify, enjoy, and adore ourselves."[20] According to Barth the Old Testament's prohibition of images protests against this, which is not to say the same thing as that "commonplace of the science of religion" that the image of God is only the "representative" of the deity but not identical with it. *For this reason,* God "cannot be represented by any human work, . . . for . . . in His revelation . . . He wills to give exclusive testimony to Himself," "because it is

19. Karl Barth, *Der Römerbrief,* 2nd ed. (Munich, 1922; 12th ed., 1978), pp. 372-73; ET: *The Epistle to the Romans* (Oxford, 1933), p. 389.

20. Karl Barth, *Der Römerbrief,* 2nd ed., p. 1; ET: *Epistle to the Romans,* p. 44.

only through truth that truth can come to man. If man tries to grasp at truth of himself, he will from the outset grasp wide of the mark." Thus the human only catches hold of himself, as a being that is separated from God. "Because it is a *grasping*, religion is the contradiction of revelation. . . . It is . . . an arrogant but hopeless attempt . . . to make something which man can only make because and when God makes it for him: the knowledge of the truth, the knowledge of God" (I/2 330f. = 302-304 rev.).

The second aspect is that revelation tells the human that he, in his efforts to achieve justification and sanctification, is only fooling himself that *this* is his intention, because in truth he is only attempting "to justify and sanctify himself" (I/2 338 = 309). To attempt this in his religion is probably his only option because he really means himself when he is talking about God. Caught up in this attempt, she must contradict revelation, for she imagines that she can attain on her own the salvation which revelation promises her. But when revelation promises salvation to the human, it contradicts this attempt made by religion. For Barth this is the significance of the Old Testament and New Testament witness against work righteousness (I/2 339-343 = 310-314). Man "cannot in any sense declare to himself that he is righteous and holy, and therefore saved, for in his own mouth as his own judgment of himself it would be a lie. It is truth as the revealed knowledge of God. It is truth in Jesus Christ. . . . He replaces all the different attempts of man to reconcile God to the world," for "God reconciles the world to Himself in Him" (I/2 336 = 308).

The statement that the lie is unmasked only by the truth and not by itself — it willfully conceals itself in a sham truth — corresponds to the statement that religion is not capable of uncovering itself as a concern of godless humans — it also conceals itself behind images of "the true, the good, and the beautiful." Barth admits, of course, that religion "can be called in question from within" (I/2 343 = 314). As indications of its "ultimate nonnecessity" (I/2 345 = 315) and "weakness" (I/2 345 = 316), one could consider mysticism, for which "everything external is only a form and picture" of indwelling reality (I/2 349 = 319), and atheism, which with its "negation of the over-world of religion" succumbs all the more easily to the "disguised religions" with their very different "dogmas of truth" (I/2 351f. = 321). Yet neither of these can abrogate religion, in part because they need it in order to negate it, and in part because they live out of the innermost marrow of religion, namely, "man's faith in himself" (I/2 343 = 314). It is an illusion to think that one can live without religion. "If a religion died, it died because of the victory of another religion, not because of the . . . attack of mysticism or atheism" (I/2 353 = 323). "The revelation of God denies that any religion is true. . . . As the self-offering and self-manifestation of God, as the work of peace which God Himself has concluded between Himself and man, revelation is the truth . . . over against which there is only lying" (I/2 356 = 325). Christians, who are aware of this, cannot, any more than can religion, evade the judgment spoken over them all in the revelation. They are "most acutely" aware that it applies to them, and "to non-Christians only in so far as we recognize ourselves in them . . . in the solidarity . . . in which, anticipating them in both repentance and hope, we accept this judgment and participate in the promise of revelation" (I/2 358 = 327).

So, "the abolishing of religion by revelation" must not mean its negation. "Religion can *certainly* be preserved in revelation, although and in that the judgment still stands. It can be upheld by it and concealed in it. It can be justified by it and . . . sanctified." In virtue, not of its own self-consciousness, but of the grace of God, there can be "a true religion: just as there are justified sinners" (I/2 357 = 326 rev.). Its truth will now lie in the fact not that religion links us to God but that God links himself to us, justifying and sanctifying us, in spite of and in our religion. In our religion and despite our religion, we are liberated to honor God in that we live by his justification and sanctification, and we are free also to interact with the adherents of non-Christian religions in solidarity and hope.

Witness to the Truth

The "great craft and power" of the lie is not crafty and powerful enough to obstruct the human knowledge of truth. We would be denying that revelation is the "truth of truth" if we could not rely on true knowledge of the truth. We could not recognize as a lie the lie that feigns to be the truth, and confess that we are unmasked liars, if the limits to its power and craft and thus the distinction between truth and lie were completely unknown. Counting on the knowledge of the truth does not have for Barth a postulate as its basis. Its basis is the reality that the truth has come into the world. Jesus Christ is "the true Witness" (IV/3 425 = 368). "He attests this truth as He attests Himself" (IV/3 507 = 440), himself as the one who is "full of grace and truth" (John 1:14), whose grace is truth, and whose truth is grace. He is "the Guarantor" of the truth (IV/1 150 = 137), and he guarantees it to us as the "contemporary" of every human (IV/3 572 = 497). So, it is not that "there is knowledge of the truth," but that *he* gives the knowledge of the truth. He does so as his witness to the truth announces it, evokes it, calls us to it. He calls *sinners* to it (IV/3 588 = 588), and as they follow his call, they do not step out of their connectedness with all other people "in full solidarity" (IV/3 610f. = 531), because they recognize that they are guilty of the lie. The fact that they *recognize*, however, what previously they denied shows that they have been touched by that witness to the truth and participate in it "by the liberation which comes from the truth itself" (II/1 234 = 208). This does not take place automatically. "The great and critical moments in the history . . . were and are those in which there may be . . . not by the perspicacity or profundity of man, but in the power of the Word of the true Witness again received by man, and therefore in the power of the Holy Spirit, certain provisional discoveries . . . of the glorious (in its simplicity), unsettling yet deeply consoling fact that even in its supreme form falsehood is only falsehood" (IV/3 506f. = 440).

Those whose eyes have been opened to the truth by this Witness to the truth, and to the difference between truth and falsehood that appears to be true, are themselves *also* witnesses to the truth with Christ although not simply the way he is. That they, in contrast to him, are witnesses as called *sinners* demonstrates that they are so in another way than he is. They bear witness to the truth which is never identical with them, which is even alien to them, and which is only "guaranteed" to them. They are by all account mere *witnesses* to this truth (IV/3 700 = 611), "mere" in the sense that they neither are nor possess the truth. They cannot control or manipulate it. They are dependent upon it, upon its constantly opening itself to them anew. When it opens up before them, they can only point to it. That is what they *can* do and *ought* to do. The truth is not made known to them as an "end in itself," let alone an "object of their self-seeking" (IV/3 650 = 566f. rev.), as if they were permitted to hoard it away from others, to conceal it and deny them access to it. "To be called means being given a task" (IV/3 658 = 573), which is to be witnesses to the truth to these other people. "As witnesses they have to repeat what God Himself has first said to them" (IV/3 661 = 576). They have to do this with careful attention to what has been said to them, yet also with a freedom that displays the "acquiring of the courage exalted by Kant as the essence of true enlightenment, to use his own understanding" (IV/3 608f. = 529).

The fact that they are simply witnesses to the truth, with no control over it, is illuminated anew through Barth's thought that not only *within* Christendom but also *outside* it, in the secular world, genuine testimonies to the truth, "true Words" are to be found. The community may and "must accept the fact that there are such words and that it must hear them too" (IV/3 128 = 114-5). These words cannot, of course, replace or even supplement the true Word of that one true witness. But insofar as they correspond to the true Word, the community must recognize them as "true words . . . which, whatever their subjective presuppositions, stand objectively in a supremely direct relationship with the one true Word, a relationship that they certainly did not create out of themselves and that certainly might also speak against them" (IV/3 141 = 125 rev.). "We cannot see or understand how a man may be, or come to be, in a position to speak true words in this qualified sense from the outer or inner spheres of secular darkness" (IV/3 139 = 124). There can be only one reason for it. "In the world reconciled to God in Jesus Christ there is no secular sphere abandoned by Him or withdrawn from His control, even where from the human standpoint it seems to approximate most dangerously to the pure and absolute form of utter godlessness" (IV/3 133 = 119). The sphere of his influence is much wider than that of the church and really lies outside it. We Christians must "have ears to hear the voice of the Good Shepherd even there too, distinguishing it from other clamant voices, and therefore . . . placing ourselves more definitely and deeply [in the ministry of his Word] that we may be the better and more attentive and more convincing servants of this Word" (IV/3 131 = 117).

But what if humans witness to the truth in diverse ways that appear to be or are really in disagreement with each other; what if they argue or ask what is really or only allegedly true? It is like the assumption made by G. E. Lessing in his parable of the three identical rings. Only one of the three is the genuine one, and each of the owners looks upon his ring as the genuine one and regards the others as false, but "the right ring could not be proven." Barth found Lessing's answer illuminating: certainly there is the genuine ring in comparison with which the others are false. The point is that one cannot announce, since they all look alike, that it is a matter of indifference whether they are genuine or false. Nor can one of the participants assert that his ring is genuine simply because it happens to be in his hand. For this, only the "Proofs of the Spirit and the Power" can be cited.[21] With regard to the freeing of the Christian to become a witness to the truth, "it must be noted rather than proclaimed that liberation has come to him too, and to him specifically. Inevitably this will, in fact, be perceived in his witness, not merely in the convincing note and ring of his voice as a witness, but also in the fact that it is made explicit that the work of God is the Word of God . . . whose truth may be experienced in his own life by each of those to whom it is attested" (IV/3 775 = 676).

We cannot, of course, prove that what our words *attest* as the truth really *is* the truth. The truth does not have "its source in man, so that to know and declare the truth, to establish the truth as such, to live by the truth and in

21. Karl Barth, *Protestantische Theologie,* pp. 228ff.; ET: *Protestant Theology,* pp. 256-262; cf. CD IV/1 726 = 650.

the truth, does not lie in man's capacity and existence. But properly and decisively, and therefore in truth, the truth is seen throughout as a predicate of the prerogative of God as the Lord who speaks and acts in Israel. . . . In the truth and therefore the faithfulness of God, that of man has its origin as well as its object and criterion" (II/1 233 = 207). God alone can give this proof, the demonstration of the Spirit and of power (cf. IV/1 726 = 650). "The perfect work of truth will always be God's own work and not ours" (II/1 234 = 208).

Barth distinguishes three aspects of human witness to the truth that correspond to the three aspects in which the truth makes itself known to us. First, he points out that this witness does not validate a principle, a formal rightness, a simple agreement between our perceptions and our terms. The witness cannot be divorced from the living Giver of the truth commandment and thus from a certain, basically helpful content, which must be respected ever anew in concrete relationships. What is meant can be clarified with reference to Barth's reply to Kant's question, May one tell a lie to save the life of a friend? Barth differed from Kant, who responded in the negative with the argument that the honesty called for in the truth command could not itself be the cause of the mortal danger of a friend. Barth responded differently to the question addressed to him from the Dutch resistance in 1942: whether in the context of the struggle for a just state and against a rogue state there might be "a special relationship" to the truth command.[22] Barth responded to this in the affirmative, not because the command could be suspended, but because "the true discourse commanded of humans" was to be understood as "the active confession of God's revealed will." Those who were committed in conscience to fulfill this confession in the form of participation in this struggle "could only speak the truth in such a way that one's speech takes place in that participation. . . . In all circumstances one owes one's neighbor *the* word as the word of truth that is demanded of him in and with that struggle. . . . The end did not justify the means, but obedience to the known will of God did, and disobedience to this will, even though it took the form of truthfulness, would desecrate the means and make it a form of sin."

Second, according to Barth, it is characteristic of the person who is the witness to the truth that his testimony tends to bring him into *distress* although, and perhaps because, "he will more often be recognized by his absence on certain occasions than by his counteractions, by his silence than by his words" (IV/3 712f. = 622). Even when she does not want to cause offense, simply by testifying to the truth that is alien to the world in its lie, that unmasks its sham truth as falsehood, that is crucified for the sake of its libera-

22. Karl Barth, *Eine Schweizer Stimme*, pp. 248-49.

tion from its lie, she causes offense. If a Christian "discharges his ministry of witness . . . he cannot avoid disturbing those around, exerting upon them by his witness a pressure to which they can and will react with counter-pressure" (IV/3 706 = 617). Then she will prefer to bring to remembrance "forgotten truths" (H. Stoevesandt). "The world can tolerate . . . a good deal in the way of religion" (IV/3 711 = 621), but not this witness. "The world usu-ally wonders in what diluted form it might tolerate all this" (IV/3 714 = 623), or it attempts to defame the witness as a "disturber of the peace" (IV/3 715 = 624). The Christian, however, cannot cease to be a witness and "retreat into an island of inwardness" (IV/3 706 = 616). He is indeed "a man who is help-less and vulnerable," whose "witness . . . is his *only* instrument of justice and force" (IV/3 719f. = 627, 629), and in whose "little passion" the passion of Christ "goes forward" (IV/3 729 = 636).

Although the Christian "is oppressed by his environment" (IV/3 709 = 619), he is not "troubled" (IV/3 759 = 662), because his affliction is "one of ministry" (IV/3 704 = 615). She would not be a witness to the truth if she were not "absolutely secured" (IV/3 738 = 645). She can confidently put her "trust in the Holy Spirit, who will see to it . . . that the truth always remains the truth no matter what people may say against it."[23] If the church is a witness of this sort, then it has "the wonderful possibility, peacefully and joyfully, of having the upper hand over against the totalitarian state and the totalitarian world, not always going around with clenched fists. The church can wait. And it knows that it does not wait in vain." For it knows "that all the totalities of the world and society and the state, which are in truth false gods, are lies. Ultimately one cannot be afraid of lies. 'The truth will out.' In the church one can know this. If the church takes these lies seriously, it is lost. It must quietly and peacefully treat them as lies. The more its life is characterized by humil-ity, by the knowledge that its members are only human and themselves given up to lying, the more certain it will be in its knowledge that 'God is in charge' over against the lie." Then even under the most difficult conditions the church "will stick to its task and regard it as forbidden to be anxious about its future."[24]

Third, Barth defines the witnesses to the truth as those who manifest their liberation through the truth by showing that they are irresistibly *claimed* by it. They are delivered "from the ocean of apparently unlimited possibilities by transference to the rock of the one necessity which as such is [their] only possibility" (IV/3 762 = 665). Because the truth is inflexible, the

23. Karl Barth, *Gespräche 1964-1968* (Zurich, 1997), p. 425.
24. Karl Barth, *Gespräche 1959-1962* (Zurich, 1995), pp. 353-54.

human must always render honor to it, and not simply to *one's* knowledge of it. We must validate it decisively yet also modestly, for "whatever we think and say has its limitations."[25] Since the truth cannot be detached from its good content, the witness will be led out of "the "miseries . . . of self-dependence" and "the desire for a purely private existence" and "drawn . . . into fellowship" (IV/3 761 = 664). Under the claim of this truth, the witness will certainly not testify *against* someone else, nor to someone in such a way as to make him the object of one's skill. "A witness will not intrude on his neighbor. He will not 'handle' him. He will not make him the object of his activity, even with the best intention" (I/2 488 = 441). The truth to which he is to testify leads "from the forcible dominion of things to the free territory of man and the human." Since God "became a man and not even the most important or resplendent of things . . . the smallest sigh or laugh of a man is surely more important to Him than the support of the most important institutions, the construction and working of the most marvelous apparatus, the development of the most lofty or profound ideas" (IV/3 763 = 666). Since on the one side the claim of truth cannot be made into a claim that we raise for ourselves, and yet on the other side we do have to reckon with the possibility that others will speak "words that are true," dialogue is obviously the natural form in which witness will be given to the truth.

"I and Thou must both speak and hear, and speak with one another and hear one another. No element must be lacking. This is the human significance of speech. . . . And speech means comprehensively reciprocal expression and its reciprocal reception, reciprocal address and its reciprocal reception" (III/2 302f. = 252-53). "Most of our words, spoken or heard, are an inhuman and barbaric affair because we will not speak or listen to one another. We speak them without seeking ourselves, without wanting to help ourselves. And we hear them, without our finding ourselves, without wanting to be helped" (III/2 311 = 260 rev.). The witnesses to the truth, however, may not derive from the *form* of conversation the permission to divorce the truth to which they are to testify from its good *content*. The reason for their unlimited openness to others is their "unlimited readiness to see in the aliens of today the brothers of tomorrow, and to love them as such and not simply as men," for "neither the Old Testament nor the New" knows "anything of a general love for humanity"; that is "Christian communication" (IV/3 568 = 494). In like manner, they cannot conclude from the form of dialogue that truth is relative and not binding. They can conduct this conversation only un-

---

25. Karl Barth, *Letzte Zeugnisse* (Zurich, 1969), p. 35; ET: *Final Testimonies* (Grand Rapids, 1977), p. 34.

der the presupposition that the claim of truth is binding on all parties. Barth could thus boldly state, "It is only where adversaries are opposed with genuine dogmatic intolerance that there is the possibility of genuine and profitable discussion. For it is only there that one . . . has something to *say* to the other" (I/2 924 = 827).

Exacting Exhortation — Gospel and Law, Ethics

The Connection of Gospel and Law

The starting point of Barth's Christian ethics is to be found in the formula "Gospel and Law," which was for him part of the "basic substance" of his dogmatics (IV/3 427 = 370). The gospel speaks about God's will *for* us and the law tells us what God wills *from* us. They are two things, but in both it is the same God who has to do with the human and with whom the human has to do. Hence the two are not to be separated. God does not make an offer without his offering including a *command* — his grace is not cheap grace. But he does not command without enclosing that command in the offer of his *grace.* His command is not a burdensome "law." The grace of God commands, and the command of God is gracious.

> The Word of God is both Gospel and Law. It is not Law by itself and independent of the Gospel. But it is not Gospel without Law. . . . It is first Gospel and then Law. It is the Gospel which contains and encloses the Law as the ark of the covenant the tables of Sinai. . . . The one Word of God which is . . . the work of His grace is also Law. That is, it is a prior decision concerning man's self-determination. It is the claiming of his freedom. It regulates and judges the use that is made of this freedom. . . . As the one Word of God which is . . . the work of His grace reaches us, its aim is that our being and action should be conformed to His. . . . The truth of the evangelical indicative means that the full stop with which it concludes becomes an exclamation mark. It becomes itself an imperative. (II/2 567 = 511-12)

These statements conflict with a Christianity that separated from Judaism as a religion of law on the ground that it now possessed the gospel. They conflict with a Christianity that, under the cloak of a grace that is only received passively, absorbed entire peoples and kept its lay members passive, satisfied when they did not withdraw from clerical grace and also from the "gracious" authorities. The statements conflict, too, with Luther's insight concerning the distinction between faith and the righteousness of works, though Barth did say that "it might well be asked whether I am not quite a good Lutheran after all" (IV/3 428 = 371). Yet his position did run into Lutheran criticism. "The Christocentric confession that there is salvation in no other one has essentially the antithetical sense that righteousness before God is never based upon works of the law. Only when the gospel of justification by faith alone is free of any legal provisos . . . can it grant the peace and freedom that it promises."[1] This criticism does not directly affect Barth's thesis, because the "evangelical indicative" is affirmed and is not dependent upon legal provisos. But the critique is referring to something else: the consolation of the gospel depends upon the fact that it does *not* enclose *any* law, that it is a law-free reality which God's law precedes, with the twofold function (1) of preventing external outbreaks of sin by the sinner through the force of legal statutes and (2) of causing the sinner internal despair at one's own inability, and thus making one ready to hear the gospel.

According to this view, the law conversely has to be understood as a grace-less and gospel-free reality. It follows, then, that its divinity is not located in the content that is commanded but in its character as "legal" coercion. The biblical, the "Jewish" commands can be arbitrarily replaced by any other kind of "law," such as the statutes of any "authority," the inexorability of natural laws, the social "orders," or technical or economic pressures. Since legalities of this kind include steps to eliminate their violation, it might be asked what is the "sin" that the gospel of grace forgives. This gospel must, in any event, have no effect on these legalities and participation in them. A *Christian* ethics is therefore impossible except insofar as it might help us to do more conscientiously what we can do without it. For Christians as for all others ethical action is that which is in keeping with the legalities of the world.

Can such a conception truly appeal to Luther? It surely took on its contours only in the context of the modern emancipation of ethics from the obligation to observe God's commands. It has both promoted this emancipation and reacted against it. For the result of this emancipation, which Lutherans

1. Gerhard Ebeling, *Lutherstudien,* vol. 3 (Tübingen, 1985), p. 566.

call "irreversible,"[2] was the formulation of the thesis of the immanent "autonomy of all life's spheres": political, economic, and other kinds of action must be governed by this autonomy and its forces, as a rule in conflict between opposing demands, yet according to "objective," universally acknowledged criteria, which must function effectively without any dependence upon the Christian confession of faith.[3] Acknowledging this thesis, modern theologians have withdrawn faith into the private sphere, while simultaneously surrendering ethics to that autonomy of the secular world. Thus W. Herrmann, the teacher of Barth, based his thinking upon the view that the reality of the world is controlled by universally understandable laws that should guide our actions, whereas the province of religion is the individual inner life of the human person.[4]

This emancipation of ethics, of course, plunged ethics into a permanent crisis. What is obligatorily commanded of us if the question, "What should we do?", is no longer held to be answered by God's commandment? Should the very human who claims in his "fallenness as sinner" to "know what is good and evil" (Gen. 3:5; IV/1 254 = 231, 497f. = 447-448; III/4 356 = 315) be allowed to be his own lawgiver and judge? Can she do that? For, "of ourselves we may well know what we want to do, but not what we ought to do" (II/2 727 = 653). In reaction to the ethical caprice that surely threatens here, and to hold it in check, theological ethics had all the more cause to insist upon those immanent "autonomies" and "orders" as inevitable. It did so at the cost of the assertion that, because the issue here was *laws,* they were *God's* law — although they were not able to explain to what extent it is *God* and not some other authority making these commands.

Barth developed his thesis of "gospel and law" in reaction to this modern emancipation of ethics from the gospel of grace. Yet he did not do this merely as polemics, and thus he did not promote a specifically "Christian" ethics detached from that ethic and hence beyond correction (II/2 577ff. = 520ff.). He was looking at that ethic which had been removed from the acknowledgement of the gospel (II/2 569ff. = 513-515), when he set up the following double thesis. The existence of a non-Christian ethic "confirms the truth of the grace of God which as it is addressed to man puts the question of the good with such priority over all others that man cannot evade it." *And,* such an ethic "confirms that man tries to escape the *grace* of God by which

2. Cf. Wolfgang Trillhaas, *Ethik,* 2nd ed. (Berlin, 1965), p. 12.
3. Max Weber, *Gesammelte Aufsätze zur Religionssoziologie,* 6th ed., vol. 1 (Tübingen, 1972), p. 552; ET: *From Max Weber: Essays in Sociology* (New York, 1946), p. 339.
4. Wilhelm Herrmann, *Ethik,* 5th ed. (Tübingen, 1913), pp. 92ff.

the question of the good is put. . . . Strange as it may seem, that general conception of *ethics* coincides exactly with the conception of *sin*" (II/2 574 = 518). These two statements belong together. The first demonstrates the openness of a Christian ethics with which it can learn from non-Christian ethics and even be corrected by it. This is not because we are of ourselves able to say adequately what the good is. It is because, thanks to the grace of God, a consistently closed "autonomy" is simply not possible for us. The second statement maintains that this experience may not lead Christians to the erroneous thought that the standard for what they might receive into their ethic from non-Christian ethics is a general concept of the good, but rather only *the* good that God does and makes knowable in the revelation of his grace. Taken together, the two statements signal a critical openness in relation to ethics that is self-consciously non-theological.

Barth is, on the other hand, polemical in dealing with a certain way that modern theology has approached the task of ethics (I/2 877ff. = 782ff.). Just as he thought that theology shared responsibility for the development of modern atheism, he also saw a theological responsibility for the emancipation of ethics from theology — and the two things are related to each other. His *indirect* debate with atheism involved a theological critique of the false picture of God offered by theology, and similarly his *indirect* debate with that emancipation involved a theological critique of the questionable way that *theology* dealt with ethics. The theology of the seventeenth century was already pointing in the wrong direction. It "did not understand how to make it clear that it is not only in this or that aspect of Christian doctrine, but in dogmatics as a whole and throughout, that we have to do with ethics, that is, with the being and conduct of man" (I/2 877 = 784). Hence it left the impression that the human person already knew what the good is, and did so from different sources other than the knowledge of the good that God does for us. Thus this theology also fostered the suspicion that dogmatics is a "teaching" that is distant from life, and that it is only in ethics that life becomes an important theme. A development was thus set in motion whose result was "that . . . the separation of the two disciplines and also . . . the basic subordination of theology to ethics became and remained the rule" (I/2 879 = 786). As a consequence, theology must share responsibility for the emancipation from the divine command that marks the modern era. Barth handled the problems that derived from this emancipation by pointing to the responsibility of theology for what took place. He put the question to theology: Can we really delegate the command of the biblically attested God to an immanent autonomy? His own basic thesis was that the correctness of a Christian ethics stands or falls on whether or not it relates to the law of God, that is, not just to law alone, but to the law *of God.*

The Antithesis of God and Mammon

Let us look again at Barth's thesis on "gospel and law," and at what corresponds to it theologically, namely, that "dogmatics itself is ethics; and ethics is also dogmatics" (I/2 888 = 793), in the context of his discovery of it! In 1933 and 1934 the category of the law divorced from the gospel made it possible for Protestant theologians to affirm the authoritarian and racially nationalistic Führer-state. The theologians at Erlangen University stated that there is not *one* but there are *two* words of God, the law and the gospel. The gospel of forgiveness, free from every divine command, is preceded by the law, which as "the unchangeable will of God" encounters us in "reality as a whole" and "obligates us to the natural orders to which we are subjected, such as family, people, race," and to the "devout and faithful" Führer, through whom God "will confer" upon us "a good government marked by discipline and honor."[5] Friedrich Gogarten declared that the law of God "encounters the modern generation concretely in the form of the national socialist movement in both state and people," as a "hard" but for this reason an "authentic law."[6] This would exclude a "specifically 'Christian' or 'biblical' law." Instead, the church must be the "nurse and guardian" of the law that is given in nationhood. It must also preach the gospel of forgiveness, though this does not relate to offenses against that external "law" — the "authorities" will deal with those. This would mean, then, that the gospel itself carries within itself a command of God against which we might offend. Forgiveness relates to a different and more general form of inward despair.

In response to all of that, Barth discovered that the gospel and law *belong together* and that equating obedience to the Führer with obedience to God was the fruit of an older theological error. He set forth his new understanding in a sermon delivered in September 1935, on the text which should always be heard together with his thesis — Matthew 6:24: "You cannot serve God and mammon." He remarked on this, "A law without gospel hopelessly places us in the service of both God and mammon. But there is no law without gospel; there is only the law in the gospel."[7] Barth retained this image of the division of life into a partial service of God and partial service of mammon that results with the repudiation of ethics as a theological task. If we do not see that the grace of God is a commanding grace, then "far too easily, and indeed inevitably, we begin to look for the indispensable *norm* of the

5. Cf. Joachim Gauger, *Chronik der Kirchenwirren*, vol. 2 (1935), p. 222.

6. Friedrich Gogarten, *Einheit von Evangelium und Volkstum?* (Hamburg, 1933), pp. 17, 21.

7. Karl Barth, *Fürchte dich nicht!* (Munich, 1949), p. 97.

Christian way of life elsewhere than in the Gospel (in which we think we have only the consoling word of justifying grace), and are forced to seek and grasp a *law* formed either by considerations drawn from the Bible or natural law, or by historical convenience. But this means that we are involved in a double bookkeeping, and . . . we are subjected to other lords in a kingdom on the left as well as to the Lord Jesus Christ whose competence extends only, as we think, to the forgiveness of sins" (IV/2 571 = 504; cf. III/1 571 = 414). "Mammon" is for Barth the epitome of these other lords.

Barth's discovery means, then, that we may not identify the law of God with either the accidental magnitude of the Nazi state nor with any demands of worldly authority *of any kind,* just as we may not combine obedience towards God with that toward *any* form of "mammon." "Mammon" is the lord, the god, "the spirit of our resources or possessions attempting self-absolutization" (CL 380 = 222; cf. IV/2 189 = 168-69), and thus the decisive embodiment of what Barth calls "the lordless powers" (CL 378ff. = 222).[8] These are real and sinister *forces.* They impose upon humanity coercive pressures and inexorabilities; they repress and exploit us. According to Barth's diagnosis they do what is intolerable (truly intolerable wherever the human inwardly affirms their power!) because they exercise *false* lordship, *illegal* power, *usurped* might. What we are dealing with in them are the *human* possibilities that, in consequence of the human separation from God, then separate themselves from the human, so that she no longer has them but they have her (CL 365f. = 215). They dominate her, although their demands, which are those of a false lordship, cannot be conceived of as genuine, divine commandments. And if they are not divinely commanded, then there is nothing to that double bookkeeping, as though it were the divine will in his law to subject us to "lordless powers" and make us submissive to them.

To obey God means not to obey mammon. Yet how are we to distinguish their claims? We can do this, Barth thinks, when we see that the reality of God's relatedness to humanity, in which he reveals himself, places us before a certain and inseparable linkage of pardon and claim. *This* linkage rules out any double bookkeeping, makes any serving of both God and mammon *impossible* ("you *cannot* . . ."). Barth put to the theological sanctioning of Nazi domination as the category of law this basic question: How am I to tell whether something commanded is of *God* rather than of the idol "mammon"? The question itself makes it clear that Barth's thesis of the interrelationship of gospel and law does not signify a mingling of the two, but rather ascertains that both the gospel and the law *belong* within the realm of God's determina-

---

8. Cf. above, II.4, and the context discussed in n. 17, pp. 141, 154.

tion and of nothing or no one else. By expressing that question Barth rejected the view that *every* law is the law of God because it is the commanding character of the *law* itself that makes it into God's law, rather than the fact that *God* commands it. Barth was not just looking for a desirable definition of the content and function of law. He was raising the *fundamental* question: What is it that makes the *law* of God the law of *God?* His first inquiry, then, is not about the quality of the *law* but about its *Giver.* We can not decide what his law is nor if his law is really to be reduced to the function of compulsion, regardless of what compels us and to what end, until it has become clear Who is the One who is to be seen as the Giver of his commandment.

Our starting point is that we can know God, and know him as the giver of the law, and therefore know his law, only when God reveals himself to us. The fact that God turns to us and reveals himself to us is his grace. God and his grace and his law are all declared to us *together.* Hence we have to say that the very same God who offers us his grace is also the God who commands us. As his grace comes to us, so does his command. How does this take place? According to Barth the revelation of God is definitively the Easter revelation. With the resurrection of Jesus Christ from the dead the verdict of God went forth by which he identified himself with the one who had sacrificed himself on the cross. Therefore, the cross is revealed as the event of our reconciliation with God, the event of his *grace.* At the same time, the One who was sacrificed is revealed as the Exalted One, to whom "all authority is given" (Mt. 28:18): the authority to claim for himself and for the will of God those who are reconciled with God. Here, then, is the *command* of God.

Just as, in his gift to us, God does not merely give us something but rather his very self, so in his command to us, he does not will that we should offer him just anything but rather our very selves. "[God] and his will, and thus the Law, are, however, not manifest to us in all things, in every occurrence, that is, so very manifest that our apprehensions of it could claim to be more and something different than our own theories and interpretations. . . . It is not only uncertain and dangerous but perverse to want to understand the Law of God on the basis of any other things, of any other event which is different from the event in which the will of God, tearing in two the veil of our theories and interpretations, is visible in grace. . . . Because this occurrence of the will of God, therefore the occurrence of his grace, becomes *manifest* to us, the *Law* becomes manifest to us."[9] We know the *law* of God,

9. Karl Barth, *Evangelium und Gesetz* (*Theologische Existenz heute!* 32) (Munich, 1935), p. 9; ET: "Gospel and Law," in *Community, State, and Church: Three Essays* (Gloucester, Mass., 1968), pp. 77-78.

therefore, only when we know *God.* We know God only in his *revelation,* and thus we know his *commandment* rightly only in connection with his *grace.*

This will help us to understand why obedience to God rules out obedience to mammon. In our obedience towards God, the issue is not submission to *this* "Lord" rather than that one, as though God and mammon shared the same denominator "lordship," and those who command were exchangeable entities, and the exclusiveness in which God desires obedience to *himself* were based on his competitive envy of another commander. God is not just another lord alongside mammon. He is lord in a totally different way, not one in a series of "lordless powers," but so different that one cannot obey him without being freed by him from such powers. *His* command is related to his gracious *covenant* will, whose "purpose" and "meaning" it is that the God who has become our partner should also make us his "real partners" even in all our "non-deity" (III/1 207 = 184; II/2 134 = 125), that is, independently active partners and not "mere objects of divine action" (III/3 74 = 64-65; IV/3 1082 = 941).

The goodness of God is that he does not oppress us with his command but rather wants to have us join him in his covenant. As Barth sees it, our independent action is not that we *institute* the covenant of grace but that we *confess* our partnership in the covenant that God has graciously instituted. As God *does* that, he in his grace lays *claim* upon the human person. Precisely in the *grace* of God, genuine, legitimate, and commanding lordship encounters the human. It commands her that she *should be* and should thankfully prove that she is what she is thanks to God's graciously instituted covenant: God's partner. This lordship makes no alien claim to her, but makes the claim on one who already belongs to the covenant God. To obey this God is actively to affirm our membership in his covenant as partners of God. "Grace does not will only to be received and known . . . as it works itself out as the favor which it is, it wills also to rule. But it rules by offering God to His covenant-partner as Lord of the covenant. . . . There is no grace without the lordship and claim of grace" (II/2 10f. = 12). Hence the command of God rules out the nonsense of serving both God *and* mammon.

Fulfilled Law

Our task now is to explain in greater detail in what sense we can know God's law in his revelation. If that revelation unveils for us the pure grace of God, how can it also meet us as a command without causing uncertainty about grace by reason of the attached conditions? How can God be gracious to us in such a way that his grace also includes a command? Clearly it could not have been Barth's intent to define the *relationship* of "gospel and law" to each other as much as it was to define *each* in entirely new ways — in such a way that God's grace is to be understood as commanding and his law as gracious.

This is the point where we must address his much debated statement that the "Word of God is both Gospel and Law. . . . In its content, it is Gospel; in its form and fashion, it is Law" (II/2 567 = 511). Barth does not use the terms "content" and "form" in an Aristotelian sense, as though the mere matter of the gospel first achieved its true being through the form of the law. Nor is the objection valid that the gospel was legalized, if it did not have its own nonlegal form.[10] In defining the *gospel* Barth asserts that it has "priority over the law,"[11] for it proclaims what *only* the God who relates himself to us does for us and to us.[12] The term "form" first plays a role in the understanding of the *law,* and it tells us that the form of the law is not to be separated from the "content" of the gospel which fulfills it — to separate it is to abuse it terribly. Note here Barth's criticism of the German Christians. According to them the gospel today must "adopt a very specific form," meaning that it should be adapted to the slogans of race and people, which had to be respected as the already given "law of God."[13] Note should also be taken of Barth's "No!" to Emil Brunner's thesis, according to whom "the revelation of God [is] some kind of 'matter,'" in relation to which the (already) responsible human is the appropriate "form" into which then this "content" is to be fitted.[14] According to Barth, that content would, in either instance, be essentially *de*formed. He could not reject this without also attacking the "Lutheran" thesis that the divine aspect of the law was only its *mere* form as demand, whereby it is a matter of indifference what content fills that form. Barth's counter-thesis is as follows: When God also commands us in his revelation, his command is no *mere* form of a demand which can be arbitrarily filled with any particular content. This command has only the *one* content, and this content cannot be separated from the command without the command ceasing to be the law — the law of *God.* That content is the gospel of God's gracious pardon and comforting address.

---

10. Eberhard Jüngel, "Zum Verhältnis von Kirche und Staat nach Karl Barth," *Zeitschrift für Theologie und Kirche* 6 (1986): 103.

11. Karl Barth, *Evangelium und Gesetz,* p. 5; ET: "Gospel and Law," p. 73.

12. Karl Barth, *Evangelium und Gesetz,* p. 11; ET: "Gospel and Law," p. 80.

13. Karl Barth, *Für die Freiheit des Evangeliums* (*Theologische Existenz heute!* 2) (Munich, 1933), p. 11.

14. Karl Barth, *Nein! Antwort an Emil Brunner* (*Theologische Existenz heute!* 14) (Munich, 1934), p. 25; ET: *Natural Theology* (London, 1946 [with Brunner's article]), p. 88.

The command of God is always a command that is already filled and thus cannot be filled arbitrarily by us — it is filled by the gospel. Just as the sense of the Ten Commandments lies in the fact that God first speaks of all that he has done for the people, God's command always issues forth in connection with his beneficence toward those whom he commands. The "form" of his law thus *conforms* to the gospel, for it aims at conformity with the kindly will of God toward his own. "Man is determined only to be the partner of the gracious God. . . . He must be the one to whom God is gracious and think and speak and act as such." God's grace "determines his action to correspondence, conformity . . . with God's action. . . . What are we to do? We are to do what corresponds to this grace" (II/2 639f. = 575-576).

Barth, therefore, rejects any "works righteousness." If the human's *response* to the grace of God turned toward her is demanded of her, how could she then earn this grace or its validity by first of all fulfilling some condition? Yet Barth's rejection of works righteousness has an accent of its own. Already in 1922 he could say that "grace . . . means neither that men can and ought to do something, nor that they can and ought to do nothing. Grace means that God does something," to be sure, not "everything" but "something quite definite." He could say, too, that "grace is sufficient, even for ethics!"[15] What is wrong about works righteousness is not the fact that the human *does* something, so that in her passivity she would be in concordance with the grace of God. The wrong thing is that human action stands in contradiction to grace, competes with it rather than conforms to it. Thus, even humans themselves negate works righteousness when they say "yes" to grace, and *thereby do* what accords with that grace.

Barth thus advances a qualified definition of good and evil. Active affirmation of grace is good, and active negation of grace is evil. Thus, unrighteous people are not the most difficult ethical problem, but those self-righteous who allege that they are doing "good." For Barth, the very *core* of sin is hostility to grace. It is unbelief as "the original form and source of all sins" (IV/1 460 = 414). It is hostility to grace in the twofold form of pride and sloth. In *pride* the human presumes to do what only God can do and does (IV/1 458ff. = 413ff.). We thus contradict the *gospel* of God, which tells us that we can live only by what God in his grace does for us. Rather than being content with that, the human (who cannot do what God does) replaces this gracious God with another, a graceless, "legalistic" God, through whom the human imagines that he lives on the basis of his performance, on what he must

---

15. Karl Barth, *Der Römerbrief,* 2nd ed. (Munich, 1922; 12th ed., 1978), pp. 196, 423; ET: *The Epistle to the Romans* (Oxford, 1933), pp. 215, 437.

produce, and on his graciousness to himself. In so doing his actions are graceless, not only ungodly but also inhuman. In trying to do what she neither can do nor should do, she does not do what she both may and should. This is the sin of *sloth* (IV/2 452ff. = 403ff.). In this sin, the human contradicts the *law* of God that conforms to the gospel, the law in which God permits and empowers and commands her to do what she can now do because of the grace that has happened to her and which is her only possible action: the active presentation of her grateful response to that grace. Instead of acknowledging the claim of God that we should confess him as those who belong to him, we resist that claim as those who have not received the blessing of grace, those left to their own devices, people whose actions are defined by their "withdrawal into ourselves," who lag behind themselves and what God has graciously made possible for them (IV/1 475 = 407). To do this is also to contend against God's grace.

How can the law of God move us toward conformity with the gospel? It does so as the "form" of the gospel, that is, as the form fashioned and shaped by the gospel.[16] This form corresponds to the gospel and does so in that in accordance with the gospel it is fulfilled *in and of itself,* is essentially *fulfilled* law. It is fulfilled as Barth sees it in a twofold way, in keeping with the twofold covenant of grace.

First, through the action of the gracious God: "God has first bound Himself to man" (II/2 821 = 735), who thus *claims himself* for man and "makes Himself responsible for man" (II/2 567 = 511). His law then encounters us, not as an abstract decree but as the law followed and fulfilled by him in his own action. It is the law that decides so fundamentally what is good and what is evil that we no longer have to make this decision. It is the law in which those at whom it is directed from the outset are treated as his possession because he makes himself responsible for them. "The proposition: 'There is a command of God,' is quite inadequate as a description of what concerns us. . . . What 'there is' is not as such the command of God. . . . the core of the matter is that *God* gives His command. . . . We cannot emphasize too strongly the fact that . . . by the sanctifying *command* of God . . . we have to understand a divine *action*" (II/2 608f. = 548). God's command is not an abstract demand placed by a placid God upon the human who is also placid and who only occasionally emerges from his placidity to ask about what is now commanded. For "God exists in His act," so much so that "alone in His act He is who He is" (II/1 305 = 272). God *is* gracious and righteous and free as he *acts* graciously, righteously, and freely. His grace as the *content* of his will al-

---

16. Karl Barth, *Evangelium und Gesetz,* p. 11; ET: "Gospel and Law," p. 80.

ways takes the *form* of his *acts* of grace toward us. The command of God as the *form* of his gospel is in the first instance the praxis of God (II/2 609-548), and thus necessarily the form with this *content*. The command of God does not speak abstractly about a praxis demanded of us; it speaks first of all of the praxis of God which precedes all our praxis. It encounters us only as the command that God for his part has actively fulfilled. It is "given" to us only in God's own fulfillment of his command. The command, then, is not alien to God's grace, but is the form of his grace.

Second, the command was also fulfilled on the *human* side — by the one who took *our place*. Precisely there where we are disobedient to God, he accepted God's No to our disobedience, and he was *obedient* to God "unto death, even death on a cross" (Phil. 2:8). "It is precisely this God who has authority for Jesus. . . . It is to Him that He is obedient. It is not a matter of any kind of subjection to a power of fate, nor of any kind of subordination to a self-imposed rule. It is a matter of the obedience of the One who is received and accepted by God in free grace, and who for that very reason is terrified to the depths at the majesty of God and placed completely at His disposal. It is a matter of the obedience of the free man to the free God. And for that very reason it is a matter of real obedience" (II/2 623 = 561). God "is the God who has summoned man by Himself becoming man and as such not only demanding obedience but rendering it: He has spoken of the good by *doing* it . . . by *delivering* Himself up for us" (II/2 627 = 565).

The decisive act of the obedience of Jesus is found by Barth in his *prayers,* for these show that his obedience is accountable and free, not blind or slavish, and because in his own response to God, in this humanly conducted interaction with God the covenant is concluded on the human side (II/2 134 = 125-126). In that Jesus renders this obedience *in our place,* the law of God *is fulfilled in our place.* The law, *fulfilled* not only by the praxis of God but also by corresponding human praxis, now meets *us* as the command of the gracious God, "the law of the Spirit of life" (Rom. 8:2; II/2 643 = 579).

The law is fulfilled, according to Barth, not only *by* the gospel but also *as* law. It is *formed* so much by the gospel that it encounters us only as a law that has been already *graciously fulfilled.* The only thing we can do is to confirm its fulfillment in that we let ourselves be told, "*Be* what you *are!*" We can now see why Barth concludes that to separate the law from its fulfillment is to make of it the *mere* form of a demand. It then becomes an ideal that the human must fulfill because it has not been fulfilled in itself. We are then "*misusing*" the law[17] whether it is observed or regarded as unfulfillable. We are

---

17. Karl Barth, *Evangelium und Gesetz,* p. 17; ET: "Gospel and Law," p. 85.

obeying someone else and not God — "A law apart from the gospel hopelessly enmires us to the service of both God and mammon."[18] Here sin produces its "master stroke."[19] For the true problem of sin is not the transgression of "laws," so that it would be erased with the observance of such laws. Again, the true problem of sin is self-righteousness. This consists of the idea that the command of God is a law that *we* must first fulfill, while *in itself* it is unfulfilled and graceless. For Barth self-righteousness is not just the confidence that we can keep the law; it is also the hopelessness of not being able to keep it. When, however, we accept the law as one that has been fulfilled, we also accept the claim of God that our "action should become and be always that of those who accept God's action as right" (II/2 638 = 575). "When Israel does keep the commandments of God, . . . it will necessarily appreciate that the knowledge and experience that He is its salvation and righteousness . . . are God's free grace" (IV/1 25 = 26). The fact that the gospel has the "form" of the law does not mean that we must do "something" to make the gospel apply to us. It means that the gospel encounters us, that it lays claim on us as the possession of God that we already are, so that we may correspond to that responsibly.

Responsibility

"It is as He makes Himself responsible for man that God makes man, too, responsible" (II/2 567 = 511), and "constitutes this 'being responsible' the whole meaning of his existence" (II/2 11 = 12). Hence the command of God cannot encounter us without already being fulfilled for us, instead of our first having to fulfill it. Nor can the grace of God encounter us without claiming us for the God who claims us for himself. Hence we have to reject the "Lutheran" view that the grace of God could be reduced to the forgiveness of sins whereas the law leaves us to ourselves anew, subjecting us to the worldly "ordinances," or, in today's terms, to the "competence of experts." The grace of the command of God lies in the fact that "it is simply not true" that the human person "is thrown back on himself. He belongs to the Head, Jesus Christ, of whose body he is or is to become a member, the Lord of the Church who is also the Lord of the cosmos, and therefore the Lord of those who so far do not believe in Him, or do so no longer" (II/2 599 = 539). Through the God who lays claim graciously upon himself for the human, she

18. Karl Barth, *Fürchte dich nicht!* p. 97.
19. Karl Barth, *Evangelium und Gesetz*, p. 17; ET: "Gospel and Law," p. 85.

is so claimed that that claim precedes all her faith. Faith, then, cannot be mere receptive passivity. In faith the human is *addressed* by the God who lays claim upon himself for her in such a way that this God finds an answer in her. God makes her responsible, answerable.

In making the human responsible, God summons him into a specific correspondence to God — his "being is in act." "It is as he acts that man exists as a person" (II/2 572 = 516). "What we do, we are. It is not as if man first exists and then acts. He exists in that he acts" (I/2 887 = 793). We are close here to the existentialism of Sartre, who said: "I am my deed."[20] The difference is that here the human is elected to freedom of action, and not condemned. Another difference also becomes clear here. Whereas "Luther's understanding of the gospel requires human passivity and receptivity . . . Barth's anthropology has an entirely different orientation. The human is understood by definition to be constituted by action and self-determination." This anthropology "permits the gospel to be transformed immediately into the form of law which demands human action."[21] One might ask, of course, whether the difference from Luther is so great, for in his own way Barth accepted the basic proposition of Luther that the person makes the works, not the works the person. The person, however, does not constitute one's own self. The grace of God constitutes it as God thinks us worthy of fellowship with himself.

Since the grace of God carries with it God's laying of a claim upon himself for us, his grace toward *us* also includes his claim upon *our* action in which we exist. The communication of grace does not abrogate God's law, as Luther seems to say, but rather truly reveals it. Yet Barth can say this only by setting aside Luther's presupposition that the law consists of the abstract demand, "Thou shalt," without asking whether the human can do what he ought to do, without giving to him that which he needs in order to do what is commanded. This graceless command is not the law of God for Barth. The law of God is always a graciously filled form, and never grace-less. As God graciously lays claim upon himself for the human, and therewith fulfills the command he lays upon us, his command always encounters us as a fulfilled command. It does not say to us that we must fulfill a law otherwise not fulfilled. It tells us that we should *join ourselves* responsibly, answerably, to this already fulfilled command. Once again, the command of God is not regarded as an ideal that the human "must put into practice" and thus actualize. In this case she would be left to her own devices, and constantly subject

---

20. Cf. Eberhard Jüngel, *Barth-Studien* (Zurich, Cologne, and Gütersloh, 1982), p. 203; ET: *Karl Barth: A Theological Legacy* (Philadelphia, 1986), p. 122.

21. Eberhard Jüngel, *Barth-Studien*, p. 205; ET: *A Theological Legacy*, pp. 123-124.

to excessive demands. God's law places her, rather, in a *reality* that is already opened up, in which she now is to stand and to abide, to use Johannine language. Her action can only be discipleship, following *after* Jesus.

Since the law of God is formed by the gospel of grace, it has itself a gracious *character*. The action that follows it receives the character of a free permission not a forced coercion, of a self-determination corresponding to divine praxis, not a subjection to an alien control. Paul indeed speaks of the frightful character of the law of death that kindles wrath (Rom. 8:2; 4:15), but, according to Barth, he is not speaking, as Lutheran tradition holds, of the legitimate *"use"* of the law for which God gives us his law, but he is speaking of the wicked *misuse* of God's law for *self*-righteousness.[22] The gospel of the forgiveness of sins does not regard such misuse as good, but removes it, but not the law itself. The law that is not misused, the law that God institutes in his gospel for its divinely ordained use, that law that claims us for the responsive affirmation of the gospel and thus to conformity with it, that law is, instead, given to us for life (Rom. 7:6; 8:2). It is good (Rom. 7:12).

Of this good law, which is not "legalistically" misused, we may then say:

> The form by which the command of God is distinguished from all other commands . . . consists in the fact that it is *permission* — the *granting* of a very definite *freedom*. . . . [Other commands] all mean that at some point man is interrupted and even jostled; that at some point — and worst of all when he begins to command himself — he is vexed and tormented. In one form or another they all express to man the suspicion that it might be dangerous to free him, that he would certainly misuse his liberty. . . . From the most varied angles they fill him with anxious fears. . . . They use these fears to appeal to him, instilling them into him and holding him in their grip. In essence, their bidding is a forbidding; the refusal of all possible permissions. . . . The command of God sets man free. The command of God permits. It is only in this way that it commands. It permits even though it . . . *in concreto* . . . says, 'Thou shalt' and 'Thou shalt not.' . . . The command of God and other commands do the same thing, but it is not really the same. . . . It will not compel man, but burst open the door of the compulsion under which he has been living. It will not meet him with mistrust but with trust. It will not appeal to his fear but to his courage. It will instill courage, and not fear into him. This is the case because the command . . . is itself the form of the grace of God . . . the *easy* yoke and

---

22. Karl Barth, *Evangelium und Gesetz*, pp. 15, 18; ET: "Gospel and Law," p. 85.

the *light* burden of Christ . . . the assumption of which is in every sense our *quickening* and refreshing. This is what God prepares for us when He gives us His command. (I/2 650f. = 585-586)

The "man who is not refreshed [under God's command] is not the obedient man but the man who disobeys God" (I/2 651 = 586).

Barth's ethics is therefore in its material execution an ethics of *freedom*. His *ethics of creation* puts the *Sabbath* commandment first, with his invitation not to "doing nothing," but to "non-doing" because he thinks that one cannot understand the commandment "before we have understood the holy day" and observed it (III/4 54f. = 51). This commandment "points him away from everything that he himself can will and achieve and back to what God is for him and will do for him." "The aim of the Sabbath commandment is that man shall give and allow the omnipotent grace of God to have the first and the last word at every point" of his activity. It frees man from the compulsion of trying "to live by the Yes that he can say to himself or to others or to the cosmos." This does not hinder but frees him to say an "active yes" to himself and to others in his work. This happens in such a way that his action receives the character of such a freedom, so that his "*ability* to work is not his attainment and therefore his own property, but a free gift . . . his *obligation* to work is not his invention but God's commission" (III/4 58f. = 53-54).

Barth's ethics of reconciliation should stand on the basic concept of the "invocation of the gracious God" (CL 67f. = 43-44). The point is that prayer, modeled on the prayer of Jesus, is the primal *act* in which humans demonstrate their *accountability*. This does not mean our emancipation from God, but rather the freedom of fellowship, the liberty of the *children of God* (CL 113ff. = 71-73). All further action, now both possible and expected, is defined as activity that does not forsake the grace of God in order to transition into its own work, but rather relies upon that grace and responds to it — just as, conversely, through this grace "man is not run down and overpowered, but set on his own feet" (IV/4 25 = 22).

The "should" of God's command is a *"may."* Yet Barth also says that conversely a true "may" is a *"should."* Does this then restrict or even retract that free "may"? What we find here is an exact analogy to the relationship between freedom and fellowship according to which freedom is self-determination for coexistence. Just as Barth distanced himself there from the freedom that means individual independence, he does here from the distortion of "may" into the human caprice that assumes that one may allow *oneself* anything at all. Such caprice conflicts with the command of God, "not because it does not wish man to be really free . . . but . . . because God does want this, because he cannot really be free . . . in his self-will" and can end up under the slavish law of a "strange lord and tyrant." The law of God "is against us only in so far as we are against ourselves" (II/2 66of. = 594-95). Caprice is present when freedom detaches itself from relationships, especially the relationship to God, in which freedom can be truly freedom. "May" means "should" to the extent that it holds us firmly to the fact that we are free only in fellowship with God, who for his part graciously maintains fellowship with us. The basis of the fact that "may" means "should" is that with this permission we are in a commitment in which *everything* is permitted to us that *God* permits us in his love.

Barth combines the concepts "may" and "should" — concepts that characterize the actions that follow God's law — in the apparently paradoxical concept of "free obedience." The point is that a forced or blind obedience is no more real obedience than a disobedient freedom would really be freedom (cf. II/1 38f. = 36; III/4 12 = 13-14). What we have here is true freedom, the freedom practiced by "independently active and free subjects" (IV/3 383 = 332). The existence of "a marionette pulled by wires in a group of dependent men who all share the same illusion of independence" is an existence in *sin* (IV/1 517 = 465 rev.). God's grace frees one from that sin in that through grace the human is not "deprived of his accountability but is pronounced and treated as accountable" (IV/4 25 = 22-23 rev.). This freedom, however, is a *gift* to us. We *owe* it to the grace by which God has made himself responsible for us, as the grounds for our own responsibility, and so this freedom consists in the active presentation of thanksgiving for this grace. The human's freedom, then, is his self-activity *in* the relationships that God has instituted, so that he chooses that, only that, which corresponds to what God has chosen both for himself and for him: his self-determination is within God's covenant to which he belongs through God's determination that preceded his self-determination (II/2 192ff. = 175ff.). Hence this *freedom* is free *obedience*.

Just as "may" and "should" characterize the *doing* of what God commands, two concepts characterize the issuing forth of God's command, according to Barth: the *concreteness* and *constancy* of the divine commanding (II/2 737ff. = 661ff.; III/4 5-34 = 6-31; CL 3-9 = 4-7). This terminological doublet corresponds to the knowledge of freedom in fellowship. It is appropriate to the freedom of God that his command always encounters us as a concrete command. The constancy of his commanding is appropriate to the fellowship for which he determines himself. In the first instance, Barth rejects the view that the divine command is a universal statute that one must always follow "literally" whether it fits the situation or not, or when it really does not fit, is made to fit as we use our skills of adjustment. In such cases we would certainly obey a statute, but not by a long way would we be obeying God himself. (For instance, the attempt to assassinate Hitler was obedience to God, whereas the abstract application of the command not to kill to this situation could have been disobedience toward God.)[23] In the second instance, in our concrete following of the command we would in actual fact not be following God but rather our own *interpretation* of what *we* now regard as imperative. In both cases God's command functions as something in our hands, and we know, either in advance or instinctively, what God desires of us. In both cases we stand *in* our actions not really before the God who commands us, but are left to ourselves. The term Barth uses for this view is *casuistry*, and his main objection to it is that the command of God is from the very first a *concrete* command. The living God is always free to determine afresh what is in keeping with his will. Concrete commands must therefore be received each time afresh. We must always ask anew how we are to obey God in each situation. Both the clarification of that and the resulting execution must be an act of obedience toward God, or it would otherwise be an act of autonomy which removes itself from the divine command.

On the other side Barth rejects *decisionism,* that is, the reduction of what is commanded to single isolated acts. He does so in such a way that he also distances himself from the neo-Lutheran doctrine of the orders of creation or of preservation that themselves opposed decisionism. What was meant by these orders were constants such as authority, family, people, and in 1933 race, all of which, it was claimed, were part of creation, even if it were fallen and independent of God's revelation of grace, and which as such allegedly were divine commands to which one was to submit. Barth held that the assertion of such orders was arbitrary; he disputed that such alleged orders could have any kind of command character for us. In this case someone other than the God of revelation would be issuing commands. Barth offers a very different definition of the constancy of the divine commanding, which is in spite of all that must be addressed. This constancy consists of the fact that the command of the God to whom the Bible bears witness, in the concrete form that it assumes, makes certain constant conditions visible in which it is made. These are not orders, but *"relationships."* "It is in these very relationships that his command always finds us and that we will always encounter Him in such and such a way with our conduct" (III/4 23 = 22). For Barth, these relationships are those between God and human, between human and co-human, of the person to himself, and those of the history of God with temporally limited humanity. These relationships are not themselves the command of God; they

---

23. Cf. CD III/4 513 = 449 for the attempt to assassinate Hitler.

are the field on which that command regularly encounters us. They indicate the lines along which the commands of God will flow. Thus, the concrete commands of God, since they are made in these relationships, will be appropriate to the relationships and the fellowship. For that reason, no distinction should be made "between individual and social ethics" (III/4 532 = 464-465)!

Christian Action in the "World"

Since a Christian cannot serve God and mammon, and since basically no other command is binding on her than that of the self-revealing God, Barth asks the question which was already lurking in the context of his discovery of "gospel and law," the question of the relation of the church to the *polis*. With that discovery, he placed himself outside the dominant pattern of the time according to which the church had only to proclaim the simple gospel, while the law was externally enforced by the state, or, more precisely, the "authorities." (This was a term that Barth replaced with "civil community" in 1946, in order to describe the responsibility of all engaged in the public affairs; we shall simply call it *polis*.) Yet if the state as such does not embody the law of God, if God's law is made known only in the context of the revelation of his gospel, what, then, is the relation between the church and the *polis?* Is the church an island isolated from the rest of the world? Can justification be found for a Christian dominion over the *polis?* And are the members of the church in a position to cooperate with those who feel committed to a different law from that of God?

Barth undoubtedly acknowledged the modern secular *polis*. Just as a state that does not limit itself to the tasks of state can "only [become] an idolatrous church," a church that did more than act as a church would result in a "clerical state."[24] In 1935 Barth stated that the Constantinian alliance of church and state, "the *Christian*-bourgeois or *bourgeois*-Christian age has come to an end, . . . that is, Christendom no longer exists in the form we have known. . . . The world is reclaiming . . . its freedom (from the church). . . . But with that, the gospel's freedom over against the world has been restored to it." For the church this did not mean freedom *from* the world, but a " freedom *in* the world" that that alliance had never afforded.[25]

This freedom includes the renunciation of the desire for a "Christian

---

24. Karl Barth, *Rechtfertigung und Recht* (Zollikon, 1938), p. 31; ET: "Church and State," in *Community, State, and Church: Three Essays* (Gloucester, Mass., 1968), p. 132.

25. Karl Barth, *Das Evangelium in der Gegenwart (Theologische Existenz heute!)* 25 (Munich, 1935), pp. 33-34.

state," and as well for a doctrine which claims to be "*the* Christian doctrine of the just state."[26] This renunciation presupposes the renunciation of a churchly claim to be the promised kingdom of God to which it is to testify, a claim that would legitimatize its dominion over the world.[27] The *polis,* the kingdom of the "world," is not the kingdom of God either, yet this kingdom is also promised to it. But that is also "concealed" in it because it is not the church, and because it is the realm of human life together, regardless of what they or if they believe.[28] For the church, precisely if she is not allowed "freedom from the world," this means that its members, in keeping with the hiddenness of the promised kingdom of God in the kingdom of the world, will be known there only by their fruits. They can only be active "anonymously," not displaying their Christian name but showing forth their faith by convincing arguments and actions.[29]

Is there not a contradiction when Barth then says that "this Gospel . . . is political from the very outset"?[30] How can he, in light of all that was just said, then state that "from the belief in God's righteousness there follows logically a very definite political problem and task" (II/1 434 = 386)? What we learn from statements of this kind is that while there is no freedom from the world, there is freedom *in* the world. Notwithstanding the distinction, therefore, a positive relation exists between Christianity and the task of the *polis.* This is not a relation arbitrarily instituted and adjusted by Christians. Nor is it a relation that they can evade. God himself has instituted it. If his kingdom is hidden in the kingdom of the world, then it is present as "its promise in the midst of the chaos of the worldly kingdom." For Jesus Christ is "not just the Lord of the church, but . . . in the form of the claim upon the political order he is also the Lord of the world. The claim upon this order, made to all people, is not based upon a specific secular law but on the law of *God* that is proclaimed in the church and also valid for the world."[31] This means, however,

26. Karl Barth, *Christengemeinde und Bürgergemeinde* (*Theologische Studien* 20) (Stuttgart, 1946), pp. 18-19; ET: "The Christian Community and the Civil Community," in *Community, State, and Church: Three Essays* (Gloucester, Mass., 1968), and *Church and State* (Macon, Ga., 1991), p. 160.

27. Karl Barth, *Christengemeinde und Bürgergemeinde,* pp. 10-11, 15; ET: "Christian Community and Civil Community, pp. 153-54, 157-58.

28. Karl Barth, *Christengemeinde und Bürgergemeinde,* p. 7; ET: "Christian Community and Civil Community," p. 184.

29. Karl Barth, *Christengemeinde und Bürgergemeinde,* p. 48; ET: "Christian Community and Civil Community," p. 184.

30. Karl Barth, *Christengemeinde und Bürgergemeinde,* p. 49; ET: "Christian Community and Civil Community," p. 184.

31. Karl Barth, *Gotteserkenntnis und Gottesdienst* (Zollikon, 1938), p. 205; ET: *The Knowledge of God and the Service of God* (London, 1938), p. 223.

that the *polis* owes its existence to an ordinance of divine *grace*.[32] It corresponds to this grace when it outwardly works and cares for justice, peace, and freedom. Insofar as it does this, "there does exist a service of God in the *world*, a *political* service of God," and according to Romans 13:1 those who administer it are "ministers of God *(leitourgoi)*."[33] This is not due to the political actions of Christians. It is true whether Christians individually participate or not.

Nevertheless, Christians do not do anything that is alien either to their faith in the God who graciously commands or to those who are responsible in the secular *polis*, when they too participate in this political service of God. They should not try to evade this duty on the grounds that it would involve digression from their "proper" task. If they do not want to deny their freedom in the world, they should never restrict their obedience to the command of God to an inner sphere, in order to subject themselves externally to the laws of some other authority. Just as the kingdom of God is hidden in the *polis* but still present, Christians, even when acting "anonymously" in the *polis*, may not suspend the one standard of the command of the God who reigns both here and there. They will "be citizens . . . because they are not merely or primarily or finally citizens . . . because their service of God is not simply to be equated with political service. It only includes the latter" (II/2 808 = 723). It includes it because the goodness of the divine command consists of its determining them for fellowship (II/2 794 = 711). "We recognize the divine command in all times and places, nations and spheres of life, by the fact that it is good in the full sense of the term. For this reason, the divine command cannot be split up even in view of the fact that it concerns both our relationship to God and our relationship to other men, our natural being and our being under grace, our outer life and our inner life, our position in the Church, and our position in the state. It cannot be divided into the Christian command on the one side and natural ordinances on the other. However varied it may be in its concrete content, it is the same in both connections," the good command of the gracious God (II/2 795 = 712).

For what purpose should Christians become involved in their political service of God? Not "for themselves,"[34] nor for the church's issues and its protection. Even in extreme cases when the church has to oppose the state

---

32. Karl Barth, *Christengemeinde und Bürgergemeinde*, pp. 13, 19; ET: "Christian Community and Civil Community," pp. 156, 160-61.

33. Karl Barth, *Gotteserkenntnis und Gottesdienst*, p. 207; ET: *The Knowledge of God and the Service of God*, pp. 222-23.

34. Karl Barth, *Christengemeinde und Bürgergemeinde*, p. 25; ET: "Christian Community and Civil Community," p. 165.

because in totalitarian fashion the state threatens to take away its freedom, it must carry out its opposition for the sake of the just *state* that is not to be permitted to become totalitarian. The church becomes involved here for the "righteousness of the state," that it might correspond in *human* fashion to the kingdom of God that the church proclaims.[35]

Two things are involved. (1) In keeping with the freedom of God's command, the church will always become involved for something specifically *concrete*. The command of God is not to be confused with principles. The church "owes allegiance not to some natural law but to its living Lord. It must never think or speak or act according to 'principles.' ... It will therefore reject all systematizing of political history and of its participation in it. It will protect its freedom to evaluate new phenomena in new ways. Yesterday it might have rolled along these rails, but it is not committed to rolling along the same rails today."[36]

(2) In keeping with the constancy of God's command, there are certain "lines" that the church must follow[37] when it becomes involved in something concrete in the *polis*. The basic line may be summed up in the slogan: "freedom in fellowship." The issue here is the church's engagement so that the state might serve "the general welfare ... on the basis of freedom."[38] For this, democracy is appropriate, but it should be a democracy that consists of more than replacing the rule of the few with the rule of the "people"; it is, rather, where "the law and the duty of fellowship and freedom" rule.[39] Accordingly, *causes* are not to dominate over humans here. When the human serves things rather than they serve him, he quickly becomes someone governed by bureaucracy and the media, as well as economically exploited.[40] The true needs of life yield to artificially originated desires for more things we do not need, and the ground is cut from under humane existence (III/4 616f. = 538). In the *polis* Christians must resolutely follow the line that "man is the measure of all things (!)."[41] In keeping with this, Christians must act to resist the power

---

35. Karl Barth, *Christengemeinde und Bürgergemeinde,* p. 29; ET: "Christian Community and Civil Community," p. 169 rev.

36. Karl Barth, *Offene Briefe 1945-1968* (Zurich, 1984), p. 159.

37. Karl Barth, *Christengemeinde und Bürgergemeinde,* p. 22; ET: "Christian Community and Civil Community," p. 163.

38. Karl Barth, *Texte zur Barmer Theologischen Erklärung* (Zurich, 1984), p. 300.

39. Karl Barth, *Eine Schweizer Stimme: 1938-1945* (Zollikon-Zurich, 1945), p. 165.

40. Karl Barth, *Christengemeinde und Bürgergemeinde,* pp. 32-33; ET: "Christian Community and Civil Community," pp. 171-72.

41. Karl Barth, *Christengemeinde und Bürgergemeinde,* p. 33; ET: "Christian Community and Civil Community," p. 172.

exercised by humans over humans that robs them of freedom and pushes them onto the margin of society. Following Christ's *solidarity* with the lost — "casting all false impartiality aside"[42] — Christians must "look downward" upon the socially and economically weak. They must "summon the world to reflect on social injustice . . . and to alter the conditions and relationships in question" (IV/3 1023 = 892).

How is the church to become involved in this way? For Barth this was not a specifically ethical question, but about its entire orientation to God. "The Church would not be the Church if, in her very existence . . . the Law of God, its commands, its questions, its admonitions and its accusations would not become visible and apprehensible also for the world, for state and society."[43] Only the church that *is* indeed the church can do what is right in its relations with the *polis*. In Barth's eyes its action will then be twofold.

The first and *critical* form corresponds to the freedom of the divine command and consists of the church's "prophetic office of watchman." The church itself, or some of its members, with a clear appeal to God and thus not anonymously, gives courageous witness in a current political question. It does so not as a lobby for the church, but to press the state to be a *just* state in this matter. Such witness is not ongoing, but is rendered "from case to case."[44] It presupposes that the church, in its commitment to its living Commander, must be prepared to assess the constantly changing situation anew. Essential to the office of a watchman is that it should not promote the religious exaggeration of something about which most people are in agreement. It speaks because the rest are silent, knowing that silence is in this instance sin. For that reason it is essentially a critical witness with which Christians "swim against the stream."[45]

"Positive cooperation" is the second form of the political service of God.[46] It corresponds to the constancy and the fellowship-relatedness of the divine command. Christians in this instance do not oppose the *polis*, but are directly within it. In this situation, they do *not* appeal directly to the standard of their own action, but can only act by applying the consequences of what they know from their standard, ". . . only . . . in the form of decisions which could be the decisions of any other citizens . . . regardless of their religious

42. Karl Barth, *Christengemeinde und Bürgergemeinde*, p. 34; ET: "Christian Community and Civil Community," p. 173.

43. Karl Barth, *Evangelium und Gesetz*, p. 11; ET: "Gospel and Law," p. 79.

44. Karl Barth, *Offene Briefe*, p. 159.

45. Often used by Barth; cf. Karl Barth, *Predigten 1913* (Zurich, 1976), p. 595.

46. Karl Barth, *Gotteserkenntnis und Gottesdienst*, p. 212; ET: *The Knowledge of God and the Service of God*, p. 228.

profession."[47] Sharing a common life with non-Christians, they have to demonstrate that their freedom in the world does not mean freedom from it but allows them a capacity for fellowship with others. Precisely because God is not absent there, which they believe, no other standard is possible for them in their cooperation in the *polis* than the commands of God. That same standard allows them, therefore, even if their appeal to it must remain silent, to act with others in genuine cooperation and to enter into coalitions whose purpose is to seek "what is best for the civil community."[48] They have this "freedom in the world" which is in accordance with the gospel and with the gracious command of God enclosed within it.

47. Karl Barth, *Christengemeinde und Bürgergemeinde,* p. 49; ET: "Christian Community and Civil Community," p. 184.

48. Karl Barth, *Christengemeinde und Bürgergemeinde,* p. 53; ET: "Christian Community and Civil Community," p. 187.

The Good Creation — Its Basis and Preservation

The Peril of Thinking of the Creation as Godless

Kornelis Heiko Miskotte[1] found the greatness of Barth's doctrine of creation in its assertion that we first recognize that creation is a work of *God* only as we apprehend it to be an irrevocably *good* reality. Barth does indeed say: "We are not free to think and speak in this matter otherwise or even uncertainly and equivocally. . . . The Christian apprehension of creation . . . shows us God's good-pleasure as the root, the foundation and the end of divine creation. . . . Creation, as it is known by the Christian, is benefit" (III/1 379 = 331-32). That gives us pause. Was not Barth well known as one who fought against "natural theology"? Did that not mean that his own theology would have a broken relationship to the article about creation? Has he not been called a new Marcion,[2] one for whom the God of creation seemed to be an Anti-God in the light of the Redeemer? And now, a thoughtful song of praise to the Creator from one who was not forgetting his "No" to "natural theology," but who instead thought that this theology was not even capable of such a song of praise!

We pause again when we remember that Barth was writing this from 1942 onward, precisely as the naked horror of war was happening. Was his theology that far removed from earthly distress if in *that* situation he could

---

1. Kornelis Heiko Miskotte, *Über Barths Kirchliche Dogmatik* (*Theologische Existenz heute!* n.s. 89) (Munich, 1961): 141.

2. Adolf Jülicher, "Ein moderner Paulusausleger," in *Anfänge der dialektischen Theologie*, ed. Jürgen Moltmann, part 1: *Karl Barth, Heinrich Barth, Emil Brunner* (Munich, 1962), p. 94.

praise the irrevocable goodness of the God of creation? Barth certainly perceived those terrors and was deeply shaken by them. He spoke of God's goodness like the prophet who extolled the unceasing "good works of the Lord" while gazing upon "the ruins of Jerusalem":[3] "Its inhabitants are killed or deported. . . . The temple of God lies in ruins, and God himself has become an alien and an enemy to the people of Israel and to the prophets. How close to us" is this — we are confronted by untold ruins, including that "of the Christianity as we have known and preached and applied it until now. And it is an incomprehensible and dark face that we perceive today at the place where we have been used to looking at what we regarded as God." In speaking of the ruin of *Christianity,* what Barth has to say theologically about creation cannot be unaffected. There is need for real wrestling if we are to find again the face *of God* behind the picture of him "whom we regarded as God." Is not the face of God, which is now to be rediscovered, the "Yes of God the Creator" that alone is able to bring light into an encompassing darkness? We cannot overlook the great amount of destruction. "The human encounter with nothingness has taken place in our day in an extraordinary way." "Whoever is ignorant of the shock . . . is surely incapable of thinking and speaking as a modern man and unable to make himself understood by his contemporaries" (III/3 397 = 345).

In the ocean of suffering[4] and killing how are we to rediscover the face of the Creator and his goodness? Barth believed that the senseless events since 1933 were simply "the bad fruit" produced by an old and "bad tree" (III/1 476 = 414). It is thus understandable that in the process of his attempt to rediscover the Creator's Yes, he grapples with modern thought more tenaciously than with any other theme in his work, defining line by line that bad tree that produced such wicked fruit. He looked back upon a fateful path in the history of thought, that had been followed since the 17th century.

This path began with the view that we know God in creation in a way more generally valid than in his historical revelation of grace, and thus in a way normative for it. The result is that God is not only known via another *way,* but is known as *another* God:[5] not the God who graciously links himself to humans but a God who, over against the world, exists abstractly *for himself.* This God does not have to turn in grace toward the human, for humans can know him without his gracious turning, since the human is also one who exists for himself and is thus all too similar to God. For the self-existing and

3. Karl Barth, sermon on Lam. 3:21 (1944); *Fürchte dich nicht!* (Munich, 1949), p. 280.

4. Barth, *Fürchte dich nicht!* p. 277.

5. Cf. the discussion of Descartes, CD III/2 401-415 = 350-363.

relationless human person, God is not the *Opposite* who establishes a relationship with her, but a *conceptual thing* already present. Yes, the God who is thought of as non-related does in fact *have* no relationship with the world. It functions in such a way "ut ne a Deo quidem mutari queat" [= that it cannot even be changed by God].[6] Thus, "nature" as the medium now in which we know God, is imagined with neither "grace" nor relationship. The eighteenth century thought of the world as a machine, which in the nineteenth century produced a gigantic world of machines (III/1 466 = 405) that treats "nature" as an object of humans. It does so with a *science* that either never asks (cf. II/2 733 = 657-658) whether what can be made should be made, or understands everything makeable as the ethically desirable. It is all accompanied by a "fever of work" that "is a symptom of the approaching and gigantic ruin of at least a stage of civilization. There is at least a possibility that it cannot continue very much longer" (III/4 638 = 556).

> We can, we will, we do achieve much, constantly more, but to a large extent the wheels are secretly turning in vain because we desire and use a power which we do not basically need at all and which in some respects it would be better if we had never even known, far less wanted and unleashed. The technical mastery which goes beyond what is vitally necessary, which at bottom has its meaning and purpose in itself, and which in order to exist and augment itself, must always evoke new and doubtful needs, inevitably becomes the monster which in many ways we now see it to be, so that finally and ridiculously it is little more than a technique of disorder and destruction, of war and annihilation. Nevertheless, man should not accuse technical skill of being "soulless"; he should accuse himself and his irrational will for power. He himself is the problem of modern technical skill. (III/4 451 = 395 rev.)

He is this as he *makes* creation into a "world" that is *conceived* of without God, and *managed* without God. It is the world of *things,* of the Non-Self,[7] which is there in order that the self should understand it as part of itself. Nature is the mass of manageable things that is accessible to human grasp. The human can either grasp it to himself or reject it, either treat it as valuable or destroy it. This is what Barth finds in Schopenhauer (III/1 383ff. = 335-37). Schopenhauer thought that it is the most direct act of freedom to af-

---

6. H. Grotius according to Ernst Wolf, *Grosse Rechtsdenker der deutschen Geistesgeschichte: Ein Entwicklungsbild unser Rechtsanschauung* (Tübingen, 1939), p. 247.

7. This is how Barth understands J. G. Fichte, CD III/2 113-128 = 96-109.

firm the return to nothing of what is nothing anyway, and to extol *this* as redemption. "It is obviously no great gain to man that . . . he has usurped the place of God" (III/1 388 = 339). Schopenhauer is followed by Nietzsche with his "humanity without the fellow man" (III/2 276-290 = 231-242). The human becomes here boundary-less, ruthless, leaving good and evil behind, incapable of bearing with weakness, the superman who steps over the poor and lowly and who is the inhuman brute. Darwinism, too, fits in here (III/2 92ff. = 79ff.). The problem with Darwinism is not that it sees the relation between humans and animals, but that it defines humanity in terms of the animal. Losing their distinction from the animals, humans also lose the capacity for a genuine *relation* to the environment, for they seek their humanity in the exercising of instinctive drives. "Today we are reaping the evil fruits" of this world-view. "To try to deny man his humanity, and to understand him as the expression of a universal dynamic, was to do something which could only avenge itself, and has done so" (III/4 98 = 84).

These thinkers did not conjure up chaos. They are simply the interpreters of modern society. At the beginning of this aberration Barth discerns a fault on the part of Christian theology. The "double bookkeeping" of the older theology was one of the "historical causes." Certainly this theology spoke about God's covenant of grace with humanity in Christ with regard to the complex of sin and forgiveness. Nevertheless, in broad areas — in the doctrines of the state and of creation — this theology could not say much at all. For these themes, it opened up other books, and its discourse, even when speaking about God, ignored the God who relates himself to us in grace. The "sun of the Enlightenment ruthlessly exposed what must always come to light sooner or later when the double system is used. . . . No man can serve two masters. And if we once serve another master alongside Christ, as will always be the effect of this procedure, we must not be surprised to see bad fruit growing on the bad tree" (III/1 476 = 414).

To summarize the steps in this entire path: first the interpretation of the covenant of grace in terms of the creation, and then creation without reference to this covenant, and ultimately without any reference at all to God; the understanding of "nature" as humanity's mass of manageable things and then its negatability by humans; the understanding of the human person without reference to the fellow person and then in terms of the animal — this entire pathway began, for Barth, in a *theology* that thought of God without the human and the world, saw him in relation to creation as one not essentially connected to it. A theology that thought along these lines shared responsibility for this path, and had to watch helplessly as it then unfolded one step after another, and even had to affirm its progress because of that well-practiced "double bookkeeping." We can thus see why Barth thought it a "very serious and responsible undertaking" (III/2 282 = 236) to break away from this wrong path.

One's only option, he thinks, is to oppose this wrong path from *the very start*. Criticism must be directed against the theology that culpably opened up this path with its system of "double bookkeeping" and its factual assertion of a *worldless* God. "The pressure exerted by worldly science on theology would have been more bearable later on, if earlier on it had submitted more energetically and effectively to the pressure from its own science of God (which it solemnly emphasized in theory)" (III/1 5 = 6 rev.). It was a matter of "pressure" because it is not the existence of God that is at stake when humans portray themselves as godless, but the existence of the human, when one's theology conceives of God as both separated from and surrendered to the human. Barth locates his theology of creation in the context of what he took to be the main theological task during the war years: "The confession of the sole dominion of Jesus Christ in the church" had now "to be continued and completed as confession of the sole dominion of Jesus Christ in the world."[8] Only along these lines could theology find itself able to resist the *other* error, "natural theology." Natural theology thinks of God and his revelation and grace in terms of the "world," and the outcome is that natural theology does not really think of God and his revelation and grace, but of a godless, graceless, and inhuman world. In contrast, the theological doctrine of creation must insist that "in faith in God's particular revelation man sees God before he sees the general history of creation," the "history of nature" (III/3, 51 = 44; III/1 172 = 154).

The Covenant God as Creator

Certainly the issue in the doctrine of creation is not to fabricate a new picture of God based on the boundaries drawn against these two errors. It is an illusion to think that by concocting a new view of creation and of the way *we* can move from a badly to a well-treated nature, theology could defeat that fateful development! The idea of a worldless God and a godless world is to be disputed because it *has* already been disputed — through the Word of God testified in Scripture. In that light we can really see that the two paths are *wrong* pathways. The problems that they cause simply act as a spur to listen anew to the Word of God testified in Scripture. When we do this, we can *discover* that

---

8. Karl Barth, *Eine Schweizer Stimme: 1938-1945* (Zollikon-Zurich, 1945), p. 6.

the *reality* of God's creation, which our thinking did not devise, contradicts the view that holds sway along those two paths. For this reason Barth's doctrine of creation consists primarily of an exposition of Genesis 1 and 2.

The content of the Word of God focuses on the covenant by which God relates himself to his (fallen) creature, in order thereby to relate that creature to himself. This comprises the dual emphasis, which for Barth grounds the reality and the goodness of creation, that God is not a worldless God, and thus his creation is not a godless world. To know this, we must understand the following:

1. We have to know *God* in order to recognize him as the *Creator.* Indeed, we must learn first from his revelation that he is the God of this *covenant,* and we cannot learn that from the creation viewed in distinction from the revelation of the covenant.

2. Because God defines *himself* in his revelation, he is never another God. Even though he acts differently in creation, he is still *the same God* who wills to bind himself to the creature and the creature to himself.

Here, then, we have the twofold principle that permeates Barth's doctrine of creation. "The history of God's covenant with man which has its beginning, its center and its culmination in Jesus Christ . . . is as much the goal of creation as creation itself is the beginning of this history" (III/1 44 = 42). Creation is "the *external* basis of the covenant" (III/1 107 = 97), and the covenant is "the *internal* basis of creation" (III/1 261 = 231). The first statement *distinguishes* between creation and the covenant and says that creation can be understood only in terms of the covenant. According to the second statement creation is "a specific work, or a special element in the one divine work, in which, by reason of His own inner will and determination, God turns outward" (III/1 44 = 42). We must *not,* therefore, *separate* creation and the covenant.

That the covenant presupposes the creation as its *external* basis is what Barth calls a *formal* presupposition of the covenant. That the creation presupposes the covenant as its *internal* basis is what he calls the *material* presupposition of the creation (III/1 262 = 232). We are reminded here of Barth's thesis that the law is the form of the gospel and the gospel is the content of the law.[9] As the law is not a "form" that can be randomly filled, but rather the law *of God* only as the form of the *gospel,* creation is not a neutral thing that can be randomly defined. As *God's* creation, it must be understood solely in terms of the *covenant.* Just as the gospel materially precedes the law and thus gives the law a form that conforms to the gospel, the covenant materially

9. Cf. ch. 5 above.

precedes the creation and defines it as a beneficial act. If the law is terribly abused when it is abstracted from the gospel, similarly a dreadful abuse of the good creation happens when it is put in the hands of sinners instead of in the hands of the God who in love binds himself to the creature. As God in the reconciling work of Christ protects his good law against misuse with his gospel, so he does his creation by the very same event.

The point of the statement that creation is the external basis of the covenant is to make the *distinction* between creation and the covenant. The belief of Israel in the covenant God *subsequently* caused it to confess God the Creator. We, too, can recognize in creation the work of the Creator *only* if we know God *first* as the one who binds himself to us by fulfilling the covenant in Christ. *For this reason* Barth says that creation is *merely the form* of the covenant of grace. "Creation provides the *space* for the story of the covenant of grace. This story requires a space corresponding to it: the existence of man and his world. Creation provides this" (III/1 46 = 44 rev.). The purpose and meaning of creation "is to make possible the history of God's covenant with man" (III/1, 44 = 42).

This *formal* definition of creation upholds the irreversible distinction that we can know creation as the work of the covenant God and his goodness only when we already know God's love from the revelation of his gracious covenant, and not from creation viewed in isolation from it. The formal definition keeps us aware of the recognition that God created the creature purely *in order that* he might love it and cause it to be loved by him, so that it might then love him for its part. The meaning of creaturely existence becomes clear only as the covenant unfolds, to be the provision of the external presupposition *for it*. This presupposition is not a condition *brought by* humans, which would provide God reason to love them. It was created by God alone, so that he might love them. *God himself* presupposes the creature for his covenant. He guarantees the reality of its existence, something that the creature could neither set aside nor maintain — as with covenant itself.

The statement that the covenant is the internal basis of creation denotes the *interrelationship* of the covenant and creation. As the first statement guards against natural theology, the second guards against a "double bookkeeping" between the reality that God has filled and a godless and graceless secular autonomy. It tells us that since the covenant is the internal basis of creation, *the same God* is at work in creation as is active in the covenant with Israel fulfilled in Christ. It says further that as God presupposes the existence of the creature, he *is* its *precedent;* he precedes it as the covenant God who has determined the creature to be his partner. There is no neutral existence, no randomly manipulable existence. For the *love* of God for the creature *precedes* its existence. It cannot enter into existence without being loved. *On this ground* a decision has already been made that it is *good* for the creature to exist.

It is not the case, as some more recent criticism alleges based on an abstract reading of Barth's first proposition, that Barth himself had made concessions to that "double bookkeeping." According to these critiques, creation is viewed as an empty space in which the filling of the reality of the divine covenant of love could be lacking, or which might be accessible to very different fillings, perhaps through arbitrary human dispositions. As the "formal" presupposition of the covenant, creation must con-form to it to such an extent that it is inseparable from this filling. "The fact that the covenant is the goal of creation is not something which is added later to the reality of the creature, as though the history of creation might equally have been succeeded by any other history. It already characterizes creation itself and as such, and therefore the being and existence of the creature." *For that reason* creation, instead of being *merely* the external presupposition, is the anticipation of the covenant history which follows, and it contains "all the elements which will subsequently meet and be unified . . . in the history of Israel, and finally and supremely in the history of the incarnation of the Son of God" (III/1 262 = 231-32).

The two statements belong together. The first one says that creation has no autonomous special life of its own. The second tells us that the grace of the covenant God has no special sphere of its own. The first one guards against the idea of a worldless God; the second against the idea of a godless world. The first orients "*everything* toward faith"; the second orients "faith in relation to *all* of reality." The two together say that there is in "the realm of nature . . . for all its distinctiveness . . . nothing which does not point to grace and therefore already come from grace; nothing which can enjoy independent life or exercise independent dominion. And conversely, for all the newness and particularity of the realm of grace, there is no place in it for anything unnatural, but from the creation everything is also nature" (III/1 67 = 62).

The two statements are for Barth a recognition in faith that God made a covenant with Israel and fulfilled it in Jesus Christ. Through his covenant two things are established: that creation and the covenant are not identical, and that they are related to each other. When we take into account both statements, it is clear that this nonidentity does not posit a "world" that is emptied of God and his grace. The world is grounded in the fact that the relation between creation and the covenant is defined by the covenant, not one projected initially in abstraction from it. The assertion that both were identical would always mean, not that the same thing was being thought in another "paradigm,"[10] but that *another* God is being set in the place of the covenant God. This other God would be accessible to us through impressions to which, if we are to speak about them, we must ascribe elements of divinity. For the knowledge of this other God we do not need faith in the Word in which God discloses himself in his covenant. This is a *different* God, who, in contrast with the free grace of his action with Israel and in Jesus Christ, is a graceless God. This might either mean that he is thought of as abstractly superior to those dependent on him, or, if such a view seems not to be opportune, the distinction between Creator and creature is blurred, the Creator is made dependent upon the creature, the creature is declared to be a cocreator, and we, notorious vandals, are at once made the guarantors of the goodness of creation. These things then become the preliminary condition for the word and work of the covenant God, to which they must now correspond. For Barth this was a dangerous misunderstanding of God's word and work. Since God's covenant of grace opposes all views of this type, Barth maintains the nonidentity of the covenant and creation.

Yet there is no loosening of the relation between them. There is, in fact, a clear and sure connection, which is not, however, a generally given thing, but is given by the God who acts in his covenant. Thus, creation is not a preexisting something which precedes the covenant so that the covenant has to correspond to it. The opposite is the case. In his word and work the covenant God makes *himself* the presupposition of creation and causes it to correspond to himself. Creation is neither the covenant itself nor a neutral setting for it. It *corresponds* to it. The delimitation that creation and the covenant are neither to be merged into one nor to be separated, follows from the positive knowledge that the creation is the reality which is *appropriate* to the *covenant*. As such, it discloses itself solely from that to which it corresponds: the *analogatum* [= that which is brought into correspondence through a relationship to another] of the *analogans* [= that which an other brings into correspondence with itself] of the covenant and of its fulfillment in Christ. This is the *analogia revelationis* [= a relationship of correspondence established by revelation] (III/3 59 = 51). Barth opposes this to the *analogia entis* [a relationship of correspondence based on shared being], which views the covenant in the light of a general outlook upon creation, and in which we can deduce our relationship to God based on a commonalty found in shared being.[11] To

---

10. Cf. Jürgen Moltmann, "Schöpfung, Bund und Herrlichkeit," *Zeitschrift für dialektische Theologie* 3 (1987): 212.

11. Cf. Eberhard Jüngel, *Barth-Studien* (Zurich, Cologne, and Gütersloh, 1982), pp. 210ff.

what extent does creation correspond to the covenant? If the covenant fulfilled in Christ consists of the fellowship of God who is linked with humans and of humans linked with God, then creation *corresponds* to the covenant in this twofold truth: (1) "God is not alone" and (2) "man is not alone" (III/1 26f. = 25-26).

If God is not alone, this means (1.) that he grants existence to something distinct from himself. He *grants* it. He did not *have* to make the creature in order not to be alone. As the Trinitarian God he is eternally not alone. It was a pure favor that God granted existence to something distinct from himself. And, if God wills "really not to be alone" with this other, it follows that this other is truly *distinct* from himself, and is not a divine "emanation." The fact that God is not alone is the basis of the fact that the creaturely world has its *own reality*. Barth delimits himself from an ever-recurring pantheism. Pantheism denies the distinction between Creator and creature, and thus denies God's gracious granting as well as what is granted to humanity. "In all its forms pantheism is a conception which does violence and injustice not only to God but also to the creature" (III/3 98 = 86). Barth also opposes the understanding of the world as an appearance, as something that is merely thought, an idea that results from the modern concept that it is an element in our human ego-consciousness which we can control, attracting it to us, or rejecting it, or tolerating it as we please. Take away the *Creator* and we also forfeit the *reality* of the creature. God alone, and the fact that God "is really not alone" is the guarantee of the reality of the creature. "The creature may be because God is" (III/1 395 = 345).

2. That "man is not alone" does not merely mean that he essentially is in relationship to *one* other. It means that she is dependent upon *God*. The human is not "self-grounded." God does not need humans in order to be God, but humans need God in order to be human. Man "lives, because God lives" (III/1 27 = 26). Yet the issue here is not his abstract "absolute *dependence*" (Schleiermacher). For the one from whom she exists is — thus the first step comes first — the God who *grants* existence to his creatures. In that God's love for his creature precedes her existence, in that she owes her existence to the fact that God grants it to her, her dependence upon God means that her existence *as such* is a being-that-is-not-forsaken-by-God. The main concern, then, is not what God *will* one day make of his creatures; it is therefore good to exist *as such*. Thus, the limitations of the creature belong to the goodness of its being created. For that reason, evil is not a creation of God. Creaturely existence as such is praise for the love of God and for his favor (IV/3 796 = 695-696). The fact that "God is not alone" guarantees the *reality* of creation, and the fact that "man is not alone" demonstrates the *goodness* of this reality.

As the former rules out that the creation is merely something thought, the latter rules that existence is fallenness in sin (Tillich). As little as the creature can guarantee its own reality itself, so little can it give itself the goodness of its reality — nor, of course, take it away.

3. How do we know that God is not alone, that humans are not alone, that therefore creation is both real and good and thus the reality that is appropriate to the covenant? This truth is no mere postulate, nor is it generally evident. It is a truth *of faith,* and we can know it only as it is disclosed to us by the Word of God. In this Word, in the history of Israel and the incarnate Jesus Christ who took our nature upon him (John 1:14), the one God who is also the Creator addresses us. In the believing knowledge that is grounded in this Word, we know that this God is our Creator and that we are his creatures. This includes the knowledge that the work of creation is *in itself* not "dumb destiny," not "irrational energy," not "a silent brute fact" open to all kinds of arbitrary interpretations and "world views," but rather that the selfsame Word is at work in it (III/1 122 = 110; cf. III/2 390 = 323-24). God does not simply "act" here without telling us what he is doing. To be sure, creation is a work of the triune God, also of his Spirit at work in us — and thus it is a truth of faith (III/1 59ff. = 56ff.). Barth adopts here the insight of Calvin that we are not to detach the Spirit from the "Word" of God. For this reason even in matters of creation "we will unavoidably fall into error, both generally and in detail, if we move away from Christ."[12] He affirms Hebrews 11:3 ("By *faith* we understand that the world was created *by the Word of God*")[13] when he says, "Jesus Christ is the Word by which the knowledge of creation is mediated to us because He is the Word by which God has fulfilled creation" (III/1 29 = 28). "Encountering the creature, the Word really comes into its own." As the possession of God, the creature is "the work of the *Word* of God *corresponding* to His utterance" (III/1 122 = 110). In the revelation of the Word we know creation as the reality that is appropriate to the covenant.

God's Constant Yes to His Creation

Knowledge of the goodness of creation, according to Barth, is threatened by the neo-Protestant view that draws the creation into its own "preservation," in order to understand this process as "an ongoing creation" *(creatio con-*

---

12. Calvin on Genesis; cf. CD III/1 32f. = 30-31.
13. Cf. CD III/1 2, 5, 17, 19 = 4, 6, 17, 19; and John 1:3.

tinua).[14] As the source of its knowing, this view turns not to the faith in the biblically attested Creator, but to the general experience of a becoming or a being caused. Its necessary content is the thought of a *reciprocal* relation between God and the world in which God becomes part of the world and is himself always in a *process of becoming,* while the human threatens to be divinized and to become the solemn *co-creator.* As such he is able to improve creation, but also to destroy it as well as to protect it against such misuse. The goodness of creation depends upon human cooperation. For this reason, the human person can never be certain that it is really good, because she can constantly render that uncertain. On the basis of a human's self-confidence she can thus imagine (but only imagine) that it is good or on the best route to goodness. For this reason the human has difficulty explaining to what extent she is a *creature* because she is constantly reaching beyond her createdness. For the same reason, she finds it hard to say who then the *Creator* is, unless she simply regards as divine that becoming, that "vital" process of causing and being caused. Is not this view the intellectual motor that drives the self-*created* belief of humanity in unrestricted progress?

Why does Barth reject the modern doctrine of continuous creation when he acknowledges its *particula veri* [= particles of truth], such as that the Creator *is* and not just *was* (I/2 771f. = 688-89; III/1 64 = 60)? Why does he find a beneficial significance in the fact that according to Genesis 1:31–2:3 God, with his judgment of the goodness of the completion of heaven and earth and with his resting "from all his work," did not continue his work of creation? Barth's response is that the "Creator-God of the Bible is not a world-principle developing in an infinite series of productions. His freedom is demonstrated in the fact that His creative activity has a limit appointed by Himself, and His love in the fact that He is content with His creature as a definite and limited object, and has addressed Himself only but totally to it as such" (III/3 6 = 7). The world principle that would animate us, *too,* to develop "in an infinite series of productions" would not "belong to itself"; it is inevitably "subjected to its higher necessity. A being is only free when it can determine and limit its activity." Although such a world-principle "might seem to be an ocean of love, it would not really be love at all. Missing every possible object of love, at bottom it would be condemned to pursue its own shadow. Love has a definite, limited object. It is in this way that God loves" (III/1 242f. = 215).

That God limits his creative activity corresponds to the fact that being

---

14. Cf. Friedrich Schleiermacher, *Der christliche Glaube nach den Grundsätzen der evangelischen Kirche im Zusammenhange dargestellt,* 3rd ed. (Berlin, 1835/36), pp. 188ff.

created means being "within its limits. . . . It may begin at one point and end at another. . . . It may be free here, but bound there; open at this point, closed at that. It may understand one thing, but not another; be capable of one thing, but not another. . . . That it may be in this way, within its limits, is not an imperfection . . . an obscure fate." Its limitation is the opportunity that it is given to experience its freedom "and accomplish that which is proper to it, to do that which it can do, and to be satisfied. . . . It is in this freedom that it comes directly from God and moves toward Him." Being given this freedom, "it is the object of the goodness of God," and "by making a right use of it, it magnifies the Creator. 'I will . . . sing praise to my God while I have my being' (Ps. 104:33). . . . The creature will only stumble at a supposed imperfection or obscure fate . . . when it does not admit or accept these limits. . . . Of all creatures only man seems to have this impossible possibility of repudiating his preservation by God as a preservation within appointed limits. But he cannot alter the fact that like all creatures he is in fact preserved in this way, and rightly so" (III/3 96f. = 85-86).

That God limits his creative activity also means that he wants only that reality (distinct from himself) that is the reality of the creature he has made. He does in fact want that reality. He desires to be *faithful* to it and to provide for the proper preservation of its existence within its given limits. If God were a mere "manufacturer," he would "easily leave what he makes to itself, and the more easily the more perfect it is. But the Creator cannot do this in relation to his creature" (III/3 8 = 9). He cannot do it because — we have to see this first in faith in order then to see the other — he wills to be in covenant with his creature, the covenant made with Israel and fulfilled for all in Jesus Christ. Just as he presupposed for himself the existence of the creature when making this covenant, and just as his saying "yes" to the creature in this covenant is his affirmation of the *very existence* of the creature, so he wills, in the faithfulness with which he stands to his covenant, that the creature should *always be there* within its limits. And so he "orders" his care in relation to the history of the covenant so that the creature can live out his days (III/3 43 = 38). If we detach his providence from its inner purpose in covenant history, then it is no longer the "King of Israel" who only *as such* is the one who reigns providentially as the "King of the world" (III/3 200 = 176). Then there reigns a fateful destiny (first of all for Israel itself) that either appeals to "the word 'providence' . . . a favorite one on the lips of Adolf Hitler" (III/3 33), or rebels against it in the persuasion that "it is the better for the freedom . . . of the creature the more it can call its own a sphere marked off from God" (III/3 166 = 146). If, however, it is the God of the *covenant* who preserves and rules the world, then the creature profoundly *owes* the external preservation of its existence to this God. It can then be seen as the good intention of the limitation of the creative activity of God that instead of leaving the creature to its own device, "to its fate," God as "the Lord of its history . . . has *associated* Himself with His creature . . . and is *faithful* to it as such." God's freedom can also be recognized in the fact that the creature "may serve Him in His immediate presence and under His immediate guardianship and direction, thus fulfilling its own meaning and purpose, having its own honor and existing to its own joy" (III/3 12 = 12-13).

Does not the fact of evil challenge the goodness of creation and also its preservation? Or must not Barth otherwise, as is often alleged,[15] make evil innocuous? His term for evil is "nothingness" (III/3 217ff. = 289ff.), not because it is nothing or non-being, but in the twofold sense that it has annihilating force for the creature, and that the Creator has the power to reduce it to nothing. It is a "factor" that is "subordinate" to God and "superior" to the creature (III/3 87 = 76). Barth does not deduce this from an abstract omnipotence of God nor from an abstract frailty of the creature. God is superior to evil because he allows the No of Nothingness towards the *creature* to engage God in the death of Jesus Christ. He "takes up the cause of the creature" (III/3 89 = 79) in such a way, that the threat made by the negating power of nothingness is no longer the human's concern. The human is, then, inferior to evil and falls victim to its annihilating power when he looks away from the God who can reduce it to nothing, when he sees the "controversy" with nothingness as "his own cause" — at that, the "great catastrophe" occurs (III/3 413 = 358).

For one thing, the human falls victim to a "misconception of nothingness" (III/3 295ff. = 335ff.) that *plays down* the "intolerable" character of the "dreadful fact" of evil (III/3 408, 329 = 354, 291). She underestimates it by thinking either that she is able to cope with it or that she can reach an agreement with it. The automatic consequence is that the human no longer has that evil in view which is superior to her, but makes the mistake of regarding something as evil over which she feels herself to be superior.

For another thing, the human fights against God and his grace, falling victim to evil precisely by seeking to contend against it, and thus "maintains" it by "direct cooperation" with it (III/3 341 = 300), which only ensures its superiority over him. In so doing, the human denies that God in his merciful solidarity with his threatened creature has made the negation of nothingness

---

15. Cf. Gerrit Cornelis Berkouwer, *Der Triumph der Gnade in der Theologie Karl Barths* (Neukirchen and Moers, 1957), pp. 198ff., 235; ET: *The Triumph of Grace in the Theology of Karl Barth* (Grand Rapids, 1956), pp. 215ff., 253; see also p. 222, note 35.

his own affair. Fortunately, all he can do is to deny it. The human's effort cannot render ineffective the fact that God is "superior" both over nothingness and over that human battle against nothingness that only serves to strengthen it.

Our only option as those who are threatened by destruction is *conversion* from our belief in the power to heal ourselves to belief in the God who can annihilate nothingness and thus create for all the necessary courage to be! This is the courage to turn away from evil so that the human turns towards *God's* total affirmation of his creature, which includes *God's* total negation of evil.

Like creation and its goodness, nothingness and its impotence to destroy this goodness are grounded in the covenant of God and its fulfillment in Jesus Christ, and it is in this way alone that we can know them. The statement about the impotence of nothingness falls into doubt "in proportion as we dissociate covenant and creation (and . . . the Old and New Testaments)" and fail to see that the "truth of the covenant is already the secret of creation, that the secret of the covenant includes the benefit of creation" (III/1 380f. = 332-333). Creation corresponds to the covenant, in that the latter presupposes creation for itself and its action. God created the creature "out of nothing," which means that he distinguished "that which He willed from that which He did not will" and gave it "existence on the basis of that distinction." "By *preserving* the distinction God preserves the creature" (III/3 83 = 73). Nothingness does not emerge "by a chance . . . and therefore without God, but in a sense *by means of God*" (III/3 87 = 76-77). God would not will the creature that he affirms without also *willing* that which negates the creature, a negating that he does not *will*. But He wills it only because he negates it, and he negates it because it negates the creature. It is therefore not one of his creatures. It *exists* only in virtue of his distinguishing between the creature that he affirms and that which he negates because nothingness itself negates the creature's existence and the good will of God declared therein. He negates it, not in order to "preserve" it in its negativity, but in order to determine that it will disappear and to deprive it of all substance (III/3 416f. = 366).

We can venture statements of this kind only on the basis of the covenant and its fulfillment in the atonement. If the covenant is the inner basis of creation, it follows that the spoken Yes of God to the creature that had fallen victim to nothingness reveals and confirms God's original resolve in relation to the creature. Just as his Yes to the creature precedes its existence, so God's No to the creature's destruction also precedes its existence. With this initial Yes God speaks this No first, and not only after nothingness is there. The creature cannot exist at all unless it is affirmed by God, and therefore nothingness cannot exist as something that can claim a right to existence as that which is grounded in either Creator or creature. As that which has always been rejected by God, it has only the "being of *non-being*" (III/3 87 = 77).

For this reason creation is *irrefutably* good. The *preservation* of the creation by God consists of the fact that God *stands* by his affirmation of the creature. The promised "new creation" does not then replace the good creation of God with another one. It is the definitive removal of all negation of the good creation by evil, a removal which is impossible in terms of the internal world but accomplished alone by God (IV/1 52 = 49-50; IV/3 259-226), with the result that the "being of non-being" is sentenced to *non*-existence. The fulfillment of the covenant saw the incursion of the new creation into the world (IV/1 343 = 311). "Reconciling it to Himself, God has given it a corresponding *future*" (IV/3 363 = 315).

The Creature

Surprisingly enough, Barth's doctrine of the divinely created creature is not a doctrine of the cosmos. It is almost identical with the doctrine of the *human person* (anthropology). That sounds like an affirmation of modern anthropocentricity, which in a fateful way disparages the nonhuman creation as a negligible quantity, or at least regards it as something that we humans can exploit as we wish. Yet to criticize Barth along these lines is erroneous even though he very definitely does not espouse the biocentricity that is thought to be today the only alternative to anthropocentricity. In his debate with Darwin, however, he is open to consider that "animals much lower in the level of creation have possibilities which put those of man in the shade," in relation to which the human has no "right" to ascribe to oneself a "higher and better" being. Why should not "the much boasted mind of man," by which he is alleged to be superior to the animal, be understood as the human "disease" (III/2 104 = 89)? For Barth, a proper anthropology will make it clear that, "in the plenitude" of creatures, "man is only a component part, very inconsiderable in some important ways and deeply dependent on creaturely elements and factors which are greatly superior to him" (III/2 2 = 3-4). In expounding Genesis 1 he stresses the fact that the creation of plants before animals tells us that the plant world was created for itself, and that since plants can live without humans but humans not without them, the human is "the neediest of all creatures" (III/1 160 = 143 rev.). Along with Schweitzer, Barth declares: "Those who handle life as a divine loan will above all treat it with respect. . . . Respect is man's astonishment, humility and awe at a fact in which he meets something superior — majesty, dignity and holiness, a mystery which compels him to withdraw and keep his distance, to handle it modestly, circumspectly and carefully" (III/4 338-39). Over every slaughterhouse there should be "written in letters of fire" the statement (Rom. 8:18f.) concerning the "eager longing" of the creature, namely for the liberation of those who bring them from life to death (III/4 404 = 355). Barth does indeed contest an anthropocentricity that tries to understand man while overlooking that "he must remain *loyal* to the earth" (III/2 2 = 4).

This certainly rules out, therefore, any idea that the human differs from all the rest of creation because of his immanent qualities, intelligence, or immortal soul. Those who hold such a view despise the physical. If the human person is a creature like all the rest of God's creatures, there is no reason for that kind of disparagement, though it has had a long history in the church and has provoked by way of reaction the "soulless image of man" in materialism. "Has it not always stood on the side of the 'ruling classes'? . . . And has it not with its doctrine of soul and body at least shown a culpable indifference toward the problem of matter, of bodily life, and therefore of contemporary economics? Has it not made a point of teaching the immortality of the soul instead of attesting to society . . . that the judgment and promise of God compass the whole man?" (III/2 467 = 389-390). The human is a creature in that she is "wholly and simultaneously both soul and body" (III/2 446 = 372).

Why, *then,* does Barth limit his doctrine of the creature to humanity? Negatively, he contests the theory that goes back to Aristotle, that is still held widely today, and that is a dangerous speculation, namely, that the human is a microcosm that contains the macrocosm, and is thus one part of the whole. This is the basis of much of the new ecological ethics. According to this view, the human finds in oneself everything that lies outside in the creaturely world, so that she can deduce the creaturely world from herself and therefore project her concept of life upon it (III/4 376f. = 332-333). This view means that "the essence of the cosmos is contained within the life of man, as though the cosmos could not exist over and above its special relation to man, in quite other dimensions and in quite another sense. But we do not know these other dimensions. . . . We know the cosmos only through this relation. . . . Yet this does not justify us in supposing that its life is necessarily exhausted in this relation" (III/2 15f. = 15 rev.). This view is dangerous because it is only in appearance that it avoids anthropocentricity. In a subtle way it understands the human as "the measure and epitome of all things" (III/2 16 = 16). The limitation of the doctrine of the creature is an act of human modesty in relation to non-human creatures, in profound respect of their mystery and of the fact that the meaning of their existence is not exhausted in the human relation to them. The modesty goes along with the acknowledgment that *God* has created them, that they are not "alien to God" but present to him, that his very distinctive praise is found in them, and that there are distinctive "relations between God and other creatures" that are not mediated by humans (III/2 17 = 17 rev.). Insofar as the human in faith in God recognizes the fact of these relations, she indeed recognizes that these creatures are "in the covenant" with her and are thus her "companions" (III/1 199 = 178). Because the manner and the inner core of these relations are hidden from her, she must take seriously that these other creatures receive from God the meaning of their existence, and that they are not there merely for the sake of humans. Therefore, "any proud or arrogant usurpation on the part of man is rendered impossible at the very root" (III/1 170 = 152). Limiting the doctrine of the creature to anthropology thus has significant ecological relevance.

The positive basis for this limitation consists of the fact that the measure for everything that theology can responsibly say is certainly not the human person, nor a concept for what the human holds to be "life." The "measure of all things" for humans is the *Word of God,* the Word directed to *them.* This summons us to a knowledge that we may not evade even by arguing in advance that we are just part of a greater biological totality. Human knowledge learns something here, for the Word of God primarily tells us who God is and, secondarily, who we are to whom this Word is directed. God is God in covenant with humans, and the human is human in covenant with God.

The fact that this covenant focuses upon *humans* cannot be deduced from a previously observed advantage of humans over other creatures, nor does it entail the sanctioning of such an advantage. In her way, the human person is the least and most dependent form of life, so that there is no basis for God's covenant with her other than the fact that God has made this covenant with humans, and there is nothing to commend us apart from the fact that God has concluded this covenant with us. This does, of course, constitute a "peculiar distinction" on the part of the human person (III/2 18 = 18). It is to be seen in the fact that the human person has thereby been qualified as God's covenant partner. The corollary that the human's qualification through God's covenant reveals is that human createdness means that the human is intended for *co-existence.* If that is the createdness of the human, then God's good will in the creation of all creatures is revealed in this intention for humanity. As creatures, however, we have to see in this determination the good will of God in creating every creature. "As God's covenant with him [the human] is disclosed, the cosmos is shown to be embraced by the same covenant," for "the Creator of man is also the Creator of the cosmos, and His purpose toward the latter, although hidden as such, is none other than His revealed purpose for us" (III/2 19 = 18-19). If God's covenant with humanity also reveals the meaning of the cosmos, then the intention that species shall co-exist is the meaning of the cosmos. With that, the human in particular is made responsible for such co-existence. Thus humans properly practice their genuine human responsibility only when they *themselves* co-exist with the other species. "It is also true that man for his part is possible and actual only as man in the cosmos" (III/2 15 = 14).

Co-Humanity

In his anthropological teaching Barth very definitely declared that even in dealing with nonhuman creatures, we as creatures are always in relation, for in ourselves first of all we are destined for coexistence and are, therefore, *relational* beings. As thus destined, according to Barth, we are in correspondence, in an *analogia relationis* [= analogy of relationship] to God (III/2 390f. = 322-323). Just as God can relate himself outwardly toward humanity, because in himself as the Triune One he is being-in-relation, the human can as well. Moreover, because God, who is so rich in relationships, has set himself in relation to humanity in the covenant that found fulfillment in Christ, the human becomes a relational being, destined for coexistence in correspondence with the covenant. Barth makes this point on the basis of the revelation of Christ.

The "true man," that is, Jesus Christ, is not an ideal human with whom the sinner could be contrasted as "the real human," but is identical with the "real human" against whom the sinner contends but into which he cannot make himself. Nor is this true man a being whom we pre-define — out of our own experience of ourselves or through a filtering out of those elements in us that seem to us to be untouched by sin — in order then to discover it in Jesus. The true and real human is neither the human nor the sinner *in and of himself,* but rather the human as God in Jesus Christ sees him, creates her, ensures that he cannot be lost. That is the person to whom God turns, the human in covenant with him. "Our self-knowledge can only be an act of discipleship" (III/2 61 = 53). Our creaturely humanity consists of the fact that God causes it to correspond to this human in covenant relationship. Thus, God's covenant with the human, whom he makes into the covenant partner of God and thereby truly makes human in the first place, takes place "on the presupposition and in the framework of certain relationships of the being of man which are influenced by sin but not structurally modified by it" (III/2 46 = 40). Barth defines the creaturely being of the human in this way: It is the human's being that is conferred by God in his relationship with humanity in particular settings, against which the human may well sin but which he cannot remove. The creaturely human is essentially a being in relationship, and only as such is he free. According to Barth, this human person exists in four relations, first to God, then to other people, then to the self (as the soul of the body), and finally to time.

What is meant is made particularly clear in the second relation and its thesis. The thesis here is that the humanity of the human person consists of one's relation to fellow humans. "In its basic form humanity is *fellow-humanity*" (III/2 344 = 285).

> He *is* in fact in the encounter of I and Thou. This is true even though he may contradict it both in theory and in practice; even though he may pretend to be man in isolation and produce anthropologies to match. In so doing he merely proves that he is contradicting himself, not that he can divest himself of this basic form of humanity. He has no choice to be fellow-human or something else. His being has this basic form. (III/2, 344 = 285-286)

Humanity as co-humanity is not a virtue; one cannot cultivate it in order to be regarded as even more human. "The man who is not the fellow of others is no real man at all" (IV/2 474 = 421). This person contradicts his or her own being, "but provision is made that man should not break loose from this human factor" (III/2 344 = 285). Insofar as we cannot break loose from it, our humanity is a *likeness* that reflects the reality of the covenant between God and us, and a *hope* that the covenant will find fulfillment in Jesus Christ (III/2 344 = 285). Because we cannot separate ourselves from our fellows, we are *commanded* to correspond to our true being and thus to demonstrate co-humanity. How would all our knowledge of divine forgiveness help us if co-humanity is lacking? "Between tyrant and slave there is no genuine encounter, and even genuine encounter ceases to be genuine to the extent that it is understood and actualized on the one side or the other as the encounter of tyrant and slave. Only in the atmosphere of freedom can it be genuine. Companions are free. . . . Only what takes place between such as these is humanity" (III/2 326 = 271).

Barth differs from the I-Thou personalism of Buber by saying that co-humanity belongs to the *essence* of the human creature and is thus "the center of the human" (III/2 348 = 289). That is why offenses against co-humanity are so devastating. In Barth's view the problem of modern scholarship belongs here. It developed out of the medieval "cloister cell," that is, out of a masculine "I-speculation that left out the Thou." "A world of the I wandering without limit or object," in which the feminine Thou had no place, is "a demonic and tyrannical world" (III/2 349f. = 290). After the disasters of the twentieth century, it was for Barth very important that there has been "posed afresh the problem of humanity from the particular angle of the question of the rights, dignity and sanctity of the fellow man," and "the hostility, neutrality and antithesis between man and man" can be radically "known and rejected as inhumanity" (III/2 273 = 228-29). Theological anthropology carries a special responsibility in this regard, for it can and should demonstrate that co-humanity is indeed an "inviolable constant of human existence" and not just a demand (III/2 349 = 289). The inhumane person cannot break away from that demand, any more than godless people can break away from God.

To what degree will we not be able to divorce ourselves from our co-human, even when we shamefully offend against our co-humanity? To the degree, says Barth, that there is no such thing as the human *in and for himself,* but rather he always exists in the duality of male and female. This means that all the *other* distinctions between people are relativized by this "structural differentiation of human existence" (III/2 344 = 286), which casts a new and helpful light on these distinctions. The fact that God created humanity as *male and female* (Gen. 1:26-31; 2:18-25) is the "Magna Carta of humanity" (III/2 351 = 291), for it shows that intrinsically, and not in consequence of an imperative, humanity is co-humanity, no matter whether we contradict or correspond to our nature. Indeed, Barth finds in this dual form of our existence the vulnerable but still irrevocable definition of humanity as made in the image of God, in relation to the God who, for his part, exists only in co-existence. If we are to understand this much debated thesis of Barth,[16] we should note that he formulates his statements in analogy to the divine work of creation.

1. As creation has *reality* because God grants it an existence that *differs* from his own, there can also only be co-humanity because there is between humans an authentic and irrevocable distinction, that is, because man and woman are different. In this regard Barth stresses the fact that we cannot define what constitutes this distinction. When we try to do so, the price we pay is to make intolerable ascriptions of roles (even if they are tolerated in their intolerability), which as a rule favor the domination of the man over the woman (which is still intact where the woman strives for a share of this "domination") (III/4 168ff. = 154ff.).

16. CD III/1 202ff. = 181-182; 329ff. = 288-290; III/2 344ff. = 285; III/4 127-272 = 116-243.

2. Just as the reality of the creature, whose being is derived from God, is a *good* reality, the togetherness of man and woman demonstrates that it is in fact not good for the human person to be alone (Gen. 2:18). "Here everything is fundamentally two-sided in character: a back and forth . . . between two partners of equal essence and dignity" (III/2 387 = 321). These two could really be *themselves* only as they freely affirmed their "being in fellowship" (III/4 184 = 165) with one another in a mutual seeing, questioning, and accepting of responsibility for one another, whether within marriage or outside it (III/4 185-187 = 167-168).

3. Since the structures of the reality and goodness of creation are disclosed to us only in the biblical witness, the same applies to the distinctiveness of male and female in differing from, yet relating to, one another. This is revealed in what may seem to be patriarchal but is in fact the characteristic speech of the Bible when it refers to the male's leading the way and to the female's following after him. To be sure, "it is nowhere said that men should assume a position of superiority in relation to women," nor that the woman should be "an object surrendered to the sheer power of the superior partner" (III/4 192 = 172). Barth interprets the Biblical passages as saying that the man is "utterly to her" and the woman is "utterly from man" (III/2, 352 = 292). He understands this in this way: the man is and would be in his "being utterly to the woman" — this is his "primacy of service" (III/4 190 = 170) — the witness to the woman of the first one named, witness of the "reality" of her counterpart; he is first of all responsible for the respecting of her authentic, free, accountable existence (contrary to the repressive rendering of the woman invisible). And the woman is and would be in her "being utterly from man" — that is the "primacy of woman" (III/4 195 = 175) — witness of the second one named, witness of the "humanity" of their relationship (III/4 190f. = 171-72); she is first of all responsible for the good significance of their being in fellowship (contrary to the inhumane drive of man to be alone). In this way Barth attempts to show that precisely in their differentiation they both *need* each other for their common humanity.

Barth's concern here is to make it plain that humanity is essentially co-humanity, and that any humanity that denies this is inhumanity. Co-humanity bears witness that God is not really alone and therefore the human is not really alone either. It also bears witness that our creatureliness corresponds to the making of God's covenant with us. It testifies, too, that it is good to be human, and that all God's creation is good. In face of the threat that chaos launches against creation, it is most urgent that we should have a resolute belief in God the Creator who is identical with God the Merciful. If the human wanted to put an end to the chaos without relying on faith in *this*

God, he would actually participate in that which summons up the chaos, the destructive power of nothingness (III/3 409ff. = 354-356). Faced with this threat, it is crucial to believe that God is the Creator and that his creation is good. When we consider the interrelation of gospel and law, it will be clear that in this faith we will receive all kinds of things to do. Yet this will never mean that we are to try to make an imperfect or bad creation better, but rather that we are to confess the reality and goodness of God's creation against the enemies of humanity and against those who scorn God's gift.

The Critical Reconciliation —
The Doctrines of Sin and Justification

Repressed Sin

In the period after World War II, as Barth was writing his doctrine of sin, he commented: "Six million Jews were murdered. Fire fell down from heaven. . . . Horror and agony of every kind fell upon humanity. But all that has come and gone as a wind blows over the . . . flowers: they are bowed for a while, but when the wind stops, they raise themselves again." Yet all of that did not confront us with "our lostness and condemnation" so "that we can no longer escape it."[1] To be sure, an excess of wickedness has taken place. "Man collectively may take on a terrifying and monstrous appearance" (IV/2, 496f. = 440-41). Yet this has not produced in us a true consciousness of sin. What all this evil we have done ultimately reveals is our "inability to mourn" (A. M. Mitscherlich). Barth composed his doctrine of sin in the face of this alarming disconnect between the gigantic nature of the violence committed in our century and contemporary humanity's loss of a consciousness of guilt. Himmler gave classical formulation to this disconnect when, referring to the horrors of the holocaust, he stated, "To have persisted through all that and remained respectable in the process has made us strong."

The question might be raised whether the two things were not basically connected, whether there could be such an excess of evil in our time because there was such a deficit in the knowledge of sin. At any rate, the concept of sin has landed in a crisis in this modern age. We can see this if we

---

1. Karl Barth, *Die christliche Lehre nach dem Heidelberger Katechismus* (Zollikon-Zurich, 1948), p. 38; ET: *The Heidelberg Catechism Today* (Richmond, 1964), p. 44; cf. CD III/3 397 = 345.

consider the following questions. Can what the church used to call sin be explained as a breaking of the rules of social conventions, so that what the majority calls wicked relates primarily to those who deviate from the average norm? A further consequence is that what is regarded as wicked can be dealt with by the sanctions of society without any need for God and the atonement! Is not the norm of wickedness always changing historically so that what was frowned upon yesterday is moral today and vice versa (cf. IV/1 443 = 400-401)? Can we offer a biological understanding of "so-called wickedness" (Konrad Lorenz) as an inadequate human adjustment to evolution? Or a psychological interpretation as false shame at turning away from an internalized father or mother figure? Or a sociological understanding as unavoidable damage caused by one's environment? Or a political interpretation as a cudgel used by the ruling classes to keep the smaller folk passive? If we entertain questions like these, does not the church, in what it says about sin, breathe very thin air?

Barth certainly never thought that such interpretations banished sin from the world. But he was not interested in confronting those who explained away sin with "problems" with which they could not deal alone but which would make them dependent upon a "grace" mediated by the church. He was so little interested that he could be regarded as one who made sin innocuous or even denied it.[2] He saw no sense in trying to change such people's minds through the efforts of theologians to ascribe to sin some enormous character of reality alleged to be generally illuminating. Instead, he made the disappearance of a sense of sin, which goes hand in hand with the excesses of humanity's evil, the main theme in his doctrine of sin. He advanced the thesis that the highest accomplishment of sin, "the sin in all sins" (II/2 839 = 751), consists of one's "refusing the name of the sinner," that is, denying, contesting, or repressing it. That also means that sin is most sinister where it is most secret. Its power is most dangerous when it dons the mantle of the respectable, of the normal, or even of the unavoidable, not when, according to human judgment, it ostensibly offends against something, but when sin has the ability to explain itself as an act that is "the genuine *good*" (IV/1 443 = 400). The *corruptio boni* [= corruption of the good], even *optimi* [= of the best] (IV/1 549 = 493), is the real problem in the doctrine of sin. Indeed, Barth will say that the worst form of sin occurs when for the sake of doing good people resist the grace of God. If, however, sin has the

---

2. C. van Til according to Gerrit Cornelis Berkouwer, *Der Triumph der Gnade in der Theologie Karl Barths* (Neukirchen and Moers, 1957), p. 305; ET: *The Triumph of Grace in the Theology of Karl Barth* (Grand Rapids, 1956), p. 385.

ability to conceal itself in the appearance of what is not sin, how is it to be unmasked?

According to Barth the decline in the knowledge of sin goes along with the decline in the knowledge of God. "In the knowledge of sin we have to do basically and in general with a specific variation of the knowledge *of God*" (IV/1 397 = 359). With its responsibility to speak about God, theology is also responsible for speaking about sin. Yet Barth does not think that theology in its current state would be the fitting teacher to disclose "to the world" its sin. This is because modern theology has, in its own way, made a big contribution to the decline in the consciousness of sin. His thinking here proceeds then in such a way that he grapples only indirectly with secularization outside the church, but all the more intensively with secularization within the church. He deals only indirectly with the crisis in the knowledge of sin, but very directly with theology's co-responsibility for this crisis (III/3 355 = 312ff.; IV/1 413ff. = 374ff.). "If we do not want the consequences" (the innocuousness of sin), "we must not want the presupposition" (theology's failure in relation to the doctrine of sin) (IV/1 430 = 389). Some materially related quotations will show how he viewed theology's co-responsibility.

We read, for example, that "there are few heresies so pernicious as that of a God who faces nothingness more or less unaffected and unconcerned, and the parallel doctrine of man as one who must engage in independent conflict against it" (III/3 415 = 360). This heresy had, according to Barth, gained ground in the doctrine of sin of modern theology. Nor was the Reformation, he thought, without guilt in this regard, for it failed to achieve clarity in its understanding of the law of God (IV/1 404ff. = 366-67). Barth acknowledges that according to the Reformation the human cannot know sin on her own, but only in that God discloses it to her through his law. Yet his criticism was that the law that unmasks the sinner was thought of as "emptied" of the gospel (IV/1 403 = 365) according to which God is subsequently "affected" by sin. In the law itself that is isolated from and precedes the gospel, God stands over against evil as one who is "unaffected and uninvolved." This would have to have fatal consequences at the moment from the 17th century on that the law, which the reformers still viewed as bound to the Bible, was now equated with the natural law that is innate to the human and identical with the moral law in the human. Thus, even as sinners we have something good in us, namely, the standard by which to judge what is sinful. This also means that even as sinners we have the ability, indeed, the good will, to distance ourselves from sin. The knowledge of sin that expresses itself as human self-assessment must necessarily result in human self-pardoning (IV/1 429 = 388-89). If God is excluded from the assessing of guilt, then he must also be excluded when the guilt is removed through pardon. Our self-exculpation functions in such a way that we counter our sin, now understood as an "accident on the job," with our morality, the "good core" in us, our having meant well after all. What we of necessity cannot see is that this supposedly good kernel is the source of evil, for it causes us always to find excuses for our individual failings, to separate ourselves from them, and to obliterate or rather repress them (IV/1 447f. = 403ff.). When the human is seen as "one who must engage in independent conflict against" sin, the result will be that decline in the consciousness of sin.

The second citation looks at the problem from a different aspect. Barth tells us that "there is no doctrine more dangerous than the Christian doctrine of reconciliation . . . if we do not consider it with this warning in view," namely, that "the fact that it speaks of God making good what we have spoiled does not mean that we can call evil good (unless we would also call good evil)" (IV/1 74 = 70 rev.; cf. II/2 847 = 757). The error of our saying that what is evil is good rests on the even greater error of saying that if God makes good our evil deeds, then it is God who calls the evil we do good. The mistake here is that of thinking that God's reconciliation is a reconciliation with sin. Barth thought that the reformers were again in some sense guilty here, for they did not sufficiently explain the significance of Christ's atonement for us. The answer they gave was that we are "simultaneously righteous and sinners." Barth regarded this answer as correct and often repeated it, but he also had questions about the way it was formulated. Did it not lead to a stabilization of life under a double bookkeeping in which, "either tacitly or openly, we are subjected to other lords in a kingdom on the left as well as to the Lord Jesus Christ whose competence extends only, as we think, to the forgiveness of sins" (IV/2 571 = 504)? Furthermore, does not our life in these two spheres become a "possible, and even perhaps a not wholly uncomfortable shelter" in which this "simultaneously" appears to the Christian not as "monstrous . . . but as normal, congenial and respectable" (CL 316, 256 = 187, 154)? What kind of reconciliation is it that stands under the shadow of the suspicion that it was only "verbal," took place only as an "as if," because "simultaneously" it validates the sinner's continuing to live as sinner?

Barth raised the question in view of the new interpretation of the relation between sin and grace in the further course of theological history. As God's law was implanted now in the human person as the standard of self-judgment given to him, so now his being under sin and under grace was understood as two entities given in his spiritual reality, contending with each other. It could now be seen how fateful it was that the Reformation had not very definitely ruled out that double bookkeeping. For in that now both sin and grace were incorporated simultaneously into the same psychic reality, they were no longer seen as being in conflict and contradiction, but as mutually compatible entities (IV/1 417 = 377-78). Sin could now be seen as something imperfect and immature in the human, and grace as an impulse toward betterment also residing in a person. Both could thus be regarded as elements in a meaningful ongoing process. The thought was not far distant that even in its negativity sin could be regarded as something positive and indeed necessary for progress to what is better. Or it could be viewed as a possibility that we must grasp if we seriously want to be free. Either way it is understood as a possibility that is part of our human existence, not isolated from what is good but participating in it. If it is something bad, then it is a tolerable badness which neither can nor must be rejected — life can be lived with it.

The two aspects of the outcome of the modern doctrines of sin are, in Barth's view, the theological factor that has promoted the disappearance of a consciousness of sin in modernity. In both instances, sin is thought to be so harmless that at bottom we do not need divine reconciliation. Either we are capable of excusing our sin or we can tolerate it as a transitional element leading on to higher things. We ourselves can deal with what we call sin if it proves to be too disruptive, or we can make allowance for it without having to find it disruptive. Barth thought that such a concept of harmless sin was very dangerous, for real sin is by no means harmless. Under the mask of harmlessness, it can lay waste to everything around it. It would, of course, simply be a dead end to try to correct this theological doctrine of sin directly by a less harmless view of sin, as long as its damage is not seen and corrected at its roots. In some sense, indeed, these teachings have helped to confirm negatively the basic insight that we are not aware of our real sin, that we hide it from ourselves in a harmless picture, even if we depict it far more realistically than is the case in these doctrines. This will happen as long as we understand ourselves as the subject who must "engage in independent conflict against it."

The Sympathetic Judge

We recall again Barth's statement that "there are few heresies so pernicious as that of a God who faces nothingness more or less unaffected and unconcerned, and the parallel doctrine of man as one who must engage in independent conflict against it." We see and correct the defect at the very root when we see and correct this error, the error of a God who is "unaffected and uninvolved" when he faces evil. That God does contend with sin means that its reality and mystery become recognizable for us only where *God himself engages it*. Only then is sin brought out of the concealment with which it seeks to make itself invisible to us, and the mask of its apparent harmlessness is torn off. Only then can we make the statement that the "sin in all sins" consists of our human denial that we are sinners, of our making our real sin harmless and invisible. We can know sin where God himself is in active conflict with it, and not at that point where he allegedly *forbids* it, while remaining himself unaffected and uninvolved. No law divorced from the gospel that God subjects himself to sin in order to contend with it will ever show us sin in all its sinister reality.

The event in which God is "affected and involved" with sin, and in which he wrestles with it, is identical — Barth's decisive discovery — with the event of the *reconciliation* of the world with God in Jesus Christ on the cross (2 Cor. 5:19). We can attain to the knowledge of sin only when the knowledge of the reality of this reconciliation is our starting point. We must, above all, understand its *reality,* and in so doing we will then unavoidably understand its *necessity:* the fact that we are sinners and stand in need of this reconciliation. The proof of its necessity lies here and not in needs ascertained independent of it. Its reality carries with it the proof of its indispensability. Its reality consists of the fact that in Jesus Christ God on our behalf has taken to himself the sin that separates us from him. Since it is *God* himself who acts vicariously for us, we realize that the true knowledge of sin can come only when it is recognized to be so intolerable that we can neither bear it nor get rid of it ourselves. "The serious and terrible nature of human corruption . . . can be measured by the fact that . . . God could react and reply to this event only by . . . His giving up of Jesus Christ Himself to overcome . . . it" (IV/1 456 = 412).

The reality of the reconciliation of the sinner with God reveals that it is our sin that requires God's intervention in order to overcome it; we cannot excuse ourselves for it, and we cannot wrestle with it ourselves. Or, to put it another way, what we think that we ourselves can grapple with is, in fact, not our real sin. Much greater than the sin that we might otherwise commit is the sin of thinking that we ourselves could grapple with it alone. Our sin reaches its climax when we deny it, when we claim that there is in us a good kernel that enables us to separate ourselves from our sin and in that way to rid ourselves of it. This is the greater sin, for it directly contradicts the reconciliation in which *God* reconciles himself with us. If we are truly reconciled by the fact that God does not remain uninvolved over against our sin, then we are no longer able "to make a distinction between ourselves and our sin" (IV/1 447 = 403 rev.). We have, then, not just *committed* sins; we *are* ourselves sinners. It is not that God has merely forgiven us for something; we are *ourselves* being reconciled with God, and nothing less than that.

The fact that God is not uninvolved in his encounter with our sin, in that he reconciled us to himself in the suffering of Jesus Christ, means further that God *himself*, in unity with the One who suffers there, is in the *lowliness* of this suffering, and is so without "any alteration or diminution of His divine nature" (IV/1 200 = 183) yet also without any weakening of the gravity of his humiliation. In this regard we must "learn to correct our notions of the being of God" (IV/1 203 = 186), notions that are deeply rooted. Is it not blasphemous to state that this humiliation was not external to God, indeed, that the deity of Christ is manifested precisely in his humiliation? That is "the complaint of Judaism and Islam against the Christian confession" (IV/1 200 = 183). Yet that is in fact the Christian confession. "That God can and must only be absolute in contrast to all that is relative, . . . exalted in contrast to all that is lowly . . . such beliefs are shown to be quite untenable . . . by the fact that God does in fact *be* and *do* this in Jesus Christ. . . . By doing this God proves to us . . . that to do it is within His *nature*": to surrender himself in such a way without ceasing to be God (IV/1 203-204 = 186).

God is not uninvolved when he faces the dreadful character of the cross.

> With the eternal Son the eternal Father has also to bear what falls on the Son as He gives Himself to identity with the man Jesus of Nazareth, thus lifting it away from us to Himself in order that it should not fall on us. In Jesus Christ God Himself, the God who is the one true God, the Father with the Son in the unity of the Spirit, has suffered what it befell this man to suffer to the bitter end. It was first and supremely in Himself that the conflict between Himself and this man, and the affliction which threatened this man, were experienced and borne. What are all the sufferings in the world, even those of Job, compared with this fellow-suffering of God Himself which is the meaning of the event of Gethsemane and Golgotha? (IV/3 478 = 414)

It is obviously proper to God to be able to be both fully above and fully below (IV/1 213 = 195). The objection that this projects on God earthly ideas of the relations between above and below, and sanctions them,[3] overlooks the whole point, namely, a radicalizing of the decision that the church made

---

3. Jürgen Moltmann, *Gott in der Schöpfung* (Munich, 1985), p. 258; ET: *God in Creation* (London, 1985), p. 17, n. 14 (322).

against subordinationism (the Son of God is less than God the Father) and modalism (the Son of God is a mere mode in which the God who is apart from this world appears). These two errors suffer from the fact that "they try to evade the cross of Jesus Christ" (IV/1 218 = 199), for in the former the Humiliated One is *God* only in a non-essential way, and in the latter God is the *Humiliated One* only in a non-essential way. We really understand the reconciliation only when we understand both as *essential.*

We then also understand that "in it as a passion we have to do with an action . . . an act of God which is coincident with the free action and suffering of a man, but in such a way that this human action and suffering has to be represented and understood as the action and, therefore, the passion of God Himself" (IV/1 269f. = 245). If we fail to see this, we would not understand the New Testament message of reconciliation. According to this message the Humiliated One in his passion suffers as we do in solidarity with this man in his misery of sin. If the mercy of God for this man were only an impotent pity, his suffering would be made permanent, however much it might be regretted. The decisive point, however, is that the mercy of God toward us and his participation in relation to evil mean that the Humiliated One suffered *"for us,"* that he did and suffered that which we could not do and suffer, so that it all took place purely on our behalf. By virtue of this event "for the men of all times and places," their situation as the sinners that they are "has objectively been decisively changed" (IV/1 270 = 245). In stead of making the situation into a permanent one, this is the "revolution of God" (IV/1 609, 627 = 546, 562).

One thing that we must clearly see is that reconciliation does not merely mean that God's attitude toward us is conciliatory. The reconciliation of the world with God in Christ takes place in the form of a real *conflict* of God with sin and sinners. As God exposed himself to sin, he wrestled with it and differentiated himself from it, and since this was done for us, he also differentiated us, too, from sin. In Barth's view reconciliation takes place as the ruthless nonreconciliation of God with the wrong. It is the negation and not the affirmation, the condemnation and not the validation, indeed the destruction of sin and of the subject who has fallen victim to it and now practices it. If reconciliation were to take place in some other form than this, it would practice a "cheap grace" (IV/1 238 = 216) that regards sin as harmless. "The very heart of the atonement is the *overcoming* of sin" (IV/1 278 = 253). This is *not* "out of any desire for vengeance and retribution on the part of God," seeking satisfaction through some sacrificial victim, in order then to become more conciliatory. What we see here is "the radical nature of the divine *love,* which could 'satisfy' itself only in the outworking of its wrath against the man of sin" (IV/1 280 = 254). The wrath of God does not extinguish the love of God; it is the "redemptive fire of his love" (IV/1 546 = 490). It expresses the *righteousness* that is the will of his love. His love "does not rejoice in wrongdoing" (1 Cor. 13:6). It practices righteousness. It is a distorted love that labels the wrong as, in fact, the right. It is graceless to become an accomplice of the wrong, even if it is only passively suffering under it. The reconciling mercy of God, Barth stresses, is an incomparable right act in which God graciously overcomes sin through the exercise of the right. The issue is not that wrong should be "punished"; what is at stake is its removal. He caps it at its wellspring, where it constantly bubbles up, instead of raging at what emerges from the spring (IV/1 279 = 254). We do not know either grace or right if we do not see that in the reality of reconciliation grace and right are not two things, let alone an antithesis, but they are *one* and the same thing (see IV/1 260 = 236-237).

The way in which God's gracious act of right is executed in reconciliation finds expression in Barth's formulation, "The Judge Judged in Our Place" (IV/1 231 = 211). If we are to understand that the Crucified suffered "for us," that he "took our place" and interceded for us, then we have to see that in so doing he *acted* toward us as the divine and definitive and "last day" *Judge,* making and executing his ultimate judgment (IV/1 240 = 218). If we do not say this first, then his solidarity with us would appear to be complicity with the wrongdoing of our sin or would reduce it to mere solidarity with those who suffer wrong at the hands of others. Either way there would be no judgment of the wrong by him. By him! For he as our Judge "took our place," and this means that we are released from and relieved of the function of judge which we think we are permitted to exercise. Man "has no more say even in this home of his, this place where the flesh is most intensively and happily and seriously flesh" (IV/1 254 = 232), for "all sin has its being and origin in the fact that man wants to be his own judge" (IV/1 241 = 220). It is not merely that someone other than ourselves is the Judge. He is the Judge as one who is empathically other than we. He is the *true* Judge. When we judge ourselves, the final result will be to make sin innocuous, while his judgment will result in the condemnation of sin. The verdict he passes is one of grace, but this is not at the cost of a righteous condemnation of the wrongness of sin. "If he were not the Judge, he would not be the . . . Saviour of the world" (IV/1 238 = 217). There is no contradiction here. For it is a "favor" that he as the Judge, whatever he does in detail, is "the One whose concern is for . . . peace, who must uphold the right and prevent the wrong" (IV/1 238 = 217). Barth's answer to the age-long question of why God became man is thus that he did so "in order to *judge* the world" (IV/1 243 = 222). But there is more: he is this

Judge not by creating respect for a norm superior to himself, let alone posited by us, but by establishing right in his very person and in the fullness of his judgment. This Judge is "the measure of all righteousness" (IV/1 240 = 219).

"He is the Saviour of the world in so far as in a . . . most astonishing way He is also its Judge" (IV/1 238 = 217). The judgment he passes on sinners is their pardon. Nor can anyone gainsay it, for his judgment is that of the supreme Judge. The divine Yes is, of course, hidden in the divine No, for this Yes is pronounced when and as the No encounters the man of sin, the one who "suffered for us," and who "entered into our place." He, the Judge, did this by making himself liable for those whom he had to negate as wrongdoers (IV/1 259 = 235-236). His purpose was "to do right at the very place where man had done wrong" (IV/1 261 = 237). He did it "by treading the way of sinners to its bitter end in death, in destruction, in the limitless anguish of separation from God, by delivering up sinful man and sin in His own person to the nonbeing which is properly theirs" (IV/1 278 = 253). In this way he is the Judge who is "judged in our place." The verdict that ought to have been ours was pronounced and executed on him, so that an end was made with us as sinners so that as such we have no more future. We are no longer in the place we occupied when we were sinners. This place is now occupied by him. "Our sin is no longer our own. It is His sin, the sin of Jesus Christ. God — He Himself as the obedient Son of the Father — has made it His own. And in that way He has judged it and judged us as those who committed it" (IV/1 261 = 238). "Our *being in sin* is now in *His* hands" (IV/1 266 = 242). If we do not want to go back before Good Friday and thus fall prey to hopeless abstraction, then we have here the decisive reason that we will find the right knowledge of sin only in him, and not in vain reflection or a "law" abstracted from it. In that he, in our place, trod the way of sinners to its end, he did no wrong, but rather, in keeping with the will of the Father, "He has done this before God and has therefore done *right*" (IV/1 282 = 256). He has acknowledged God's right against himself and against the evildoer on whose behalf he intervened. As such he is "the new man," and *we* are the right man "in that place" where he stands for us (IV/1 283f. = 257-58).

Barth describes this great "day of atonement" as "the day of the dawn of a new heaven and a new earth" (IV/1 285 = 259), for it is the day when the eternal will of God is done in time, the will whose intention is fellowship between God and us and us and God. Since we are sinners, of course, the doing of this will means that "God wills to lose in order that man may gain" (II/2 177 = 162). He executes this will in the atonement, surrendering "His own impassibility" when "facing the world of evil" (II/2 178 = 163). "He elects the cross of Golgotha as His kingly throne. He elects the tomb in the garden as the scene of His being as the living God. That is how God loved the world" (II/2 180 = 165). This love is the justification of us sinners. Yet it is much more. "In this work of the justification of unrighteous man God also and in the first instance *justifies Himself*" (IV/1 626 = 561). Sin is not merely a question for us. "It is a menacing of the whole work of God, the whole world as created by Him," the covenant He has made with the world he created, "a menacing which is . . . quite intolerable to God" (IV/1 455 = 411). The question raised by sin is not whether we can appease an angry God but whether God is really the world's Creator and Lord in view of the chaos that has broken into creation (IV/1 627 = 562). In choosing us to be his covenant-partners, has "God stretched out His hand to [man] in vain" (IV/1 628 = 563)? Since it is God himself whose work is threatened by sin, only he can contend with it. He has done his reconciling work in such a way that he has removed those questions and transformed them into a positive answer. In so doing he has justified himself.

"The Justice of Grace"[4]

The reconciliation of God has the purpose that the human person be justified, that the wrongdoer of sin become right before God. "There never was and there never can be any true Christian Church without the doctrine of justification" (IV/1 583 = 523). Yet how is this truth to be understood? Further, if we assume that the sinner becomes a justified person only through God's grace, is she not the one or the other solely in a nominal sense? Does grace consist of our being called righteous "as though" we were when all the time we are not? Or does it consist of calling its recipients sinners "as though" they were that although they are not that any more? We recall a statement we quoted earlier: "There is no doctrine more dangerous than the Christian doctrine of the reconciliation . . . if we do not consider it with this warning in view. The fact that it speaks of God making good what we have spoiled does not mean that we can call evil good (unless we would also call good evil)" (IV/1 74 = 70 rev.). The warning results from what has been said: God makes good what we do wrong, not by validating but by condemning our wrongdoing. God in his reconciliation says Yes to the human in that he says to his sin and its doer a "No in which there is no hidden Yes" (cf. IV/1 453 = 409). Because all that is true, in our understanding of justification we may

4. CD IV/1 244 = 223.

indeed say Yes to what God has made good, but we must surely never call evil good.

Our protection against the misunderstanding that would allow us to call evil good is the fact that in the justification of man grace does not replace right but that grace happens in the form of a divine right act. "The God who is present and active in the justification of man, and therefore the gracious God, has right and is in the right. . . . This is the backbone of the event of justification" (IV/1 592 = 530-31). The right that God has is his irrevocable "right over man and to man." God "is unchanged in His right, the right of the One who has elected and made Himself the Creator and the Lord of the covenant. . . . Man may fall," but even in his "fall into the abyss he cannot fall out of the sphere of God and therefore out of the right which God has over him and to him." We err if we think that the wrong we do is a private matter not subject to God's jurisdiction. God's right "is not merely a valid right but one which is exercised. It is the right which God exercises for His own sake (because He is . . . the living God) and for the sake of the creature and covenant-partner who even as a transgressor is still subject to His right" (IV/1 596f. = 534-35).

The right act of justification that brings blessing to the sinner has for Barth two aspects. On the one hand, justification means divine *judgment*. It means that "man's wrong, i.e., man himself as a wrongdoer cannot stand in the judgment of God. The righteousness of God means God's negating and overcoming and taking away and destroying wrong and man as the doer of it" (IV/1 597 = 535). Since justification involves judgment, by no means is it that "weak remission" (IV/1 666 = 597) that leaves alone what it has pardoned, whether in the sense of that double bookkeeping or in the modern view of sin and grace as two entities that can tolerate one another. The concept of divine judgment in Barth's writings has often been misunderstood, either with the opinion that he doesn't have one, or that it works for him as a counterpart to the concept of the grace of God, as in an older tradition. Barth does indeed give a new interpretation to a concept that for him is indispensable. As he sees it, the judgment of God is an act of the divine right that is not in opposition to grace but is rather *that* form of grace in which it cannot be reconciled with human wrong. It is no abstract God who opposes this wrong, which is then weakened and rendered harmless by grace. Precisely the gracious God must be thought of solely as "the act of opposition" to sin (IV/2 449 = 400). Divine judgment is that *element* in God's grace by virtue of which that grace is an "act of opposition" to the wrong of sin, and the doer of sin, neither of which God can ever call good. Therefore, God's "grace would not be grace without His judgment" (IV/1 545 = 490). For this reason the judgment of God, even when we cannot know it as such (IV/1 601 = 539), is never without grace, but is rather "the redemptive fire of His love" (IV/1 546 = 490, cf. 242 = 221). For Barth, indeed, the divine judgment is the "sum of every temporal realization" of the divine election of grace in which it is the will of God to treat us as his own even in the No that he says to the sinner who is alienated from him (II/2 819 = 733). Thus, Barth can assert that "it is therefore grace if he [that sinner] has to perish and die as such" (IV/1 604 = 542).

This is why justification has a second aspect, not by virtue of an immanent inevitability, but by virtue of the grace of God in the right act of justification. "The justification of man is the *establishment* of his *right,* the introduction of the life of a new man who is righteous before God" (IV/1 619 = 554). Would not God have renounced his right over us and to us if he had given up sinners to destruction? Certainly we ourselves have no claim upon God that he should do more than execute his righteousness in the form of judgment. Moreover, for such sinners, who having done wrong must surely "die" based on the divine execution of right, there can be nothing beyond one's wrongness, unless it be in the wonder of the "resurrection from the dead" (IV/1 620 = 555). The message of justification proclaims this wonder. It does not speak of the immanent transformation of a person from one that was wrong into one that is now right. And yet it does speak of "the transition of man from his wrong to his right, from death to life" (IV/1 621 = 557), of a *"creatio ex contrario,* but a *creatio!"* [= creation out of its opposite]. It speaks about God's judgment in which "those who are in the wrong are set in the right and the dead are raised again and are alive" (IV/1 661 = 593). Justification means "the establishment of the lordship of God over this man, fulfilled in majestic defiance of the supposed necessity of our sin and in irresistible contradiction of the claim that we can and must continue in it" (II/2 863 = 771).

For Barth everything depends upon our not regarding the killing of sinners as "only nominal." If we were to take that view, then a "dualism" would result in which we could "alternately" assess ourselves as still more or less sinful, or as no longer sinful at all. This will lead on finally to "the basic schema which underlies every religion of redemption and every philosophy of life": the contrast between an *"empirical* reality" in which man knows himself to be imperfect, and an *"ideal* truth" toward which he strives to form himself according to the idea of a right person as his authentic being. For Barth it is most important that we understand that God "does not work either here or there"; neither in the removal of the wrong nor in the production of the right man does God fashion a "mere 'as if,' but actualities" both here and there (IV/1 605-608 = 542-45 rev.). The killing of the former and the resurrecting of the latter person actually *take place.* They have occurred already, not in us but in Jesus Christ, who took our place. Our righteousness with its two sides is to that degree "always a *strange* righteousness" (IV/1 613 = 549). Nevertheless, as Barth emphasizes, it is *our* righteousness, for Jesus Christ stands in *our* place, and we then also stand in that place. "His history is as such our history . . . the history that is most authentically ours" (IV/1 612 = 547 rev.). With his death "our wrong is extinguished" (IV/1 617f. = 553). "His right is *our* right" (IV/1 620 = 556). We cannot take all this in an exclusively Christological sense, as though the "fire of his love" were no longer something that concerned us. What happened in him directly concerns us. "In Him we are quite alone . . . torn away . . . from the whole world of fairytale and myth, taken right beyond all our empirical and ideal pictures of ourselves, *genuinely alone,* and therefore [are] the men who stand in that judgment and transition" (IV/1 612 = 548).

As the history that "concerns us," what we experience here is not, of course, identical with the history of Jesus Christ. "We are in Him . . . but we are still not He Himself" (IV/1 613 = 549). What he did *for* us, what he suffered and received must not constantly be repeated anew. We need to recognize and acknowledge it, and to do so not merely in an act of our minds but in an act of our lives, by which we grasp that the concluding stroke drawn in Christ across our old life need not constantly be drawn anew, and the door to a new life opened to us in his resurrection does not constantly need to be opened anew. As history that concerns us, both that stroke and that door intervene in our life in a way that puts us on a new road and directs us to walk forward along it. It is the road on which our old life, thanks to that concluding stroke, remains our past always, and our new life, thanks to that opened door, remains always our future. As we stride forward along this road we are those who have *simultaneously* "in every present . . . both this past and this future" (IV/1 639 = 573). We are still in the *full sense* sinners, but we are also in the *full sense* pardoned and righteous (IV/1 643, 672 = 576, 602). Our striding along this road is not a constant running around in circles. "A garden path may be circular. But a garden path is not a true way. A true way has a beginning and an end which is different from it" (IV/1 622f. = 558). This road has as its goal our being before God as those who are right, and not an eternal combination of right and wrong (IV/1 673 = 603).

All of this casts a light upon Barth's controversial description of sin as that which is "absolutely impossible" (IV/1 454 = 410). This implies neither in an abstract sense the impossibility of the sin which in fact continues to take place, nor its theoretical inexplicability. The meaning of that formulation is that God, by drawing in Christ the concluding stroke through our sin, has taken away from us all reason for sin. He has done this so radically that the human can find no basis for sin in herself. If, nevertheless, she still sins, then she is doing something for which there is no basis, "something which has been eternally removed and destroyed" (IV/1 618 = 553). One is not merely doing something that one has been ordered not to do. Just as our righteous acts do not have a demand as their basis but the law of God filled by the gospel and fulfilled in Christ, so sin is not just the doing of what is forbidden, but an act which has been made groundless in the killing of the old man in Christ. The core of sin is not "immorality"; it is hostility to grace.

Does this mean that there can be no true knowledge of sin because such knowledge merely means that sin is considered "no longer relevant in actuality"?[5] If, for Barth, we can know the intolerability of sin only from the fact that God has actually borne it in Christ, then we can obviously know sin only as that which has been set aside. Indeed, "it is only of forgiven sin that we know . . . that it is sin" (II/2 860 = 768). Yet is not this taking too light a view of sin? That is an overly hasty conclusion, for it overlooks the decisive fact that so long as we believe that we can wrestle with sin ourselves and thus the Reconciler is concealed from us, so long is our sin also concealed to us, according to Barth. Yet when the reconciliation of God is manifested to us, our sin is also for the first time made manifest to us. In God's pardoning of us we have both behind us: the unforgiven *and* unrecognized sin, and we have both at the same time before us: the forgiven sin *and* the sin made plain to us in the light of forgiveness. "Forgiven sin does not mean sin . . . forgotten. . . . The statement that it is forgiven does not mean . . . that penitence is no longer required. We . . . [are not] acquitted and justified in God's judgment, if we do not acknowledge and confess our sin, if it does not grieve us to the heart, if we do not remain under the accusation of the command, if we do not maintain the responsibility which we owe to God for what we are and do and which shatters all our assurance" (II/2 845 = 756). We do not have to bear our sin one more time. But, corresponding to the critical reconciliation in which Christ has borne our sin, we do have something to bear: such a self-critical responsibility. We correspond to the reconciling Yes of God to us sinners, and his implacable No to our sin, when in gratitude to his grace we live a life of penitence. For Barth penitence is not the condition but the consequence of the gracious pardon of the sinner that makes it possible to begin with. The goodness of God leads us to repentance (Rom. 2:4; cf. II/2 860 = 768).

For one thing, this makes plain a special significance of the knowledge

5. Gerhard Ebeling, *Lutherstudien*, vol. 3 (Tübingen, 1985), p. 564.

of the law implied in the gospel. It is not mere demanding that one stand up to one's sin, but rather the gospel of reconciliation that is able to overcome our "inability to lament." Only when we know that we are accepted are we free to admit our reversion, whereas in our former anxiety at the exposure we would encounter we would do everything to trivialize or dismiss or repress it. When our nakedness is covered, we no longer need to find ways of escape. Guilt forgiven is the opposite of guilt repressed, where guilt is not really removed but pushed into the subconscious where it continues to work in sinister fashion. Life in the repression of guilt is an existence without grace. Life in gratitude for God's grace manifests itself in the fact that guilt no longer needs to be repressed.

For another thing, this also means that true penitence is not something that we first expect of others, but is rather our own penitence. That Christians know they are reconciled is first demonstrated in that they continuingly beat their "mea culpa" on their own breasts. They then deal with the guilt of others only in solidarity with them. "The New Testament knows very fully and with great exactitude what goes on outside, but basically it does not look or talk through the window ('*You* who are evil,' Matt. 7:11). The interesting sinner is not the worldly man but the *Christian....* The Christian knows and says this first and decisively about himself and only then about others" (CL 36f. = 25).

The Validity of Reconciliation

We turn now to Barth's central definition: "Reconciliation is the *fulfillment* of the *covenant* between God and man" (IV/1 22). This means that reconciliation takes place with the covenant as its presupposition and its context. Reconciliation is God's reaction to human sin. If one merely reacts, however, there is always the danger of being sucked into the undertow of that against which we are reacting (cf. I/2 709 = 633!). If reconciliation were *only* a reaction to sin, could not sin constantly "make it questionable" and even "make it impossible"? (IV/1, 71 = 67). The covenant will of God is, by contrast, not a reaction; it is itself the action of the eternal will of God that precedes all sin. Sin arrives on the scene too late to make that will questionable. In that God's action in carrying out his covenant will then confronts the obstacle of sin, it takes on in fact the form of a reaction to sin. "The *reaction* as such takes place along the line of that *action* determined from the first and already initiated." Therefore, "even in this particular form it is the accomplishment of His covenant will" (IV/1 37 = 36).

The point is that God does not engage humanity merely *on account of human sin*. That would make sin into the presupposition of God's action. God would be, on the one hand, so dependent upon sin that it would be made eternal. On the other hand, if humanity had not sinned, God would be a God separate from humanity, an inhumane deity. The point, further, is that sin certainly *cannot prevent* God from uniting himself to us and that reconciliation can only mean that its implementation takes on the character of a "notwithstanding," a divine *protest* (IV/1 73 = 68). Because as a reaction to sin, reconciliation falls within the context of the original action of God's covenant will, it cannot be vanquished by sin but can itself vanquish sin. This obstacle can only mean for God *even more cause* to relate himself to humanity (IV/1 73 = 68).

If reconciliation, then, takes place only within the implementation of the covenant will of God and inseparable from it, then for Barth reconciliation is no incidental occurrence in the covenant, which could be lacking and without which the covenant would stand. That covenant would be threatened with pointing towards "the void," toward "emptiness" (IV/1 72 = 68), if it were not "fulfilled" with the reconciliation. We recall our earlier statement that for Barth God's covenant was not originally between "God and humanity" in general, but concretely between God and *Israel*. By the "grace that elected Israel," Israel became God's covenant partner, Yahweh's son (IV/1 181f. = 165-66). That the reconciliation takes place within the covenant means then just as concretely and with "divine necessity" (IV/1 184f. = 168-169) that "The Word did not simply become any 'flesh' . . . it became Jewish flesh" (IV/1 181 = 166). If, like Anselm, we ask why God became man, we answer: for the reason that, as the Old Testament discloses, the covenant became "a fellowship threatened with destruction and abrogation" because the human partner had broken it. In this connection the coming of Jesus Christ does not mean that the covenant with Israel is *replaced* by another, but that it is *fulfilled* — with reconciliation! Reconciliation is the "confirmation" of the covenant (IV/1 71 = 67), without which the covenant would, indeed, have been pointing into the void. But it is not pointing towards the void because its fulfillment by reconciliation cannot be reversed. This is because reconciliation means that the covenant grace of God "shows itself and acts as His free grace to the undeserving, as grace for lost sinners" (IV/1 73 = 69). For this reason, the No that Israel outside the church says to Christ can not only not set aside this fulfillment of the covenant made with it, but rather confirms it. In virtue of this fulfillment, Israel is eternally elected. Since the covenant with Israel has been fulfilled in this way, it has now been opened up to the truly undeserving peoples. It has become a covenant between "God and *humanity*."

At this point Barth makes a far-reaching correction of the Christian tradition. Those who are brought into the covenant from the nations can be sure of the *validity* of reconciliation as grace "for lost sinners" only if they confess that it is valid first for Israel, yes, for the Israel that rejected Christ, and thus confess Israel's eternal election. A Christianity that does not confess this would necessarily become so unsure of the covenant's validity that it would constantly run the risk of trying to create certainty for itself through the surrogates of self-confirmation, self-activity, and self-commendation, as well as through separation from any who might disrupt such activities.

Reconciliation, then, as the basis for the permanent and eternal election of Israel into God's covenant — making all those surrogates unnecessary — is indeed the basis for the reconciling of the *world* with God. Barth thinks of the general here in terms of the priority of the particular. The fact that the "world" is reconciled to God means that, through it, "for the men of all times and places . . . their situation has objectively been decisively *changed*, whether they are aware of it or not" (IV/1 270 = 245). Their awareness of it, of course, is not an indifferent matter, for those who are not aware of reconciliation live unreconciled lives in relation to God, to others, and to themselves. For Barth, then, it is "necessarily the case that the knowledge of it as the act of God and the knowledge of the change in the world situation brought about by it can come about individually only in the decision of faith, in which this act becomes to the individual . . . the Word of God accepted in obedience, in which the passion of Jesus Christ is attested as having happened for him, and therefore in very truth for the world" (IV/1 270 = 245).

According to Barth faith is the acknowledgment, recognition, and confession of the reality of reconciliation (IV/1 847ff. = 758ff.). To be sure, God "creates the presupposition" (IV/1 841 = 753). As a human act, faith is *accepting as true*, not *making true* something that would not be true without it. Faith is not a pre-condition but rather a consequence of the validity of reconciliation. Its urgency is not due to a demand that argues that without it reconciliation would lose its validity. Because reconciliation is indeed *valid*, valid for the believer as well, it is then the invitation to accept it as true. Because the believer cannot accept it as true without seeing that it is also valid for those who do not yet accept it as true, he cannot believe without immediately accepting as true the responsibility to witness to it to all people. Since, however, he does not have to make it true, this witness is profoundly different from that surrogate that only served one's own activity and the "self-commendation" that is so oppressive to others (I/2 368 = 336).

Reconciliation does not have validity because we ascribe validity to it. We must not understand faith in this way either. Faith, when rightly understood, rejects this notion. Reconciliation has validity because God ascribes validity to it by virtue of the fact that it is his act. We need to acknowledge it, then, as the temporal fulfillment of "the eternal will of God" (II/2 176ff. = 161ff.). Yet its validity is not like that of an immovable rock from which we may distance ourselves at will, or like that of a perhaps significant historical fact from which, whether we "know it or not," we may gradually move away. It took place not only at one time but "once and for all, the history of a decision which has been taken and cannot be reversed or superseded. . . . That is how God loved the world, and *it* is so, it is in *force,* and must and will be, whether there be few or many who know the fact, and whatever attitude the world may take to it. . . . Reconciliation in itself and as such is not a process which has to be kept in motion towards some goal which is still far distant. It does not need to be repeated or extended or perfected. It is a unique history, but as such — because God in Christ was its subject — it is present in all its fullness in every age. It is also the immediate future in every age" (IV/1 81 = 76). It is valid because it creates validity *for itself* always and everywhere. "It reaches beyond its own particular sphere, which embraces our sphere, the sphere of human life generally, which comprehends every man virtually, prospectively and *de iure* and the Christian actually, effectively and *de facto,* which assigns to him a receptive and spontaneous share" (IV/3 322 = 279). In virtue of this event, because Christ and not the church is its subject, the Reconciler God is not just unknown but is "very well *known*" to the "non-Christian world" (CL 194 = 119). Similarly, he is not just *"known"* to the church, but *"also unknown"* (CL 222 = 134). These facts show us that in this event "He has not yet reached His goal. He is still moving towards it" (IV/3 377 = 327). At the level where what is already valid must still contend for its validity, he still suffers, and the evil, which in reconciliation has been made into "nothingness" yet is still possible as the "impossible possibility," still endeavors as "an elusive shadow" to draw us into its negating wickedness. But only as an elusive shadow, only as an impossible possibility, only as the resistance waged against the validity that is already superior to it, which can neither change nor put in question the goal toward which the Reconciler is still underway.

Does Barth's train of thought then require that this goal must be a "universal reconciliation"? Three comments should be made with regard to his thought at this point. First, a doctrine of universal reconciliation means that a human sets himself or herself on the throne of the divine Judge, whose judgment is certainly one of grace, albeit his free grace. Our sole task in the "ministry of reconciliation" is to be its witnesses (IV/1 81 = 76). This ministry sets us in the *"open . . . situation of proclamation"* (II/2 528 = 476). The situation is open not so much because it is always open with regard to how many believe or not in response to it, but because it must always proceed with "respect [for] the *freedom* of divine grace" (II/2 462 = 417) — that freedom to elect and to call those to whom God in his grace grants it. "No right or necessity can legitimately be deduced. Just as the gracious God does not need to elect or call any single man, so He does not need to elect or call all mankind. His election and calling do not give rise to any historical metaphysics, but only to the necessity of attesting them . . ." (II/2 462 = 417f.).

Second, since God's grace without his judgment would not be grace, we can not know his grace if we first see under his judgment those others in regard to whom a doctrine of universal reconciliation seems questionable to us. We must *first* see the judgment of divine grace falling upon *ourselves*. Why, then, have we been given that grace? Why have we not been excluded? This question shatters for Barth the worst, the Christian form of "desecration of the name of God," namely, an "attempted *nostrification* of God," in which Christians equate their cause with God's and God's cause with theirs (CL 214f. = 130). It also shakes up the traditional distribution of humanity into those who have faith, ourselves usually included, and those who do not, whereby we tend to think here of definite others. The question reminds us of the sovereignty of God in which he demonstrates his grace by making the first last and the last first (cf. II/2 330f. = 300f.).

Third, "there is no good reason why we should forbid ourselves, or be forbidden, openness to the possibility that in the reality of God and man in Jesus Christ there is contained . . . the supremely unexpected withdrawal of the final threat. . . . If for a moment we accept the unfalsified truth of the reality which even now so forcefully limits the perverted human situation, does it not point plainly in the direction of a truly *eternal* divine patience and deliverance and therefore of a . . . universal reconciliation? If we are forbidden to count on this . . . we are surely commanded the more definitely to *hope* and *pray* for this." Appearances to the contrary, "His mercies never come to an end" (Lam. 3:22-23, 31; IV/3 550f. = 478).

The Prevailing Spirit — Pneumatology

Forgetting the Spirit?

A common complaint has plagued Barth's theology, namely, that he does not speak enough about the Holy Spirit and his working in us and to us. Different reasons are given for this complaint. In 1981 it was argued that the "overshadowing" of pneumatology by Christology failed to satisfy the pneumocentric concerns of the modern charismatic movement.[1] In 1936 it was claimed that his theology was unable "really to perceive the powerful work of the Holy Spirit" as it was being demonstrated in the "Führer" of the Nordic race.[2] Be that as it may, when Barth at the end of his career gave serious consideration to "the possibility of a theology of the third article, . . . a theology predominantly and decisively of the Holy Spirit,"[3] was he not pointing to a gap in his thought as others had done?

He had much earlier considered this "possibility" and wrote about it:[4] Christian theology "is aware of God as the *Word* of the Father which is spoken to man and as the *Spirit* of the Father and of the Word which enables man to hear the Word. It cannot seek to have merely one centre . . . just be-

---

1. Philip Joseph Rosato, *The Spirit as the Lord: The Pneumatology of Karl Barth* (Edinburgh, 1981), pp. 181, 183.

2. Fritz Mund, *Pietismus: Eine Schicksalsfrage an die Kirche heute,* 2nd ed. (Marburg, 1938), pp. 14ff.

3. Karl Barth, "Nachwort," in *Friedrich Schleiermacher* (Munich and Hamburg, 1968), p. 311; ET: "Concluding Unscientific Postscript on Schleiermacher," *The Theology of Schleiermacher* (Grand Rapids, 1982), p. 278.

4. Karl Barth, *Die protestantische Theologie im 19. Jahrhundert: Ihre Vorgeschichte und ihre Geschichte* (Zurich, 1947), pp. 410ff.; ET: *Protestant Theology in the Nineteenth Century: Its Background and History* (Valley Forge, 1972), pp. 458-459, 460.

cause its subject is God." If it were to make either the former or the latter the center, it would become either metaphysics or mysticism. "A pure teaching of the Word will take into account the Holy Spirit as the divine reality in which the Word is heard, just as a pure teaching of the Spirit of the Son will take into account the Word of God as the divine reality in which the Word is given to us." The former is the Christological theology of the Word of God that Barth develops, whose goodness is dependent upon the demonstration of its inclusion of a theology of the Spirit. The latter would be for him the "theology of the Holy Spirit" — he could speak of it as the theology promoted by the Reformers (I/2 228 = 208-9) — that would be "the teaching of man brought face to face with God by God, of man granted grace by grace." Such a theology's worth, if it is not to be "theology [that] was now no longer theology," depends upon whether or not it demonstrates that the "*divinity* of the Holy Spirit" is truly its center. When it is, then such a theology of the Spirit is "just as much justified" as the former. The two are both saying the same thing, although in different ways.

There were good reasons why Barth should give the preference to the Christological theology of the Word of God in his thinking. The main reason was this: he feared that in the modern situation a theology of the Spirit would be open to serious misunderstandings. Although he often asked whether such a theology *could* have been the "desire" of Neo-Protestantism,[5] he concluded that, in fact, "it was at this point that Neo-Protestantism failed," for it "forgot the divinity of the Holy Spirit" by making our human freedom for God "a more precise establishing of the all-dominating 'freedom from man's side'" (I/2 228 = 209). Its forgetting the Spirit did not consist of not talking enough about the Spirit but of no longer respecting its divinity. The Spirit was "equated . . . with that which we know as our own created spirit or soul."[6] It is precisely in the "fullness of the 'life of the Spirit' that the concept of the Holy Spirit has become impossible for our epoch." For "the Spirit is God and thus the subject of faith; therein lies the boundary of Christian thought . . . over against our modern and fully unfounded assumption that we possess a spirit that permeates all culture."[7] That was how the philosopher H. Barth put it when backing up his brother.

Karl Barth sees J. G. Herder as responsible for this modern concept of

---

5. CD I/2 228 = 208; 275 = 252f.; Karl Barth, *Protestantische Theologie,* pp. 411-12; ET: *Protestant Theology,* pp. 459f.; Barth, "Nachwort," p. 311; ET: "Concluding Unscientific Postscript," p. 278.

6. Karl Barth, with Heinrich Barth, "Zur Lehre vom Heiligen Geist," *Zwischen den Zeiten* I (1930): p. 41.

7. Karl Barth, "Zur Lehre vom Heiligen Geist," pp. 33, 35.

the Spirit with his idea of life — oriented against Kant's "intellectualism" and focusing on "sensibility" and "experience" — that bubbles up through all living things, God and creature alike, through the "medium of the living Spirit": "'Tis only when the mind, which seeks to live / In all men's souls, o'erlooks the narrow bounds / Of self, when heart beats with a thousand more / That you are made immortal, powerful, like God. . . ."[8] In Schleiermacher, too, Barth sees a concept of the Spirit as "identical with subjective stimulation," a view which knows about the "supreme enhancement" of the human spirit, but no longer knows that "God is really God and the Spirit is really the Spirit and not the stream of life."[9] Barth found in this whole epoch a "reinterpretation of the Holy Spirit into the creative power of our own spirit," into a human self-understanding that is "upwardly open," and "a long and melancholy development" into Troeltsch's equation of the Holy Spirit with the "direct religious productivity of the individual."[10]

Both the younger and the later Barth saw in such teachings about the Spirit a forgetting of the Holy Spirit that was not a theology of the Holy Spirit. Here the Spirit is not conceived of as the Spirit *of God*. The human spirit thinks only about itself, seeing itself as either divine or as intrinsically open to God. This approach avenges itself, for now the Word or the Son of God cannot be thought of any longer as truly God, but at most as a "demigod" since the human is open to God anyway and thus no longer really needs God's self-disclosure. Again, "if the Christ of the New Testament is a demigod from above or below, then naturally faith in Him becomes a human possibility. . . . But in this case there is in fact no need for the deity of the Holy Spirit who creates this faith. On this view the name 'Holy Spirit' may very well be a mere name for a particularly profound, serious and vital conviction of truth or experience of conscience" (I/1 482 = 460). How dangerous such a view is, and why the church must necessarily reject it, came to light when at the beginning of 1934 Barth exclaimed to the German Christians in Berlin, "We have another Spirit."[11]

If he saw in this concept of the Spirit not a deficiency in talk about the Spirit but a loss of the knowledge of the deity of the Holy Spirit, then it must be clear that he was not engaged in neglecting the doctrine of the Spirit even

8. Karl Barth, *Protestantische Theologie,* pp. 285-86; ET: *Protestant Theology,* pp. 320f.

9. Karl Barth, *Die Theologie Schleiermachers* (Munich, 1933), pp. 62-63, 429; ET: *The Theology of Schleiermacher* (Grand Rapids, 1982), pp. 30, 31, 240-41.

10. Karl Barth, "Zur Lehre vom Heiligen Geist," pp. 41, 44, 46.

11. Karl Barth, *Gottes Wille und unsere Wünsche* (*Theologische Existenz heute!* 7) (Munich, 1934), p. 4; cf. Karl Barth, *Reformation als Entscheidung* (*Theologische Existenz heute!* 3) (Munich, 1933), p. 22.

if his No appeared to do so to the proponents of this concept of the Spirit. His concern, albeit succinctly addressed by him, was the critical reclamation of the knowledge of the *deity* of the Spirit. If that is correct, then it clearly follows that if his theology sought to be a Christology of the Word of God, as the first possibility we discussed, then it can hardly be claimed that he sought to remedy Neo-Protestantism's forgetfulness of the *deity* of the Spirit by himself forgetting the Spirit — so that the pendulum would react to his proposal of a Christological theology by swinging back to a theology centered on the concept of the Spirit. Rather, careful attention should be given to the fact that Barth's Christologically formulated theology includes within itself a certain doctrine of the Holy Spirit *and* that he clearly was endeavoring to rediscover the knowledge of the deity of the Holy Spirit that had been lost in the pneumatology of Neo-Protestantism. Whoever wants to develop a theology of the Holy Spirit, which Barth certainly regarded as possible, will have then to take Barth's question about the deity of the Spirit with utmost seriousness.

Whether theology is a theology of the Word or of the Spirit, for Barth one "can never more mistake the work of the Holy Spirit . . . than by making it the object of an independent investigation." The result "will certainly be *either* that we merely find something extremely human in which Christ is unrecognizable, . . . *or* that we most inappropriately confuse and equate the occurrence which we know . . . with Christ Himself." "Where the Holy Spirit is sundered from Christ, sooner or later He is always transmuted into quite a different spirit, the spirit of the religious man, and finally the human spirit in general," or, indeed, a universal creaturely spirit (I/2 271, 273 = 248, 251).

A *mere* theology of revelation, of course, that is abstracted from the work of the Holy Spirit, would become for Barth a metaphysics. It would look at revelation objectively as a self-enclosed datum placed before the human, who would then have the task of deciding what to do with it. Barth suspected that such an objectivistic theology contributed to the more recent theology characterized by that concept of the Spirit. That modern theology of the Spirit should then be understood as a reaction trying to correct the damage done by the earlier theology. It caused further damage, however, by adding to the given revelation an extra revelation that united the divine and human spirits. This means that the damage done by such a view of the Spirit can be dealt with only by removing the earlier problems that led to it — based on the insight that "an objective revelation as such . . . a revelation that does not penetrate to man . . . would be an idol like all the rest, and perhaps the worst of all idols. . . . If we think of the subjective as something which has later to be added, then necessarily we have thought of the objective as an idol, and it is hardly likely that the added subjective will not also be portrayed as an idol" (I/2 258-260 = 237-38).

The Deity of the Spirit

When we acknowledge that the Holy Spirit is *God,* then in this first step a decision has already been made. It means that the normative source of the knowledge of the Holy Spirit cannot consist of various experiences and sensibilities ascertained by the human person on her own. They are intrinsically ambiguous. If "the Holy Spirit acting upon man is also *God,*" then the decision means that "His work upon us is also *revelation,* and knowledge of Him is knowledge of *revelation....* We have no right, then, to expect to import into the reality of God's process of revelation to and among men any contribution learned from a source of knowledge different from Holy Scripture. In this respect also we must realize the adequacy of Holy Scripture as the source of our knowledge" (I/2 227 = 207-8).

Yet how are we to understand revelation if it is not to be understood as "an objective revelation as such"? Barth tells us that "the fact that God gives His *pneuma* to man or that man receives this *pneuma* implies that God comes to man, that He discloses Himself to man and man to Himself" (I/1 472 = 450). What does this mean? After all, God has already come to us in the incarnation of the Word (John 1:14)! It means that in the Holy Spirit the One who has come to humanity already comes to us again. We are to see two acts in the one and same revelation. Yes, in the one and the same revelation! We find here a rejection of the doctrine of a "third kingdom of the Holy Spirit" that arose in the Middle Ages and was given a modern form by Lessing. This doctrine "imagined that the historical Christ could now be left behind as something antiquated." Barth held that this separating of the Spirit from Christ led to the absorption of the Spirit into the human spirit (I/2 273 = 250). Further, when appeal was made to the "spirit that obviously lives in us all," faith was enlisted in "an alien service," that of "Mammon" and even of nationalism.[12] Barth's thesis is a repudiation of the idea that there is a revelation of the Spirit separate from the revelation of Christ, whose content is something new and totally different from the revelation of Christ.

Yet in the one revelation there are two things to be distinguished. Just

---

12. Karl Barth, *Reformation als Entscheidung* (*Theologische Existenz heute!* 3) (Munich, 1933), p. 20; ET: "Reformation as Decision," in L. W. Spitz, *The Reformation: Basic Interpretations* (Lexington, Mass., 1972), pp. 166-67.

as we find the law of God in the gospel, and just as what God wills to do with us is "enclosed" in what he does for us, correspondingly and in a related fashion, the work of the Holy Spirit is "enclosed" in the revelation of Christ (I/2 262 = 240). Barth uses different pairs of concepts to describe the distinction between the two acts in the one revelation. He says, for example, that "the once in time . . . history of Jesus Christ" *(illic et tunc)* becomes "for certain men" in the Holy Spirit *(hic et nunc)* "the event of their renewing" (IV/4 29 = 26). Or he puts it this way: as God has revealed himself in Christ as the speaker of his Word, so he in the Holy Spirit makes humans into the recipients of his Word (I/1 270 = 247). Or again, what has taken place in Christ *de iure* for everyone becomes in the Holy Spirit an event that is valid *de facto* for concrete individuals (IV/2 578 = 511). Or again, the reconciliation of the world with God in Christ is the valid "objective revelation" irrespective of human concurrence, and the "subjective revelation" is the outworking of this reconciliation in humans through the Holy Spirit that evokes our concurrence (I/2 260 = 238). Or again, whereas the revelation of Christ is simultaneously the concealment of God, for God does not put himself at our disposal and opposes a natural ability to know God, in the Holy Spirit we are dealing with a form of divine revelation that opens itself up to us (I/1 350f. = 331-332).

The distinctions make it clear that we profoundly misunderstand God's revelation if we view it only as objective revelation or as a brute fact of the past, as something that can become actual and present and vital only through human manipulation. A view of this kind automatically combines with a righteousness of works or with a mystical immediacy to God through appropriation of the divine. Revelation rules out such a view, for it is an event that "moves out and communicates itself" (IV/3 7 = 8), an event in which the "objective revelation" bears witness to itself in the Spirit, makes itself present and shows itself to be alive, makes itself man's "contemporary" (IV/3 571f. = 497). It does not stand outside humanity as an alien counterpart but "imparts" itself to us (IV/3 618 = 538; IV/2 737 = 651-652). It also has the character of a something "perfect": "It is finished" (John 19:30; I/2 260 = 238). This perfected character means that the subjective work of the Spirit adds no content that leads beyond it, but is rather "enclosed" in it. But it does not mean that revelation is something closed in upon itself. In that its content has to do with the fellowship into which God sets himself with the human so that she might be set in fellowship with him, in that this has happened "for us," in that the Crucified One as the Living One *reveals* the act of reconciliation accomplished on the cross, this revelation presses outward beyond itself to the humanity of all ages, presses itself as a work of the Spirit into the life of humanity as a dynamic event that concerns all people at all times and in all places. The fact that the "objective revelation" takes the form of concealment means that "God's self-unveiling remains an act of sovereign divine freedom" (I/1 339 = 321). This does not mean that God could retract his having come to humanity. What it means is that the objective aspect of the objective revelation discloses itself from within, and thus it is not an object that is open to our capricious human grasping. If it were, then revelation would in fact be an idol in our human hands.

The good meaning of the fact that the work of the Spirit "is not to be regarded . . . as a new instruction, illumination and stimulation of man that goes beyond Christ" (I/1 475 = 452-53) is that its work is Christ's coming to us, the *revelation* of the revelation to definite people, the "irruption" of objective revelation "into the subjective, . . . the impress of objective revelation upon us" (I/2 261 = 239). Thus the Spirit's work upon humans aims at their recognition of revelation, but at a "noetic which has all the force of a divine ontic" (IV/3 343 = 297) which "should . . . alter the whole man" (IV/3 211 = 184). It is creative in that God *makes* us for the first time into recipients of revelation (I/2 230 = 210), creates an entry for himself where there was none,[13] and thus guarantees man's participation in revelation (I/1 475 = 453). It is not a church institution that does this although God does it in "the area of the church" (I/2 230 = 210), making use of "definite signs of its objective reality" given by God (I/2 243 = 223). It does not take place through personal appropriation, although the subjective revelation aims at "man's participation" (I/2 289 = 266). "God Himself and God alone" does it (I/2 230 = 210).

It thus follows that "the statements about the operations of the Holy Spirit are statements whose subject is God and not man, and in no circumstances can they be transformed into statements about man" (I/1 485 = 462). The work of the Holy Spirit discloses that God does that which the human person is unable to do. "It is real in the Holy Spirit that we are free for God. And this settles the fact that we are not free for God except in the Holy Spirit" (I/2 265f. = 243). As Barth sees it, the Holy Spirit overturns the pillar of the modern doctrine of the spirit, namely, the assertion that there is a capacity for God as a given in the human person. The human incapacity to make oneself into a participant in revelation is not a universally acknowledged truth. Humans will dispute it hotly. Only in the experience of the Holy Spirit does God's Word "rid him of any idea that he possesses a possibility of his own for such a meeting" (I/2 280 = 234 rev.). Indeed, the whole idea that

---

13. Karl Barth, *Unterricht in der christlichen Religion,* vol. 1 (Zurich, 1985), p. 243; ET: *Göttingen Dogmatics* (Grand Rapids, 1990), p. 197.

the Holy Spirit sanctions the view that we are equal partners with God is un-masked as a lie (IV/3 513 = 445-446). If a person's presence at revelation were based upon one's innate capacity for it, then one would be "in his own way the lord in revelation," and would "confront" it "as an object," competent to "gain control over it." In that the human person is enabled by the Spirit alone to be present at revelation, he is told what he "does not want . . . to be true"; "man is, as it were, challenged in his own house" (I/1 491 = 468).

This negative is only the reverse side of a positive, so that "there is not the slightest contradiction between the offices of the Holy Spirit as Com-forter and as Judge" (I/2 267 = 245). That God himself sees to it that we are present at his revelation is the perfection of his *grace* in his turning to us. Full and free grace is his turning to us in his "objective revelation"; full and free grace is his making of us into addressees of that revelation. Where the divine Spirit is united with the human spirit, the result is either the "disappearance of the true confrontation of God and man," which distorts *free* grace, in a mysticism in which man discovers divinity in himself and himself as divine, in "an experience of union induced" by him.[14] Or, the "evil spirit" of works righteousness, distorting *all* of grace, breaks out in the person who proffers his ability to transcend himself as his movement toward God.[15]

Conversely, Barth thought that the history of theology had followed a sensible course in the early church. "It is logical that this doctrine had to be the last stage in the development of the trinitarian dogma. It had to be reached before the doctrine of grace . . . could become a problem. The Refor-mation with its doctrine of justification by faith alone can also be under-stood only against the background of this specific dogma" (I/1 491 = 468). If the "dedication and appropriation" of revelation is pure grace, then it is *God* who provides this for man, just as God shows himself to man as the God of real *grace* by giving himself directly for man's appropriation as the One who is turned to man in his revelation. The *grace* that conducts revelation to its goal demonstrates the deity of the Spirit. The Spirit displays his deity in the fact that he *corresponds* to the "objective revelation" — in which God deter-mines himself graciously for fellowship with us and us for fellowship with him — by his graciously bringing us into correspondence with this goal. He demonstrates his deity in the fact that he is the Spirit of Jesus Christ: "The Holy Spirit is the Spirit of God, because He is the Spirit of the Word. And that is the very reason and the only reason why we acquire eyes and ears for God in the Holy Spirit" (I/2 271 = 248).

14. CD IV/3 620 = 539-40; I/1 505 = 481.
15. Karl Barth, "Zur Lehre vom Heiligen Geist," pp. 63-64.

If, like the Speaker of the Word, and like the Word (the Son) that is spoken, the Spirit as the Word achieving its goal is *God,* then we have to think of God in Trinitarian terms. God is God in that he acts toward us in this way. The "Father" reveals himself in the "Son" through the "Spirit." Or, as Barth translates it, the Speaker of the Word addresses us in the form of his Word in that he makes us both those who are addressed by him and those who respond to him (cf. I/1 493 = 469-71). We have to say that the Spirit "does not first *become* the Holy Spirit . . . in the event of revelation." He works in revelation as the Spirit of God, because "the subjective element in this event is of the essence of God Himself" (I/1 489 = 466). If God were only to *become* God through the relationship with the created, then he would himself be a creature or even a creation of the self-deifying creature. If the Spirit were not "the actuality of God himself," then the setting of the creature in relationship with God would be something alien to God, something that could be achieved only with the help of creaturely possibilities. The Trinitarian being of God, however, is the condition that makes it possible for God himself and God alone to bring himself into fellowship with us and us into fellowship with him.

If we are not dealing with three revelations of God, then we also should not understand the Trinity as a collective of three ego-like persons "in the modern sense of the term," but rather as the three "modes of being . . . of the one divine Subject" as Barth puts it (I/1 493 = 469). And if the Holy Spirit is not another revelation distinct from that of the Word, then we should also not think of the Trinity as though the Father were producing two different "sons" or "words," but rather that the Spirit is the divine reality in the relationship of "Father" and "Son." What does this mean? For Barth the doctrine of the Trinity is an explanation of the saying that God is love. This means that "God already negates in Himself, from eternity, . . . solitary existence, self-sufficiency, self-reliance." For (as the "Father") "God is oriented to the Other" (to the "Son"), "God is oriented to the Other, . . . will have Himself only as He has Himself with the Other and indeed in the Other," is at the same time essentially the Other who correspondingly does not desire himself without the One "out of whom He is." Thus, in this back and forth being in God, the "Father" and the "Son" bring forth the "Spirit," "the negation of solitary existence," "the law and the reality of love," which is not an entity superior to God, since "the law and the reality of love" is God himself. "The love which meets us in reconciliation, and then retrospectively in creation, is real love . . . because God is antecedently love in Himself" (I/1 507f. = 483-84 rev.).

Love meets us in reconciliation inasmuch as God the Spirit lets humans participate in it *de facto.* Yet it also encounters us "retrospectively" in creation. The knowledge of it "can be known and confessed only on the basis of revelation and faith," and cannot be "the theme of a natural theology" (I/1 495 = 472). It is certainly true that creation must exist as a reality distinct from God, and that the created must live in order that God may encounter it in love. This presupposition, however, is not to be regarded as something that the creature posits, into which the divine encounter in love can inscribe itself after the fact, submitting itself to the creaturely initiative directed to it. God Himself *creates* this presupposition. In his loving encounter with us he presupposes that love in and for himself and his action, and for this reason we can only see it "retrospectively." God presupposes the creature in such a way that from the very first he affirms and favors it in its own reality — that is creation "through the Word"; he also does so in such a way that he confers and preserves its own life — that is the work of the Spirit as the "Creator Spirit" (I/1 495 = 472; III/2 429 = 356). As the Creator Spirit he cannot be equated with the so-called "created spirit." The Spirit is not the principle of pantheism that intermingles Creator and creature in an exchange of roles. The Spirit is *God,* God alone as the sole "source of life" (III/2 425 = 353-354), even the life of animals. "It is only by the Spirit of God the Creator that they also live and are soul of their body" (III/2 431 = 359). This applies especially to the human creature whom God addresses directly in his revelation. He cannot live as a created one without God, who is not a part of the human nature (III/2 414 = 344-45). In order to live the human is dependent upon God. Man lives not because he "is Spirit," but only in that "he has Spirit," or rather, "as the Spirit has him" (III/2 425 = 354), the Spirit that makes "man into a subject," "embodied soul and ensouled body" (III/2 437 = 364; 426 = 354-55). "In this respect already Spirit means that man may live, and lack of the Spirit that he must die" (III/2 432 = 360). "The creature needs the *Creator* to be able to live. It thus needs the *relation* to Him. But it cannot create this relation. God *creates* it by His own presence in the creature. . . . The Spirit of God is God in His freedom to be present to the creature, and therefore to create this relation, and therefore to be the life of the creature" (I/1 473 = 450). As the Creator Spirit He gives life to the human in order that he might truly do his own work towards humanity in the divine operation of God's covenant and reconciliation.

The Presence of the Spirit

One result of the knowledge of the deity of the Spirit is that the gift cannot be "abstracted from its Giver" and be considered in and of itself. We have to say this when facing the "obvious danger of confusing the subject and object of faith and love" (I/1 513 = 488). The gift of the Spirit enables us to see the distinction between God and ourselves. "The Spirit is not identical, and does not become identical, with ourselves" (I/1 476 = 454). No matter what the Spirit does in a person, ". . . the Holy Spirit never becomes his spirit but is . . . always the spirit *of* God." "His mighty action on and in man is the work of His *good-pleasure* which He neither owes to any, nor comes to owe when it takes place" (IV/3 1082 = 942). The gift of the Spirit has nothing to do with "a quality of grace poured into man" (I/2 289 = 265-66). These negations are not merely the bracket within which everything positive about the gift of the Spirit is to be said; they make truly plain just what this positive consists of. The distinction between God's Spirit and the human's spirit that is demonstrated by the gift of the Spirit is not an abstract distance. It signifies that the divine is not swallowed up by the human spirit, nor the human by the divine Spirit. This makes it possible for the human person, in the encounter of the Spirit, to become specifically alive and active ". . . in his *own* spirit . . . together with the Holy Spirit" (IV/3 1082 = 942).

What does the Spirit actually do in human persons? Through the Spirit they are "led by God Himself to a certain conviction. They believe that objective reality in revelation exists for them . . . in such a way that they can no longer understand their own existence by itself, but only in the light of that reality: not apart from it, therefore, but only in relation to it" (I/2 253 = 232). This relation, which is the new thing that the Spirit brings in its work in us, is our own participation in the divine possibility of perceiving revelation. It is our "true and concrete participation . . . in the great context of the history of God with the world" (IV/3 687 = 599), but "participation in it does not signify an abolition of our identity with ourselves. It is a frightful misunderstanding to try to interpret it along the lines of a possession or a trance. There are such states, but only when the consciousness of identity is removed. For that reason we must not interpret the miracle of the divine possibility along the lines of such unusual but not miraculous phenomena. In this miracle we are dealing with the miracle of God which is performed upon ourselves in our own identity with ourselves. . . . This participation is achieved in our own experience and activity, in that act of self-determination which we call our human existence" (I/2 290 = 266).

This human person, identical with and determining himself, comes through the work of the Spirit in him into a relationship in which he now can be human only through the Spirit's determination of him. In that determination the human is free for God's revelation. "That freedom exists where the Word of God or Jesus Christ is to man the Master, and unavoidably the Master. . . . To stand unavoidably under any other master is a sign of sickness. But to stand under this Master is not only the normal thing, it is the only possible thing. The outpouring of the Holy Spirit exalts the Word of God to be the Master over men, puts man unavoidably under His mastery. . . . The 'God became man' is actualized in us as 'man has God.' . . . In this event man is a participator in this divine possibility. Through God he is free for God" (I/2 294f. = 269-70).

The "mastery" of the Word of God is not in contradiction with the freedom for which the Spirit "makes us free." It is in contradiction with a specific human slavery, that is, with our inability to make ourselves the recipients of revelation. "Because man is bound in this way he is not able nor free to receive real revelation"; "because he is not free for real revelation, he is in bondage." The freedom that the Spirit gives cannot "consist merely in freedom from that servitude. It must also consist — and decisively so — in freedom from that powerlessness, for the real revelation of God. . . . The reference is not to any kind of freedom or any kind of ability. In accordance with the freedom of God Himself . . . what is at issue here is man's freedom for God. . . . A real hearer of the Word of God . . . is free. . . . The truly free are free . . . as the servants of God (1 Pet. 2:16). . . . The work of the Spirit . . . consists in freedom, freedom to have . . . God as Lord" (I/1 478-480 = 456-457).

That there is no contradiction between freedom and being God's servant is shown by the concept of our being the children of God, which is the chief way to define the gift of the Holy Spirit. The Spirit's creation is "the life of the children of God" (I/2 404 = 362). Everything aims at this, everything effected by that Spirit who "had spoken through the prophets" and who is especially the origin of the human Jesus who was taken up into unity with the Son of God. "To be such a child of God and to receive the Holy Spirit is one and the same thing" (I/1 481 = 458). It is with this concept that Barth answers the question how we can become free to follow God and his Word. We *become* free in that by the Holy Spirit we *are* the children of God (I/1 480 = 457). In that the Holy Spirit makes our being God's children into our very essence, this essence comprehensively determines this childhood in a way that comprehends its entire life: in its actions, its inward and outward life, as an individual and in the mutuality of life with others (I/2 405f. = 369-70).

If the Holy Spirit grants to humans the freedom of those who are bound to God, but in this binding to God freedom, the freedom of the children of God, then this means the liberation of man "to run to the God whom he previously sought to evade," as well as the prevention of the attempt to evade himself. "It means that he finally comes to himself, to rationality," and he may be himself (IV/4 31 = 28). That the Spirit

causes His divine power to come on him does not mean that He over-
takes and overwhelms and crushes him, forcing him to be what He
would have him be. He does not dispose of him like a mere object. He
treats him, and indeed establishes him, as a free subject. He sets him on
his own feet as His partner. He wills that he should stand and walk on his
own feet. He thus wills that he should believe and love and hope. . . . He is
thus God in His power which enlightens the heart of man, which con-
victs his conscience, which persuades his understanding, which does not
win him . . . from without, but "logically" from within. (IV/3 1081f. = 942)

"There is no more intimate friend of sound human understanding than the
Holy Spirit" (IV/4 31 = 28). "To this revelation there belongs the wonderful
revelation which is particularly dear to His Holy Spirit that two and two
make four and not five" (III/3 183 = 161).

Selection

Where the Spirit is not understood as the Spirit of God that is distinct from
our human spirit, then a view of the Spirit develops that justifies a syncretis-
tic identification of Christians with the surrounding world. Yet when the
Spirit is seen to be the Spirit of God, then the gift of the Spirit carries with it
a summons not to be identified with this "world." The *pneuma* of God is
called holy "because its purpose is the *sanctification,* i.e., the setting apart,
the seizing, appropriating and distinguishing of the men who receive it, the
distinguishing by which they become that which in and of themselves they
neither are nor can be, men who belong to God, who are in real fellowship
with Him, who live before God and with God" (I/1 472 = 450). In Jesus
Christ God joins himself in fellowship with sinners and sinners in fellowship
with him. That is the gospel. In that the Holy Spirit brings about our opening
up to this God, he selects us for that fellowship. He encounters us in the form
of the lawful and challenging claim of God upon us as those who belong to
him.

> To other authorities we may make the most profound surrender. . . . But
> over against all of them we can still remain independent. . . . For every
> other authority is the kind which we still have to choose and recognize as
> such. . . . But the outpouring of the Holy Spirit means that man is placed
> under the Word, because it is God's Word. . . . [God] rules over him. . . .
> Everything else is simply the working out of the reality that irresistibly

and definitively man has acquired his King. The occurrence of revelation takes place within and on the basis of this basic relationship. . . . It is the very atmosphere and setting in which reconciliation, grace, assistance, even judgment . . . can arise on God's side — and faith and unbelief, obedience and disobedience on man's. (I/2 296 = 271)

In the Holy Spirit a claim is put upon us because the "Word that God directs to man" reaches us in him: "the Word which concerns man, which claims man, and which completely absorbs his attention" (I/2 886 = 792 rev.). Barth likes to speak of direction here. "To receive and have the Holy Spirit has nothing whatever to do with an obscure and romanticized being. It is simply to receive and have direction. To be or to walk in Him is to be under direction and to stand or walk as determined by it. . . . The Christian community exists as the people which is built up under this direction. Whether a man is a Christian . . . is continually decided by whether his existence . . . is determined by this direction" (IV/2 404f. = 362). The "'saints' are those whose existence is . . . radically altered . . . by the fact that they receive direction in a particular address of the One who alone is holy" (IV/2 591 = 522-23). For Barth, the concept of "direction" — as his designation of the process of human sanctification by the Holy Spirit — has three aspects: placement [in CD, "indication"], correction, and instruction.

1. The term "placement" has a character that "fix[es] or establish[es]," describing a "place of departure." It tells us that we are to be what we already *are*. The Spirit "makes the power and lordship of the man Jesus, the fact that He lives, and lives for us, so that we also live in Him, the presupposition which obtains here and now for us. He shows us where we always and unreservedly belong because we are already there and have no other location" (IV/2 405 = 363). The presupposition is that our sanctification is already a reality, not a mere ideal demand which we would have to make into reality. "The exaltation of man to fellowship with God as it took place in [Jesus Christ]" is this reality. In "the true and new man in virtue of this exaltation . . . there has taken place, and is actualized, the sanctification of all men" (IV/2 173 = 155). The direction that the Holy Spirit gives us is the form of "the grace that happens to man" (IV/2 605 = 534). It places us there where we can let the already realized sanctification be valid for us, and thus only be "witnesses of His holiness" (IV/2 590 = 522), following after the One who is holy. "They are already His people even as He calls them." Over against Jesus' call into discipleship, when it confronts us in the direction of the Spirit, there is thus "no legitimate contradiction and resistance," nor is there any appeal to present or lacking abilities in order to follow him. In this placement by the Holy Spirit, we encounter "grace

in the form of command" (IV/2 605 = 535 rev.), "startling" us, while we continue to "act" as though we were not placed in that point of departure, with the call to "*Be* what thou art" (IV/2 407 = 364).

2. The term "correction" bears a "critical character" (IV/2 413 = 370), relating to man's "non-use of the freedom which he is granted at that point of departure." This is that un-freedom in which man may well choose from a range of possibilities, but practices his un-freedom by not choosing "that which is solely possible for him at that point of departure, but rather the impossible, that which is rejected in Christ" (IV/2 410f. = 367-68). The Spirit works critically because he "separates in the man to and in whom He works . . . the *new* man which . . . he may be, and in truth . . . from the old man who is already superseded in the existence of the man Jesus, [but] who continually stirs and moves in us as if he still had a right and place there. . . . And the Holy Spirit affirms the one man and negates the other. He fights for the new man against the old. He champions freedom against unfreedom, obedience against disobedience, our life against our death, the one possible thing against the many impossible. And His work may be known by the merciless and uncompromising way in which . . . He wages this war and plunges man himself into the battle" (IV/2 411 = 368).

The correction of the Spirit specifically reveals that sin also consists of sloth. Sloth in itself is not questionable. Why should we not erect "in a side-chapel a small altar to idleness" (III/4 636 = 554)? Yet sloth is a sin to the extent that, in distinction from the pride with which we dream for ourselves the role of a false absolute God (IV/1 468f. = 422-23), in its exercise one lags behind oneself, behind the person one is permitted to be as the one who is exalted into fellowship with God. It is sin insofar as it directs itself against the gospel command, fulfilled by the man Jesus and thus fulfillable, according to which the dignity that God has given humanity consists of our not being crestfallen, not cowering, but of our being able to stand up and walk upright (IV/2 427ff., 453ff. = 382ff., 403ff.). "The man who contradicts God and therefore contradicts and hopelessly jeopardizes himself . . . would be lost . . . if in this self-contradiction which he achieves he were not confronted, in the man Jesus on whom he stumbles and falls, by the superior contradiction of God" (IV/2 459 = 409), that is, if the Holy Spirit did not correct him. Those to whom that happens are in their sloth "disturbed" sinners. "The unreconciled man . . . is an undisturbed sinner," though he, too, "has his own restraints and periods of unrest. But he is able to surmount and master them. . . . The direction of the Son of Man, the work of the Holy Spirit, is needed if he is to be disturbed in a way which cannot be overcome" (IV/2 593 = 524), by "awakening to conversion" (IV/2 626 = 553).

3. The term "instruction" has a "positive character" (cf. IV/2 405 = 362) in that it directs toward a specific action. The instruction of the Spirit causes us or summons us "to test ourselves and our situation, to consider most carefully our possibilities and choices. This is the task of theological ethics," which is theological when it "leads us, in face of the many possibilities with which we are confronted, to ask what *God* wills of us.... But the Holy Spirit is rather more than a professor of theological ethics. He is the One ... who actually reveals and makes known and imparts ... the will of God as it applies to us concretely here and now. ... The Holy Spirit *does,* therefore, that concerning which we ourselves, even in the very best theological ethics, can only *ask. ...* In face of the instruction of the Holy Spirit there can be only the most concrete obedience" (IV/2 416 = 372). In this instruction there comes to us the summons of Jesus, now exalted to fellowship with God. Jesus here opposes his kingdom to the kingdom of the world that is the victim of its sloth, and calls out: "Get out of the box of everything that ... appeared to be self-evident up till now! And then, get out of the box of a merely inward ... movement in which he ... just chatters away about ... all kinds of deliberations and projects concerning this or that which he could do, would like to do, but at the moment really can't and won't do because he is not that far along ... in his thinking about it" (IV/2 611 = 540 rev.). Yes, out of a world of "given factors" that rule "with the claim of absolute validity and worth," and whose rule makes the world into "the world of the slothful man," a world "which strives against God and which is for this very reason in a state of hopeless disintegration and in need of reconciliation with God and of His peace." "What man does of himself" even in rebellion against this world "will always serve to confirm and strengthen it." The call of Jesus, however, "calls man out" of this bondage and this "conformity," for through that call the break with the world has already been made, and thus man becomes "an offence" to that world and suffers at its hands, even though he will not provoke it (IV/2 614-618 = 543-46).

Sending

If we do not regard the new life that the Holy Spirit gives as God's pure grace, then reception of the Spirit will end up in the standstill of "holy egoism" (IV/3 878 = 767), resulting in a tacit or open self-elevation over others, an appropriating and possessive thinking in a kind of higher "capitalism," a beneficiary's existence legitimized by the Spirit, a way of being which basically has no need of other people (cf. IV/3 874 = 764). "The work of the Holy Spirit in the gathering and building up the community ... cannot merely lead to the blind alley of a new qualification, enhancement, deepening and enrichment of this being of the community as such." Its existence "is not an end in itself. . . ." "Called *out* of the world, the community is genuinely called *into* it. And the genuineness of that 'called out' is essentially defined by that fact that there is no break between it and the 'called into' which infallibly follows it; its separation from the world and its turning to the world take place in one unbroken movement" (IV/3 874 = 764 rev.). All its "distinction" *in relation to* the world is its "preparation" for the work *in* the world entrusted to it (cf. IV/3 657 = 573-74). This must be probed further.

First, sanctification through the Holy Spirit does not happen solely and primarily to individual persons. Sanctification "takes place as God fashions a people of holy men, i.e., those who in spite of their sin have the freedom, which they have *received* from Him, to *live* in it, to represent Him among all other men. . . ." The special existence of this people is not an end in itself. "It is the witness of the love with which God has loved the world." The community is separated as "the creaturely reflection of the holiness in which God confronts . . . both itself and the world, addressing it even as He is distinct from it" — in the Old Testament the "holy people" and in the New Testament the *"sancta ecclesia"* [= holy church]. With regard to the ministry for which this people exists it is important to note that "the saints of the New Testament exist only in *plurality.* Sanctity belongs to them, but only in their common life, not as individuals. . . . *The* Holy One *creates* the saints" (IV/2 578-80 = 511-513 rev.).

What makes this plurality into a Christian congregation? It is not an urge for fellowship, or a feeling of kinship, or in this sense a "communal spirit" (Schleiermacher). It is the Holy Spirit who makes them into a Christian congregation. He does this not merely by bringing together different people, but rather by "bringing and holding together" Jesus Christ and these people (who are apparently constantly moving away from him): "divine and human working, heavenly and earthly working, being and action, creative and created freedom and deed. . . . His work is to bring and to hold them together, not to identify, intermingle nor confound them, not to change the one into the other nor to merge the one into the other, but to coordinate them, to make them parallel, to bring them into harmony and therefore to bind them into a true unity" (IV/3 871 = 761). In doing this, the Holy Spirit as "the bond of peace" (IV/3 870 = 760) accords with its inner-Trinitarian being in the work of revelation. "In virtue of this gracious act it is always true and actual that the Head does not live without His body nor the body without its Head, but that the Head, Jesus Christ, lives *with and in* His community, and the body, His community, *with and in* Him" (IV/3 872 = 762).

The Holy Spirit does not just bring and hold together Christ and "the" church in general, but rather Christ and concretely the speech and action of both the community and its members. It is in this way that its speech and action *become* what he calls both the congregation and its members to, to the "ministry of the Word" of God, to *"witness"* (I/1 477f. = 454-55) — "the church means the service of testimony" (I/2 468 = 424). It cannot be more than this (its service is not identical with God's action), but it also cannot be less (no mute "reception" of God's action). "You shall receive the power of the Holy Spirit and be my witnesses" (Acts 1:8).[16] For through the Spirit Christ becomes the "contemporary" of specific people. He "addresses and claims them as partners in His covenant" (IV/3 577 = 502). "The Christian is a witness," and "the question is not . . . whether he regards himself as able or worthy, nor whether he is willing, nor whether he can guarantee specific results" (IV/3 698 = 609). That is not the question because he *becomes* a witness solely through the fact that Jesus Christ by the Spirit, in His speech and action, witnesses *Himself* to him.

The members of the community first of all bear witness to each other within the community. They do this in *love* because the love to which they are to witness is to be demonstrated in their mutuality, in their integration into a fellowship (IV/2 922 = 812-13). This love "begins . . . at the very point where the pleasure which men have in one another, and the favors which they may show in consequence, do not necessarily cease, but may very well do so . . ." (IV/2 930 = 819). It arises, then, when my fellow-human becomes my "neighbor," thereby causing me "a really mortal headache, because I cannot withdraw myself from him and because I would really prefer to exist in some other way than in this co-existence" (I/2 476 = 431). Testifying to the love of God, "to the law and the reality" of love which is precisely the Holy Spirit, consists of "one guaranteeing to the other that God loves His people, that He therefore loves the two concerned, and that they may both love Him in return" (IV/2 929 = 819). ". . . none can do it. . . ." But "by the Holy Spirit . . . they *become* free for *this* action, . . . the individual becomes free for existence in an active relationship with the other in which he is loved and finds that he may love in return. The one who is most deeply filled with the Spirit is the one who is richest in love. . . . There can be no question of their activity dispensing them from living by forgiveness. But it is a matter of practicing faith in this forgiveness where one sinner (his own sin notwithstanding!) may love as a neighbor . . . another sinner (his own sin notwithstanding!)" (IV/2 928 = 815 rev.).

16. Cf. CD I/1 477 = 455; I/2 468 = 424f.; IV/3 698 = 609, 715 = 624-25, 915 = 799-800.

The mutual testifying of the gospel to one another, however, is now the community's "equipment for its mission to the world" (IV/2 944 = 832). "They are to one another witnesses of that which as the people of God they have commonly to attest to every man" (IV/2 924 = 814). It is precisely in this sense that the community of Christ is not an end in itself but rather "community for the world." "It exists ecstatically, eccentrically: within the world to which it belongs, it relates not to itself but completely to the world, to its surroundings. It saves and maintains its own life as it interposes and gives itself for all other human creatures. . . . First and supremely God is there for the world. And since the community of Jesus Christ is there first and supremely for God, it has no option but . . . to be there for the world. . . . The centre around which it moves eccentrically is not, then, simply the world as such, but the world for which God is there" (IV/3 872 = 762 rev.).

The sending of the community into the world around it does not rest on an urge to promote or commend or confirm itself by incorporating those who differ from it. The reverse is the case: "It would manifest a remarkable conformity to the world if concern for its purity and reputation forbid it to compromise with it. The world only too easily sees itself reflected in a community which has no care but for its own life and rights and manner and which thus tries to separate itself from those around. The world itself constantly divides into individual cliques, interest groups, cultural movements, nations, religions, parties and sects of all kinds, each of which is sure of the goodness of its own cause and each anxious within its limits to maintain and assert itself in face of all the rest" (IV/3 886f. = 775 rev.).

The basis of the sending of the community into the world is the fact that God loves the world, that he has reconciled it to himself in Christ, and that the Holy Spirit "draws and impels and presses" the community "beyond its being as such, beyond all the reception and experience of its members, and only as it *follows* this drawing and impelling is it the real community of Jesus Christ" (IV/3 874f. = 764). It is, once more, "the work of the Holy Spirit" that in his strength, not ours, he endows this people "with the power, freedom and capacity to do its human work, to bear the witness entrusted to it" (IV/3 869 = 759). And that defines the way in which the community gives its witness in the "world." Although it is "very unlike" the world, since by the Spirit its eyes have been opened to the light of life which shines in Jesus for the world, it must "know and practice [its] solidarity with the world. . . . Solidarity with the world means full commitment to it, unreserved participation in its situation, in the promise given it by creation, in its responsibility for the arrogance, sloth and falsehood which reign within it, in its suffering under the resultant distress, but primarily and supremely in the free grace of God demonstrated and addressed to it in Jesus Christ, and therefore in its hope" (IV/3 884f. = 773). The slogan of the worker priests may describe this solidarity: *"Les saints vont en enfer"* ["The saints go down into hell"] (IV/3 886 = 774). We practice this solidarity when we see others as those whom God has already reconciled in Christ as our brothers and sisters, and we are "directly affected by their misery" (IV/3 393 = 341). We practice solidarity, when we "expect to find the witness of Jesus Christ, and therefore, our neighbour, not only in the Church, but . . . in *every* man," when we are open to the fact that "the unconverted [could be] sometimes dearer to [Christ] than the converted" (I/2 468 = 424-25; IV/3 422 = 365).

Moving Out

Since the Holy Spirit is the Spirit of God as of the full and free grace of Jesus Christ, he summons us out of compromising with the world, out of thinking that we are ends in ourselves, and out of the mentality of having and possessing. He stands thus in direct conflict with the modern teachings about the spirit that support such a mentality by interchanging the divine spirit with the human. This is not by chance. Since the presence of God among humans is the issue with the Holy Spirit, modern man could focus on this point in order to strengthen his desire for grasping, appropriating, and taking possession. "Individualization" was Barth's term for the "spirit" of this desire, referring to the human's self-understanding as an individual. By this, he means a being who is "undivided and indivisible . . . related to the ultimate reality of God," finding in himself "something eternal, almighty, wise, good, glorious, whose presence . . . allows and requires him" to elevate himself to being "the secret, yet for himself supremely real king. . . ." "Individualization means . . . the making inward of what is external, objective to man, by which it is robbed of its objectivity, so to speak eaten up and digested, made into something within man." This means at the same time "externalization, in so far as it is a question of man projecting what is within him externally in such a way that it is now also quite outside him, so that he obtrudes himself upon the object, identifies himself with it."[17]

    If the Holy Spirit is the Spirit of God as of the full and free grace in Jesus Christ, then it contradicts this mentality by evoking a new mode of thinking. This Spirit forms no basis for "having." He *takes away* the spirit of "having," the "spirit of capitalism" (M. Weber). "To have the Holy Spirit is to

---

17. Karl Barth, *Protestantische Theologie,* pp. 92-93; ET: *Protestant Theology,* p. 113.

let God rather than our having God be our confidence" (I/1 485 = 462). Participation in the Spirit's holiness is participation in an *aliena sanctitas* [= alien holiness] (IV/2 527 = 518), and thus not in "the transmission of a material addition" to God's gracious turning to humanity. Thus it is not the confirmation of a "selfish desire for salvation" nor "the satisfaction of the private religious needs of man" (I/2 258 = 237). In the Holy Spirit we are to come to know "God the Redeemer," and can understand redemption "in so far as [it] implies our own being [as the redeemed] . . . only as future, i.e. as the redemption that comes to us from God" (I/1 486 = 463). We are thus not to conceive of the attitude of persons so defined with the image of living "on the interest from a capital amassed yesterday,"[18] but rather as pilgrims always living from hand to mouth. "All the gifts of the Holy Spirit . . . are designed to empower the people of God and its members for this . . . pilgrimage." Deriving from Easter, they stretch into the "eternal future" and our "participation in the eternal life of God" (IV/2 948 = 836). "The existence of the Christian community as the pilgrim people of God" is neither "an end in itself" nor a "private affair. . . . It is a public affair" that tells the world of "the coming of its new form and the passing of its old." Hence it invites others, too, to join in the pilgrimage (IV/3 397f. = 344-45).

Why does it go on this pilgrimage? Is it because it feels that something is lacking when measured by self-appointed and attainable ideals? Depending on its mood at any given time, would this pilgrimage be able to slow down its pace if people preferred to stop and enjoy what they had already attained? Or, conversely, one could ask whether "it is possible to live a life exposed . . . to the incessant pressure of this call to advance" (IV/3 397 = 344). In this case the present would be regarded primarily as a "vacuum," in which Christ, as the one who came once and will come again, would now only occur "on the margin," resulting indeed in "a replacement of Jesus Christ by Christianity." Then it would "naturally" be man, "the Christian in particular," who would be "the vicar of the living Jesus Christ who is not Himself present . . . in this vacuum." And it would be this particular man's task to deal with the controversy or the overcoming of this experience of absence, whereby Christ himself would only "play the role which humans accorded to him" (IV/3 404 = 349 rev.).

The impulse toward pilgrimage is the very thing that contends against the idea of a present-day "vacuum," namely, the "promise of the Spirit" as Jesus Christ's "direct and immediate presence and action among and with and

18. Karl Barth, *Einführung in die evangelische Theologie* (Zurich, 1962), p. 182; ET: *Evangelical Theology: An Introduction* (Grand Rapids, 1963), p. 165.

in us" in which he affirms himself as the hope of us all in our present situation (IV/3 405 = 350). The given promise of the Spirit means that our present cannot be a vacuum. "The fact that in this time we and all creation look forward with groaning . . . to the redemption and consummation and therefore to the coming of Jesus Christ" does not mean "that Christians have cause to complain of an inadequacy of the Spirit who is given them as the pledge and firstfruits of the ultimate future." If our present were only "a day of small things" and not one that is filled by the promise of the Spirit, "there would be a serious threat that . . . in our expectant longing for the coming new world and its order we should be disillusioned rather than genuinely comforted and encouraged" (IV/3 414f. = 359-60).

What pushes us forward is the Spirit, who is not absent in our present situation, but is given to us, given as *promise*. Barth takes this in two ways. First, *"the Spirit promises."* To those who already know Christ he promises his coming as Redeemer and Perfecter along with "the new cosmic form . . . as the future of the world and their own ultimate future." The Spirit promises his coming in connection with the affirmation of his presence and his help on our way as we move toward the future (IV/3 406 = 351). Jesus Christ is the hope of these people in that as those who are "not yet redeemed and perfected, who are still on the way like others," they "are already recipients . . . of the promise" of the Spirit with whose power they are moving toward this future (IV/3 408 = 353).

Second, *"the Spirit is promised."* He is promised to those who do not yet know Jesus Christ, who are not simply "not" recipients of the promise of the Spirit, but "not yet," and who on their pathway are "referred to the caprice, accident or fate of their own inventions or obscure impulses. . . . One thing, however, they do not lack. And this one thing is more important than all the things they do lack. For the Holy Spirit, as Jesus Christ is risen, is promised to them too. . . . They are not condemned to the unspiritual life in which they exist as non-Christians." Jesus Christ is the hope of these people as well (IV/3 408-410 = 353-354).

The "one thing in distinction," the promise of the Spirit, divides *and* unites Christians and non-Christians. Our present, therefore, is not empty because it is not empty of the promise, *and* because it impels Christians to move out beyond the present into the future, which is what the promise is about. They move along the way leading to the future bearing hope for all people, that way on which the Spirit's promise puts them and on which it accompanies them — as the "sure pledge that this is the way, and that they may and should tread it" (IV/3 406f. = 352 rev.). They move out along this path not with a sense that the present is empty, but because Jesus Christ walks this path in his revelation "from its present to its future fullness," and because they may walk this path "in accompaniment of the prophetic work of Jesus Christ" (IV/3 415 = 359, 422 = 365). Yet this advantage can not make them arrogant. "Who has such deep and necessary cause for sighing as he who has received the promise of the Spirit?" (IV/3 423 = 366). "More restless than the most restless . . . he asks: 'Where art thou, peace of all the world?' and he asks it the more restlessly . . . because he is sure of this future peace . . . and moves forward to this future which is filled by it" (IV/4 221 = 201) — "obedient to the prodding of the Holy Spirit, constantly departing . . . towards a land . . . 'that I will show you' (Gen. 12:1)" (IV/4 43 = 39 rev.).

Moving Out Together —
The Doctrine of the Church

The Church's Predicament

Barth thought that he could see that in our age "Christianity in the form we have known it up to now" is ending.[1] What he had in view was the occidental Christianity as it was formed in the fourth century through its transition and entry into "a unity with people, society, state and empire" (IV/4 185 = 168; cf. IV/3 18ff. = 18ff.). The presupposition here was "the practical concurrence between civilization, culture and political power on the one side and the Church on the other." It consisted of a society "in which Christian and non-Christian existence came together, or seemed to do so." The result was a "Christianity which is automatically given and received with the rest of our inheritance" (IV/3 602f. = 524-25). "Apart from the Jews, to whom grudging toleration was extended, there were not to be . . . any persons who did not belong to the Church just as naturally and necessarily as they did to the empire, so that everybody had quickly to become a Christian" (IV/4 185 = 168). Yet this view of Christianity, "no matter how tenaciously it may linger on, . . . has now become historically *impossible*. . . . The Christian West no longer exists" (IV/3 605 = 525). The contemporary established church ("people's church"), into which the earlier unity of church and society has evolved, is in Barth's view disintegrating.

How are we to evaluate this Christianity under the sign of such unity? According to Barth, it can be understood *critically* as a concession to the temptation to adapt oneself to the powers of this world in order to negotiate

1. Karl Barth, *Das Evangelium in der Gegenwart* (*Theologische Existenz heute!* 25) (Munich, 1935), p. 33.

a guaranteed existence — which was connected with the duty that the church should also guarantee the existence of these powers.[2] The result was that "the primitive and heathen Swabian, German, Saxon, Frank, Briton, Italian, Spaniard or Hungarian, though he might dress up in priestly or even episcopal robes, did not cease to live his own virile life" (IV/3 603 = 524). In the process the salt of the church that she was meant to be for the earth lost its savor (Matt. 5:13).

The same process can also be understood *positively* as a promising parable: on the one hand as a not wholly inappropriate echo of the incarnation of God in Jesus Christ, and on the other as a distant but yet happy reflection of the coming world of God, a "provisional fulfillment of the promise . . . that the kingdoms of this world will become the kingdoms of God and his Christ."[3]

Now, however, that it is no longer self-evident that Western bourgeois existence includes one's being a Christian, Barth sees validity in *both* interpretations of this process. If that unity often sheltered the not infrequently realized danger of *unfaithfulness* toward the gospel, then Christendom need not fear "that the eventual disappearance of this form will mean the destruction of the Church and of so-called Christianity." We must "accustom ourselves to the idea that it might be better for the cause and ministry of the Church . . . if one day, without being able to rejoice in any acknowledged position . . . it had to exist again in people, society and state as a small . . . group of aliens, as a mobile brotherhood" (IV/4 185 = 168).

If that unity is a *blessing,* as is the case with the second view, Christians should be warned against the illusion that the church's shrinkage will automatically be a healthy shrinkage. They must always recall that the salt, without having to lose its savor, is meant for the earth. This interpretation makes us aware that the termination of the linkage of church and society follows a historical, not a theological, principle and thus is not a command for the formation of the church. This thesis simply lays out for our sober perception the *situation* in which the church according to human insight finds itself today, and thus it is only a stimulus, in this situation, to consider anew and with spiritual levelheadedness what it is that makes the church into the church of Christ.

In his teaching about the church Barth did not see it as his task either to provide a theory to secure the church in the form it has had until now, nor to offer a prognosis for a very different kind of church. His task was rather to

---

2. Karl Barth, *Das Evangelium in der Gegenwart,* pp. 30-31.
3. Karl Barth, *Das Evangelium in der Gegenwart,* p. 32.

investigate, in the church's existing situation, what is the promise to the church regarding its very being. He was not primarily discussing this situation itself but the two different but related conceptions that are fundamentally flawed reactions to the church's contemporary situation. He summed up these conceptions with the two thematic terms: the church in danger of alienation (secularization) and of self-glorification (sacralization) (IV/2 754 = 667), or the extroverted "church in defect" and the introverted "church in excess" (CL 224, 227 = 136ff.), or the church "looking sideways" (toward the world) and the "sleeping church" (in regard to its commission in the world).[4]

"The church in defect is the church which looks anxiously to its Lord but even more anxiously to everything else, which painfully compares itself to the world, which for this reason seeks possible points of contact from or to it; which is intent on bridges from the one place to the other. The favorite word of this church is the little word 'and'" (CL 225 = 139). It is the church in *defect* because it accommodates the gospel to the world and thus overwhelms the gospel. "It is always alienated when it allows its environment, or spontaneous reference to it, to describe and impose a *law* which is not identical with the Law of the Gospel" (IV/2 755 = 667). This happens when the church very naturally insists that this was necessary for the sake of the "addressee." Further, it becomes more obvious that when the church has the addressee in view *to such an extent,* then what it has to give him becomes more and more unclear — in fact, it becomes a question whether the church has anything to give him at all because he allegedly already has what he needs. It happens, too, when the church adopts the theory that what is alien to it is not really so alien, because, in the West, "side by side with the ancient world and the different national traditions, side by side with ancient and modern learning as it grew and blossomed and bore fruit on this soil, *Christian influence also* helped to shape and determine society in a more or less penetrating way." The problem with this is not only that fact that Christian existence and the existence of "western man" are equated, in an apparent rescue again of that medieval unity of church and society (IV/3 600 = 522). The real problem is that the church is submitted to a constant pressure to adapt and must occupy the "small space" (CL 230 = 139) left to it by society, that place at which society prescribes for the church how it can still appear to be useful, even though it otherwise is really no longer needed.

This conception processes wrongly the gradual disappearance of the self-evident character of Christian existence. It is wrong because its answer

---

4. Karl Barth, *Die Schrift und die Kirche* (*Theologische Studien* 22) (Zollikon-Zurich, 1947), pp. 29-30.

to the question of the church's task is characterized by an inner loss of independence. It "is looking sideways" because at the decisive point it looks at the human "commission-giver" rather than at the divine One. In this view the church resembles a house on whose construction much care has been expended to ensure that it has many open doors and windows, in the persuasion that this effort will also have ensured that the foundation is firm enough. As Barth sees it, the church must process the fact that many areas of society now claim autonomy over against it by viewing itself as an independent church that is "summoned to an entirely new freedom of confession and knowledge."[5] This accords with the distinction made by the reformers between ecclesiastical and secular action, the impact of which was still concealed in the sixteenth century because the unity of church and society continued, upheld by the Reformers as shown by their position toward the "Enthusiasts." After the collapse of that unity, its decision must then be thought through anew, and it must be said that the church is free in that it is content, not with the space which society (still) provides it, but rather with the space which the *Gospel* clears for it. This will be a space of "freedom from all those presuppositions, attachments, and obligations thrust upon it not by the gospel but by the outside world as it takes into account the nature and direction of historical powers and forces."[6]

On the other hand there is the church of "self-glorification." "Its aim is still to develop and maintain itself in the world. But in this case it tries to do it, not by self-adaptation but by self-assertion . . . as a world of its own" (IV/2 756 = 668-69). It is the "church in *excess*," using the Lord "for its own sake," in order "to differentiate it, to give it distinction, to declare and establish its claim over against the world," "boasting about *him* in order to be able to boast about *itself*" (CL 225 = 136). It does indeed emphasize its independence over against the rest of the world, no longer today with triumphal arrogance, but perhaps now in an amicable offer to the "world": What fulfills us inside the church and allows us to preserve something of the onetime glory of the church also permits us to affirm that it is obligatory for no one outside our walls nor for us. The church reacts here to the disappearance of the self-evident character of Christian existence by retreating into a reservation, that is, by becoming an "introverted church" (CL 225 = 136). For Barth this sacralization, that is, this transformation of the church into a "self-elevating" world "unto itself" is also a secularization of the church, just as that secularization of the church leads to a sacralization of the world. "It makes itself like

5. Karl Barth, *Das Evangelium in der Gegenwart,* p. 34.
6. Karl Barth, *Das Evangelium in der Gegenwart,* p. 34.

the world. And in so doing, by trying to be important and powerful . . . by trying to make pretentious claims for itself instead of soberly advocating the claims of God, it withdraws from the world" (IV/2 757 = 669). How would it "conform again to the world" if it did not want to "be in solidarity with it . . . to be worldly within it"! (IV/3 884 = 773).

In Barth's view the independence that the church seeks to uphold in this way is only a "formal independence."[7] It too is a flawed reaction to the collapse of the union between church and society. The church's true independence does not consist of withdrawal from an increasingly secular world in an attempt then to be something distinctive in and of itself. The *gospel* alone grants it this independence, and it has it "by giving the gospel its freedom,"[8] without interrupting it with a determination about the possible range of the gospel's validity. Thus, it is independent not — "laboriously suppressing its own yawning"[9] — by *protecting* and *preserving* traditions that are threatening to dissolve, but in constantly new *implementation* of the task assigned to it by the gospel.[10] It is truly free when independence is not its concern, but when in it the voice of the good Shepherd becomes audible, by whom it is called "not to a freedom . . . from its responsibility . . . in the world, but to freedom *in* the world and *for* the world, to live out its own sending, its proper responsibility."[11] This freedom is not a fence that separates it from the world. It is the precondition for its ability to be of significance in the world.

The Church That Is the Church

Barth's own view of the church, which points to its one genuine possibility in the modern collapse of the church's unity with society, can be summed up in a formula that he used in 1933: The "church *must* really *be* the church."[12] This formula does *not* mean the same thing as the slogan of the centrist faction of the church at that time, "Church must *remain* church."[13] What that meant

7. Cf. Karl Barth, *Theologische Existenz heute* (Munich, 1933), p. 32; ET: *Theological Existence Today! A Plea for Theological Freedom* (London, 1933), p. 66.

8. Karl Barth, *Für die Freiheit des Evangeliums (Theologische Existenz heute!* 2) (Munich, 1933), p. 7.

9. Karl Barth, *Die Schrift und die Kirche,* p. 29.

10. Karl Barth, *Theologische Existenz heute!,* p. 36; ET: *Theological Existence Today!,* p. 74.

11. Karl Barth, *Das Evangelium in der Gegenwart,* p. 34.

12. Karl Barth, *Für die Freiheit des Evangeliums,* p. 6.

13. Joachim Gauger, *Chronik der Kirchenwirren,* vol. 2 (1935), p. 93.

was that the church should protect itself against changes that threaten to encroach upon its substance, to alter its status quo. Barth's question was, could it not thereby insist on protecting something that truly needed renewal? By understanding its message as something to be *protected* inviolate, rather than as something that constantly *proves* itself anew, the church would deny its existence as Christ's church, even if it should be "victor."[14]

Again the formula does not say that the church must *become* the church, as though a church that is still only a church on paper would now make itself into a "true" and "vital" church through a "new ordering"[15] according to some idea of *the* ideal church. The formula does not intend that a church of fantasy be imposed upon the "truly existing church."[16] It asks whether a church formed according to self-confidently set goals, even if backed by biblical quotations, will not necessarily be an alien church, not coming from the Word of God and "out of obedience," and thus *not* a church.[17]

When we explain the formula, we will see that it is not a pointless tautology. The church meant by the first part of the sentence is the "invisible" church, the church known by the "*credo* ecclesiam" [= I believe (in) the church]. This church is not an ideal to be striven for. Precisely *this* is what Barth calls the "real" church, the church that never can be actualized by human effort, contrasted with the "sham church" ("the semblance of the church") (IV/2 695-699 = 614-618 [where "real" = "true"]) which the visible "really existing" church can *become* (and will do so if it understands itself in distinction from that "credo ecclesiam"), but which it *is* not necessarily and essentially. We see from this that when speaking of the church in which we believe, we must never "overlook the visibility of the church, explaining away its earthly and historical form as something indifferent, or angrily negating it, or treating it only as a necessary evil, in order to magnify an invisible fellowship of the Spirit and of spirits," in order thereby in fact to flee from it "in a kind of wonderland" (IV/1 729f. = 653-54). We believe the invisible church always and only *in* the "really existing" church.

Barth warns us, however, against identifying the visible church with the invisible — "woe to it" (IV/1 734 = 657). Why is this? It is not just because in its

---

14. Karl Barth, *Theologische Existenz heute!*, p. 36; ET: *Theological Existence Today,* pp. 74f.; Karl Barth, *Texte zur Barmer Theologischen Erklärung* (Zurich, 1984), p. 34.

15. For the German Christians, cf. Gauger, *Chronik der Kirchenwirren,* p. 67.

16. Contra Barth, cf. Karl Wilhelm Dahm, "Identität und Realität der Kirche," in *Unterwegs für die Volkskirche,* ed. W. L. Federlin and E. Weber (Frankfurt, 1987), pp. 80-81.

17. Karl Barth, *Theologische Existenz heute!,* p. 8; ET: *Theological Existence Today!,* p. 19.

external appearance and its representatives it always stands there as more or less "good," or not "good" at all! The decisive reason is that it is in the strict sense the church *of Jesus Christ*. That does not mean that he is the "object" that the church administers or represents, doing so in a more or less illuminating way. It certainly does not mean that it assigns to itself the predicate "Christian" out of a cultural and historical tradition. It does mean, first of all, that Christ himself is its true and proper subject, and "the being of the community is a predicate of His being" (IV/2 741 = 655). He is the one who, not representable by the church or by any of its courts, himself gathers the church, upbuilds it, and sends it forth.[18] It is *his* "body," and it is "real" as such. It is *really* the church of Jesus Christ never through itself but through him, through his creative and sustaining and propulsive working upon it and in it. He alone founds the church and builds it up and reigns over it, "whether man sets his hands to work or folds them or even lays them in his lap," whether he is perhaps, "in the words of Luther, 'drinking Wittenberg beer with Philip and Amsdorf'" (IV/2 714f. = 632). The saying is irreversible: "*It* is, because and in that *He* is" (IV/1 738 = 661 rev.). It is not absolutely invisible, but "visible" only in faith (IV/1 733 = 656-57). In that faith believes *in* Jesus Christ, it believes *the* church; it believes that Christ is not without his own (III/3 307 = 271; IV/2 717 = 634; IV/3 605 = 526-27), and that witness is borne to this in the church's visible existence (IV/2 737 = 651-52). The believer thus even believes himself to be one who belongs to Christ's people. For Barth, however, the existence of the church necessarily precedes the existence of individual believers.

The church as a visible appearance is "in its *visible* being . . . the witness of its *invisible* being" (IV/1 734 = 657). Yet "at best" it is "an equivocal witness" of that "real church" and of the Christ at work in it (IV/2 699 = 617). Nevertheless, this does not alter the fact that "the visible attests the invisible." The *credo ecclesiam* confesses "faith in *the* invisible aspect which is the secret of the *visible*. Believing in the *ecclesia invisibilis* we will enter the sphere of labour and conflict of the *ecclesia visibilis*" (IV/1 735, 730 = 658, 654). Yet why the sphere of labor and conflict? Because in the sphere of the visible the church can more or less pollute its witness to its "invisible" secret, or even completely fail to make it. Then it does not bear witness that Christ is bearing witness to himself within it and that it is itself thus "real church." It thereby contradicts rather than corresponds to the fact that it is the church of *Jesus Christ* who himself makes it into the church. It will then be a "semblance of the church." Yes, then "the church ceases to be the church."[19]

---

18. These are the three aspects of the doctrine of the church in CD IV/1-3.

19. Karl Barth, *Für die Freiheit des Evangeliums*, p. 9.

What this means is that the true threat to the church does not come from outside forces, but rather "the guilt of the church itself."[20] The converse is also true: "Where the church *is* a church, she is already delivered. No violation of it, no matter how brutal, can touch it."[21] "Fluctuat nec mergitur" [= "It is driven into the sea but does not go under"] (IV/3 967 = 843). But that statement does not imply that the church, when it puts itself in such jeopardy — as bad as that is — can accomplish more than a "plot against the substance of the church."[22] Just as it cannot make *itself* into the church, so it cannot *abrogate* itself as "real church," for Christ is its Head. "It may become a beggar, it may act like a shopkeeper, it may make itself a harlot, as has happened and still does happen, yet it is always the bride of Jesus Christ" (IV/1 772 = 691). It may contradict itself, but its true substance will contradict the contradiction, and we will always find ourselves placed in the "sphere of labor and conflict within the *ecclesia visibilis*," working and fighting that, even in its visible form, for all its ambivalence, it should no longer be in contradiction but should correspond and bear witness to the fact that it is the church of Jesus Christ, gathered and built up and called by him, grounded by him and thus hearing and heeding him. In this sense the church must, at the level of the witness of its visible existence, *be* that which it really *is* as the church of Jesus Christ.

This is the context of Barth's distinctive and sharp *criticism of the church*. As he saw it, "in the Church we may be just like a bird in a cage which is always hitting against the bars."[23] "But as far as we know, there is no one who deserves the wrath of God more abundantly than the ministers."[24] "For . . . the *church* from the beginning of the world [has] done more [with regard to the question of God] to narcotize than to stimulate."[25] Indeed, "it was the *church*, not the world, that crucified Christ."[26] Barth would often quote 1 Peter 4:17 that "the judgment of God [begins] with the household of God," because it cannot confront the unbelieving world more seriously than it will

---

20. Karl Barth, *Für die Freiheit des Evangeliums,* p. 9.

21. Karl Barth, *Theologische Existenz heute!,* p. 37; ET: *Theological Existence Today!,* p. 77.

22. Karl Barth, *"Der Götze wackelt": Zeitkritische Aufsätze, Reden und Briefe von 1930 bis 1960,* ed. K. Kupisch (Berlin, 1961), p. 29.

23. Karl Barth, *Dogmatik im Grundriss* (Munich, 1947), pp. 172-73; ET: *Dogmatics in Outline* (London, 1949), p. 147.

24. Karl Barth, *Das Wort Gottes und die Theologie* (Munich, 1929), p. 118; ET: *The Word of God and the Word of Man* (New York, 1957), p. 126.

25. Karl Barth, *Wort Gottes,* p. 72; *Word of God,* p. 54.

26. Karl Barth, *Der Römerbrief,* 2nd ed. (Munich, 1922; 12th ed., 1978), pp. 372-73; ET: *The Epistle to the Romans* (Oxford, 1933), p. 389.

the church. That is certainly the reason that Bishop Meiser tried to keep him away from the Confessing Church in 1934, because, as he put it, "church cannot be built with Karl Barth."[27] Was he not in fact promoting "the liquidation of the church"?[28] Nevertheless, statements are also found that go in a different direction, criticizing the option of "leaving it or of renouncing his orders, for that would be even less intelligent than if he were to take his own life." The critic of the church has "no friendly lifeboat into which he can clamber. . . . [he] must remain at his post in the engine-room or . . . on the bridge."[29] "We may often have a distaste for the whole of church life . . . but we don't make off."[30] Thus Barth found totally incomprehensible Bonhoeffer's proposal in 1933 to leave the church because of the Fascist nonsense going on it — instead of staying to fight against it![31] Was not this church critic in end effect himself rather more "clerical"?[32]

The apparent contradiction will become clear if we perceive that for him it was not a matter of this or that critic seeking to model the church on his own ideas and alternating between disappointment when it resists them and satisfaction when the desired results are achieved. No, for Barth "the Church stands in the fire of the criticism of its Lord" (IV/1 770 = 690). It is "the criticism to which it is subjected by its living Lord" (IV/1 773 = 692), as he speaks against the church because in its visible existence it contradicts the fact that it is the church of Jesus Christ. The criticism of the church made by its members must be only a reference to "its Lord's critique." It can be made only as they themselves in "solidarity" with the church "subject ourselves first" to this criticism by Christ. The goal of every criticism of the church is always to make the church a church that does not contradict but corresponds to the fact that it is the church of Jesus Christ, and thus "only on its *own* ground . . . with the intention of *re-establishing it more firmly* on this ground which it is perhaps on the point of denying" (IV/1 773 = 692). It would certainly be arrogant if the church were to reject the "criticism of the world," to

27. Hans Prolingheuer, *Der Fall Karl Barth, 1934-1935: Chronographie einer Vertreibung,* 2nd ed. (Neukirchen, 1984), p. 41.

28. Trutz Rendtorff, "Radikale Autonomie Gottes," in *Theorie des Christentums: Historisch-theologische Studien zu seiner neuzeitlichen Verfassung,* ed. T. Rendtorff (Gütersloh, 1972), pp. 178-79.

29. Karl Barth, *Der Römerbrief,* 2nd ed., p. 321; ET: *The Epistle to the Romans,* p. 336.

30. Karl Barth, *Dogmatik im Grundriss,* pp. 172-173; ET: *Dogmatics in Outline,* p. 147.

31. Dietrich Bonhoeffer, *Gesammelte Schriften,* vol. 2 (Munich, 1959), pp. 126ff.

32. Karl Gerhard Steck, "Theologische Existenz heute: Rückblick und Ausblick," in reprint of *Theologische Existenz heute!,* vol. 1, ed. Karl Barth and Eduard Thurneysen (Munich, 1980), p. xi.

which it is always subject, as merely "false and unjust" (IV/1 770 = 690). But it can understand this criticism only as a demand that the church must be *the church*.

Understood in this way, the criticism of the church does indeed take on a concrete form. It is directed against both secularization and sacralization, against the "misconception that the church must go along with the spirit of the age"[33] and the idea that it never becomes courageous until it is "thirty years too late."[34] The target of all such criticism must always be the same thing, because in all its forms it is the "conspiracy against the substance of the church":[35] the church's confusion of its self with its Head. When for the young Barth the question directed to all discourse about God is not "How does one do it?" but "How *can* one do it?"[36] then this criticism is the underlying issue. If we give the first form of the question independent weight, then the church presents itself as an entity that can grasp the divine and manipulate and share it, whether in introverted form, demonstrating its own distinctiveness, or in extroverted form, adjusting to common expectations. The church's "asserting eternally that it possesses something, feasts upon it, and distributes it" is "religion's blind and vicious habit."[37] It *is* reprehensible, for in the decisive act of its being the church, it treats its dependence upon, its petitioning, receiving, hearing, and obeying of its Head as something finished and under its control, something it now "has," and with this having it thinks it is standing at God's side and place. Later Barth described this evil as "an attempted nostrification of God" in which we make God's cause our own and our own cause God's. The church "integrates itself with God or God with itself" (CL 214f. = 130).

The "Lord's fiery criticism" resists this exchange in which the church thinks that it possesses that upon which it is permanently dependent, resists it so that much that the church consequently resembles more "a cemetery than a country fair."[38] The church can only point beyond itself to what is promised to us and to all; otherwise, it becomes an enterprise that peddles foolishness to the people or indulges covertly in false magic. In so doing, it simply demonstrates that it is not the Savior. "It does not 'possess' Him. It cannot create or control Him. He is promised to it. It can only receive Him

---

33. Karl Barth, *Predigten 1913* (Zurich, 1976), p. 597.

34. Karl Barth, *Die Theologie und die Kirche* (Munich, 1928), p. 102; ET: *Theology and Church: Shorter Writings, 1920-1928* (New York, 1962), p. 133.

35. Karl Barth, *"Der Götze wackelt,"* p. 28.

36. Karl Barth, *Wort Gottes,* p. 103; ET: *Word of God,* p. 103.

37. Karl Barth, *Wort Gottes,* p. 93; ET: *Word of God,* pp. 86-87.

38. Karl Barth, *Vorträge und kleinere Arbeiten 1922-1925* (Zurich, 1990), pp. 25, 312.

and then be obedient to Him" (IV/2 741 = 655) and *bear witness* to him. "But it loses the ability to do this, it becomes unserviceable to the will and act of God, to the extent that in its visible form it wants to be something more and better than the witness of its invisible being, if it . . . insists on representing and maintaining and asserting and communicating itself as a historical factor, taking itself and its doctrine and sacraments . . . and ordinances and spiritual authority and power in the more usual sense of the word to be the meaning of its existence, in place of the underlying and overruling power of Jesus Christ and His Spirit" (IV/1 734 = 657).

In this case the church no longer speaks about *him* because at the precise point where it ought to bear witness to him, it places *itself* in the spotlight. In so doing it advances a claim that it cannot support and that it will in fact have to withdraw, either by hiding within its own walls as an end in itself in order to let the world be *world,* or by adopting some stylish consumer orientation, in order to be *world* in the world. Either way it will not do justice to humanity. On the one hand, it will *neglect* them by withholding the gospel from them, and, on the other hand, it will patronize by maintaining control over what is in their best interests (IV/3 944ff. = 824ff.). In all its errors, and especially in its self-understanding, it will always contradict the fact that it is the church of *Jesus Christ.* In its confusing of itself with Christ, it presumes to do what Christ does — while neglecting to do what is its proper task — and can presume this only by making the false allegation that he has failed to do it. Confusing itself with Christ is in fact a denial of the fact that the place at which it is acting in place of Christ is occupied by Christ himself. It is a denial of the fact that he is present as the living One and the One who mediates himself to humanity. If this place is occupied because Christ is the Living One, as the church certainly must believe, then it can, and must, and may not do what he does, but only bear witness to what he does.

The concept of witness, so central in Barth's doctrine of the church, contains also its limitation to a task which *only* responds to the action of Christ, but is not to be equated with it. In reply to Bultmann *and* von Balthasar, Barth says that when the church views itself as the "field of possible and actual *representations* of the history of Jesus Christ" and "repetitions . . . of His being and activity," then it raises the question "whether in all the spiritual splendor of the saints who are supposed to represent and repeat Him Jesus Christ has not ceased . . . to be the *object* and *origin* of Christian faith. . . . The redemptive act of God and that which passes for our response to it, are not the same. . . . Everything is jeopardized if there is confusion in this respect. . . . The being and activity of Jesus Christ needs no repetition. It is present and active in its own truth and power" (IV/1 858f. = 768-69). This is what, or better, He is what makes the church into the church, and it must confess the fact that at this decisive point it is totally "defenceless" and dependent upon Him (IV/3 722 = 630).

The Church's Fellowship

The understanding of the church as the witness to Christ has above all positive significance, on the basis of which the negation just discussed becomes self-evident. The term "witness" is advantageous because it has two senses. First, the witness is a person who "has seen and heard the acts of God, or in the New Testament His one consummating . . . act, which is also as such God's Word directed to and received by" this person. Second, the witness is the person who "is called to the work of declaration, faithfully, if without any claim, addressing, imparting and proclaiming to others that which he has seen as God's act and heard as His Word" (IV/3 679 = 593). This twofold sense rules out any idea that the church itself can produce what it has to proclaim or that it exercises control over it. It also rules out any idea that the church's work is an enterprise that has its own ends. It rules out the dissection of the church's action into two separate acts, as though it first receives and thus "has," and then either enjoys what it has or shares it with others. In becoming the witness to God's act, it has already been placed at the side of those to whom it is to testify to what it has become witness, "faithfully, if without any claim." It does not give this testimony, however, as something it has understood and now possesses, but rather it *remains* constantly turned toward the One whose witness it is.

Barth can say the same thing but with different emphases. "The *community* is the human fellowship which in a particular way provisionally forms the natural and historical *environment* of the man Jesus. Its *particularity* consists in the fact that by its existence it has to witness to Him in face of the whole world, to summon the whole world to faith in Him. Its *provisional character* consists in the fact that in virtue of this office and commission it points beyond itself to the fellowship of all men in the face of which it is a witness and herald" (II/2 216 = 196). An important point for Barth here is that the church bears witness "by its existence," not through this or that singular activity but rather through the fact that the church is church. Here again we have that twofold sense. The church is a witness by the fact that Christ has made it the "environment" of his own word and work and given himself to it both to see and to hear. *And* the church is witness in that it sees and hears what it has been given to see and hear, and seeks to correspond to this given in its visible form, as well as in its various institutions and accomplishments. According to Barth, the witness given "by its existence" is the most convincing witness that the church can give to the world at large.

That it does bear witness by its existence means that it gives it through the fact that it is a *fellowship*. It is not founded through a random assembly of like-minded people. It is defined by the fact that in a special sense it is called into the "environment" of Jesus. What corresponds appropriately to Jesus, to the One in whom God has determined himself for fellowship with humanity and humanity for fellowship with him, is fellowship. "There is no legitimate private Christianity." "To be awakened to faith and to be added to the community are one and the same thing" (IV/1 768f. = 688f.). If one or the other is lacking, there will be either a religious individualism or an institution that administers and "cares for" its members. The two have to go together: "The community lives in Christians, Christians live in the community" (IV/1 769 = 688). The meaning of fellowship is that those who "are initially a highly divergent and certainly non-cooperative lot" are drawn together into a "common organism," into a "solid union but . . . a union in freedom, in which the individual does not cease to be this particular individual, united in his particularity with every man in his." They *are* so linked together by the Christ who links himself to them that they "mutually adapt themselves to be one organism which can be used in the world in His service" (IV/2 718f. = 635-36 rev.). For this reason, the service of worship "in all its elements," but "reaching its climax in the celebration of the supper," is *"communion"* (IV/2 722 = 639 rev.).

Not the different kinds of gifts in the church, nor their regional and local variety, constitute "a scandal" for Barth so much as does "every church division," because according to John 17:21 they render the church's ministry in the world unbelievable (IV/1 754-756 = 675-677). This scandal will not be overcome by an ecclesial "featurelessness" on the "way to a self-chosen supra-confessionalism." "What is demanded is the unity of the Church of Jesus Christ, not the externally satisfying coexistence and cooperation of different religious societies." There is only one way to overcome the scandal. "The confessions . . . are called upon primarily to take themselves seriously . . . not necessarily to remain in [separate existence and confession] . . . but to reach out from them to the one Church even in their distinctness" (IV/1 757-759 = 678-679). This reaching out will not take place in the form of a denominational self-assertion, but rather in a self-critical interrogation of the right by which any may understand themselves as the church of Jesus Christ, and in an authentic renewal occasioned by this interrogation. This alone will enable them all to see that the church in Jesus Christ *is* the one church, and its division is as "ontologically . . . impossible" (IV/1 756 = 677) as sin itself. It is sinful. This is not to be understood as though "Jesus Christ" were a minimal consensus of all confessions (if their divisions are serious ones, then they are disunited precisely in regard to him), but rather in the sense that the "real church," the church of the "credo ecclesiam," *is* always and already one in Christ. Therefore, the unity of the churches is not something that they themselves can *make real,* but rather something that they only can constantly *discover* by seeking to live visibly, in spite of their divisons, in proper correspondence to the unity already real in Christ.

When Barth designates the one community as the "natural and historical environment" of Jesus, then he is not referring solely to the church but — and this is his most striking thesis — to the one community in its two-fold form "as the people of Israel . . . *(ante und post Christum natum!)* [= before and after Christ's birth] and at the same time as the Church of Jews and Gentiles" (II/2 218 = 198). "It is the bow of the *one* covenant that stretches over the whole" (IV/1 749 = 670). At this point he opposes Schleiermacher's influential thesis that we have two different religions here. This thesis is effectively countered neither by the question of Jewish mission versus dialogical tolerance, nor by the question whether they are two materially opposite or historically related religions. It is countered, however, where one sees that Israel is the *"natural"* environment of Jesus, because he "is — primarily and supremely — theirs," because he elected "flesh and blood from Judah-Israel to be His tabernacle," and thus "their election is confirmed" (II/2 231f. = 210-11 rev.), the election that is valid for those who *are* members of this people. The church is the *"historical"* environment of Jesus because people are "called" into it as "guest[s] in the house of Israel, . . . taken up into its election" (IV/3 1005 = 877 rev.). In all their distinctiveness, Israel and the church are the one community of God.

They are both, in their distinctiveness, witnesses of God to one another and together to the rest of the world. In its election to be the people of God, which initially excluded the Gentiles, Israel bears witness to the "judgment of God," namely, to his judgment on "natural theology" with its assertion that there is in all of us a native fitness for God, an assertion that denies the grace of God. The church, however, bears witness to the "mercy of God," namely, to the mercy with which he called into the community of God those who were originally excluded from God's election (II/2 226ff. = 205ff.). What makes Israel and the church into *one* community and *unites* their two witnesses is precisely what Israel outside the church cannot perceive in its no to Christ: *Jesus Christ.* "He sees us as Jews contending against the true God and as Gentiles making peace with false gods, but He sees us both united as

'children of the living God.'"[39] He sees us thus because through his reconciliation the dispute between the two has become a "settled dispute" (II/2 229 =
208), and Israel, for all its rejection of Christ, remains elected. But now those
who were excluded are no longer excluded, and those who had made peace
with false gods have been called out of their "natural" attachments and summoned into the community. If *they* believe in Jesus Christ, they must do what
Israel in its rejection of Christ cannot do. They must "precede Israel with the
confession of the unity of God's community" (II/2 294 = 267). If they fail to
do this — and it will be the task of Jews in the church to prevent this from
happening — then the church "ceases to be the Church" and "has nothing
more to say to the world" (II/2 257 = 234). This failure is for Barth "the most
serious of all wounds in the body of Christ" (IV/3 1007 = 878).

The Mature Community

The church means fellowship. But do individuals have rights? Barth not only
says that "to be a Christian in and for oneself is to be . . . not a Christian" (IV/1
769 = 689). He also says that "a forced Christian is not a Christian" (IV/3 608
= 529). It is important to learn this in view of the fact that the loss of the self-
evident character of Christian existence is linked to the way that people are
less and less guided in their behavior by established patterns but by their autonomous decisions instead. In the sphere of religion this finds expression in
the thought that we may choose ourselves what belief we hold to be right.
This idea developed out of the summons of the Enlightenment that people
should emerge out of their immaturity. How are we to deal with this summons in the church?

Two answers are conceivable, corresponding to the positions already
discussed. On the one hand, I can, by declaring the process to be irreversible,
interpret this desire for the self-determination of my faith as a religious act
itself. Thus, if I decide to end my church membership, then I may be leaving
the church but, because this act is itself an act of religious self-determination,
I am not leaving religion. If remaining in the church is the expression of my
free choice, then those who leave and those who stay in the church are linked
to each other religiously. On the other hand, I can declare that self-
determination in matters of faith is un-Christian. For this position, the
boundary of the principle of self-determination is reached where faith is con-

---

39. Karl Barth, *Die Kirche Jesu Christi* (*Theologische Existenz heute!* 5) (Munich, 1933),
p. 17.

cerned, if not earlier, because the human person needs to be managed, or must be managed, much more than he thinks. At any rate, I myself cannot choose to believe in the grace of God. For man lives by God's grace alone which is always a pure gift to us, and which I could not grasp for myself.

The first position can uphold the right of self-determination only by blanking out the grace of God and therefore the basis of Christian faith. The second position can establish faith in the grace of God but only by excluding self-determination in matters of faith. If we adopt the first position, the church can survive only if it *adjusts* to the universal demand for self-determination. If we adopt the second, we must *oppose* any such adjustment.

Barth, however, follows a third path, in an attempt to think through anew, in view of the modern situation of mature self-determination, what the church is promised to be. "There is too much ready talk," says Barth, "about the world which is supposed to have come of age in relation to God. . . . My own concern is rather with the man who ought to come of age in relation to God and the world, i.e., the mature Christian and mature Christianity" (IV/4 x = ix-x). A question arises: "Had the world first to become mature in order that in its own way the Church should become mature in a positive sense?" (IV/3 21). "In its own way" involves theological reflection on the truth of the gospel. "In a positive sense" means that, in view of the demand for maturity, we need to consider to what extent the gospel itself enables maturity.

These things led Barth to oppose a broad Christian tradition that taught Christians to accept imposed rulings as "graces divinely given." He did not dispute the fact that the grace of God revealed in Jesus Christ rests solely upon a divine initiative. Nevertheless, he did challenge the idea that this grace establishes a one-sided relationship with God in which we are no more than passive objects that have lost their freedom and can no longer act.[40] Notions of this kind provoked the protests of the modern demand for self-determination. A grace of this kind would be a graceless grace. There was good reason, Barth thought, why the church should rethink this matter. If God reveals his grace to us in Jesus Christ, then in him who is "God with us" he shows that he wants us as his partner. "He does not force or suppress or disable. . . . He is not the rampaging numinous which strikes man unconditionally so that he can only be petrified and silent before it, yielding without really wanting to do so" (IV/3 607 = 528).

Then, however, God's grace is to be understood in such a way that the

---

40. Cf. Barth, *Der Römerbrief,* 2nd ed., pp. 157-58; ET: *The Epistle to the Romans,* p. 180; but contra Barth, Rendtorff, "Radikale Autonomie," p. 170.

human person "is taken seriously as an independent creature of God," "as the creature . . . which is of age" (IV/4 25, 39 = 22, 35). Grace is not "in any sense a destiny . . . in which they are fundamentally no more than instruments and objects" (IV/4 145 = 132), "a puppet" (IV/3 607 = 528), "a cog set in motion." "What the free God in His omnipotence wills and fashions in Jesus Christ in the work of the Holy Ghost is the free man who determines himself under this predetermination by God" (IV/3 39 = 35; cf. II/2 94f. = 178). The description of us as "God's partners" (IV/4 179 = 163) affirms our *maturity,* but it also means that our freedom is not the capricious freedom of isolated individuals, but it is maturity only in *partnership,* freedom in specific relationships, in fellowship with God and with others. The maturity that rests upon the grace of God means, therefore, that "man is now free . . . to live in contact, solidarity and fellowship not only with God but also . . . with his fellows . . . as companions in the partnership of reconciliation" (IV/3 285 = 248).

Barth's third way now becomes clear, particularly in view of the demand for human self-determination that so profoundly touches upon church membership. The issue is neither the mere acceptance nor rejection of this demand. It is a nuanced acceptance on the basis of the gospel that is proclaimed by the church. If such an affirmation is made, however, then it is also an orientation for the direction towards which the church is to direct its steps on its way from today into tomorrow. If the gospel itself calls for a free fellowship "in the partnership of reconciliation," then the way is shown to build it up as a "Christian democracy."[41] This also means that the commencement of the Christian life in the church, baptism, can only be an act affirmed in one's own, irreplaceable maturity (IV/4 144f., 204ff. = 131-33, 185ff.).

As long as we take the grace of God to mean that we are always passive in relation to it, the result in the church will be the stable arrangement of the ministerial office that dispenses this grace and the congregation that receives it. Yet the direct adoption of the demand for self-determination by the church has led to a rigid concept of ecclesial office. If self-determination is understood as the freedom of the consumer in the market of possibilities, and if one of those consumer needs is a religious one that the "church" is supposed to satisfy, then such a "church" consists of those officers who are competent to provide what is needed. *If,* however, the church receives its commission from the gospel, and if the maturity of all its members is in accordance with the gospel of God's grace, then, according Barth, the community will not lack the differences of varying functions (whose bearers are to be chosen

---

41. Karl Barth, *Die Theologie und die Kirche,* p. 82; ET: *Theology and Church,* p. 117.

by the community in acknowledgment of their maturity). These differences, however, should not mean the establishment of such a stable arrangement of office and congregation with orders of superiority and subordination.

"The living Lord Jesus Christ deals directly with his living community, not indirectly, not through some system of representation, not along the path of a humanly concocted chain of authority."[42] Churches that are based on systems such as these live in the "contradiction" that they entrust too much to their officials and too little to their members, "so that *over there* they cannot do enough to accommodate their concern about human arbitrariness, while *here* they carelessly 'make mere flesh their strength' [Jer. 17:5]."[43] There can be in the church "no 'clergy' and no laity,' no simply 'teaching' church and no simply 'listening' church, because there is no member of the church who would not be all of these at his place."[44] Such a mature church is the goal towards which the church has to form itself in view of the challenge raised by the demand for self-determination. One way to gauge whether the church is moving in that direction is provided when the sentiment, "I am going to church when I need something for myself" is replaced by the thought, "I am needed there."

The Open Host

The fading of the notion that being a Christian is self-evident raises a further problem. If many people need the church only exceptionally or not at all, then the question is, What is the church (still) for? Since this is a hurtful question for the church, it easily represses it, and its representatives react by enumerating all the services which the church has to offer. In doing so, one easily conceals the question, Is all of this is necessary? Could not a good proportion of these endeavors simply be dropped or be carried out by others? If there were no church, would many of its members really lack something which could not perhaps be provided at least as well or even better from another source?

An answer along the lines of those two other positions can be framed. *Either* the church sees it as its purpose to continue, in the space remaining for it, what might be its image of itself from earlier times, which would be to function as an official agency that distributes salvation to the "church peo-

---

42. Karl Barth, *Die Schrift und die Kirche,* p. 37.
43. Karl Barth, *Die Schrift und die Kirche,* pp. 42-43.
44. Karl Barth, *Die Schrift und die Kirche,* p. 39.

ple." But suppose that the church population, which at one time approximated the population as a whole, is now melting away? What about these other people? Are they excluded from salvation?

Or, the church sees it as its purpose to bear responsibility for religious needs in the area allotted to it by society. In this instance it will be dealing with *more* than just the little church flock, but it does so under the condition that the other parts of society work non-religiously and only give the religious sector over to it. There is the further presumption that an expressly *Christian* fulfillment of this religious sector must be dispensed with.

Once again Barth takes another path here on which he tries to combine the concerns of the first position, that is, what is distinctive about the Christian church, with the concerns of the second position, that is, how does the church maintain contact with those who are outside it. Further, he concludes that the church in the age of modernity has already attempted to take this path, by opening itself in an unprecedented way for the unchurched social reality and its problems by raising the question, "Why should there still be church?" (IV/3 20 = 20). Barth would like to strengthen the church, when it takes this path, by reflecting theologically on that which the church is promised to be. He focuses first on the very center of the Christian faith. What does it mean, he asks, that God in Jesus Christ did not become a Christian but became a *man,* and that in him he loved and reconciled the world (IV/3 560ff. = 487ff.)? The validity of this claim for the unchurched world does not come into effect only when the church communicates it, even though only the church knows about it. "The community of Jesus Christ has a very inadequate view of its Lord . . . if it is not prepared to recognize that even world occurrence outside takes place in His sphere and under His governance, or if it tries to imagine that in this occurrence we are concerned either with no God at all, or with another God, or with another will of the one God different from His gracious will demonstrated in Jesus Christ" (IV/3 786f. = 686). "We have to reckon with the hidden ways of God in which He may put into effect the power of the atonement made in Jesus Christ (John 10:16) even *extra ecclesiam,* i.e., other than through its ministry to the world. He may have provided and may still provide in some other way for those who are never reached, let alone called to Him, by the Church" (IV/1 769 = 688). The rejection of the thesis that the "hidden God" differed from the revealed God has great practical significance for the relationship of Christians to the "world."

The reconciliation of the *world* with God in Christ has *also* for the *church,* of course, a reality of such a sort that it need not be brought into concrete awareness by the church because in the Holy Spirit this reconciliation communicates itself and makes itself presently knowable in the church (IV/1

320f. = 290ff.; IV/2 163 = 146-47). To what purpose, then, is the church? The answer is a surprising one. There is no ultimate necessity for it, certainly not of the sort that derives from a decision made by society as a whole that there must be something like a religious sector somewhere in it. The church is not finally necessary, especially when it is viewed as a kind of religious sector of society as a whole. "The world would be lost without Jesus Christ . . . the world would not necessarily be lost if there were no Church" (IV/3 946 = 826). This does not contradict the fact that Christ is never without his people, but it does contradict the reverse of this statement. In the church there is no knowledge which is not valid outside of it as well and which thus *could* also be known.[45] What distinguishes the church from others is the fact that it *does know* that God reconciled the world in Christ. The distinction between the church and the rest of the world lies *here* and not in the claim that people in the church have salvation and those outside of it do not. Along these lines Barth corrects the saying, "Extra ecclesiam nulla salus," that there is no salvation outside the church (IV/1 769 = 688f.). This means that this distinction is a fluid and open one and sets no absolute boundary. The particular Christian maturity of which Barth speaks is based precisely upon the fact that the distinctive feature of members of the church is their *knowledge* of the reality of reconciliation. The term "knowledge" is intended to make it clear that the reality of reconciliation is not something that Christians first *make* true, but that they only *perceive* as being true (IV/3 78ff. = 72ff.). The term, then, does not designate merely an intellectual process, but rather a life-praxis in faith, love and hope that defines the entirety of human existence (IV/3 422ff. = 365ff.). And so this term underlines that what makes us Christians is not to be had more cheaply than in that "the living Jesus Christ encounters definite men at definite times in their lives as their Contemporary, makes Himself known to them as the One He is . . . and addresses and claims them" (IV/3 577 = 502).

An important point is that this knowledge is not a static communication. It sets us in *movement*. If this knowledge relates to the reconciliation of the *world* with God, then it at once moves us into *relationship* to the world outside the church. As true as it is that the world need not be lost without the church, "the Church would be lost if it had no counterpart in the world" (IV/3 946 = 826). Since the church is distinguished by its *knowledge* of the reconciliation of the world with God, it is *thereby* called to be the *witness* of this reconciliation to the world around it (IV/3 744 = 649f.). This is how Barth answers

---

45. Cf. Eberhard Mechels, *Kirche und gesellschaftliche Umwelt (Neukirchener Beiträge zur systematischen Theologie 7)* (Neukirchen, 1990), pp. 289ff.

the question: To what purpose is the church? Its purpose is to be such a witness! The fact that society and the church separate themselves from each other is no *danger* for the church, producing the reaction that it either retreats into itself or "commends" itself to society with the offer of "satisfaction of ultimate needs" (I/2 368 = 336). Barth teaches us to see this process as a real *opportunity* for the church, so that the church understands it as the emergence of a *counterpart* with which the church can now truly engage and practice solidarity with the rest of society as witness to the gospel. For Barth, the classical counterposition of clergy and laity in the church is now replaced by the over-againstness of the community and the rest of society, although the dominant pattern of the old churchly counterparts is not simply to be transferred to the new situation.

This new definition of the task of the church does not mean that it must attach the unchurched world to itself, but that *it* is prevented from understanding *itself* as an end in itself. "It is the human creature which is ordained by its very essence to exist for the other human creatures distinct from it. It . . . exists for itself, only in fulfillment of this ordination. It . . . exists . . . eccentrically, even within the world to which it belongs, not with reference to itself but wholly with reference . . . to the world around. It saves and maintains its own life as it interposes and gives itself for all other human creatures. . . . The center around which it moves eccentrically is not, then, simply the world as such" — in that case it would fall prey to a fatal pressure to conform — "but the world for which God is" — and this prevents it from expending its energies on domestic aggrandizement on the view that it is an end in itself (IV/3 872 = 762 rev.).

This then makes it understandable that the sending of the church is not something that may be absent from its existence as the church. In that the church is church and in accordance with Christ's drawing it together into a fellowship, it *is* already witness over against the "world," "provisional representation" of what God has accomplished in the reconciliation of Christ "de jure" for "all humanity" (IV/2 701f. = 620). This will help us to understand Barth's emphasis upon the maturity of the entire community. Maturity is a necessary condition if the church is to become witness in its relation as counterpart to the rest of society. It is what then makes it possible to replace the voice of *one* office with a "*multiplicity of forms* of Christian witness" (IV/3 988 = 862 rev.). For Barth, it is not only ecclesial officers who are "ordained" to such witness; "but all those baptized as Christians are . . . ordained . . . to the ministry of the Church" (IV/4 221 = 201). The conclusion is then obvious that for Barth the "external marks" of the church are not just preaching with the administration of the sacraments but that the Christian community as a whole bears this witness to the world (IV/3 883 = 771-72, 887 = 775-76, 964 = 841-42), by introducing a new "churchly worldliness or worldly churchliness" (IV/3 37 = 35 rev.).

It must be stressed, however, that in this process the church is *only* witness and not mediator of salvation. It cannot itself create the self-communicating reality of the reconciling of the world with God. God does that. Thus, in its witnessing it does not allow itself to make any alien encroachment upon the world around it. For what it witnesses to in its knowledge of reconciliation, since it is the reality of the reconciliation of the *world,* is in principle perceivable by the world around. This is what protects the church against the temptation of seeing the world apart from this reality and then re-shaping and adapting its witness to please such a "world." Also ruled out is a mission of the church understood as "self-commendation," where the issue is "the 'glory' of this or that Christianity in its relation to the needs and postulates of man" (I/2 368 = 336). This also excludes any patronizing interaction of the community with the addressees of its witness, in which it encounters them as the "owner and proper disposer" of the goods of salvation (IV/3 948 = 827). "Patronage means the human exercise of power by men against other men as though they were objects . . . treating others . . . as so much material for one's own abilities" (IV/3 950 = 829). The church must act as witness in the "solidarity of the pagans inside with the pagans outside."[46] It is "the greeting with which . . . I have to greet my neighbor, the declaration of my fellowship with one in whom I expect to find a brother of Jesus Christ and therefore my own brother. . . . A witness will not intrude on his neighbor. . . . Witness can be given only when there is the highest respect for the freedom of the grace of God, and therefore the highest respect for the other man who can expect nothing from me but everything from God" (I/2 487f. = 441 rev.), and from whom I can expect to hear "true words" (IV/3 144ff. = 128ff.). This is how the open church expresses itself.

---

46. Karl Barth, *Theologische Fragen und Antworten* (Zollikon, 1957), p. 102.

Limited Time —
Time and Eternity, Eschatology

The Loss of Time

One criticism of the younger Barth was that he opened up a "rift between time and eternity": "There is no revelation of the Eternal in time." "Eternity presses time back step by step."[1] Did not Barth in 1920 agree with Overbeck when he said: "If Christianity, then not history; if history, then not Christianity"? And again: "Historical Christianity, that is, Christianity subjected to time, is an absurdity."[2] Did not Barth reject that which Windelband regarded as the main characteristic of modern thinking: "Historicity is newly understood as humanity's basic mode of being that fatefully permeates our whole existence"?[3] Did he not abandon time to the secular world and withdraw into the distant margins while discoursing on theological reality?

All the same, the subject of time that so pre-occupies modern thinking still takes a notably large place in Barth's dogmatics. He saw the modern treatment of it as a kind of provocation that Christian theology, in his view, had to confront critically. For him, the mistake in the concept of time that was dominant in the intellectual world around him was to think of time as "absolute time," the "absolute reality," "the naked structure of the sphere" to which we belong. Viewed this way, time sets up conditions that "are not sub-

---

1. H. W. Schmidt, *Zeit und Ewigkeit: Die letzten Voraussetzungen der dialektischen Theologie* (Gütersloh, 1927), pp. 31ff., 70.

2. Karl Barth, *Die Theologie und die Kirche* (Munich, 1928), p. 9; ET: *Theology and Church: Shorter Writings, 1920-1928* (New York, 1962), p. 61.

3. Wilhelm Windelband, *Lehrbuch der Geschichte der Philosophie*, 15th ed., ed. H. Heimsoeth (Tübingen, 1957), p. 618.

ject to any condition. They are infinitely constant relationships, orders and forces, and as such presuppositions to which we are wholly and always subject. They are the indestructible walls of our prison. Our supposedly free action is only within these walls whose significance is simply to be these walls, so that our existence can have no other significance than to be existence within them. Enclosed within them, we are not merely not yet redeemed but totally unredeemed. 'There is no peace for the wicked'" (IV/3 390f. = 338).

This is a "concept of time without God" (III/2 669 = 552) that is not improved by our subsequently adding the "word 'God'" to it (III/2 668 = 551). Then God would simply be "an idealized form of creaturely existence" (III/2 667 = 558) in which the creature posits both itself and its time absolutely. In truth, this view of time allows no place for God. "Absolute time" is *godless* time. Because it is conceived of as godless, it has to be set as absolute and limitless, deified, "made into a God called Chronos" (III/2 547 = 456), and in this deification is all the more truly godless time. This understanding "finds suitable expression in the metaphysical conception of the infinity of time" (III/2 620 = 515). It is for Barth only variations upon the same theme whether, dreading the fleetingness of time, we try to endow it with an unending character, so that after the fashion of the ancient Greeks we are related to our "origin in a world of immutable being," or we conceive of a divine likeness in which we are "eternal in every 'moment'" (Schleiermacher), or in a technological era we devote ourselves to "the idea of endless progress"(III/2 622 = 516). It is not as though God jealously watches out to ensure that he may remain the infinite one in contrast to all that is finite! The true God is not the "Infinite One" at all. By revealing himself, he disputes the very "idea of the infinity of time." By clinging to this idea, we not only miss God but also ourselves in our being in time, and thus we generate a deformed time for ourselves.

It is we who deform it. Since "absolute time," that is, a time separated from God, is the product of those who posit *themselves* absolutely, they will now claim the temporal as their sovereign domain. The abstract "concept of a history of man and men and mankind apart from the will and Word and work of God is itself the product of the perverted and sinful thinking of man, one of the manifestations of human pride" (IV/1 563 = 505). With this concept man conquers his past: "When a whole generation becomes confused about its present and secretly about its faith in its future as well, then it turns to historicism, and it begins to ask romantically or precisely about what and how everything once was" (III/2 645 = 534 rev.). Why does it do this? Man "finds it intolerable that all this should have happened then, i.e., long before his own day. . . . He cannot bear to think that this dimension of life never belonged to him. Therefore he cannot leave history alone.... Therefore he fills the gap by plunging into it with his historical investigations and discoveries.... This process is usually stigmatized by its critics as a 'flight into history.'" Is it not rather an "all-out offensive, a vigorous crusade, a passionate attack on our allotted span of time in which we try to reach out into that field of the past?... It need hardly be said that this endeavor, which rightly understood is truly titanic, is nevertheless afflicted by a final impotence in all its forms.... When we try to reach out beyond our own time... we can never be in an area where we were not." We will always have only our pictures of it. "There can be no backward extension of our being in time" (III/2 700f. = 576).

We might, of course, project ourselves forward. "When a whole generation finds it impossible to make sense of the past, it glories all the more readily in the 'spirit of the age,' that is, of its own age, and succumbs to the belief in progress." Our flight now is in the opposite direction. "We flee from the cathedrals, prisons, inns and catacombs where we were yesterday, into the light of today with its promise of even greater light tomorrow" (III/2 646 = 535). "The barrier posed by the question whether everything might not turn out very differently from what we had expected, since there might be no future at all or only a threatened future, is triumphantly surmounted by the assertion that where there's a will there's a way, and our reach into the future, which has never failed us, will triumph again." But this triumph "is more like the effect of a self-administered dose of morphia.... We are no match for the future which really comes and is so terribly menacing. Our own projected images of the future, now present in us, are not the future itself" with which we have to deal (III/2 657 = 543 rev.).

As persons who are not able to limit themselves and who posit themselves as absolute, and further as persons who deal with time as a boundless and "infinite" terrain, we are in truth lonely. This loneliness reveals the godlessness of our absolute time, because by deifying this time we miss God who is by his very essence not lonely. The person of endless time is always a lonely person. This is not just because he is confronted solely by his self-projected *images* of the past and the future. It is primarily because his own product, the concept of the endlessness of time, immediately develops its own dynamic which in turn begins to seize its producer. It achieves absoluteness because it is the fitting product of the person who posits himself as absolute. His being in time thus becomes "a frantic hunt in which he is really the hunted" (IV/2 471). "Infinite, above all, is the flight which is also a chase, a chase which is also a flight" (III/2 620 = 515). The unrest and anxiety and care that overtake us are something that we Westerners try to cover over by "conscientious work" and Easterners by an attitude of "resignation" (IV/2 534f. = 473f.), although neither of these tactics, nor an exchange of these cultures, can really overcome them. For where we posit time as "absolute time," the consequence must be that "it not only slips through our fingers but carries us away with it" (IV/3 390 = 338).

The view that time is unending has for Barth a paradoxical signifi-cance, which is that the human person in such time struggles in truth with shortness of time (CL 396 = 231). "The man who lives . . . in that loss of time . . . is *alienated* from his Creator and therefore from himself, from his creaturely nature" (III/2 623 = 517). In that loss of time! The desire for unend-ing time results in the very opposite of what he promised himself from it, lost time. "The delusion of infinity" means that we must let ourselves be "ha-rassed on all sides," and we no longer have any time (III/4 674 = 587). Fur-thermore, if we have no time, then we can rob others of their time — as a "Chronophage" [= devourer of time] (IV/2 892 = 787) — but not give them any. Our history is one of "lost and wasted opportunities" (IV/2 502 = 445), which evoke the question, "What is all this if there is nothing more?" (IV/2 477 = 423). A man's life story thus goes awry:

> He is always either too soon or too late. He is asleep when he should be awake, and awake when he should be asleep. He is silent when he should speak, and he speaks when it is better to be silent. He laughs when he should weep and he weeps when he should be comforted and laugh. He always makes an exception when the rule should be kept, and subjects himself to a law when he should choose in freedom. He always toils when he should pray and prays when only work is of any avail. He always devotes himself to historical and psychological investigation when deci-sions are demanded, and rushes into decision when historical and psy-chological investigation is really required. He is always contentious when it is unnecessary and harmful, and he speaks of love and peace where he may confidently attack. (IV/2 465 = 413)

Barth asserted his criticism of the modern concept of time only *indi-rectly,* of course. The reason for this was that his criticism resulted from his seeing a fundamental contradiction to a "concept of time without God," to the view of an "absolute" and unlimited time that we both control and which controls us. This was contradicted by God and by the reality that we with such a concept of time fail to see, to our own great detriment, a reality that God has already prepared for us and that defines our time in healing ways. This reality can only function theologically as a correction of that fatal concept of time when theology itself makes a correction in its own deficient knowledge of this reality. It has to understand that a "concept of time without God" is the payment for a theological fallacy with regard to what God's *eternity* is. Theology must grasp that when it comprehends God's eternity as *timelessness,* it then provokes the thought of the *endlessness* of time. "Absolute" time, time separated from God, godless time — these are rooted theologically in an "absolute" eternity, eternity cut loose from creaturely time, inhuman eternity. There is every reason why theology should abandon the idea of such a timeless and inhuman eternity of God. Only if it does so will it do — indirectly — its part toward overcoming that fatal concept of time.

The Eternal One Has Time

"The theological concept of eternity must be *set free* from the Babylonian captivity of an abstract opposite to the concept of time" (II/1 689 = 611). It "must" be, for the God testified to in the Bible is not subject to this captivity. An eternity of God defined in contrast to time as nontemporality would be inhuman, because then human temporal existence as such would mean distance from God, and because further his temporal existence would have to allow him to exist in "independence or autonomy over against the eternal Creator" (II/1 695 = 616). Eternity in this sense would also be inhuman at a deeper level, because a god conceived of as timeless would apparently be only an idolatrous reflection of the human, who in his "loss of time" would be alienated from himself. "In fact it is an illegitimate anthropomorphism to think of God as if he did not eternally have time, and therefore time for us. . . . If this were so, if . . . abstract non-temporality were the truth about eternity, it would be far too akin to time, indeed it would be only an image in the mirror of our reflection" (II/1 690 = 612), an image of our time, lost and ruined in that "illusion of endlessness." Such an idea gave rise to "the dangerous position that there appears to be no eternity if there is no time" (II/1 689 = 611).

According to the revelation to which the Bible bears witness, the eternal God is willing and able not just to "*give* us time" but to "*take* time to Himself" (II/1 694 = 616). Indeed, "the statement, 'God reveals himself' . . . is equivalent to the statement, 'God has time for us'" (I/2 50 = 45). This does not describe merely an external condition, in order then to do this or that thing in time. "The entire fullness of the benefit of God's revelation and of the reconciliation accomplished in it lies in the fact that God had time for us" (I/2 60 = 55). The name by which God reveals himself is as such a "refutation of the idea of a God who is only timeless" (II/1 695 = 616). "God would not be my God if He were only eternally in Himself, if He had no time for me." This is witnessed to by the fact that "the message of the Old and New Testaments unlike any other religious tradition, and even more so any philosophy, is the concrete message of a *history* wrought out in time." This means that "God's relation to His creatures, as attested in Holy Scripture, is quite unlike anything we find in mythology. It is not a permanent, universal relation (as that between finite and infinite, matter and spirit, good and evil, perfection and imperfection, the sovereign and the dependent, etc.)" (III/2 630f. = 522f.). This relation comes about as God relates himself in the concrete history that has taken place and still takes place in time.

All of this does not mean, of course, that eternity and time are to be equated with each other. Time was made at creation and is a creature of God. "Only God is eternal," so that the creature does not cease to be a creature when God elevates it to participation in his eternity, does not "itself become God and therefore eternal." The eternity of God means that he is "free to be constant," and the reason for this is that "time has no power over Him.... As the One who endures He has all power over time" (II/1 687 = 609). As the Eternal One, He "is not conditioned by time, but conditions it absolutely in His freedom" (II/1 698 = 619). He does not owe his existence to time, but all temporal being owes its existence to him. This insight is obscured if the distinction between time and eternity were to be erased. If this distinction is not noted, then the eternity of God would become misunderstandable anew as a product of the projections of the human person who exists within time.

This distinction is not, however, an antithesis. Since God's eternity conditions all time, it stands in a positive relation to it. He does not have to create time first, let alone borrow (so to speak) it from a temporal being, in order to have time. "He has time, that is, true . . . time, in His eternity" (II/1 697 = 618). As the Eternally Living One, He has time, and in this time there is a genuine Before, During, and After, though these three do not separate from each other (II/1 685 = 608). God "was" before we were, he "is" while we are, and he "will be" when time is no more. Barth has three terms for these three things: God's pre-temporality, his supra-temporality, and his post-temporality (II/1 700f. = 621ff., 702 = 623, 709 = 629f.). He calls this threefold character God's eternal "readiness" to do what God does in fact do: "He gives *us* time by creating and preserving time. He takes time to Himself *for us* by Himself becoming temporal" (II/1 697 = 618). By virtue of that power, both correspond to his being and are not something alien to God. By virtue of that power God in his eternity is free and able to be actively present to all temporal beings at every moment in time. God's eternity is "that which begins in all beginnings, continues in all successions and ends in all endings. . . .

In it and from it . . . everything is which is, including all beginning, succession and end" (II/1 688 = 610). And by virtue of that power, the eternal becomes temporal in his revelation in such a way that "it is really God *Himself* who has time for us. He Himself *is* time for us" (II/1 690 = 612).

Statements of this kind are based upon divine revelation. We would not take this revelation seriously if we did not say that God's eternity does not exclude "temporal reality" but includes it: "It enters time; nay, it assumes time; nay, it creates time for itself" (I/2 55 = 50). The specific form with which God has time for us in his revelatory turning to us is his contending with our perverted, "absolute," and lost time, together with the healing of the damage it causes. God "normalizes time. He heals its wounds" (III/1 80 = 74). For revelation not only means that we can understand God's eternity in light of the way that he takes time for us in it. It also means that we are unable to understand our creaturely time apart from God and from the fact that the God who takes time for us *gives* us time — time to live with him and in the fellowship of the eternal God. *Our* time, that "godless concept of time," is not this time with God. God can not enter into this time, nor can he assume it, as he certainly does, without saying "no" to our perverted time, without rejecting it, without making it into a passing, indeed a past "old time," and without "creating" for himself and us a *new* time, a time in covenant with God in order to heal the damage of our lost time. Barth thus opposes the modern inclusion of revelation in human history when he says, "Revelation is not a predicate of history, but history is a predicate of revelation" (I/2 64 = 58). The former statement would mean that revelation would belong to that "old" time, capable only of confirming it, unable to disqualify it as "old." In point of fact, "God in time . . . is the offending thing in revelation." For "in the midst of time . . . [it is] the center of confusion" through which "we are attacked by God, as it were, in our very own sphere, namely in the delusion that we possessed time," that absolute time separated from God (I/2 68 = 61 rev.). This happens in such a way that we must recognize in revelation that "what we mean when we say 'time' is real there. . . . There and only there in contemporaneousness with Christ . . . do we really possess time," the time that is healed of our lostness, the new time, the real time, the time with God (I/2 73 = 66).

Why do we speak of contemporaneousness with *Christ?* Because it is in fellowship with him that we share in the reality of the new time that he has inaugurated. It was in him that God reconciled the world to himself. He is God's "representative to men," in whom the eternal One took on time for them in order to do away with all the wrong they had done in that lost time defined by them as "without God." He is also our "representative before God" in whom, thanks to the divine assuming of time for us, we can acquire a new time that we now have with God (cf. III/2 527 = 439). We thus need the presence of Jesus Christ, our contemporaneousness with him, in order to receive a time that is rescued from the loss of time. Yet how do we become Christ's contemporaries? "These men do not make or feel or know themselves the contemporaries of Jesus. It is not they who become or are this. It is Jesus who becomes and is their Contemporary.... Hence they can and must and actually do understand their present existence as a life of direct discipleship, as their 'being in Christ'" (III/2 561 = 467). Yet how does he become contemporary with them?

Barth understands the revelation in Christ as the "fullness of time, . . . the time of God: eternal time" (III/2 550f., 557 = 458, 462). He rejects the docetic dissolving of this revelation into a timeless, symbolic myth. "The time of Jesus Christ is also a time like all other times . . . it occurred once and once-for-all" in its "beginning, duration and end" (III/2 555 = 463). God would not have affirmed our being in time or rescued us from our lost time if the time assumed in the incarnation of the divine Son had not been a specific time "like all other times." But it would not have been valid for all at all times; it would not have been the *fullness* of time and the time *of God,* if that which otherwise in all other times is the "absolute barrier," the limitation in its once-and-for-all-ness and its then-ness, were now the "gateway" (III/2 557 = 464). That this time is not a barrier but an open gateway for every time is what makes it "eternal time."

It is here that Barth sees the special significance of Easter when *"the man Jesus was manifested* among them (his disciples) *in the mode of God"* (III/2 537 = 448). The resurrection of Jesus did not mean that he was given further time beyond the unique time of his given life on earth back then. Its meaning was that his earthly life was shown to be time "in the mode of God," that is, eternal time, time with a past, present, and future, yet without any splitting up of these tenses, but rather with the present giving fullness to the past and the future, so that "no longer" and "not yet" do not apply (III/2 573 = 477; cf. I/2 58 = 53). Jesus is in every age. He is in these three dimensions of time as the one who makes himself simultaneous in each of them — this must be said in opposition to the abstracted and dissected figure of a "historical Jesus" (III/2 562 = 468). The distinction of tenses is not erased. Jesus was different yesterday from what he is today and tomorrow. But in these tenses he is not another but always the same Jesus Christ, in whom God reconciled the world with himself. As the same One, he is according to Revelation 1:8 the One "who is and who was and who is to come" (III/2 558 = 465): the One who has come, the One who "at the beginning of time" was the One who is coming, the One who is coming today who is the One who has come and who at the end will be the One who is coming again. In this way he gives them time, time that is not without but is with him, not lost but real time.

The Gift of Real Time

Man "would not be in time if he were without God." If he should act as though he were without God — that is his sin — then he acts as though he were not in time. He is then acting as though he were relieved of time, envisions for himself the bad eternity of unending time, and envisions it without really having time at all. "But he is in time. Hence he is not without God. To say 'man' or 'time' is first and basically, even if unwillingly and unwittingly, to say 'God.' For God is for man as He has time for him. It is God who gives him his time" (III/2 634 = 525). Time is God's gift. Only time given and received as a gift is real time. If the person who in his sin is detached from God then detaches his time from the fact that it is God's gift, his time will then detach itself from him, and it will become a fleeting if not fleeing and even lost time (III/1 78 = 72).

If God in his revelation assumes time for humanity, then he is no more transforming his eternity into time than he in the incarnation of the word is transforming himself into a man. He, as the eternal One, is assuming temporal being in order that he may live in covenant with this man and make such covenant living possible. God's assuming of time does not rob us of time. It gives us our time. "The existence of the man Jesus in time is our guarantee that time as the form of human existence is in any case willed and created by God, is given by God to man, and is therefore real" (III/2 628 = 520). Since in this man God has real time for us, for all people at all times, then we each of us in our own time also have time. We have time with God. Because God is with us, time is *given* to us. This makes apparent what the sinful person detached from God cannot know, which is that it is natural for humans to have time. "It is in virtue of the presence and gift of God that temporality too belongs to human nature" (III/2 634 = 525), that is, to that *good* nature that is perverted by sin but not abolished. If the gift is a gift of *God,* then it is indestructibly a *good* gift.

Just as God's assuming of time for his creature is the quintessence of all his beneficence, humans' having of time for one another is the quintessence of all humaneness. "When I really give anyone my time, I thereby give him the last and most personal thing I have to give at all, namely, myself" (I/2 60 = 55). "Humanity is *temporality.* Temporality . . . is *humanity*" (III/2 629 = 522). It is only when a person is not alone, Barth emphasizes, that she is human. People who focus on themselves, live for themselves, lonely people are inhuman — and they have no time. However, if our being in time is a gift of God, and we know it as such, then we also see in this gift that our being is a being in relationship. Humanity is a being in relationship, first of all in relationship to God, which then makes itself evident in the co-humanity which belongs essentially the human. The co-human no more exists as a mere idea, as part of my consciousness, than does God so exist. When my I is encountered by another co-human Thou who is really distinct from me, then it exists in time and is for my I a guarantee of my own being in time, and of my own co-human humanity.

As Barth sees it, the human having of time depends upon one's really *receiving* time thanks to that gift, and that one will thereby become aware of the fact that the One in whom God has assumed time for him, Jesus Christ, is present. According to the message of Easter,

> there can be no doubt that this present day of ours is also a day of the living Jesus Christ. It may well be also a day in which all of us . . . sin in evil thoughts and words and deeds. . . . It may well be a day when the earth is covered. . . . by so much merited and unmerited suffering. It may well be a day when no moment passes in which death does not make . . . an . . . end of some human life. It may well be a day of the devil and demons. . . . This is true. But it is not decisive. The decisive thing is that it is also a day of Jesus Christ, a day of His presence, life, activity and speech . . . a day of His coming again in the full sense of the word . . . of the revelation of that which, when He came before, He enacted and accomplished in His life and speech and action and passion and death in His time as the act of God for the world and for all men. In the first instance we are not contemporaries of the great or little personages of the history of the world or culture or even the Church. . . . In the first instance we are contemporaries of Jesus Christ and direct witnesses of His action, whether with closed or open or blinking eyes, whether actively or passively. More closely and properly than any other man . . . He is the neighbor of every other man, the Good Samaritan for all of us. . . . Wittingly or unwittingly we are alongside and with Him. His today is really ours and ours His. (IV/3 418f. = 362-63)

It is not the fleetingness of time, nor any single moment measured by "the millions of identical oscillations of the clock with which we measure it" (III/2 641 = 531), but the comforting presence of God that truly makes for us a real present that is significant, urgent, and compelling.

Only now can we see that each Now is indeed a "now or never." . . . How do we know that what we now consciously or unconsciously omit is only a paltry thing and not the turning-point which determines our whole being in time both past and future? There are moments like this. Indeed, in the strict sense all moments are like this. . . . Now is no time for dreaming. . . . Now is the time to awake, to receive or act, to speak or be silent, to say Yes or No. Now is no time to send as our proxy a recollected or expected picture of ourselves, a ghost or an ideal, to act under our mask. Now we must step out and act as the men we really are. . . . Because we are under God and for Him, as we now are, there is no evading the importance of the Now, and no excuse for missing or misusing it. But there is also no absence of His grace and mercy even in our Now. Our present is indeed joyful, for in it, since God is He who is primarily and properly present . . . we are not abandoned by Him. . . . He forgives our sins, protects His erring children and causes tired wayfarers to take their halting steps. . . . His wisdom exceeds our folly and His goodness our evil. . . . He is wakeful even when we fall asleep and dream about the past and future when we ought to be buying up the Now which will never come our way again. Even in the particularity of His presence which we have failed to see or use, or perhaps misused, He will not have been present to us in vain. (III/2 641f. = 531-32)

Our past, according to Barth, is part of the gift of time. As I am today, do I have a past? It naturally seems that I have, for I can handle it as I like, remembering it or forgetting it. But is this a real past? The past means that "what and how I was then . . . — the word is cruelly clear — is passed away, 'was' in the sense of decay, of loss of being" (III/2 644 = 533-34 rev.). What is left, as of a deceased person, "is a great flood of forgotten reality . . . an island or two of memory" which the "subjective accident or skill by which we conjure up the shades of what was once present but is so no more" tries to save (III/2 617f. = 512-13). As we cannot have the present except as it is given to us by the God who is present, so we can have the past only as the past that is preserved, uncovered and also covered, and given to us in God and by God. The fact that we were those who were means that we are in the hands of God (III/2 651 = 538). "Primarily, however, it is not *we* who were, but *God*. Even then God was our Creator, Deliverer, and Preserver. He then continued to be for us in spite of our enmity against Him. . . . He was first in the heights; then we in the depths" (III/2 647 = 535-36). "He loved us even then. And this means that our then being as the object of His love . . . has not ceased to be real in His eyes and therefore in truth" (III/2 649 = 537). As the One who *is* who he was, he gives us a part in the reality and way by which our past remains the object of his love. By giving us this part he frees us to deal with our past. It may be that we are permitted to live with an "awareness of history," free from the "temptation to falsify it . . . in our own favour," and yet also from the inclination to "live *by* the past" (III/2 651f. = 539); it may be "that we are allowed to forget," but not "that we *have* to forget," or are not allowed to forget; for "enforced oblivion is as bad as enforced recollection." "How much harm comes from the forcible suppression of memories contrary to the will of God" (III/2 652f. = 540 rev.)!

As Barth sees it, the future, too, is part of the gift of time. As I now am, do I have any future at all? This too seems to be obvious, to the extent that it is possible for me in my Now. "I transcend Now's boundary moving forwards," in order to "anticipate" the future. But do I have a future? "The future of which I am full is not my real future. It is not even a pledge of it. It proves only that I now live *as if* I had a real future." It might be a "preparation leading to nothing." "The further side of my present may turn out to be the further side of my being generally" (III/2 654f. = 542f.). Again, it must be said at this juncture that like our past and our present, our future is also in God's hands. God guarantees the fact that we shall live (III/2 661 = 546). "In the first instance it is not we who will be in the next moment, tomorrow, or a year hence. It is God, our Creator, Deliverer, and Sustainer, who will still be for us and faithful to us," for this future, which is God's "in the first instance," should not be viewed as abstract, nor as detached from his good and holy purpose for his creatures as revealed and enacted in Christ. "What shall we be? Come what may, we shall be what we shall be under and with God . . . those who are loved by Him" (III/2 659f. = 545). Since God is already present as the One he will be, he also gives us a part in the reality and way by which he causes us in the future to be those who are loved by him. This sharing frees us to deal with our future; it may be by unreflectively letting our concern about it become God's concern, so that we are "free to live today responsibly for tomorrow" without any "need to suppose that we are masters of our future"; it may be that we become "reflective" about the fact that in the future we shall certainly encounter the Judge of our plans and actions, yet always with the comforting thought that "as our Judge . . . He is also the One who from the very outset has intervened . . . for us in His almighty mercy" (III/2 662-665 = 547-48, 549).

The Gracious Restriction of Time

Decisive for Barth's concept of time is the fact that creaturely time is essentially limited time. Indeed, along with the preservation of the Bible and the Jews, Barth can regard not only the preservation of humanity in its temporal limits but also its temporal end as a sign of benevolent divine providence (III/3 256ff. = 226ff.). The thought of God does not enable us to climb over the boundaries of time. The particular problem of religion, its secret pact with atheism, is shown here as God is disclosed as a mental construct to enable us to transcend our limits and to absolutize ourselves. For unrestricted and boundless and unending time is godless time, for which the converse is that humans who want to have time without God no longer have any time at all. The consequence is a certain restlessness, but also that we can not give "assent to that to which we can assent only with God . . . that one day we shall no longer exist." Apart from God, the human will try to avoid this knowledge, perhaps by ascribing "to himself, or at least to his soul, an infinitude, a so-called immortality." Or he might say that "in any case he is not yet dead," or he may console himself with the thought that the species will live if not the individual. All of this is "a typical expression of fear," a sign that those who conceive of themselves as godless cannot "face themselves," and have too weak an ego to accept the thought of their own mortality (III/4 678 = 591)! If, on the other hand, "that *Memento mori!* means concretely *Memento Domini!*" [= Remember death, remember the Lord] (III/4 679 = 591), then we can face ourselves and utter that Yes to the limitation of our time.

Since it is the gift of God and not the fleetingness of time that is the source of our knowledge that life is a unique opportunity, the fleetingness of time is also not the source of our knowledge that our lives as unique opportunity are limited, but rather the fact that *God* sets the boundary to life (III/4 669 = 583). It is not, of course, that some Absolute, infinitely superior to mankind, demonstrates its superiority by requiring that we must die! If we thought of God in this way we would have the right to flee from him into that godless time. We could invoke a Prometheus who, instead of extolling the fate of his mortality, would defy it (III/2 622 = 516). As it is, however, "there would only be cause for complaint if man wanted to be God and thus eternal, instead of being cheerfully and modestly man under and with God and therefore temporal" (III/2 649 = 537 rev.). The god that we seek to be is only a reflection of human desires, no more than an apparent god in face of whom temporal existence is a defect that we must seek to avoid. The God with whom we truly have to do, however, is the gracious God who turns to us and affirms us. If it is a benefit and not a defect to be created by this God, then it is also a benefit and not a defect to be created with temporal limits by this God. The recognition that creaturely limitation is a divine benefit enables us to accept this limitation, with the gratitude that is proper to such a benefit.

Barth recognizes, of course, that this audacious thought is open to two serious objections. It is "neither mistaken nor presumptuous" to pose a "demand for duration and protest against the barrier set by the allotting of time." Indeed, properly understood, "it is part of the disorder occasioned by the fall if . . . there is a resigned acceptance of the fact that we can only have allotted time"; and it is a self-alienation when "his demand for duration withers away" (III/2 672f. = 555 rev.). It is not an abstract desire for life but the fact that the human is destined to be with God and with other people that gives this demand plausibility, for it is apparent that a limited life provides too little time to fulfill this destiny. In the light of that destiny the demand for duration is justified. Thus, the human should want to live and not die, want to be healthy and not sick. "A little resolution, will and action . . . against sickness is better than a whole ocean of pretended Christian humility" (III/4 419 = 368). But there is more to it than that, as according to Barth the person plagued with the idea of suicide must be made to understand: "It is not that you are *obliged* to live, but that you are *permitted* to live!" (III/4 464 = 407 rev.). "*Respect* is due to [life], and, with respect, *protection* against each and every callous negation and destruction" (III/4 453 = 397). A natural urge to live does not command this, which obviously could command something else, be it the readiness to climb over bodies for the sake of one's own advantage, be it the openness to end one's own life as this urge decreases. It is the goodness of God that commands it.

How is it that the ending of earthly life on the basis of its temporal limitation can still be a divine benefit? The thought that creaturely life *cannot* be unending because God and not self is its basis is only a provisional consideration. So, too, is the thought that creaturely life *need* not be unending because to be so would not guarantee a life that accorded with its determination. The decisive insight is this. Because God is the One who both grounds and limits creaturely life, it is not *time* that abstractly limits us, rather really God who does this. God is our "Hereafter," "our Neighbour with whom we have to do on the margin of our life, on the frontiers of our time" (III/2 685 = 564). This demonstrates the significance of the fact that his eternity includes beginning and ending within itself, so that he is then present in our beginning and ending, and can even be there before we were, just as he always will be able to be there after we have come to our earthly end. "At the very point where the appointed limit can be clearly discerned at the beginning and end of our lives . . . we stand quite alone, although genuinely confronted by the eternal God" (III/2 688 = 566), by him who in time has revealed himself as the God who already was gracious, intervening wholly on our behalf and electing himself forever for fellowship with us and us for fellowship with him. This God is gracious to us both before we were *and* after we will have been, and especially at those boundaries where nothing can help us and we cannot help ourselves, and where nothingness confronts us. We see there with special clarity that nothing other than God can be our help and support in view of our perishing, and that God is truly our help then. "The fact that our time is allotted . . . simply means the natural proximity of His free grace in this clarity" (III/2 691 = 569 rev.). By his grace "the rock walls" that the limits of our temporal life would otherwise appear to signify for us "have become the protecting walls" of a created living space (III/2 683 = 563), and our earthly life is "embedded in His eternity" (III/2 690 = 568) "like a child in the arms of its mother" (II/1 703 = 623).

We must also consider another objection to the thought that the ending of temporal life is a benefit. Is it not countered by the very experience of dying as a dreadful termination of life? Indeed, "even for the Christian the end means thus far and no further. You have had your time and no more remains. You have been given your chances, possibilities and powers. . . . It is now all up with them, and you can expect no more. . . . You cannot alter anything, or improve anything, or rectify anything. . . . 'Forth thou must go, thine hour hath run its course!' . . . Have we ever done more than make a toilsome and pitiable beginning, which on close inspection is perhaps no more than a false start? Is all this really *over?* Is it finally *too late* to do anything more about it?" (IV/3 1063f. = 926). Does not all this become all the more terrible when we consider that at our ending we shall confront *God,* our final judge, and not sheer nothingness? For "between our emergence from God and our final confrontation with Him, there stands the fact of the abysmal and irreparable *guilt.* . . ." "What else can [death's] onset mean but the approach and execution of God's judgment upon us? What can this judgment mean but rejection? And what can its execution mean but the . . . expulsion of our unworthy and degenerate life from before the eyes of the Creator from whom it has already alienated itself by its guilt?" Death, "as it actually encounters us," and as the witness of the Bible sees it, "is the sign of God's judgment upon us" (III/2 724f. = 596) — surely not a benefaction but rather the "last enemy" (1 Cor. 15:26). To be sure, we are actually to fear God and not death, but for that reason death too as "an evil ordained by God as a sign of His judgment" (III/2 726 = 597).

Nevertheless, we are not only to fear. "Inconsolable as we otherwise are, we cannot fear God without finding consolation in Him, that consolation that is basic and comprehensive" (III/2 743 = 610 rev.). In his Son God has himself wrestled with death as this "final enemy" for our benefit. "God, in the death of Jesus, declares [death] to be His enemy as well, and treats [it] as such by placing Himself at the side of man in the verdict there pronounced, and snatching man from its jaws by the death of Jesus for him" (III/2 730 = 600). He did this in such a way that, thanks to the atoning intervention of Christ for mankind, death no longer has the character of a judgment that destroys us and hands us over to nothingness. This does not mean, Barth thinks, that the restriction of our temporal lives is now lifted. It means that we now have to distinguish "between end and curse, dying and punishment, death and execution" (III/2 769 = 632). In the death of Jesus Christ there is already a twofold distinction to be made between his *being able* to die and his *having* to die (cf. III/2 767f. = 630). It is not sin but free *grace* that he gave himself up to die for us, into that death in which in our place he suffered the *curse* that we in fact suffer in our death, and took the judgment of divine dereliction upon himself. Hence we are given the promise, with regard to our dying, that it will be an "ending" that is no longer a "curse." And if it is "only" an ending then, we must accordingly distinguish between both: "Death is our frontier. But our God is the frontier even of our death." "One day we shall cease to be, but even then He will be for us. Hence our future nonexistence cannot be our complete negation.... We cannot cease to be under His sovereignty, His property, the objects of His love" (III/2 743 = 611). Death thus meets us no longer as our last enemy. Even in death we are in the hands of the One who has graciously overcome that enemy. The "great darkness" of our death is "already outshone by a dazzling light. This light, however, is not our own, or under our control. It belongs to God alone.... It is the light of our life in and over death" (III/2 744 = 712).

Christian Hope

This statement made by the young Barth is famous: If "Christianity be not altogether thoroughgoing eschatology, there remains in it no relationship whatever with Christ.... All that is not hope is ... no freedom, but only imprisonment ... no God, but only a mirror of unredeemed humanity. And this is so, be there never so much progress of social reform and never so much trumpeting of the grandeur of Christian redemption! Do we desire something better than hope?"[4] A later criticism of Barth was that he had lost this

---

4. Karl Barth, *Der Römerbrief,* 2nd ed. (Munich, 1922; 12th ed., 1978), p. 298; ET: *The Epistle to the Romans* (Oxford, 1933), p. 314.

insight.[5] Yet he himself commented on that earlier statement, "Well roared, lion!" (II/1 715 = 635), even if he did add that its insight needed to be articulated in a more nuanced way. What dogmatics has to say about Christian hope is, for Barth, valid only along the lines of the above insight. Yet when we speak thematically about Christian hope we need to draw the lines a little more sharply. What we are doing materially is offering an answer to the question posed by the petition in the Lord's Prayer: "Thy kingdom come" (Matt. 6:10).

Barth thought that the concept "kingdom of God" might very well be called the "revolution of God." What did he mean by this? The kingdom, he said, introduces something absolutely *new* vis-à-vis the given world, something that inaugurates its total renewal. This is no mere idea; it is a new reality that as such can bring about something totally new, a new being that creates a new "consciousness," an ensemble of new relationships that make possible a total reversal of thought — in that order alone. With the irruption of the kingdom of God a break occurs for the given world, "the greatest, the only true and definitive break in the world and its history. . . . the destruction . . . of all the so-called 'given factors,' all the supposed natural orders, all the historical forces, which with the claim of absolute validity and worth have obtruded themselves as authorities — mythologically but very realistically described as 'gods' — between God and man, but also between man and his fellows," that is, absolutely posited possessions, worldly honor, power, family, the law of religion ("and worst of all a religion of revelation!") (IV/2 614f. = 543-44). The kingdom of God, "from the standpoint of the possibility of all other events . . . is absolutely unexpected and inconceivable. It comes down directly from above and breaks through the level of all that has taken place thus far. It thus demands and creates freedom for *human* thought and volition in a *new* dimension" (CL 402 = 235). We who belong to this world "cannot bring in the kingdom" or build it (CL 414ff. = 240). It is not the sum or epitome of human history (CL 426 = 243). "What man does of himself (against the authorities that define this world) may take the form of an attempted repudiation but it will always serve to confirm and strengthen them, continually evoking new forms of their rule. The little revolutions and attacks by which they seem to be more shaken than they really are have never succeeded in limiting, let alone destroying, their power. It is the kingdom of God, the revolution of God which breaks . . . them" (IV/2 615 = 544 rev.).[6]

---

5. Cf. Jürgen Moltmann, *Theologie der Hoffnung* (Munich, 1964, 1966), pp. 33-34; ET: *Theology of Hope* (London, 1967), pp. 39-40.

6. Cf. Karl Barth, *Der Römerbrief,* 1st ed. (Bern, 1919), pp. 24ff.

Thus, over against all that has been up to now, it is not just something new, it is *the* new. Since it can be effected by God alone, "it is the new thing *of God*" (CL 427 = 247), identical with God himself, who is to be conceived of, for his part, in the action of his confrontation with all that has been there before. "God's *kingdom* is God himself . . . as he not merely *is* somewhere and somehow . . . but as he *comes*. . . . As God's kingdom is God himself, so God is his kingdom in his own coming, his coming to meet man, to meet the whole of reality distinct from himself" (CL 404 = 236). The term "kingdom of God" conveys the same meaning as "new creation" and "end-time reality" (IV/1 343f. = 311-12; IV/2 882 = 778),[7] in which a distorted world, one that has been made "old" by the coming of God's kingdom, passes away in order to be replaced by a "new" reality, made by God and healed of all the wounds of the old world.

Barth offers a nuanced view of this concept of "new creation." It cannot mean that a better or totally different second creation will replace the first, so that in the process the first creation is destroyed. That would mean that God had not made the first creation a good one, that it was indeed a bad reality, and that would mean that the new creation could be achieved only by a negation of the created reality made by God as good. Its newness can refer only to the destruction that threatens creation, the removal of which has been God's intention from the very beginning, and not only after that destruction surfaced within creation (III/1 121 = 109-110).

On the other hand, the concept cannot mean a mere return of creation to its state before the fall. This would open the door too easily to a "natural theology" which assumes that there is a remnant of a divine-like nature, open to God, left in the human person, which remained intact and untouched by the fall. Barth did not think that creation bears within itself either its ground or its meaning. It is the divinely created external presupposition of the covenant and its fulfillment, which covenant itself makes this presupposition known for what it is. The new creation cannot, according to Barth, be a renewal that threatens or replaces the covenant, but rather, conversely, is linked with the completion of the covenant through the conquering of the destruction that threatens it.

We now approach the decisive question: How do we know about the coming of God's kingdom, and that it is and should be the ground and object of our praying and hoping? There can be no suggestion here of "a hope manufactured by people . . . the hope of a final solution of the complicated problems of world history which takes place in more or less pure transcendence,"

7. Cf. CD IV/2 696 = 588; CL 403 = 236.

of the "wishful thinking" of a utopia (CL 426f. = 247), nor also of a crowning conclusion of human progress in and through moral and other strivings (CL 416-418 = 243ff.). The Christian hope is not the "product of a need" (III/2 587 = 488 rev.), evoked by experiences of deficiencies in the present (CL 423 = 245). An eschatology developed in such a way would be dependent upon a view of the present as hopeless or would be profoundly weakened if such a view were to lose favor (cf. II/1 717 = 636). According to the Old Testament, and especially the New, Christian hope rests upon the fact that it is rooted in a definite perfect tense (in this world), breaking through our antithesis between the this-worldly and the next, and that it looks forward to a definite future tense (the next).[8]

The hope of the kingdom of God "finds its basis in the fact that the coming is not just ahead but is *already an event.... From the enacted and present coming* the New Testament looks for the future coming" (CL 427 = 247).[9] The hope of God's kingdom, that we cannot make, is not a humanly concocted idea, for the kingdom has already broken in as reality: "'The kingdom of God is at hand' means 'the Word was made flesh and dwelt among us' (John 1:14)" (CL 429 = 249). That in this Word the eternal God has assumed time for us is itself an eschatological event, and as such it is the ground for both the reality and our knowing of that reality of what the coming of the kingdom of God is and will be. The coming, the "parousia" of Jesus Christ, is not merely an image for a reality that is distinct from him; it is the coming of the kingdom of God. The eschaton of the future does not differ from the parousia of *Jesus Christ* (CL 431 = 249-50). It is not "something better or the best . . . the *Lord* is coming" (III/2 584 = 486-87), so that, however, the "new creation" could be seen in the event of his Easter advent (III/2 586 = 488; 2 Cor. 5:17). The hope of the community is set "on *Jesus himself*" and not on the "attainment merely of abstract blessings," on all further blessings only as "concomitant phenomena of His manifestation" (III/2 589 = 490). He himself is the covenant, fulfilled at his atonement, between God and us and ourselves and our neighbors. For this reason his coming is the coming of a new world. "He comes and creates righteousness . . . as the right order of the world that belongs to him. He comes and creating righteousness he abolishes the unrighteousness of people both in their relationship to him and also in their relationships to one another. He comes and sets aside not only unrighteousness but also the lordship of the lordless powers . . . restoring to man the freedom over his abilities of which they had robbed him, reinstitut-

---

8. Cf. CD III/3 175ff. = 154ff.; IV/2 238 = 214-215.
9. Cf. CD III/2 586 = 487; IV/3 1050f. = 914-15.

ing him as the lord of the earth which he may and should be as the servant of God. He comes and with him comes that 'peace on earth among men with whom he is pleased.' . . . This peace on earth, actualized when God himself comes as King and Lord and creates and establishes it, is the *kingdom of God*" (CL 405 = 237).

Yet how does the coming that has already happened press beyond itself to the hope of a future coming of God's kingdom? More precisely, how are we to understand, "abandoning any attempt to understand the New Testament better than it understood itself," that it bears witness to the kingdom "as present but also future" (CL 439f. = 254)? We are pointed first to the event of Easter, in which what was concealed in the earthly life of Jesus was made known, namely, that he is the Reconciler and the Lord of all. This has been made known in such a way that we can validly say not only that what is to be has taken place there already (III/2 588 = 490), but also that what has taken place there is what *will be*. At Easter he was perceived by the disciples "in the *future* of his completed history" (CL 440f. = 255). Then we are pointed to the event of Pentecost, when by the power of the Holy Spirit people are awakened to the knowledge that their own future is enclosed in the future of Jesus Christ (CL 442f. = 255-256). Hence the enacted fulfillment is also the promise of a future fulfillment. It is not merely the "past," but — because it is an eschatological event and thus not understandable as historical past and because it is not just a partial fulfillment! — also the fulfillment that fulfils the present and the future, already fulfillment and the inbreaking of coming fulfillment. The One who has come is then also the coming One, the One in whom we believe is the One for whom we have hoped. On the human side, our great thanksgiving is at the same time our great hope. "What *is* true in itself must still *become* true again and again," not at some indefinite time, but in the end time which is now moving towards its end, until it will simply be and remain true (IV/3 1053 = 917). There is thus no contradiction between the One who has come and the One who is coming. Nor is it an open question what will come, making us subject to the mood of fate or the future subject to the human grasp. In joyful hope, we may expect in the future the One who has come already. Thus, our waiting upon him — impatient and at the same time patient — is "expectation of what is near" (III/2 589 = 490 rev.). If the One we expect were to be changed into a distant "ideal . . . to be attained in an indefinite future," we would immediately understand his having come only historically and his present coming in the Spirit only psychologically and sociologically; we would place our hope in him as little as we would believe in him and love him (III/2 592 = 493).

Barth developed his insight that the coming of Jesus Christ is the coming of the kingdom of God in his teaching about the three forms of the parousia of Jesus Christ: his Easter appearance, the coming of the Holy Spirit, and his final "coming again" (IV/3 338ff. = 293ff.). If he could initially say that these forms of his parousia were "for us" different events, but "for him" one event (III/2 588 = 489), he would later say that His parousia was intrinsically threefold, but for us one single event. The issue is the three forms of the one parousia of Jesus Christ that together are *the* "end-time." We now live "in the time of the revelation, declaration and realization of their time in its hastening toward the end" (III/4 667 = 581). What then distinguishes the three forms?

This question arises first in relation to the Easter revelation. If the disciples were already confronted here with "the great *consummatum est* [= it is finished]" (III/2 586 = 488), if it is "the revelation of the name of God already hallowed, the kingdom of God come and the will of God done in Him, and therefore the revelation of the man already justified and sanctified in Him," then to what extent is it "moving *towards* its *fulfillment*" (IV/3 1036 = 903)? According to Barth it is not moving toward an "amplification or transcending of its content . . . which is neither necessary nor possible," but toward "a supremely radical alteration and extension of the mode . . . of its occurrence" (IV/3 1036 = 903). The alteration and extension in the second form of the parousia consists of the fact that God makes time, so that what was revealed only to the disciples at Easter but was otherwise and since then concealed from us will be made known under their ministry. To put it another way, God makes time so that what *is* true at Easter shall be perceived by people through the Holy Spirit, so that — in the "community of the last time" (III/2 612 = 504f.) — it might be proclaimed and witnessed to in the world that it might be thus awakened to faith and conversion, and the last coming of Christ may be announced. Only announced, for only a few accept it, and among them there would be not only "faith and love," but also "sin and error, sighing and tears, suffering and death" (III/2 586 = 488). Yet Barth insists that this time is already the end time, just the time *before* the eschaton, but in the power of the Spirit truly a form of the eschatological coming of Jesus Christ and the kingdom of God: "It is not a vacuum, nor a day of small things, nor a time of the delay or suspension of the *parousia*" (IV/3 1037 = 904).[10]

The first and second forms of the parousia are the nourishment of Christian hope. It is directed toward the third form, toward the last coming of Jesus Christ, after which there will be no need of a further coming. There

10. Cf. CD III/2 590 = 491; 612 = 508-509.

will accordingly also be no more need of time, since that will be the *consummation,* and thus the *end* of all time will be *permitted. "Permitted"* because "there is no history in time that can end except with Him" (II/1 710 = 630). This is the consummation, for God will be "in His Sabbath rest after the completion of all His works, the execution of all His will directed outward" (II/1 710 = 630 rev.). Since God will have nothing else to do in time, this consummation is identical with the disclosure of the fact that what he has done in time for us, in fulfillment of his covenant with us, has been done to our salvation and not in vain. "His grace (demonstrated in time) *endures for ever*" (Ps. 100:5). That grace, formerly concealed, will be *revealed* as superior to every contradiction to it and will thus bring all things into order. The ultimate future is the "triumphant *visibility* of His kingdom as it has already come" (III/2 599 = 498). It is not a revelation of the meaning and being of human history that sanctions all things. Rather, it is a revelation of the kingdom that already in time, as the new and all-renewing being, opposed the unreconciled and graceless world. It will not be "more" than a revelation of that, for otherwise the covenant of God and its fulfillment through reconciliation and its opening to all creation, the gracious self-giving of God in time as a proof of his love, would be exposed by the eschaton as a provisional, relativizable event that would make problematic the reliable faithfulness of God and his Yes to his temporal creation. Christian hope is oriented towards the revelation of God. Although we will then look back on having been temporal, we will not be lost to this God. For he will then be "all in all" (II/1 710 = 630). With the glory of this eternal revelation, man's "concluded existence, though it be only a torso or the fragment of a torso, will be seen as a ripe fruit of His atoning work, as a perfect manifestation of the will of God fulfilled in time, being thus illuminated, having and maintaining its own light, and bearing witness to God in this renewed form in which it is conformed to the image of the Son of God . . . clothed upon by His true and incorruptible and immortal being. . . . This end which is also a goal and as such a new beginning — the beginning of the exalting of his temporal existence and all its contents to *eternal* light and therefore *eternal* life — is what the Christian expects" (IV/3 1065 = 928).

In Christ's completed parousia Barth distinguishes three dimensions that correspond to the three forms. It is his last, as his "comprehensive, immediate and definitive Word," a Word that all really perceive, that excludes all opposition and contradiction, and that leaves us the one option that we should dwell eternally in his kingdom (IV/3 1036 = 922). The eschaton will be the revelation, then, of the new being in the imminent kingdom: (1) in *universal* extension, ending the situation in which it and its witnesses confront the world as a minority; (2) in *exclusive* capacity, in the removal of the conflict in which Christians are now still sinners although already justified; and (3) in *ultimate* authority, in carrying out the supreme judicial judgment, that the "absolutely *free,* absolutely *unmerited,* absolutely *sovereign*" grace of God (III/3 1059 = 922 rev.) is the reality to which all things solely and really owe their existence (III/3 1053-1059 = 917-922).

The question that is then constantly asked is, does Barth teach universalism *(apokatastasis)?* He protested against this claim to the extent that a doctrine was meant that was derived from "an optimistic estimate of man in conjunction with this postulate of the infinite potentiality of the divine being" (II/2 325 = 295), which thus reshapes the freedom of divine grace into a compulsion and the divine judgment over sin into a light-hearted appeasing.[11] The church should not "preach an apokatastasis," but "without any weakening of the contrast, and also without any arbitrary dualism, it will preach the overwhelming power of grace and the weakness of human wickedness in face of it," and not only preach it but believe and hope it, emphasizing "that in accordance with His mercy which is 'new every morning' He 'will not cast off for ever' (La. 3:22f., 31)."[12]

Hope means that the one who hopes is not yet at the place for which he hopes. In relation to it he is in a provisional and penultimate state, and thus his own action can only be the action of one who is provisional and penultimate. This is not due to a general relativism but to the insight that "to bring in this day, to cause it to dawn . . . cannot be the affair of any person." That would be "a titanism whose only result can be all kinds of greater and smaller monstrosities, wild illusions, oppressions, and suppressions of all kinds." But does our hoping for God's kingdom then not mean "to be idle in the meantime; to acquiesce for the time being in human unrighteousness and disorder and their consequences, in the mortal imperiling of life, freedom, peace, and joy on earth under the lordship of the lordless powers . . . perhaps with gloomy skeptical speculation to find comfort in the thought that until God's final and decisive intervention, the course of events will necessarily be . . . increasingly worse" (CL 455-457, 465 = 263-64, 270)? This would be the situation if those who hope have the attitude that "the sphere of the penultimate is left empty by pure hope of the ultimate, and is therefore made a place of hopelessness" (IV/3 1075 = 936). We do not have to do, however, with an empty sphere of the penultimate if in the power of the present Spirit we believe in the Easter manifestation of the

---

11. CD II/2 325 = 295, 461 = 417-18, 467 = 422.
12. CD II/2 529 = 477; IV/3 551 = 478, 560 = 487 on Col. 1:20.

kingdom that has already come, and if we expect that, in our present state, we can catch a first glimpse of the light of the new and final coming of the kingdom. If in the sphere of the penultimate we already find "intimations of the ultimate," then in our hope for the ultimate we must take the penultimate very seriously, without confusing both. Hope can then never be idle but rather active, never merely private but rather engaged in the "public" (IV/3 1077 = 938, 1070 = 931f.).

Eschatology involves ethics. In the hope for the ultimate, and in correspondence with the divine righteousness that God alone has inaugurated and made visibly compelling, the understanding of the penultimate is established for us as the "time of *responsibility* for the occurrence of *human righteousness*," for Christian action, for "effort and struggle." The "concern is with man. . . . In regard to every cause, they simply look and ask whether and how far it will relatively and provisionally serve or hurt the cause of man and his right and worth" (CL 456f, 463 = 264, 267). We proclaim the coming of the kingdom, "the appearing of *God's* righteousness on a *new* earth and under a *new* heaven . . . the setting up his ordering of human life and life together, of his creature, covenant partner, and child . . . of his order of life, right, freedom, peace, and joy which is good for man . . . which saves and keeps him" (CL 454 = 263).

His is the kingdom and the power, and *his* is the glory as well. As seen in relation to the final revelation, the glory of God is his "dignity . . . to make Himself . . . everywhere apparent as the one He is" (II/1 723 = 641). It is "the truth and power and act of His self-demonstration and therefore of His love . . . the emerging reality of all that God is" (II/1 725 = 643). In its emergence, "every lack in our life" is supplied; "all the problems and worries of our life, all the riddles of the world and the riddles of our existence . . . are . . . clarified and resolved . . . elucidated and illuminated in such a way that there can no longer be any independent reality corresponding to them. He who has God has really everything. He may not have it in the way he would choose himself. But this only means that he has it the more certainly in the way that God wills that he should have it and therefore in such a way that he can be satisfied and content" (II/1 726f. = 644).

In this manifestation "God is glorious in such a way that He radiates joy, so that He is all He is with . . . beauty" (II/1 739 = 655), and "acts as the One who gives *pleasure*, creates *desire* and rewards with *enjoyment*" (II/1 734 = 651). On this basis, the destiny of "all God's creatures" is "to offer a true if inadequate response in the temporal sphere to the jubilation with which the Godhead is filled from eternity to eternity" (II/1 730 = 648), by praising and glorifying him.

This is what is expected from all creation . . . this is their secret that will one day come out. . . . The angels do it . . . even the smallest creatures do it too. They do it along with us or without us. They do it also against us to shame us and instruct us. . . . And when man accepts again his destiny in Jesus Christ in the promise and faith of the future revelation of his participation in God's glory as it is already given him here and now, he is only like a late-comer slipping shamefacedly into creation's choir in heaven and earth, which has never ceased its praise, but merely suffered and sighed, as it still does, that in inconceivable folly and ingratitude its living center, man himself, does not hear its voice . . . its echoing of the divine glory, or rather hears it in a completely perverted way, and refuses to cooperate in the jubilation which surrounds him. . . . This his sin has already been taken away from him by Christ and "in the eternal glory before us it will not exist at all even as the past. . . . The groaning of creation will cease," because then man will live out his destiny, "rejoicing with the God who Himself has eternal joy and Himself is eternal joy." (II/1 731 = 648-49 rev.)

And just as there is an ethic that corresponds to the coming kingdom, so there is an aesthetic which accords with the glory — and both are related to each other. "Finally, in the proper sense, to be unesthetic is to be immoral." It is characteristic of this aesthetic (exemplarily in art and in humor) that in "alien character as play . . . in the midst of the seriousness of the present," it rehearses the opening scenes of what is to come, and in so doing "laughs through tears."[13]

---

13. Karl Barth, *Ethik*, vol. 2 (Zurich, 1973), pp. 438-39, 443; ET: *Ethics* (New York, 1981), pp. 510, 507.

Bibliography

I. Works of Karl Barth

Ad limina apostolorum. Zurich, 1967.

"Antwort an D. Achelis und D. Drews." *Zeitschrift für Theologie und Kirche* 19 (1909): 479-86.

Das Bekenntnis der Reformation und unser Bekennen. Theologische Existenz heute! 29. Munich, 1935.

Briefe, 1961-1968. Zurich, 1975. English translation: *Letters, 1961-1968.* Grand Rapids, 1981.

Calvin als Theologe. Zurich, 1959.

Christengemeinde und Bürgergemeinde. Theologische Studien 20. Zollikon-Zurich, 1946. English translation: *Church and State.* Macon, Ga., 1991.

Christliche Gemeinde im Wechsel der Staatsordnungen. Zollikon-Zurich, 1948.

Der christliche Glaube und die Geschichte. Schweizerische Theologische Zeitschrift 29. Zurich, 1912.

Das christliche Leben. Zurich, 1976. English translation: *The Christian Life.* Grand Rapids, 1981.

Die christliche Lehre nach dem Heidelberger Katechismus. Zollikon-Zurich, 1948. English translation: *The Heidelberg Catechism for Today.* Richmond, 1964.

Christus und wir Christen. Theologische Existenz heute! n.s. 11. Munich, 1948.

"Denken heisst: Nachdenken." *Zürcher Woche* 15 (1963).

Der deutsche Kirchenkampf. Basel, 1937.

Dogmatik im Grundriss. Zollikon-Zurich, 1947. English translation: *Dogmatics in Outline.* London, 1949.

Einführung in die evangelische Theologie. Zurich, 1962. English translation: *Evangelical Theology: An Introduction.* Grand Rapids, 1963.

Ethik. 5th ed. 2 vols. Zurich, 1973. English translation: *Ethics.* New York, 1981.

Das Evangelium in der Gegenwart. Theologische Existenz heute! 25. Munich, 1935.

Evangelium und Gesetz. Theologische Existenz heute! 32. Munich, 1935.

Fides quaerens intellectum. Munich, 1931. English translation: *Anselm: Fides quaerens intellectum.* Richmond, Va., 1960.

Freiheit. Polis 7. Zurich, 1960.

Für die Freiheit des Evangeliums. Theologische Existenz heute! 2. Munich, 1933.

Fürchte dich nicht! Munich, 1949.

Das Geschenk der Freiheit. Theologische Studien 39. Zollikon-Zurich, 1953.

"Gespräch in Brièves." 1963 (unpublished).

Gespräche 1959-1962. Zurich, 1995.

Gespräche 1964-1968. Zurich, 1997.

Gottes Wille und unsere Wünsche. Theologische Existenz heute! 7. Munich, 1934.

Gotteserkenntnis und Gottesdienst. Zollikon, 1938. English translation: *The Knowledge of God and the Service of God.* London, 1938.

"Der Götze wackelt": Zeitkritische Aufsätze, Reden und Briefe von 1930 bis 1960, ed. K. Kupisch. Berlin, 1961.

Karl Barth–Eduard Thurneysen Briefwechsel. 2 vols. Zurich, 1973, 1974.

Karl Barth–Rudolf Bultmann Briefwechsel, 1922-1966. Zurich, 1966. English translation: *Correspondence of Karl Barth and Rudolf Bultmann, 1922-1966.* Grand Rapids, 1981.

Karl Barth zum Kirchenkampf. Theologische Existenz heute! 5. Munich, 1933. English translation: *The German Church Conflict.* Richmond, Va., 1965.

"Kerl und die Bekenntniskirche." *Basler Nachrichten,* Basel 1, Beilage zu Nr. 333. 1935.

"Kirche in Erneuerung." *Freiburger Zeitschrift für Philosophie und Theologie* 15 (1968): 161-70.

Die Kirche Jesu Christi. Theologische Existenz heute! 5. Munich, 1933.

Die Kirche zwischen Ost und West. Zollikon-Zurich, 1949.

Die kirchliche Dogmatik. 4 vols. Zollikon-Zurich, 1936-68. English translation: *Church Dogmatics.* Edinburgh, 1936-69. Rev. ed., 1975.

Letzte Zeugnisse. Zurich, 1969. English translation: *Final Testimonies.* Grand Rapids, 1977.

Lutherfeier. Theologische Existenz heute! 4. Munich, 1933.

Die Menschlichkeit Gottes. Theologische Studien 48. Zollikon-Zurich, 1956. English translation: *The Humanity of God.* Richmond, Va., 1960, also containing translations of *Evangelische Theologie,* Theologische Studien 49; and *Das Geschenk der Freiheit,* Theologische Studien 39.

"Nachwort." In *Friedrich Schleiermacher.* Munich and Hamburg, 1968. English translation: appendix to *The Theology of Schleiermacher,* pp. 261-79. Grand Rapids, 1982.

Nein! Antwort an Emil Brunner. Theologische Existenz heute! 14. Munich, 1934. English translation: *Natural Theology.* London, 1946 (with Brunner's article).

Offene Briefe 1945-1968. Zurich, 1984.

Der Pfarrer. Zofingen, 1916.

Predigten 1913. Zurich, 1976.

Predigten 1914. Zurich, 1974.

Die protestantische Theologie im 19. Jahrhundert: Ihre Vorgeschichte und ihre Geschichte. Zurich, 1947. English translation: *Protestant Theology in the Nineteenth Century: Its Background and History.* Valley Forge, Pa., 1972.

Rechtfertigung und Recht. Zollikon, 1938.

Reformation als Entscheidung. Theologische Existenz heute! 3. Munich, 1933.

Der Römerbrief. 1st ed. Bern, 1919.

Der Römerbrief. 2nd ed. Munich, 1922; 12th ed. 1978. English translation: *The Epistle to the Romans.* Oxford, 1933.

Rudolf Bultmann. Theologische Studien 34. Zollikon-Zurich, 1952. English translation: in *Kerygma and Myth,* vol. 2, pp. 88-162. London, 1962.

Rufe mich an! Zurich, 1965. English translation: *Call for God.* New York, 1967.

Die Schrift und die Kirche. Theologische Studien 22. Zollikon-Zurich, 1947.

Eine Schweizer Stimme: 1938-1945. Zollikon-Zurich, 1945.

Suchet Gott, so werdet ihr leben! Bern, 1917.

Texte zur Barmer Theologischen Erklärung. Zurich, 1984.

Die Theologie Calvins. Zurich, 1922. English translation: *The Theology of Calvin.* Grand Rapids, 1995.

Die Theologie Schleiermachers. Zurich, 1978. English translation: *The Theology of Schleiermacher.* Grand Rapids, 1982.

Die Theologie und die Kirche. Munich, 1928. English translation: *Theology and Church: Shorter Writings, 1920-1928.* New York, 1962.

Theologische Existenz heute! Vol. 1. Munich, 1934.

Theologische Existenz heute: Schriftenreihe. Zwischen den Zeiten 2. Munich, 1933. English translation: *Theological Existence Today.* London, 1933.

Theologische Fragen und Antworten. Zollikon, 1957.

Unterricht in der christlichen Religion, vols. 1 and 2. Zurich, 1985, 1990. English translation: *Göttingen Dogmatics.* Grand Rapids, 1990.

Vorträge und kleinere Arbeiten 1909-1914. Zurich, 1993.

Vorträge und kleinere Arbeiten 1922-1925. Zurich, 1990.

Wolfgang Amadeus Mozart. Zollikon, 1956. English translation: in *Religion and Culture.* New York, 1959.

Das Wort Gottes und die Theologie. Munich, 1929. English translation: *The Word of God and the Word of Man.* New York, 1957.

"Zur Lehre vom Heiligen Geist." *Zwischen den Zeiten* 1 (1930) (in collaboration with Heinrich Barth).

II. Secondary Works

Amsterdamer Dokumente. Bielefeld, 1948.

Assel, Heinrich. "'Barth ist entlassen . . .' Neue Fragen im Fall Kark Barth." In *Zeitworte: Der Auftrag der Kirche im Gespräch mit der Schrift,* pp. 77-99. Nürnberg, 1994.

Balthasar, Hans Urs von. *Karl Barth: Darstellung und Deutung seiner Theologie.* Cologne, 1951. English translation: *The Theology of Karl Barth.* New York, 1971.

Beintker, Michael. *Die Dialektik in der "dialektischen Theologie" Karl Barths: Studien zur Entwicklung der Barthschen Theologie und zur Vorgeschichte der Kirchlichen Dogmatik.* Munich, 1987.

Berkouwer, Gerrit Cornelis. *Der Triumph der Gnade in der Theologie Karl Barths.* Neukirchen and Moers, 1957. English translation: *The Triumph of Grace in the Theology of Karl Barth.* Grand Rapids, 1956.

Bethge, Eberhard. *Dietrich Bonhoeffer.* Munich, 1967. English translation: *Dietrich Bonhoeffer.* London, 1970.

Blüher, Hans, and Hans Joachim Schoeps. *Streit um Israel. Ein jüdisch-christliches Gespräch.* Hamburg, 1933.

Bonhoeffer, Dietrich. *Gesammelte Schriften.* Vol. 2. Munich, 1959.

Bultmann, Rudolf. *Glauben und Verstehen: Gesammelte Aufsätze.* Vol. 1. Tübingen, 1933. English translation: *Faith and Understanding.* London, 1969.

Burgsmüller, Alfred, and Rudolf Weth. *Die Barmer Theologische Erklärung: Einführung und Dokumentation.* Neukirchen, 1983.

Busch, Eberhard. *Karl Barths Lebenslauf.* 5th ed. Gütersloh, 1994. English translation: *Karl Barth: His Life from Letters and Autobiographical Texts.* London and Philadelphia, 1976.

Calvin, John. *Commentary on Genesis.*

Dahm, Karl Wilhelm. "Identität und Realität der Kirche." In *Unterwegs für die Volkskirche,* ed. W. L. Federlin and E. Weber, pp. 71-85. Frankfurt, 1987.

Bibliography

Drewes, Hans Anton, and Hans Markus Wildi. *Bibliographie Karl Barth.* Vol. 1: *Veröffentlichungen von Karl Barth.* Zurich, 1984.

Ebeling, Gerhard. *Lutherstudien.* Vol. 3. Tübingen, 1985.

Eicher, Peter. "Gottes Wahl: Unsere Freiheit: Karl Barths Beitrag zur Theologie der Befreiung." In *Aufbrechen-Umkehren-Bekennen,* ed. Evangelische Akademie. Baden and Karlsruhe, 1986.

Evanston Dokumente. Ed. F. Lupsen. Witten, 1954.

Feuerbach, Ludwig. *Das Wesen des Christentums.* Leipzig, 1957. English translation: *The Essence of Christianity.* New York, 1957.

Frey, Christofer. *Die Theologie Karl Barths.* Frankfurt, 1988.

Gauger, Joachim. *Chronik der Kirchenwirren.* Vol. 2. 1935.

Gogarten, Friedrich. *Einheit von Evangelium und Volkstum?* Hamburg, 1933.

Graf, Friedrich Wilhelm. "'Der Götze wackelt'? Erste Überlegungen zu Karl Barths Liberalismuskritik." *Evangelische Theologie* 46 (1986): 422-41.

Greschat, Martin, ed. *Im Zeichen der Schuld: 40 Jahre Stuttgarter Schuldbekenntnis: Eine Dokumentation.* Neukirchen, 1985.

Gutiérrez, Gustavo. *Die historische Macht der Armen.* Fundamentaltheologische Studien 11. Munich, 1984.

Härle, Wilfried. *Sein und Gnade: Die Ontologie in Karl Barths Kirchlicher Dogmatik.* Berlin and New York, 1975.

Heine, Heinrich. *Werke.* Berlin and Weimar, 1967.

Herrmann, Rudolf. *Ethik.* Göttingen, 1970.

Hirsch, Emanuel. *Das kirchliche Wollen der Deutschen Christen.* Berlin, 1933.

Howe, Günter. "Gott und die Technik." In *Die Verantwortung der Christenheit für die wissenschaftlich-technische Welt,* ed. H. Timm. Hamburg and Zurich, 1971.

Jülicher, Adolf. "Ein moderner Paulusausleger." In *Anfänge der dialektischen Theologie,* ed. J. Moltmann. Part 1: *Karl Barth, Heinrich Barth, Emil Brunner,* pp. 87-98. Munich, 1962.

Jüngel, Eberhard. *Barth-Studien.* Zurich, Cologne, and Gütersloh, 1982.

―――. "Karl Barth zu Ehren." *Theologische Studien* 100 (1969): 47-50.

―――. "Zum Verhältnis von Kirche und Staat nach Karl Barth." *Zeitschrift für Theologie und Kirche* 6 (1986): 76-135.

Koch, Werner. "Karl Barths erste Auseinandersetzungen mit dem Dritten Reich." In *Richte unsere Füsse auf den Weg des Friedens,* ed. A. Baudis, pp. 491-513. Munich, 1979.

Krötke, Wolf. "Gott und Mensch als 'Partner': Zur Bedeutung einer centralen Kategorie in Karl Barths Kirchlicher Dogmatik." In *Theologie als Christologie: Zum Werk und Leben Karl Barths,* ed. H. Köckert and W. Krötke, pp. 106-30. Berlin, 1988.

Kupisch, Karl. *Karl Barth in Selbstzeugnissen und Bilddokumenten: Dargest.* Reinbek bei Hamburg, 1971.

Mann, Thomas. *Tagebücher 1933-1934.* Ed. P. de Mendelssohn. Frankfurt, 1977.

Mechels, Eberhard. *Kirche und gesellschaftliche Umwelt.* Neukirchener Beiträge zur systematischen Theologie 7. Neukirchen, 1990.

Miskotte, Kornelis Heiko. "Über Karl Barth's Kirchliche Dogmatik." *Theologische Existenz heute!* n.s. 89. Munich, 1961.

Moltmann, Jürgen. *Gott in der Schöpfung.* Munich, 1985. English translation: *God in Creation.* London, 1985.

———. "Schöpfung, Bund und Herrlichkeit." *Zeitschrift für dialektische Theologie* 3 (1987): 191-214.

———. *Theologie der Hoffnung.* Munich, 1964-66. English translation: *Theology of Hope: On the Ground and the Implications of a Christian Eschatology.* London, 1967.

Mund, Fritz. *Pietismus: Eine Schicksalsfrage an die Kirche heute.* 2nd ed. Marburg, 1938.

Prolingheuer, Hans. *Der Fall Karl Barth, 1934-1935: Chronographie einer Vertreibung.* 2nd ed. Neukirchen, 1984.

Rendtorff, Trutz. "Radikale Autonomie Gottes." In *Theorie des Christentums: Historisch-theologische Studien zu seiner neuzeitlichen Verfassung,* ed. T. Rendtorff, pp. 161-81. Gütersloh, 1972.

———, ed. *Die Realisierung der Freiheit: Beiträge zur Kritik der Theologie Karl Barths.* Gütersloh, 1975.

———, ed. *Theorie des Christentums: Historisch-theologische Studien zu seiner neuzeitlichen Verfassung.* Gütersloh, 1972.

Rosato, Philip Joseph. *The Spirit as the Lord: The Pneumatology of Karl Barth.* Edinburgh, 1981.

Schlatter, Adolf. "Karl Barth's 'Römerbrief.'" In *Anfänge der dialektischen Theologie,* ed. J. Moltmann. Part 1: *Karl Barth, Heinrich Barth, Emil Brunner,* pp. 142-47. Munich, 1962.

Schleiermacher, Friedrich. *Der christliche Glaube nach den Grundsätzen der evangelischen Kirche im Zusammenhange dargestellt.* 3rd ed. 2 vols. Berlin, 1835, 1836. English translation: *The Christian Faith.* Edinburgh, 1928.

———. *Über die Religion: Reden an die Gebildeten unter ihren Verlachtern.* Berlin, 1799. English translation: *On Religion.* London, 1894.

Schmidt, H. W. *Zeit und Ewigkeit: Die letzten Voraussetzungen der dialektischen Theologie.* Gütersloh, 1927.

Scholder, Klaus. *Die Kirchen und das Dritte Reich.* Vol. 1: *Vorgeschichte und Zeit der Illusionen.* Frankfurt, Berlin, and Vienna, 1977.

—————. "Neuere deutsche Geschichte und protestantische Theologie: Aspekte und Fragen." *Evangelische Theologie* 23 (1963): 510-36.

Sölle, Dorothee. *Stellvertretung.* Stuttgart and Berlin, 1965.

Steck, Karl Gerhard. "Theologische Existenz heute: Rückblick und Ausblick." In reprint of *Theologische Existenz heute!* Vol. 1. Ed. Karl Barth and Eduard Thurneysen. Munich, 1980.

Strauss, David Friedrich. *Der alte und der neue Glaube.* Leipzig, 1872.

Trillhaas, Wolfgang. *Ethik.* 2nd ed. Berlin, 1965.

Ullmann, Wolfgang. "Barth's zweite Wende. Ein neue Interpretationsvorschlag zu Fides quaerens intellectum." In *Theologie als Christologie: Zum Werk und Leben Karl Barths,* ed. H. Höckert and W. Krötke, pp. 71-89. Berlin, 1988.

Visser 't Hooft, Willem Adolf. "Ansprache." In *Karl Barth 1886-1968: Gedenkfeier im Basler Münster,* pp. 51-53. Zurich, 1969.

Weber, Max. *Gesammelte Aufsätze zur Religionssoziologie.* 6th ed. Vol. 1. Tübingen, 1972.

Index of Names

Anselm of Canterbury, 27f.
Aristotle, 160, 192

Balthasar, Hans Urs von, 23n.41, 26n.56, 40, 44, 252
Barth-Sartorius, Anna Katharina, 5
Barth, Heinrich, 47, 220
Barth, Johann Friedrich (Fritz), 4
Bebel, August, 10
Beintker, Michael, 26n.56
Berkouwer, Gerrit Cornelis, 189n.15
Bloch, Ernst, 84
Blumhardt, Christoph, 14, 19
Blumhardt, Johann Christoph, 38n.117
Bonhoeffer, Dietrich, 250
Boticelli, Sandro, 5
Brunner, Emil, 23, 160
Buber, Martin, 195
Bullinger, Heinrich, 5
Bultmann, Rudolf, 11, 23n.44, 72, 252
Burckhardt, Jacob, 3

Calvin, John, 4, 15, 112, 186
Cicero, 92

Dahm, Karl-Wilhelm, 247n.16
Darwin, Charles, 179, 191
Descartes, René, 26, 92, 177n.5

Ebeling, Gerhard, 153n.1, 213n.5
Eicher, Peter, 116n.13

Erasmus of Rotterdam, 4

Feuerbach, Ludwig, 58-64, 86
Fichte, Johann Gottlieb, 178n.7
Frey, Christopher, 41-42

Gogarten, Friedrich, 23, 32, 111, 156
Gollwitzer, Helmut, 74
Graf, Friedrich Wilhelm, 31n.74
Grotius, Hugo, 178n.6
Grünewald, Matthias von, 6
Gutiérrez, Gustavo, 11

Härle, Wilfried, 110n.8
Harnack, Adolf von, 12, 17
Hegel, Georg Wilhelm Friedrich, 89
Heine, Heinrich, 84
Herder, Johann Gottfried, 220-21
Herrmann, Wilhelm, 17, 154
Hilary of Poitiers, 76n.36
Himmler, Heinrich, 199
Hirsch, Emanuel, 3, 32, 33n.87, 111
Hitler, Adolf, 5, 33, 111, 126, 188
Hofmann, Johann Christian Konrad von, 27n.58
Howe, Günter, 112n.12

Jonas, Hans, 11
Jülicher, Adolf, 176n.2
Jüngel, Eberhard, 83, 84n.6, 94n.12,

296

Index of Subjects

Aesthetics, 287f.
Analogy, 26, 71, 80, 184f., 194

Baptism, 54, 258
Barmen Declaration, 33f., 65, 67

Children of God, 230f.
Church, 24, 29f., 52, 235ff., 242ff.
  Christ as Head, 248, 252
  Criticism of, 246ff.
  Fellowship, 254
  Oneness *(Einheit),* 38, 254f.
  Relation to the "World," 260ff.
  Sending of, 234ff., 259ff.
  Visible/Invisible, 247ff.
  See also Israel and Church
"Coming of Age" *(Mündigkeit),* 94,
  117f., 128, 257
Command of God, 48, 152ff., 162f., 232f.
Communication [of the Gospel], 81,
  150f.
Covenant, 51, 82, 96ff., 159
  Covenant-Partnership, 98f., 116ff.,
  197
Creation, 48ff., 176ff.
  and Covenant, 180ff., 190f.
  Preservation, 186ff.

Death, 276ff.
Dialectic, 23f.
Dogmatics, 39-42

"Double Bookkeeping," 157, 179, 202

Election, 47f., 89f., 114, 121ff.
Enlightenment, 107, 128ff.
Eschatology, 217, 239-41, 279-88
Ethics, 161ff., 287
  Casuistry/"Decisionism," 169f.
  Responsibility, 164ff.
  See also Command of God, Gospel
  and Law
Eucharist, 54, 254
European Christianity, 242
Evil/Nothingness *(das Nichtige),* 189ff.,
  217

Faith, 165, 216f.
Forgiveness 213f.

Freedom, 106ff., 166f.
  Autonomy *(Autonomie),* 116f., 119f.
  Autonomy *(Eigengesetzlichkeit),* 155,
  182
  in Coexistence, 112ff., 115ff.
  Free Will, 108f., 112

God, 21, 57f., 84f.
  Abasement *(Erniedrigung),* 88f., 205f.
  Absoluteness, 78f., 89f., 123f.
  Being-in-Act, 47
  Eternality, 268ff.
  Freedom, 106ff., 112ff., 121ff.

298

Index of Scripture References